ULTIMATE SPIDER-MAN

ULTIMATE SIX

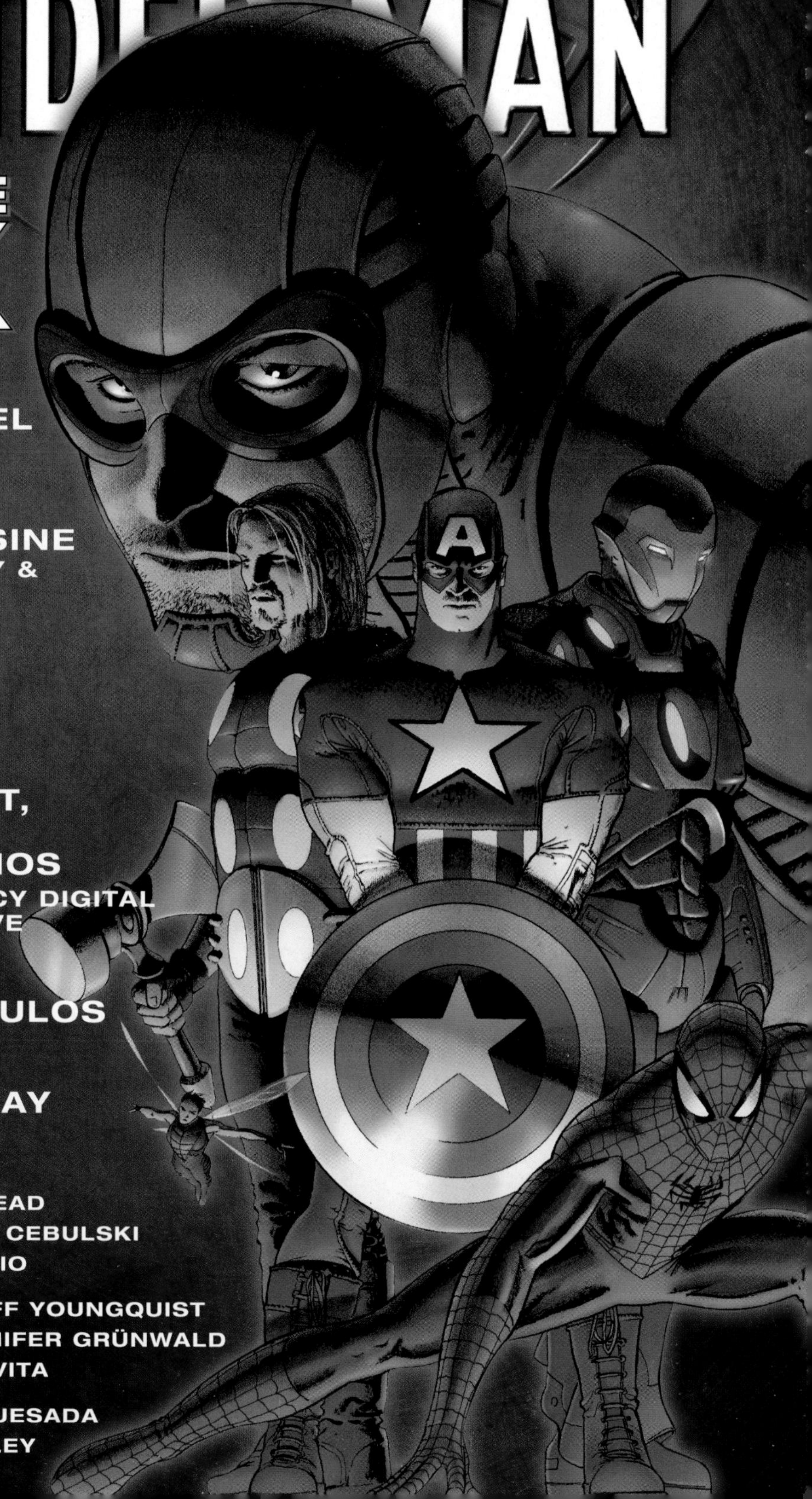

writer
BRIAN MICHAEL BENDIS

pencils
TREVOR HAIRSINE
with MARK BAGLEY & JOE QUESADA

inks
DANNY MIKI
with ART THIBERT

colors
DAVE STEWART, IAN HANNIN & AVALON STUDIOS
with TRANSPARENCY DIGITAL & RICHARD ISANOVE

letters
CHRIS ELIOPOULOS

cover art
JOHN CASSADAY

assistant editors
NICK LOWE
MACKENZIE CADENHEAD
associate editor **C.B. CEBULSKI**
editor **RALPH MACCHIO**

collections editor **JEFF YOUNGQUIST**
assistant editor **JENNIFER GRÜNWALD**
book designer **JEOF VITA**

editor in chief **JOE QUESADA**
publisher **DAN BUCKLEY**

PREVIOUSLY IN
ULTIMATE SPIDER-MAN ...

After a horrible lab accident, Dr. Otto Octavius found his body mysteriously fused to a set of metal arms that he can control with his mind. This transformation earned him the name Doctor Octopus. Having lost most of his short-term memory, he went on a rampage trying to find out who was responsible for the accident. The rampage led him to Justin Hammer, a major businessman who had hired Otto to spy on his competitor, Norman Osborn. Hammer had been funding genetic experiments with the aim of creating super-powered people to sell to the highest bidder.

In order to get revenge for what he thought Hammer did to him, Otto called a press conference to show the world what horrors Hammer had funded. After Hammer arrived in his limo, Otto got physical and attacked Hammer only to be stopped by Spider-Man.

While the fight was still raging, Sharon Carter (an agent of the American espionage agency known as S.H.I.E.L.D.) and her strike team arrived.

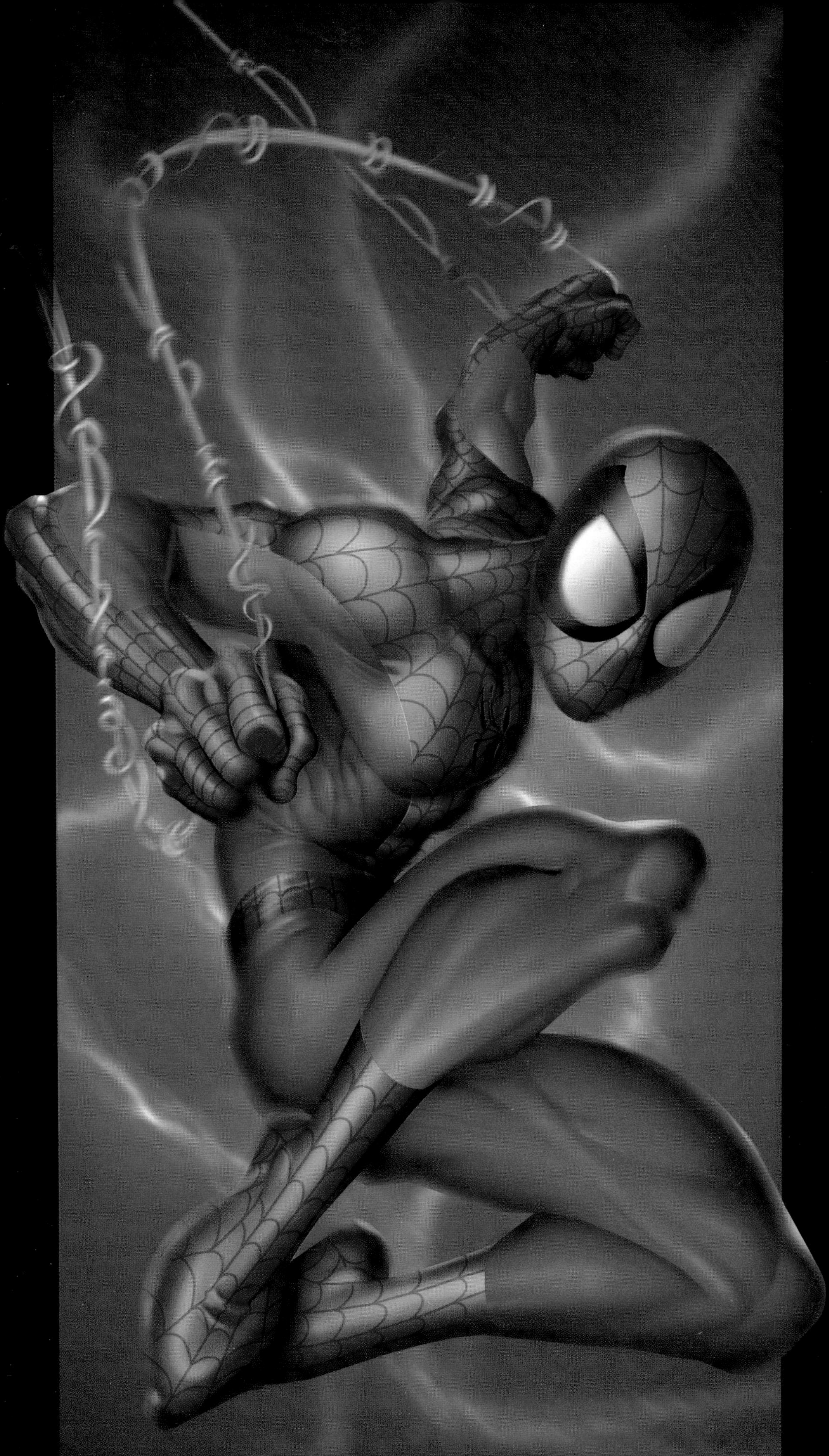

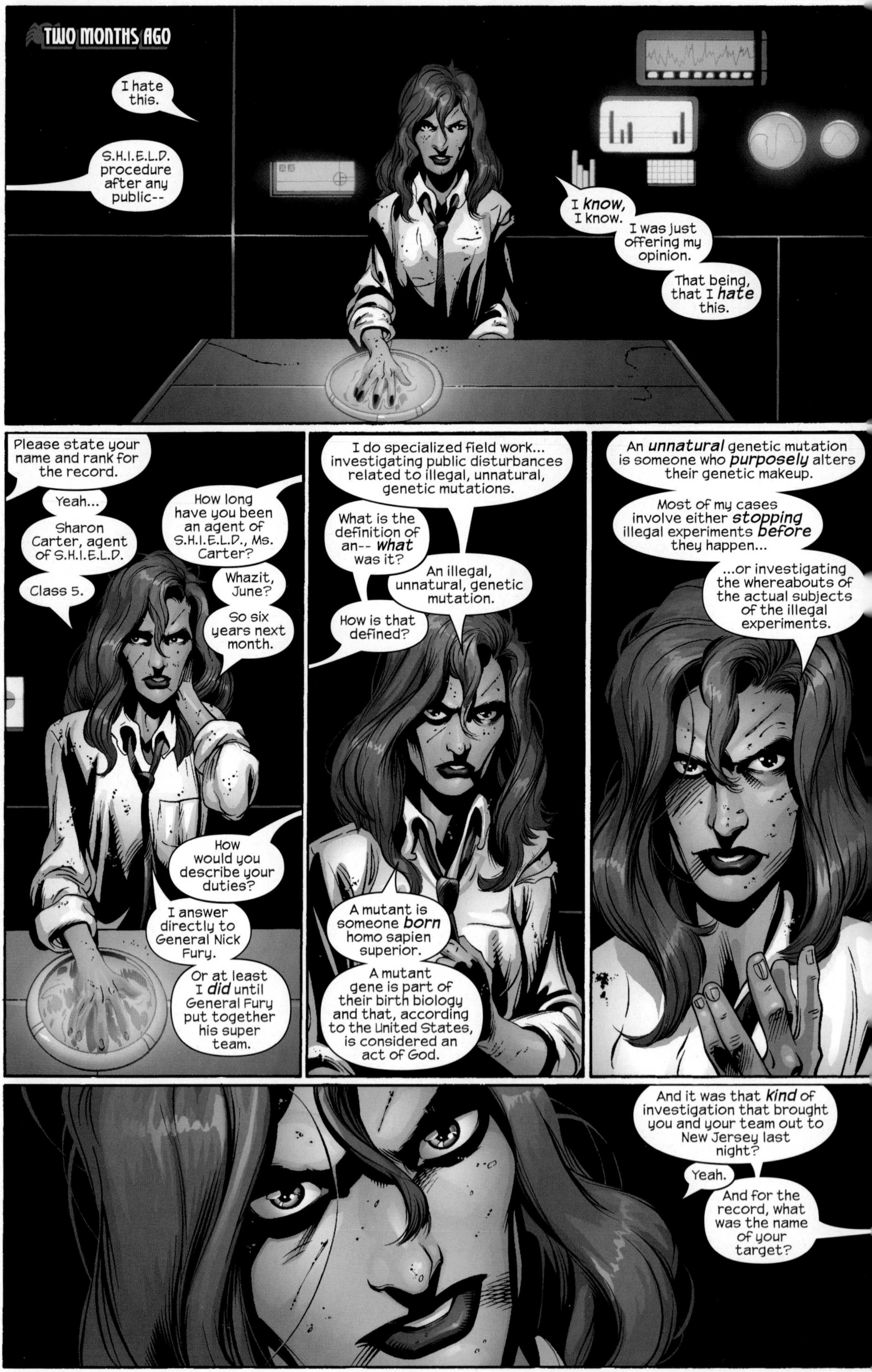
TWO MONTHS AGO
I hate this.
S.H.I.E.L.D. procedure after any public--
I know, I know.
I was just offering my opinion.
That being, that I hate this.
Please state your name and rank for the record.
Yeah...
Sharon Carter, agent of S.H.I.E.L.D.
Class 5.
How long have you been an agent of S.H.I.E.L.D., Ms. Carter?
Whazit, June?
So six years next month.
How would you describe your duties?
I answer directly to General Nick Fury.
Or at least I did until General Fury put together his super team.
I do specialized field work... investigating public disturbances related to illegal, unnatural, genetic mutations.
What is the definition of an-- what was it?
An illegal, unnatural, genetic mutation.
How is that defined?
A mutant is someone born homo sapien superior.
A mutant gene is part of their birth biology and that, according to the United States, is considered an act of God.
An unnatural genetic mutation is someone who purposely alters their genetic makeup.
Most of my cases involve either stopping illegal experiments before they happen...
...or investigating the whereabouts of the actual subjects of the illegal experiments.
And it was that kind of investigation that brought you and your team out to New Jersey last night?
Yeah.
And for the record, what was the name of your target?

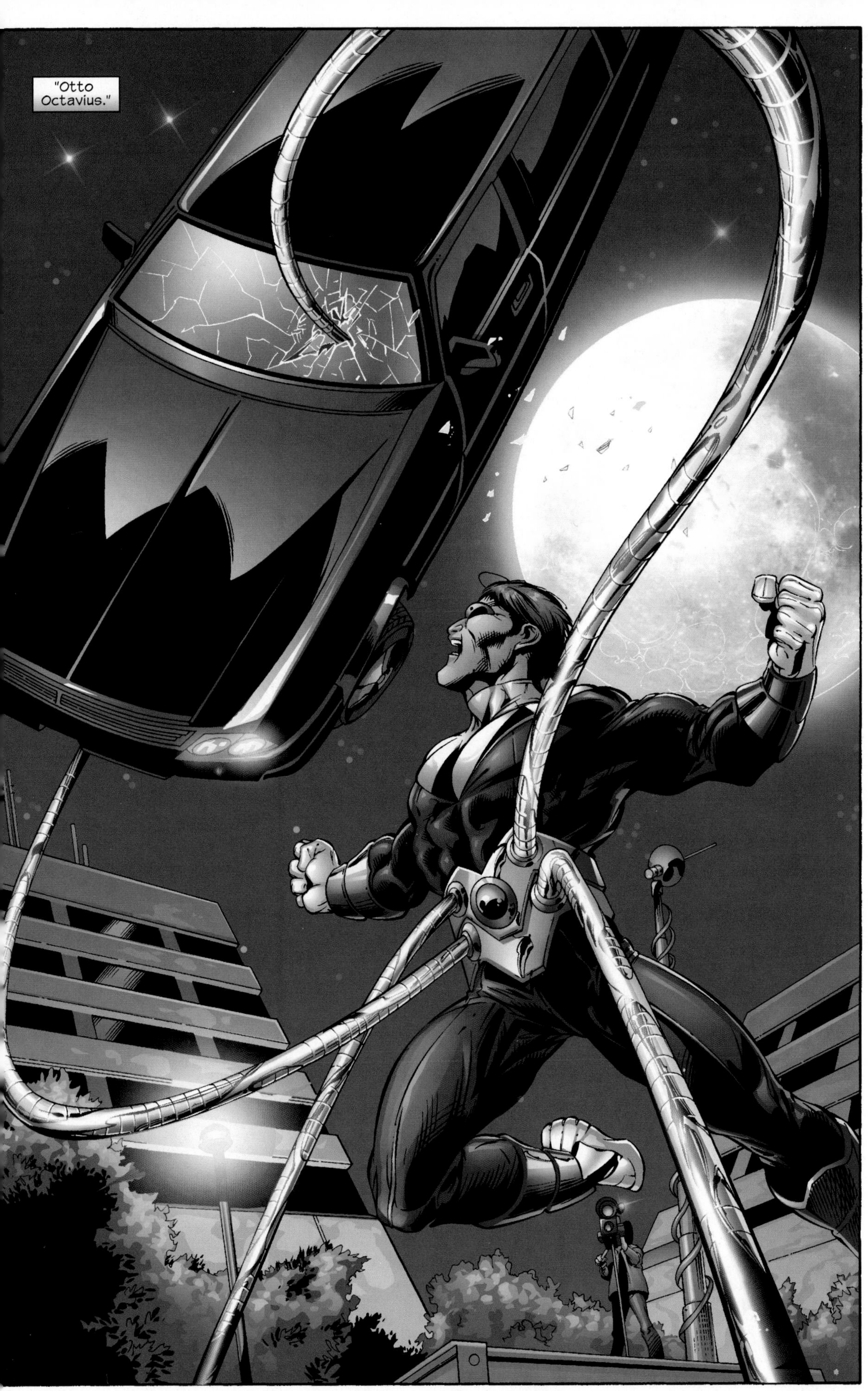
"Otto Octavius."

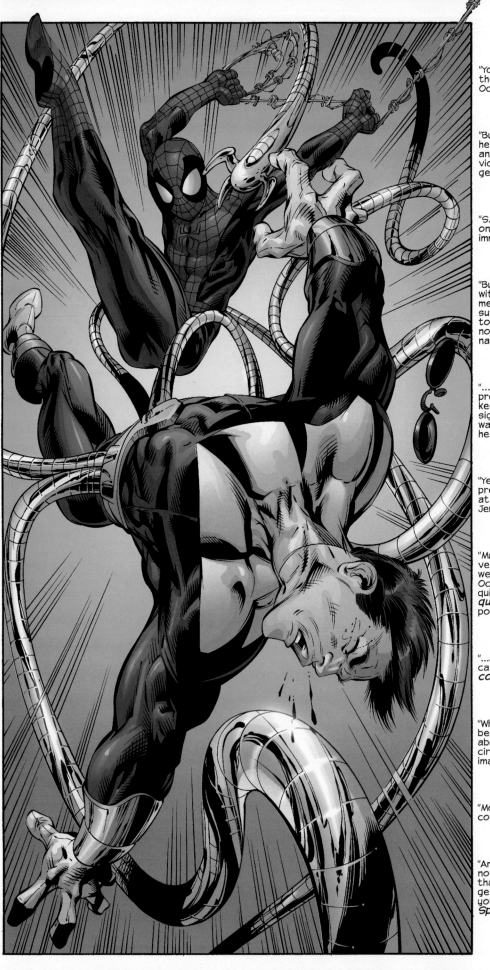

"You can read the files on Octavius.

"But at this point he was officially an escaped, violent, illegal genetic mutation.

"S.H.I.E.L.D. was on his trail immediately!

"But for someone with four, huge, metal arms surgically grafted to his body and no money to his name...

"...he was doing a pretty good job keeping out of sight until *he* wanted to be heard from.

"Yeah, he called a press conference at Hammer's New Jersey installation

"My mission was very clear in that we were to bring Octavius in as quickly and *quietly* as possible...

"...and he goes and calls a *press conference!!*

"Which, in turn, becomes just about the biggest circus you could imagine!

"Most networks covering it live!!

"And starring none other than that *other* illegal genetic mutation you know as *Spider-Man.*"

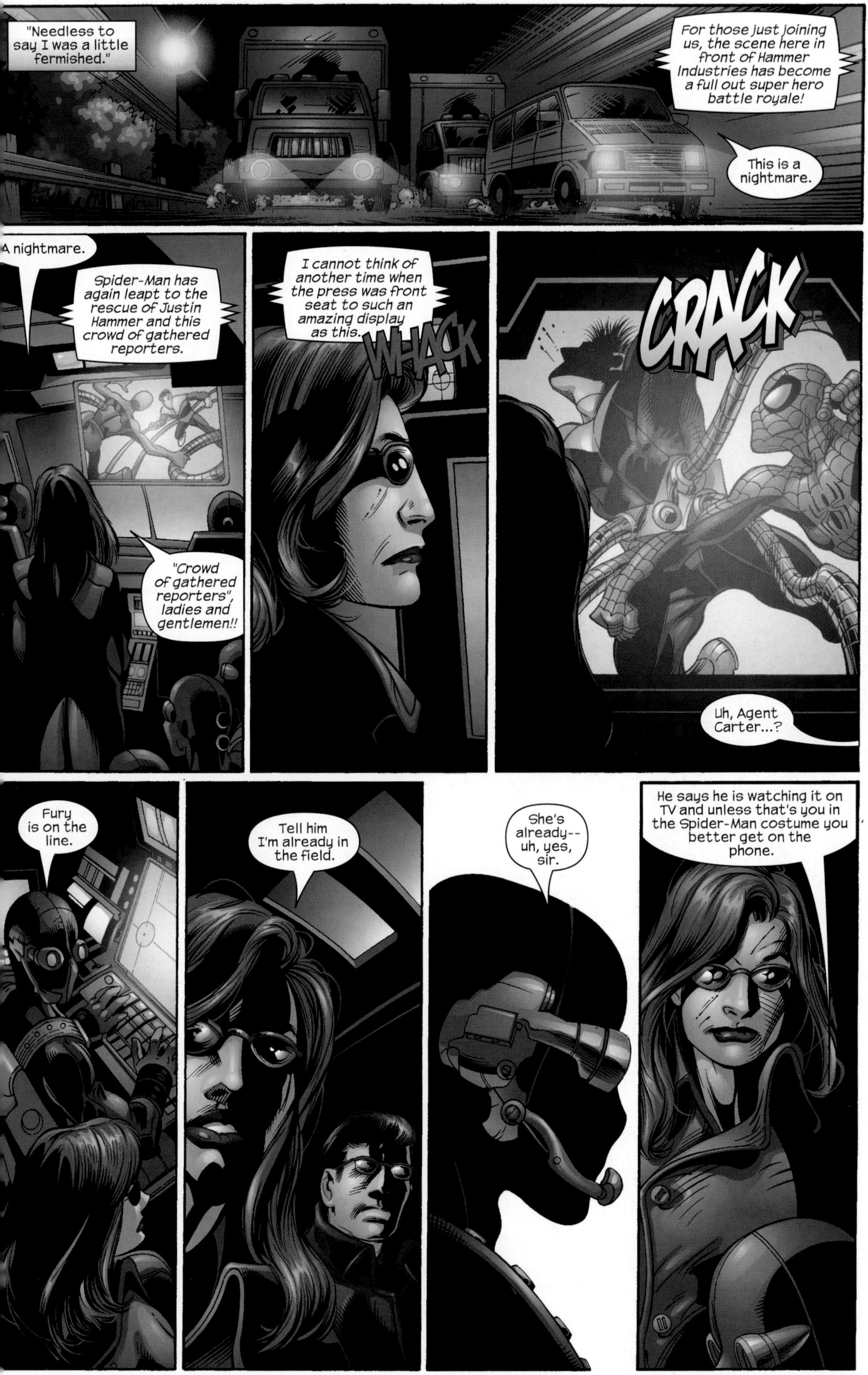
"Needless to say I was a little fermished."
For those just joining us, the scene here in front of Hammer Industries has become a full out super hero battle royale!
This is a nightmare.
A nightmare.
Spider-Man has again leapt to the rescue of Justin Hammer and this crowd of gathered reporters.
"Crowd of gathered reporters", ladies and gentlemen!!
I cannot think of another time when the press was front seat to such an amazing display as this.
WHACK
CRACK
Uh, Agent Carter...?
Fury is on the line.
Tell him I'm already in the field.
She's already-- uh, yes, sir.
He says he is watching it on TV and unless that's you in the Spider-Man costume you better get on the phone.

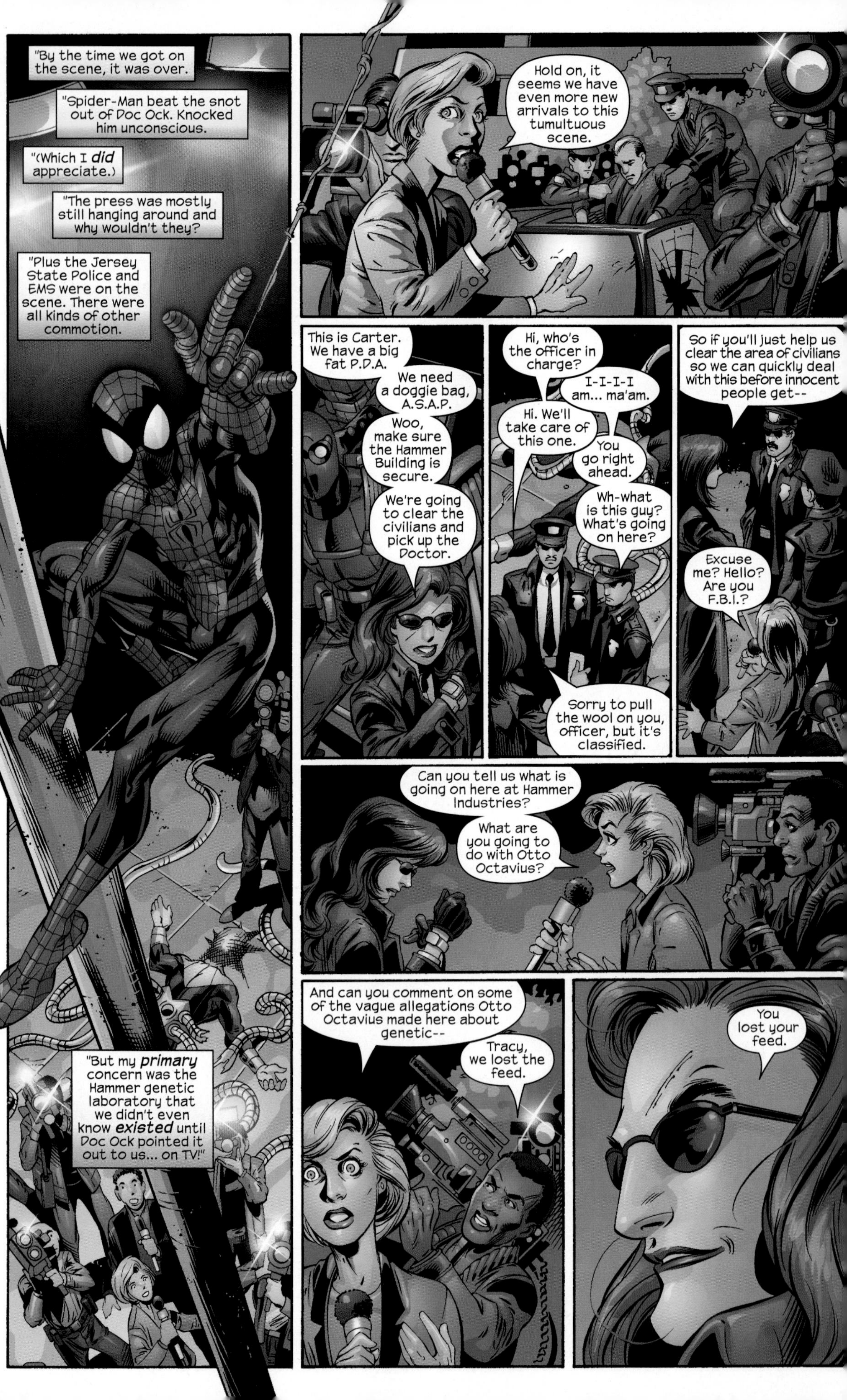
"By the time we got on the scene, it was over.
"Spider-Man beat the snot out of Doc Ock. Knocked him unconscious.
"(Which I did appreciate.)
"The press was mostly still hanging around and why wouldn't they?
"Plus the Jersey State Police and EMS were on the scene. There were all kinds of other commotion.
"But my primary concern was the Hammer genetic laboratory that we didn't even know existed until Doc Ock pointed it out to us... on TV!"
Hold on, it seems we have even more new arrivals to this tumultuous scene.
This is Carter. We have a big fat P.D.A.
We need a doggie bag, A.S.A.P.
Woo, make sure the Hammer Building is secure.
We're going to clear the civilians and pick up the Doctor.
Hi, who's the officer in charge?
I-I-I-I am... ma'am.
Hi. We'll take care of this one.
You go right ahead.
Wh-what is this guy? What's going on here?
Sorry to pull the wool on you, officer, but it's classified.
So if you'll just help us clear the area of civilians so we can quickly deal with this before innocent people get--
Excuse me? Hello? Are you F.B.I.?
Can you tell us what is going on here at Hammer Industries?
What are you going to do with Otto Octavius?
And can you comment on some of the vague allegations Otto Octavius made here about genetic--
Tracy, we lost the feed.
You lost your feed.

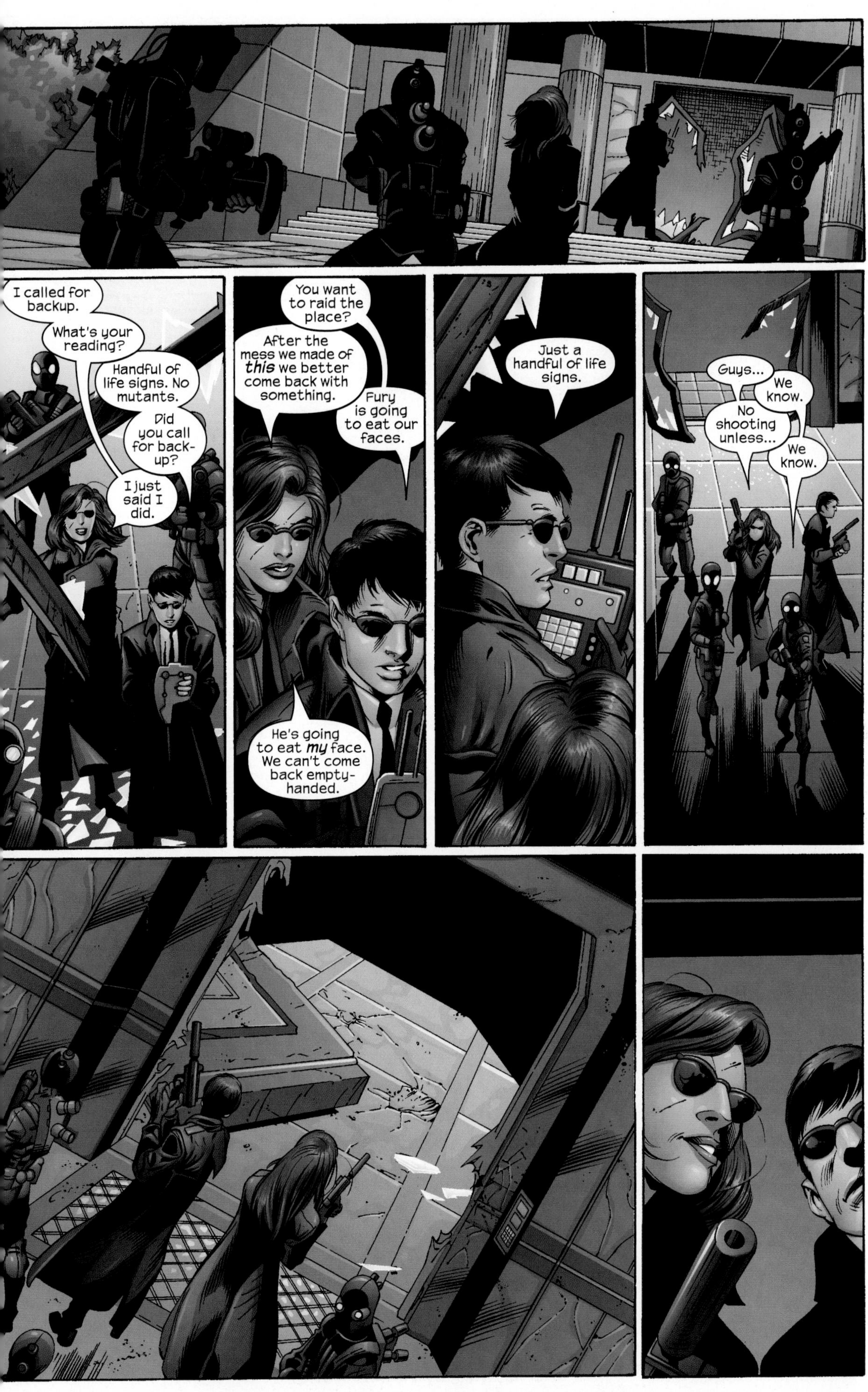
I called for backup.
What's your reading?
Handful of life signs. No mutants.
Did you call for back-up?
I just said I did.
You want to raid the place?
After the mess we made of *this* we better come back with something.
Fury is going to eat our faces.
He's going to eat *my* face. We can't come back empty-handed.
Just a handful of life signs.
Guys...
We know.
No shooting unless...
We know.

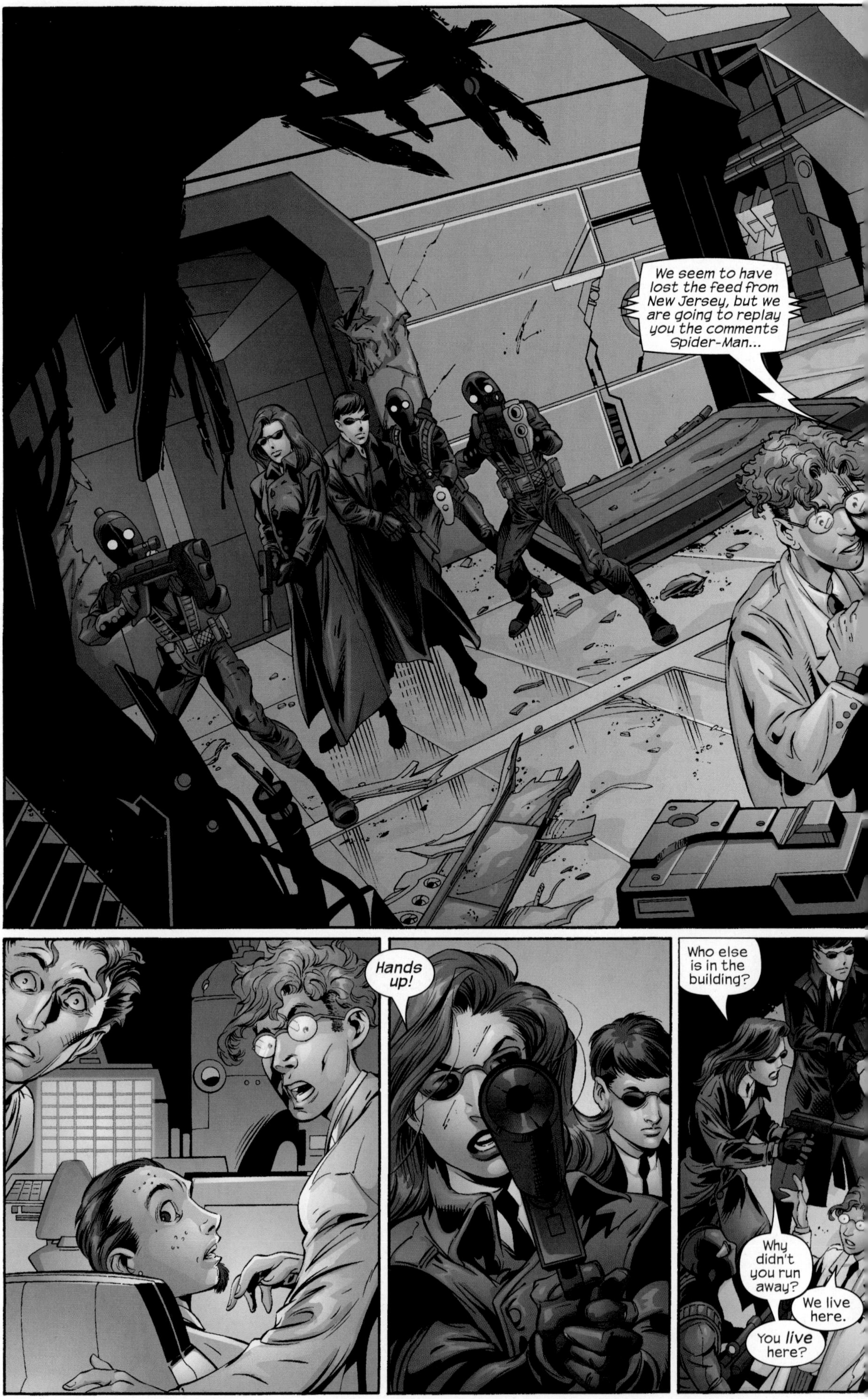
We seem to have lost the feed from New Jersey, but we are going to replay you the comments Spider-Man...
Hands up!
Who else is in the building?
Why didn't you run away?
We live here.
You live here?

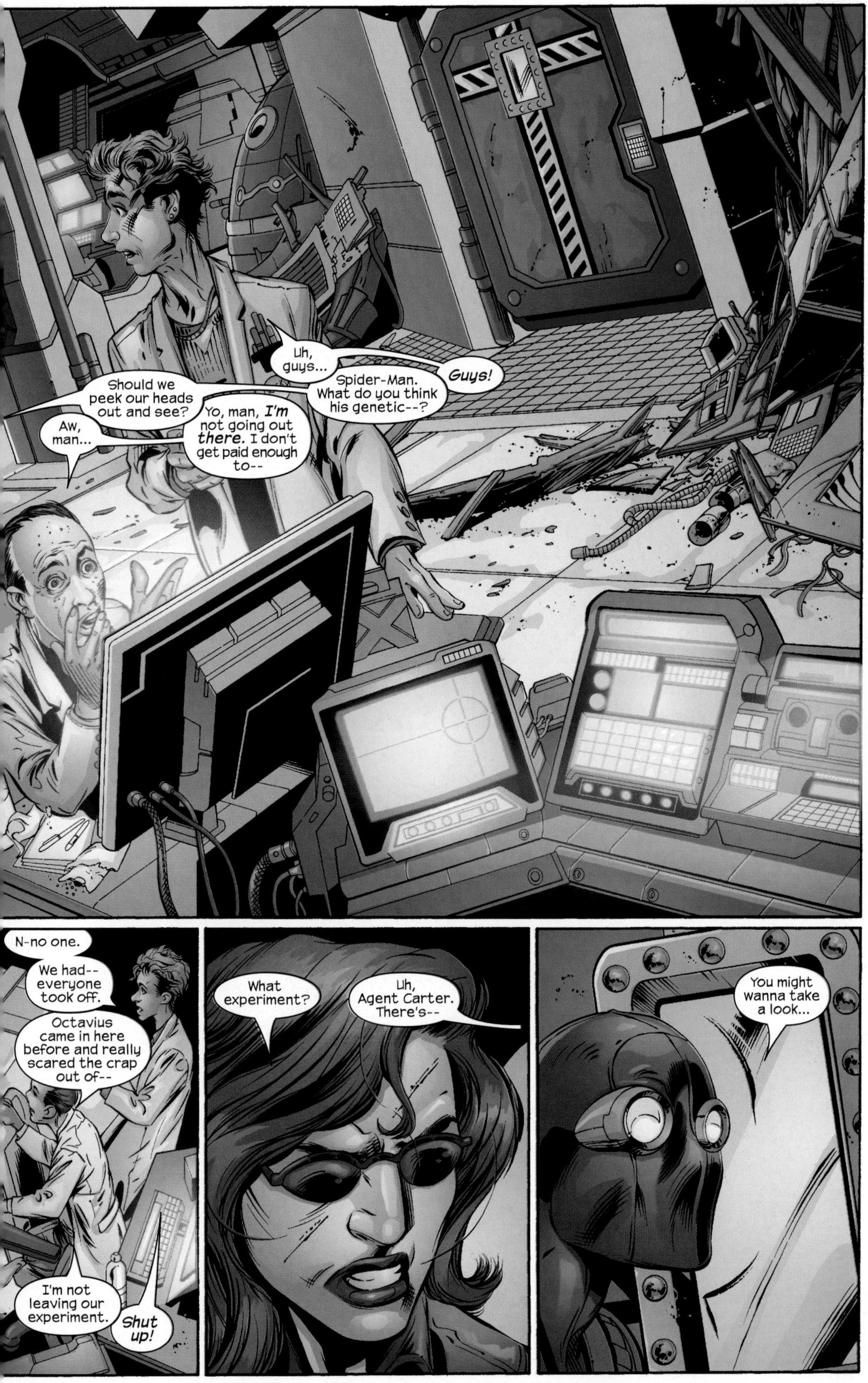
Should we peek our heads out and see?
Spider-Man. What do you think his genetic--?
Aw, man...
Yo, man, *I'm* not going out *there.* I don't get paid enough to--
Uh, guys...
Guys!
N-no one.
We had-- everyone took off.
Octavius came in here before and really scared the crap out of--
I'm not leaving our experiment.
Shut up!
What experiment?
Uh, Agent Carter. There's--
You might wanna take a look...

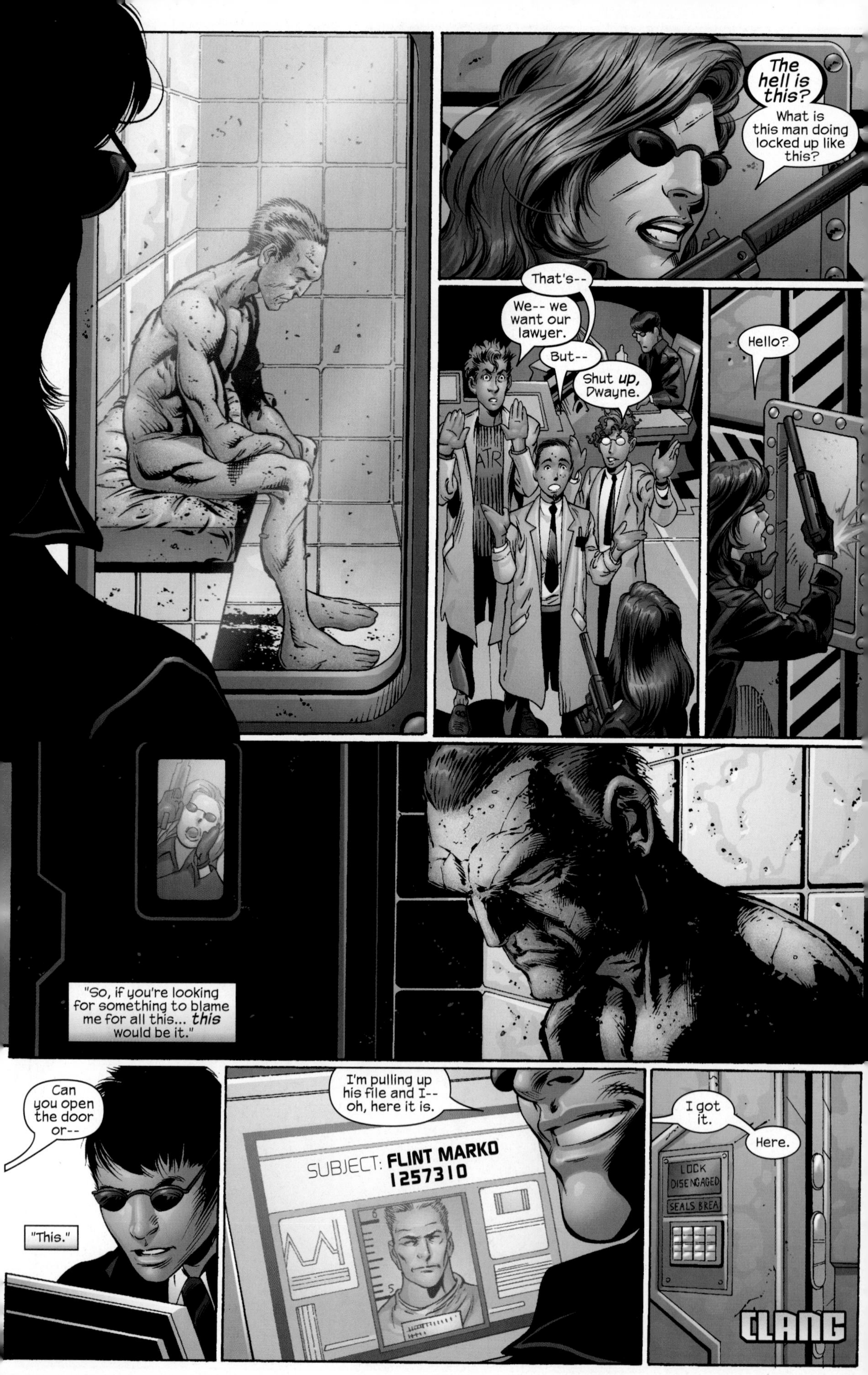
The hell is this?
What is this man doing locked up like this?
That's--
We-- we want our lawyer.
But--
Shut up, Dwayne.
Hello?
"So, if you're looking for something to blame me for all this... this would be it."
Can you open the door or--
"This."
I'm pulling up his file and I-- oh, here it is.
SUBJECT: FLINT MARKO 1257310
I got it.
Here.
LOCK DISENGAGED
SEALS BREA
CLANG

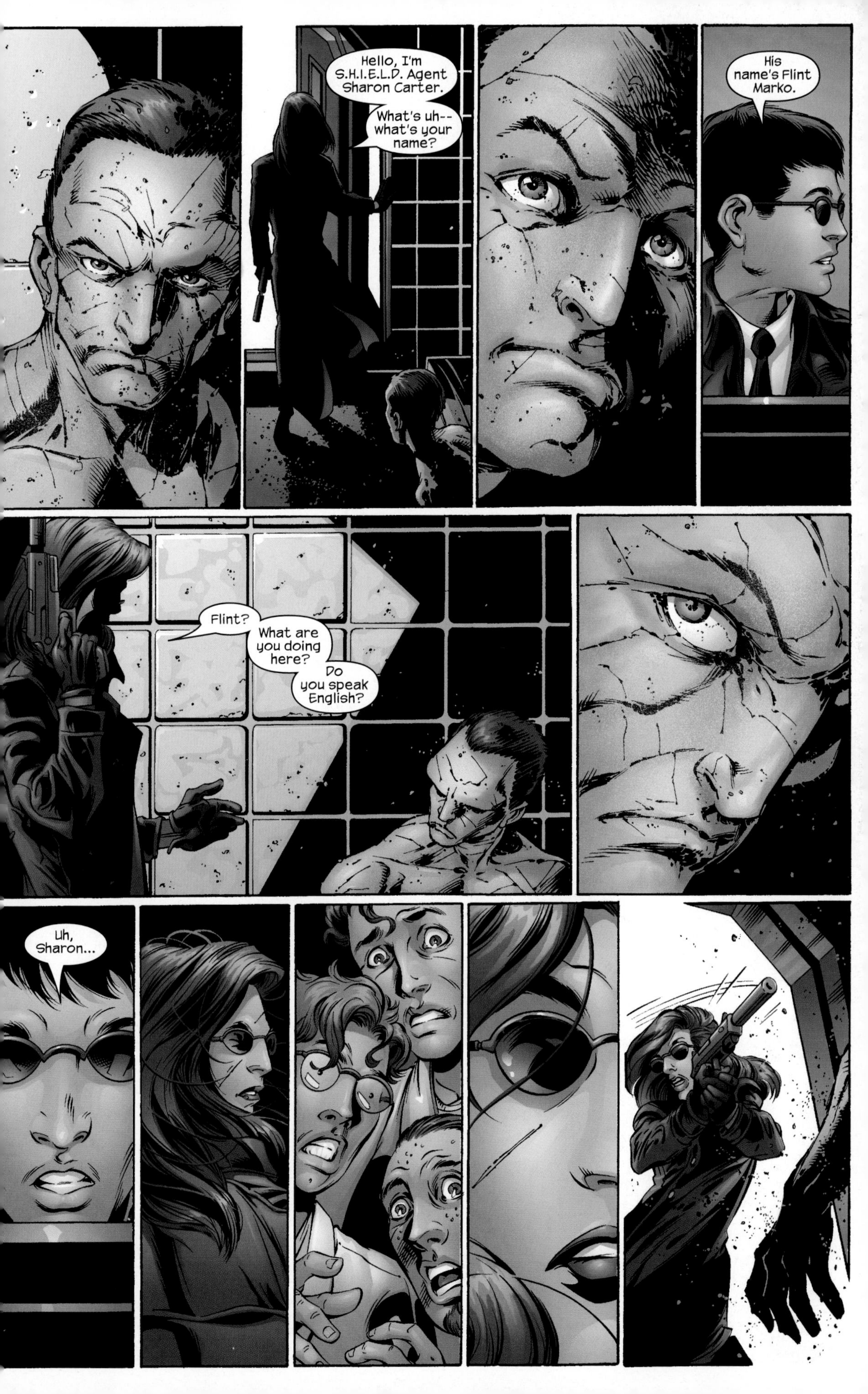
Hello, I'm S.H.I.E.L.D. Agent Sharon Carter.
What's uh-- what's your name?
His name's Flint Marko.
Flint?
What are you doing here?
Do you speak English?
Uh, Sharon...

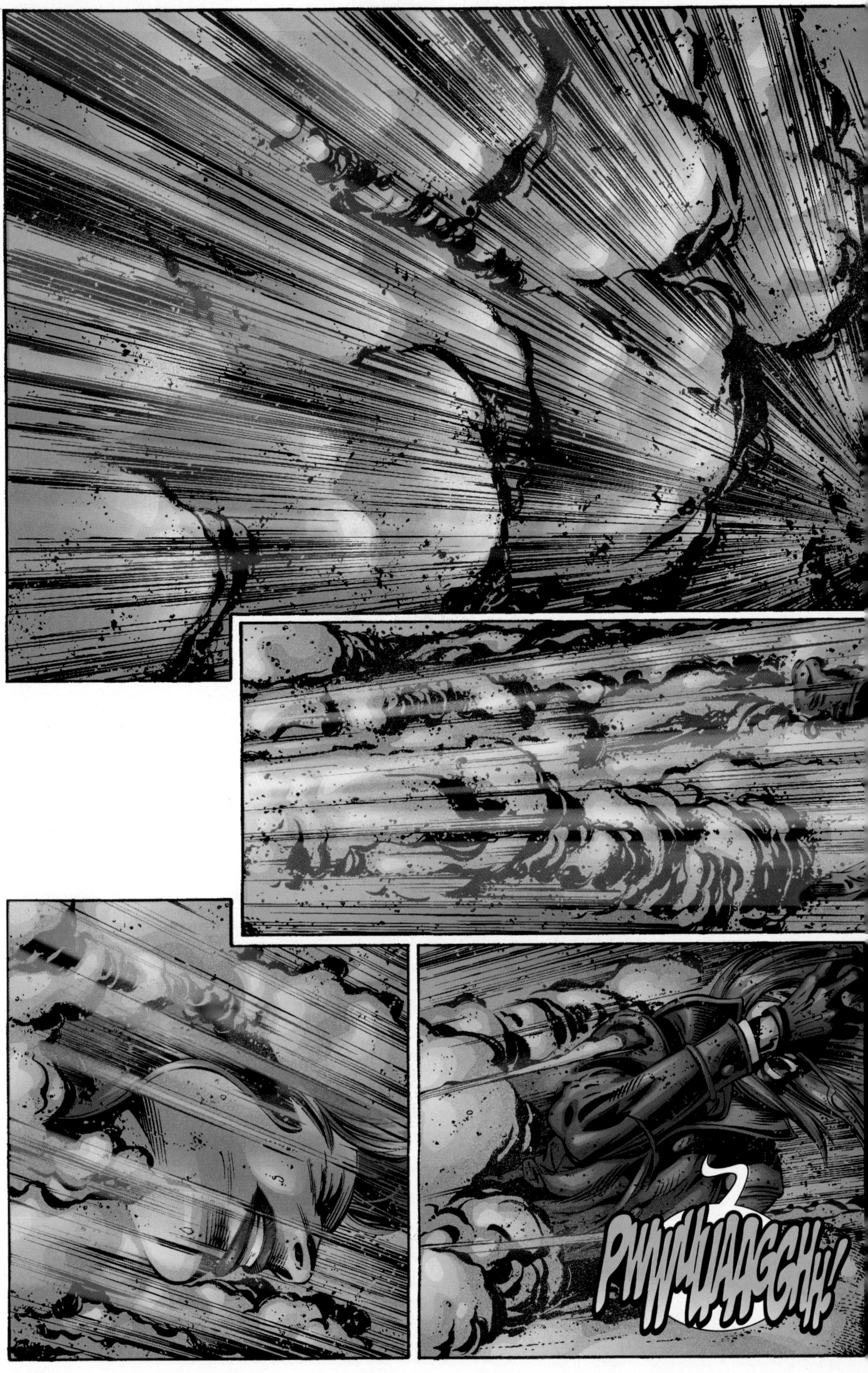
PWWAAAAGGHH!

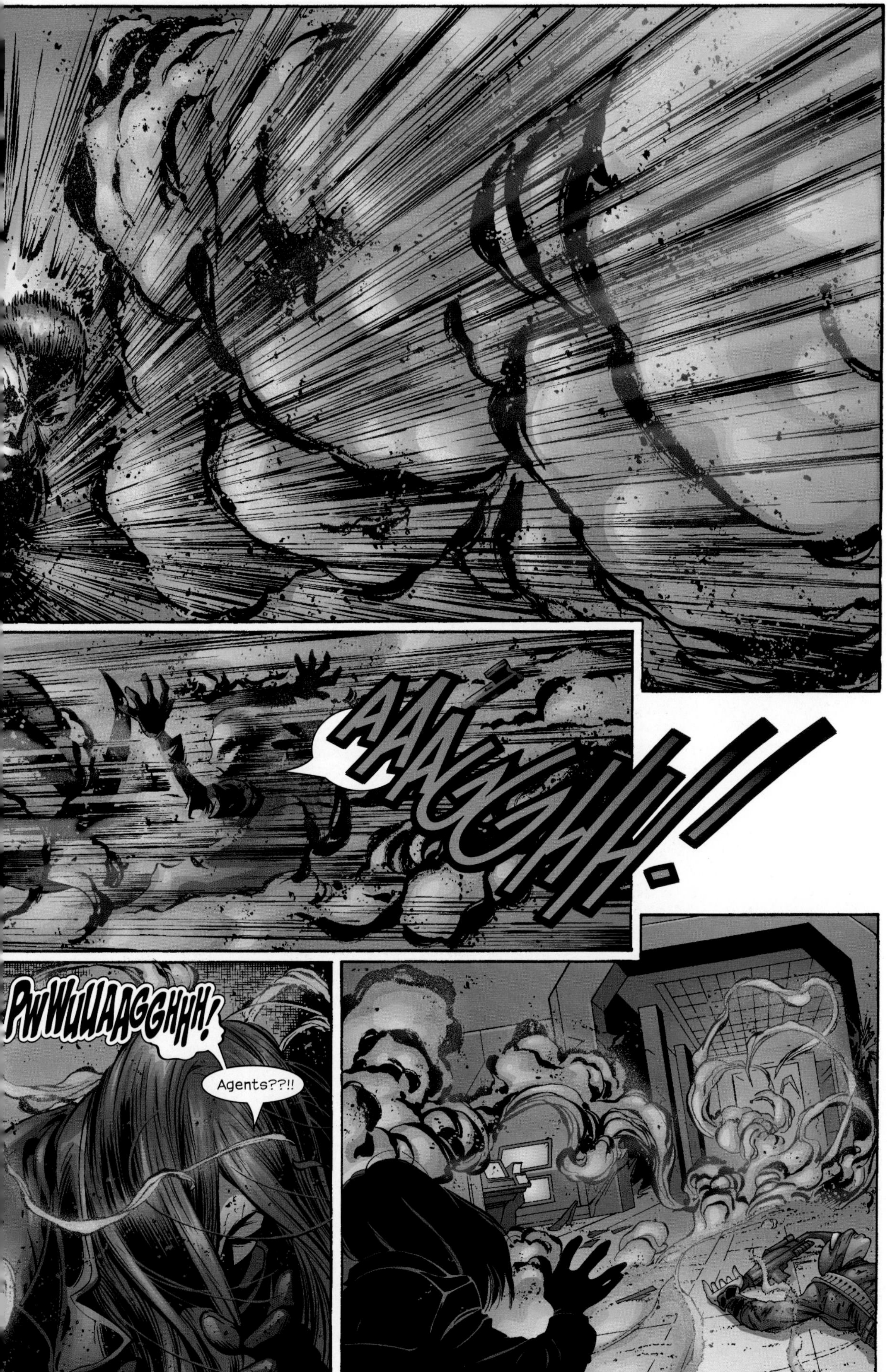
AAAGGHH!!
PWWUUAAGGHHH!
Agents??!!

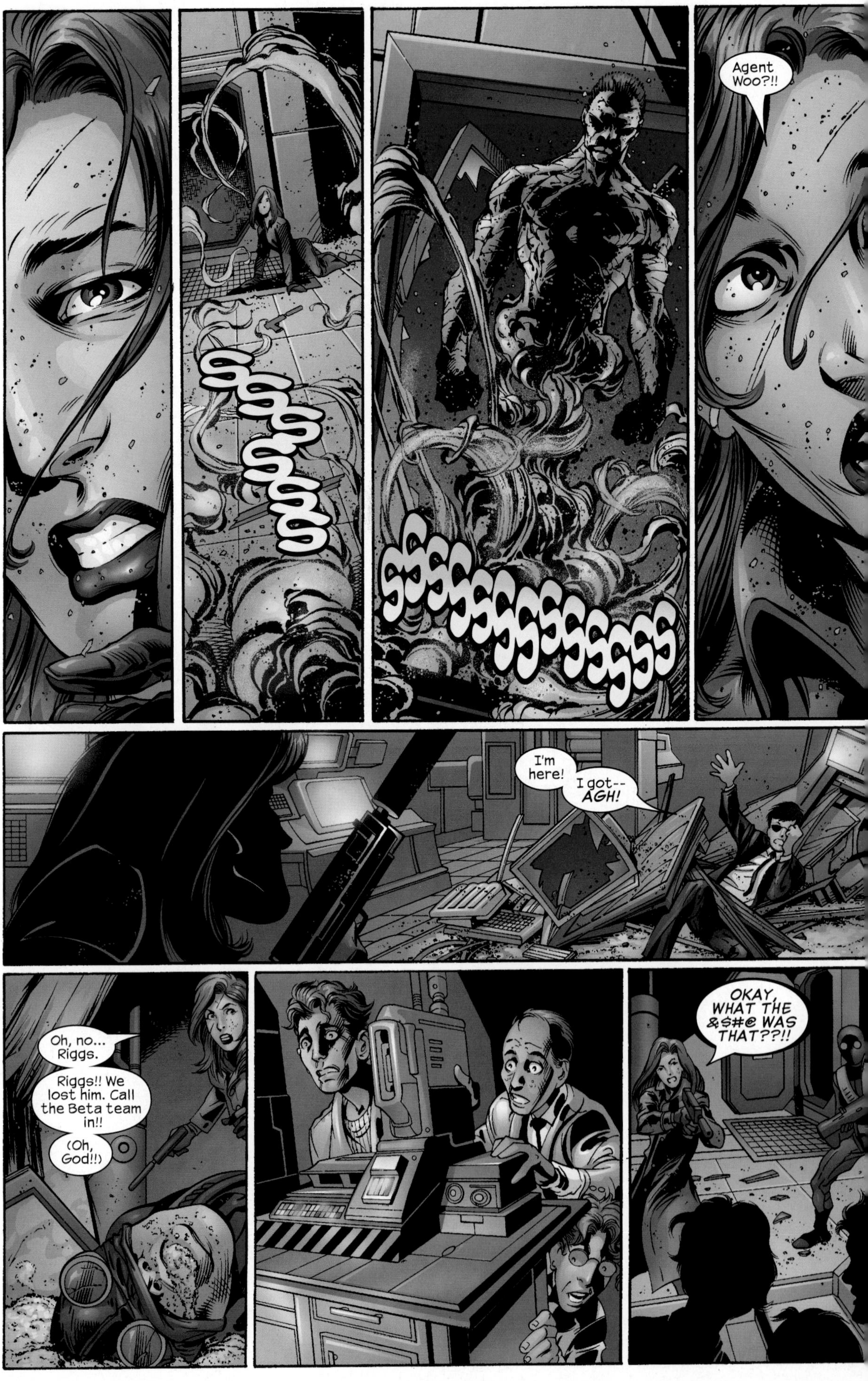
SSSSSSS
SSSSSSSSSSSSSSS
Agent Woo?!!
I'm here!
I got-- AGH!
Oh, no... Riggs.
Riggs!! We lost him. Call the Beta team in!!
(Oh, God!!)
OKAY, WHAT THE &$#@ WAS THAT??!!

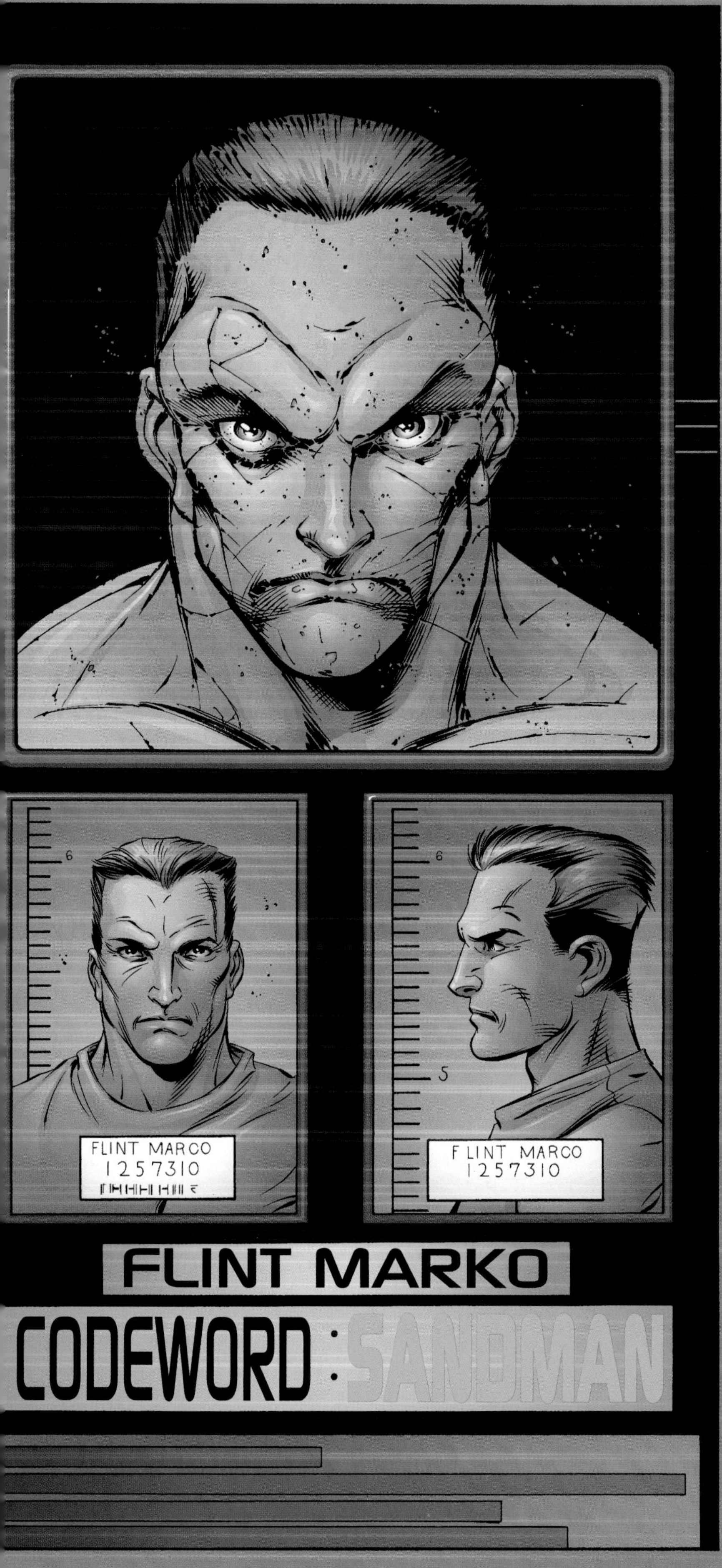
FLINT MARCO
1257310
F LINT MARCO
1257310
FLINT MARKO
CODEWORD : SANDMAN

"His file reads-- and this is, of course, information I got *after* the fact--

"The file reads: Flint Marko-- career piece of crap.

"He was sent to Ryker's for fifty years for the single worst crime spree I have *ever* seen on paper.

"He tried to rob a Brink's car, failed, ran away, went home, beat up his girlfriend...

"(In what I guess was frustration over the botched job.)

"The cops came on a call from neighbors, Marko beat up one of the cops, put him into the hospital.

"Eventually the cop dies.

"So, all that adds up to about the most disgusting human being I have ever heard of and fifty years in Ryker's.

"How he got into Hammer's custody for genetic experimentation is under investigation, but one could guess money changed hands. Deals were made.

"Marko had undergone a smattering of genetic tests and experiments--

"(You'll find the specifics enclosed in the specs report from Hammer's lab.)

"But as it stands his project, Codeword: Sandman, says it all.

"He is able to manipulate his DNA into an organic sand-like quality.

"What this has done to his brain, we don't know yet.

"As he hasn't spoken.

"But now I had an agent down and this Sandman was officially on the loose!"

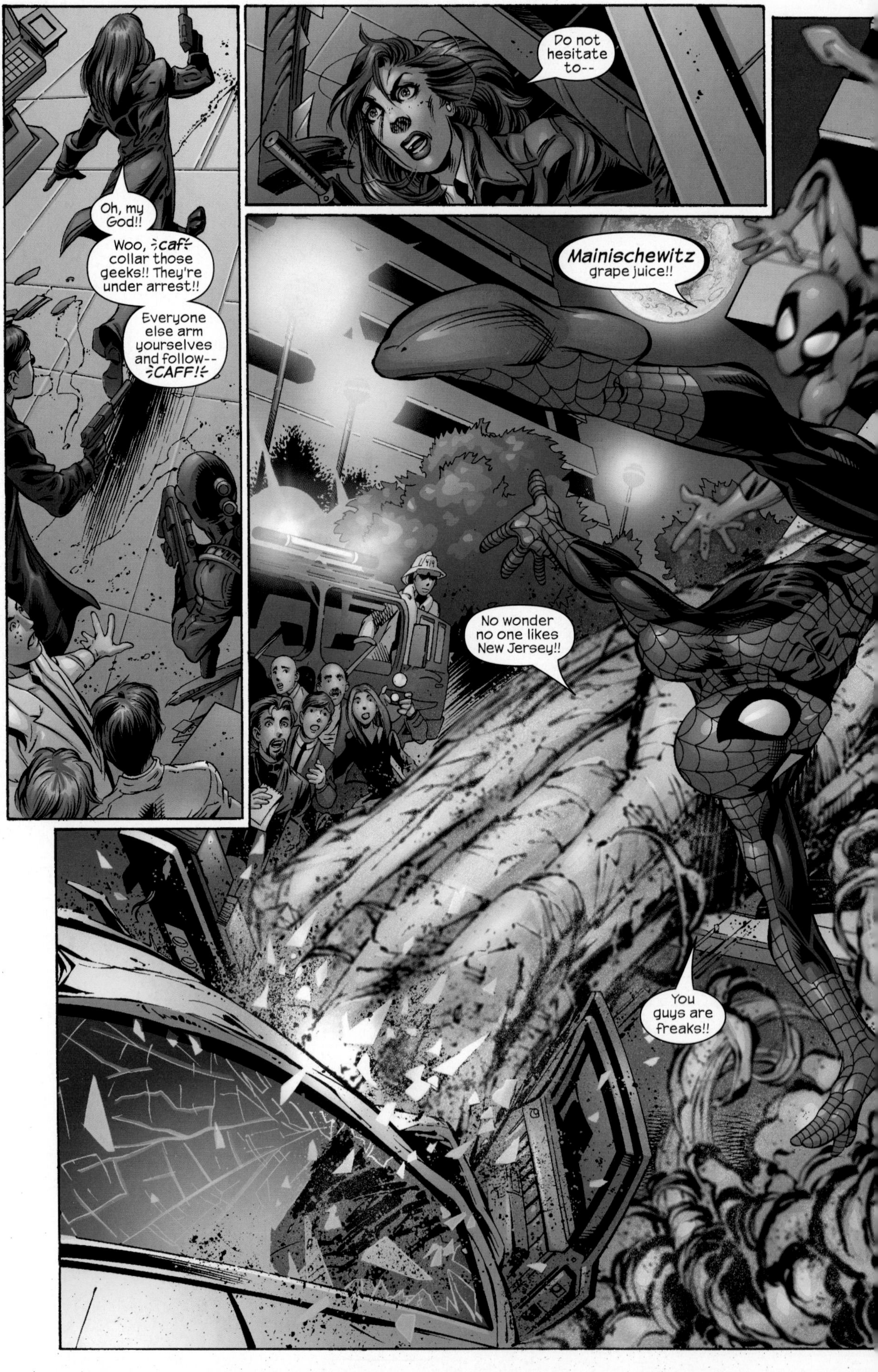
Do not hesitate to--
Oh, my God!!
Woo, *caf* collar those geeks!! They're under arrest!!
Everyone else arm yourselves and follow-- *CAFF!*
Mainischewitz grape juice!!
No wonder no one likes New Jersey!!
You guys are freaks!!

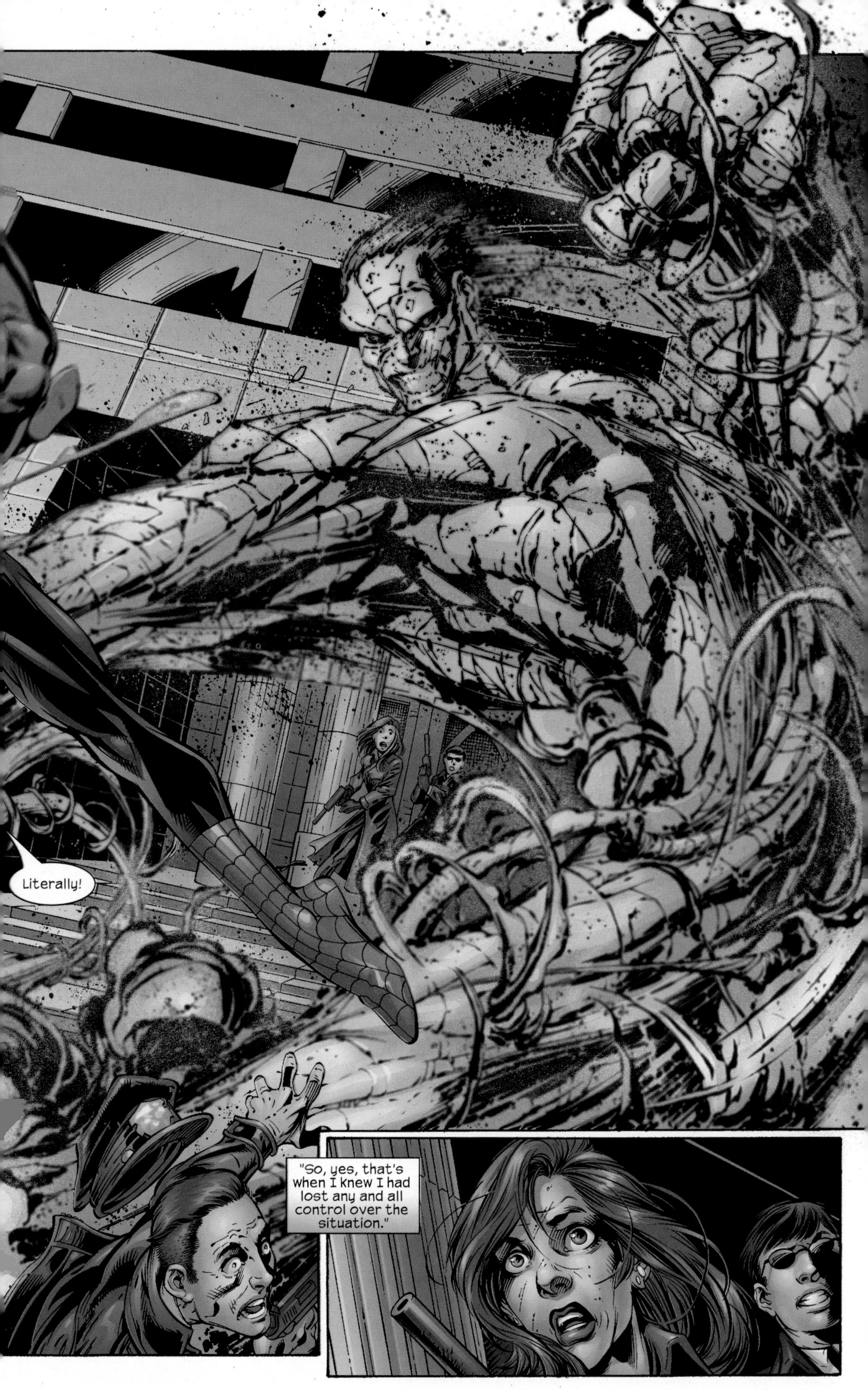
Literally!
"So, yes, that's when I knew I had lost any and all control over the situation."

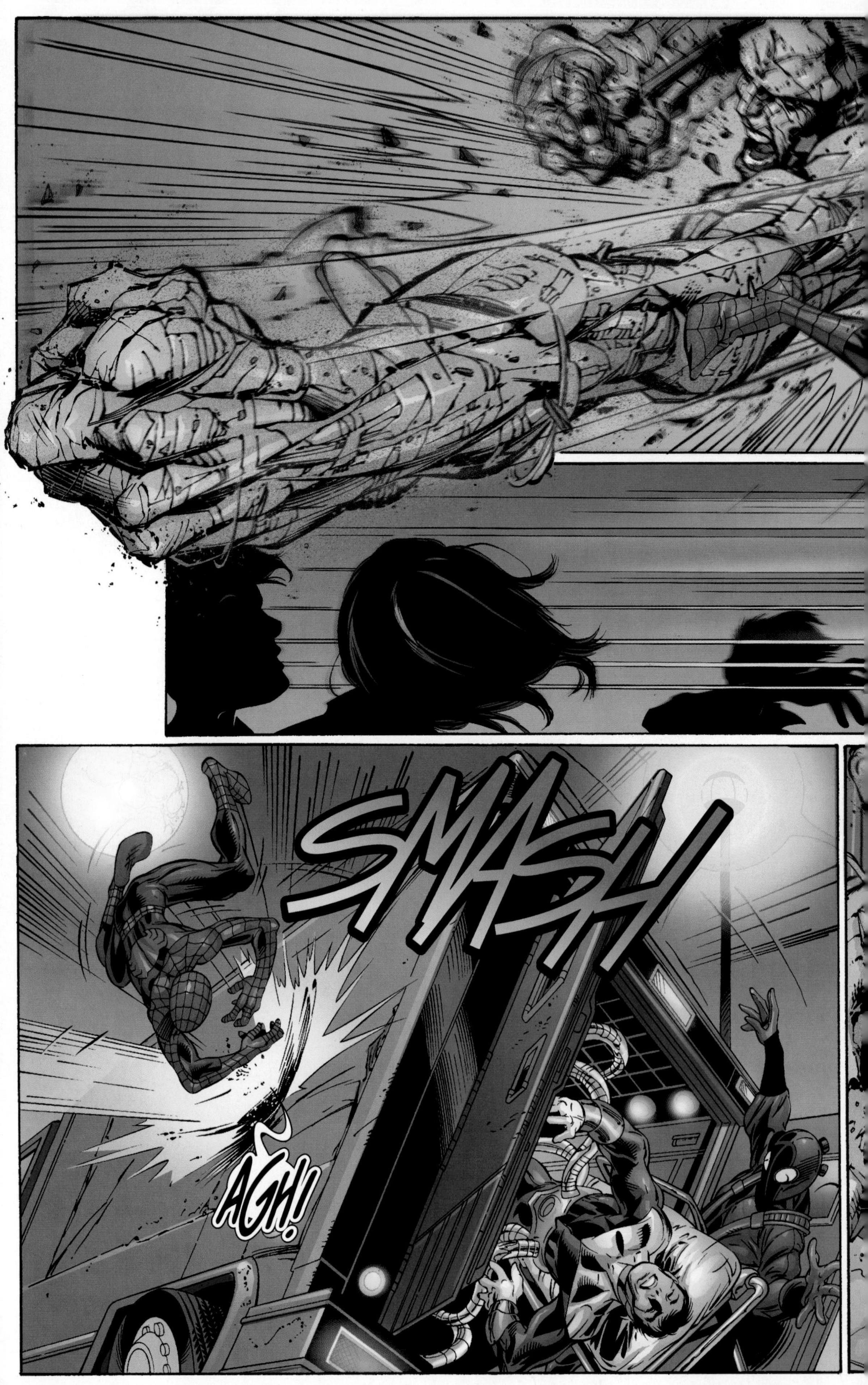
SMASH
AGH!

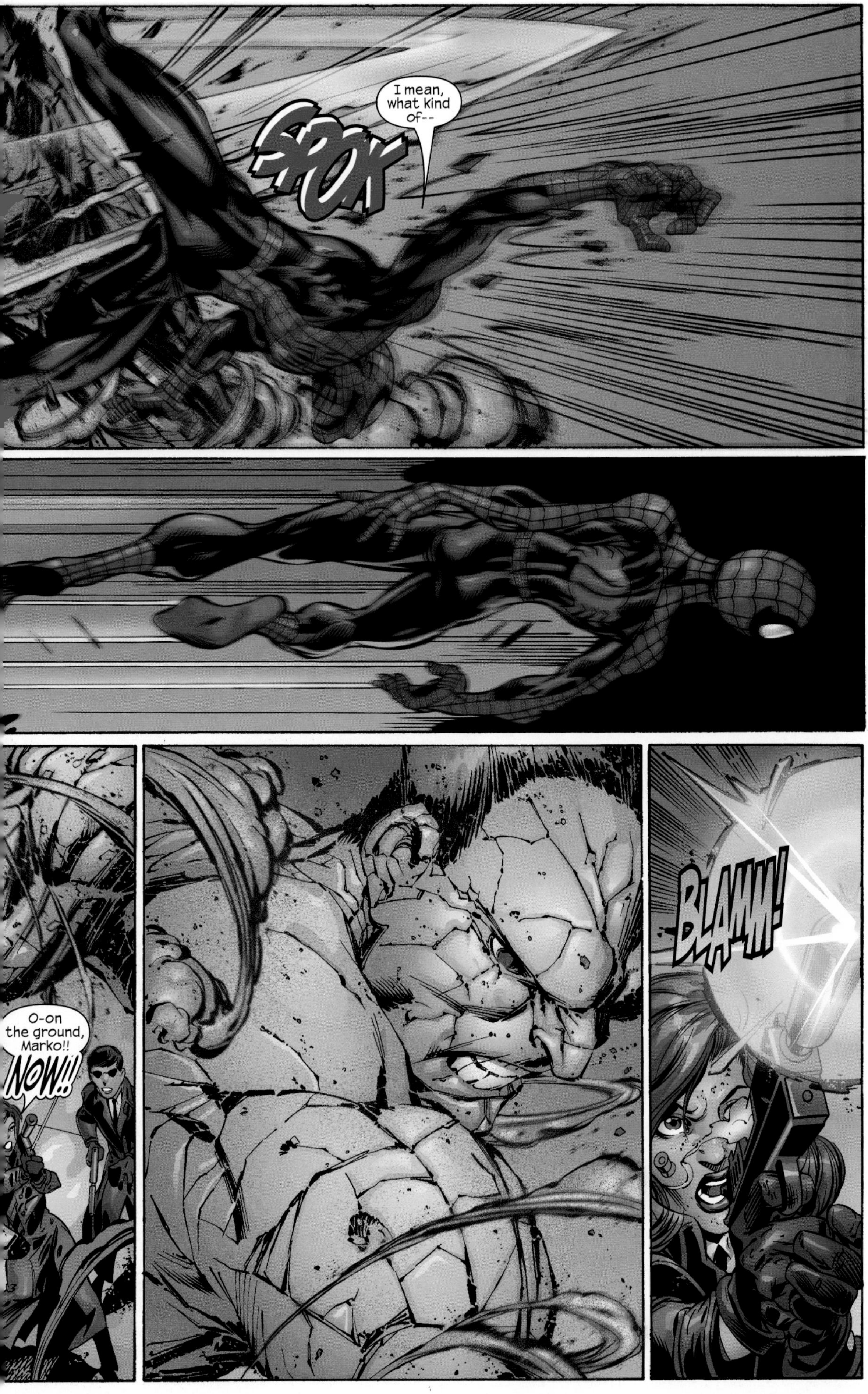
I mean, what kind of--
SPOK
O-on the ground, Marko!!
NOW!!
BLAMM!

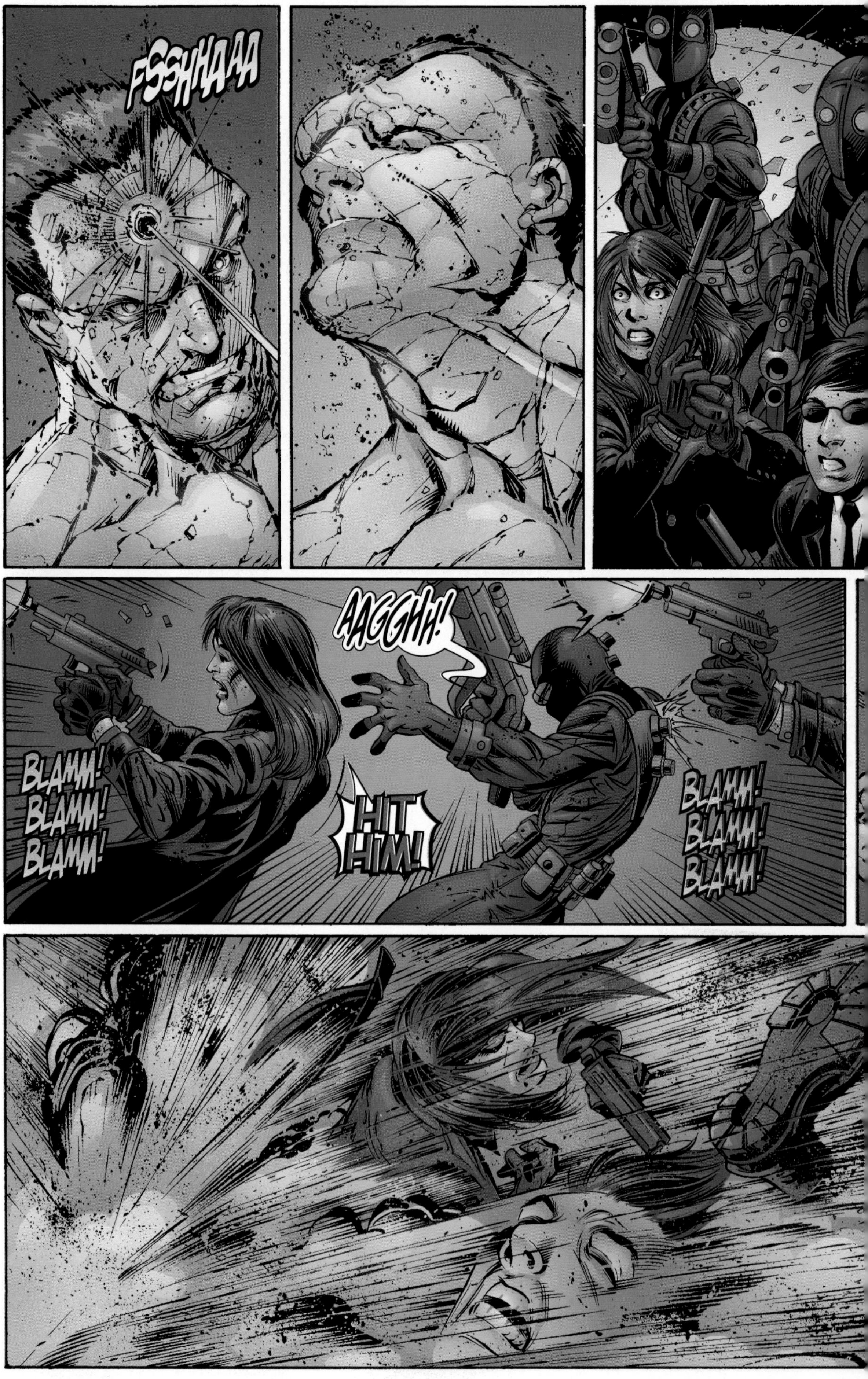
FSSHHAAA
AAGGHH!
BLAMM! BLAMM! BLAMM!
HIT HIM!
BLAMM! BLAMM! BLAMM!

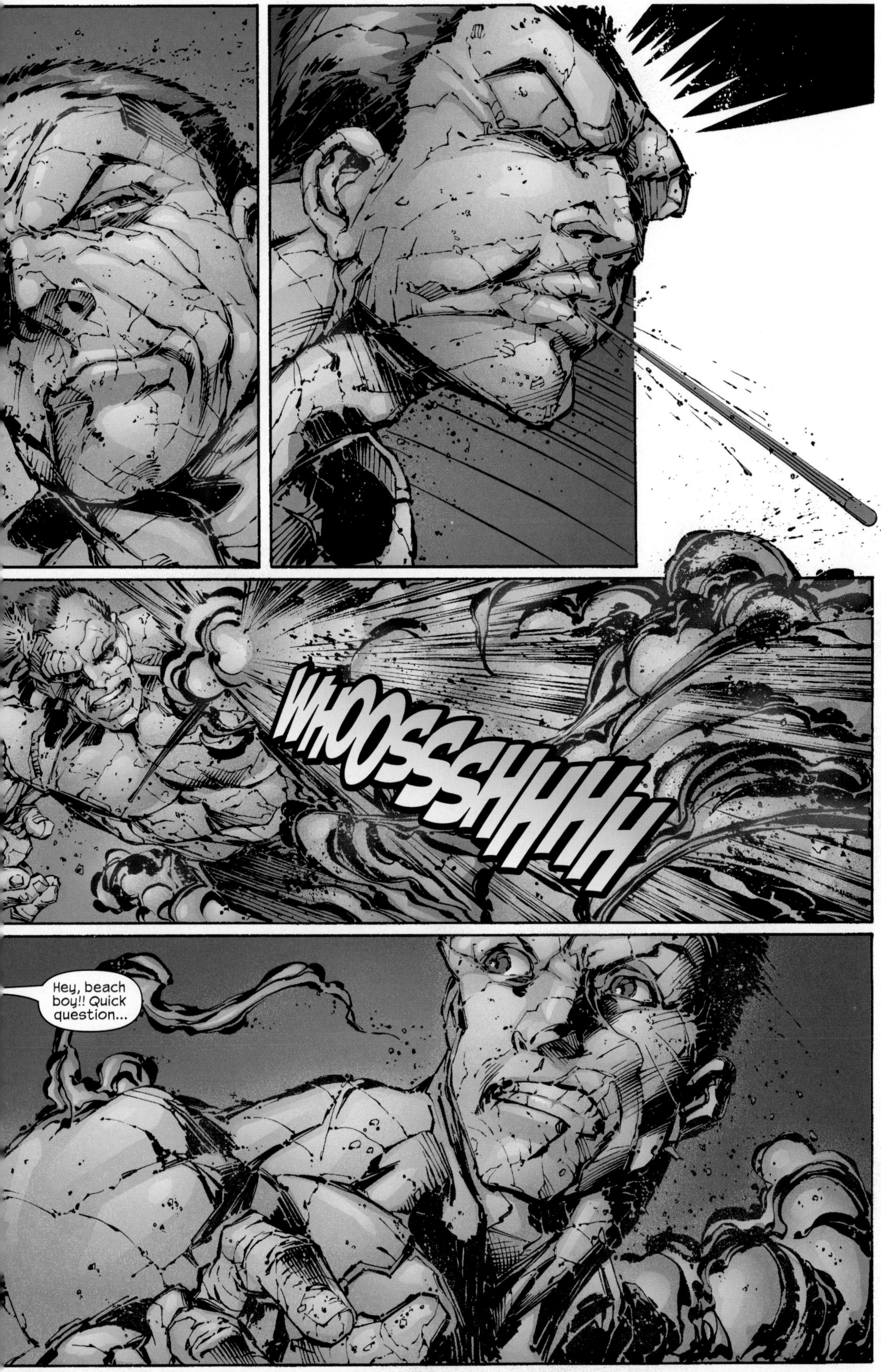
WHOOSSHHHH
Hey, beach boy!! Quick question...

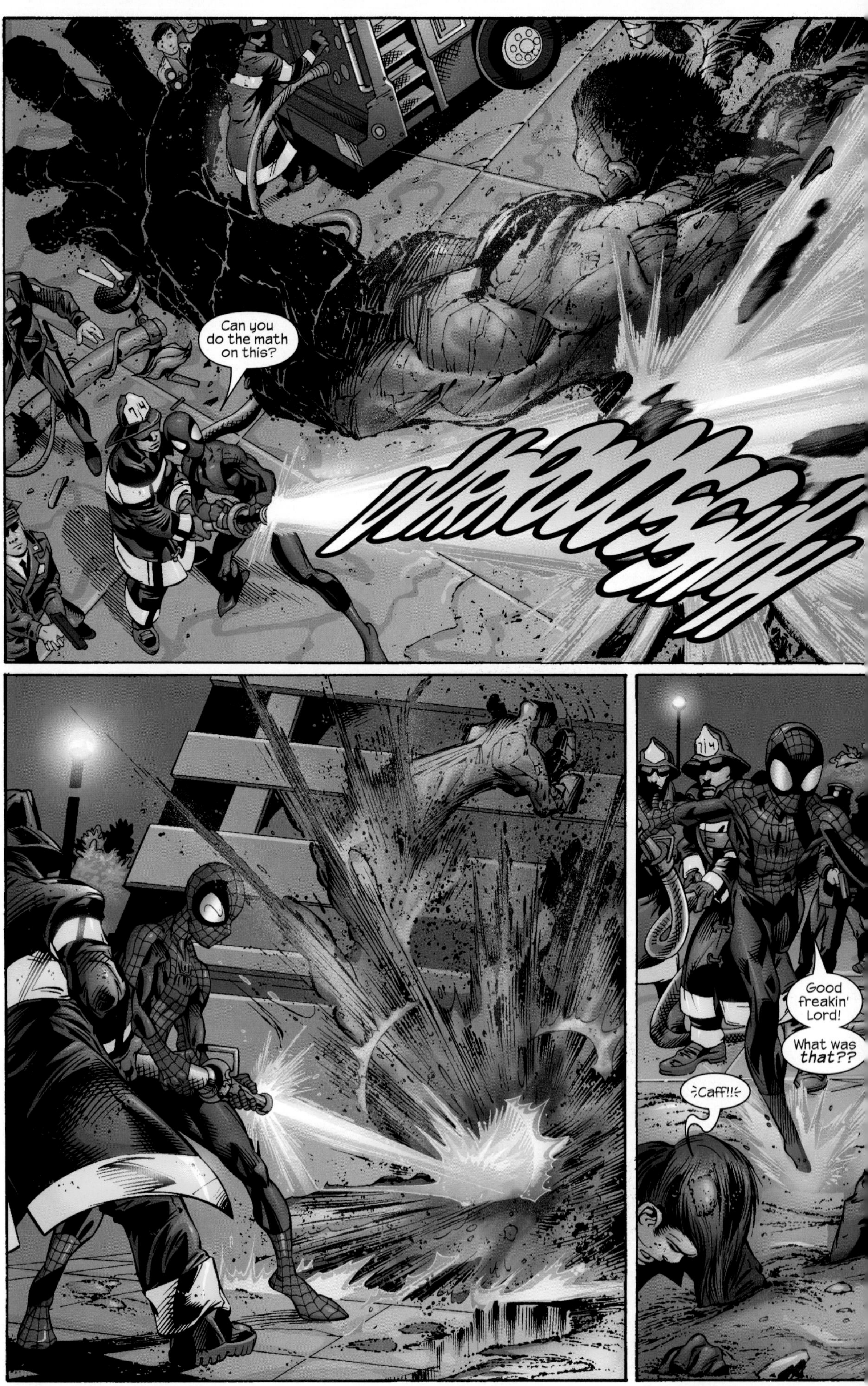
Can you do the math on this?
Good freakin' Lord!
What was *that*??
Caff!!

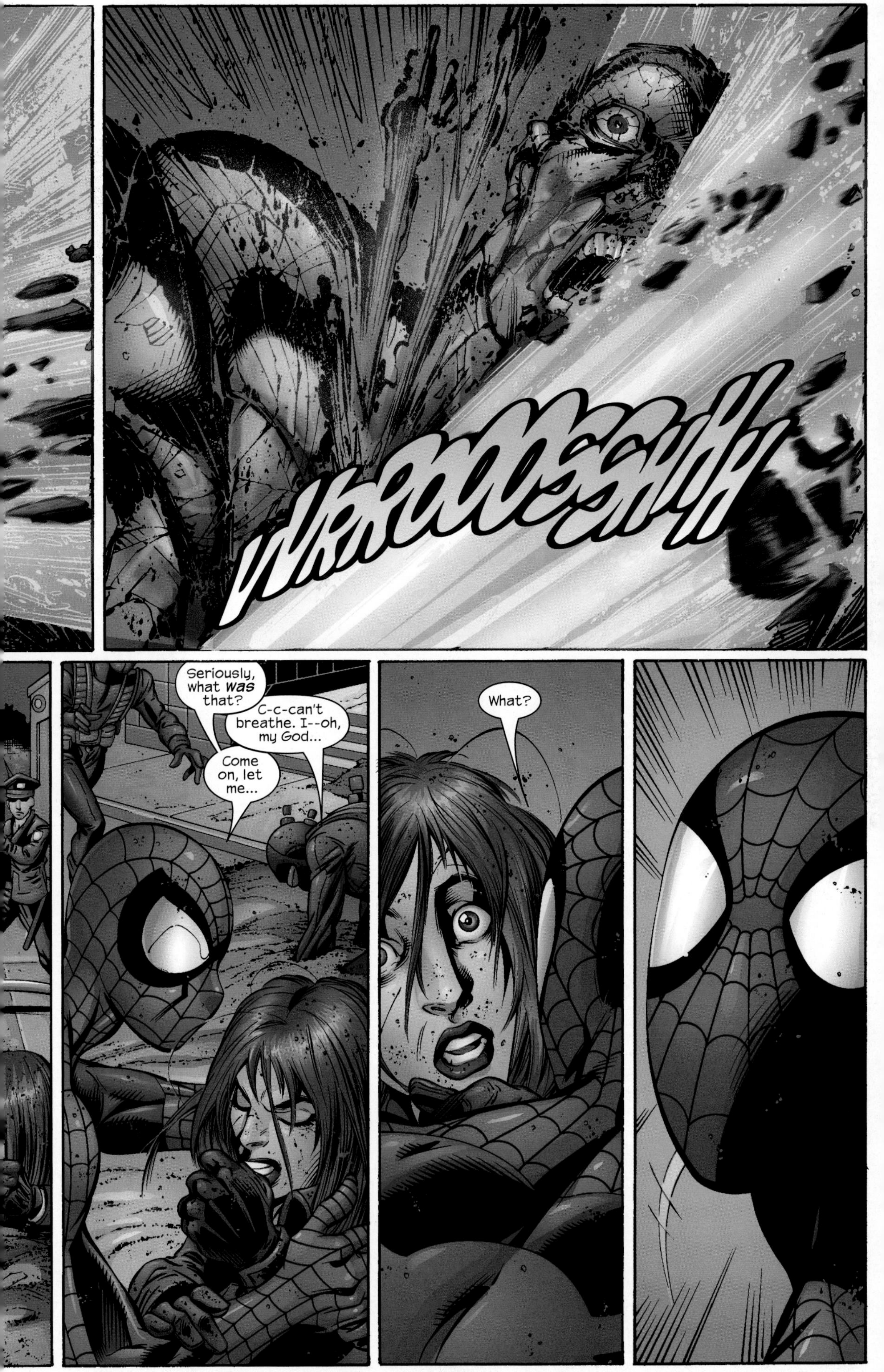
Seriously, what *was* that?
C-c-can't breathe. I--oh, my God...
Come on, let me...
What?

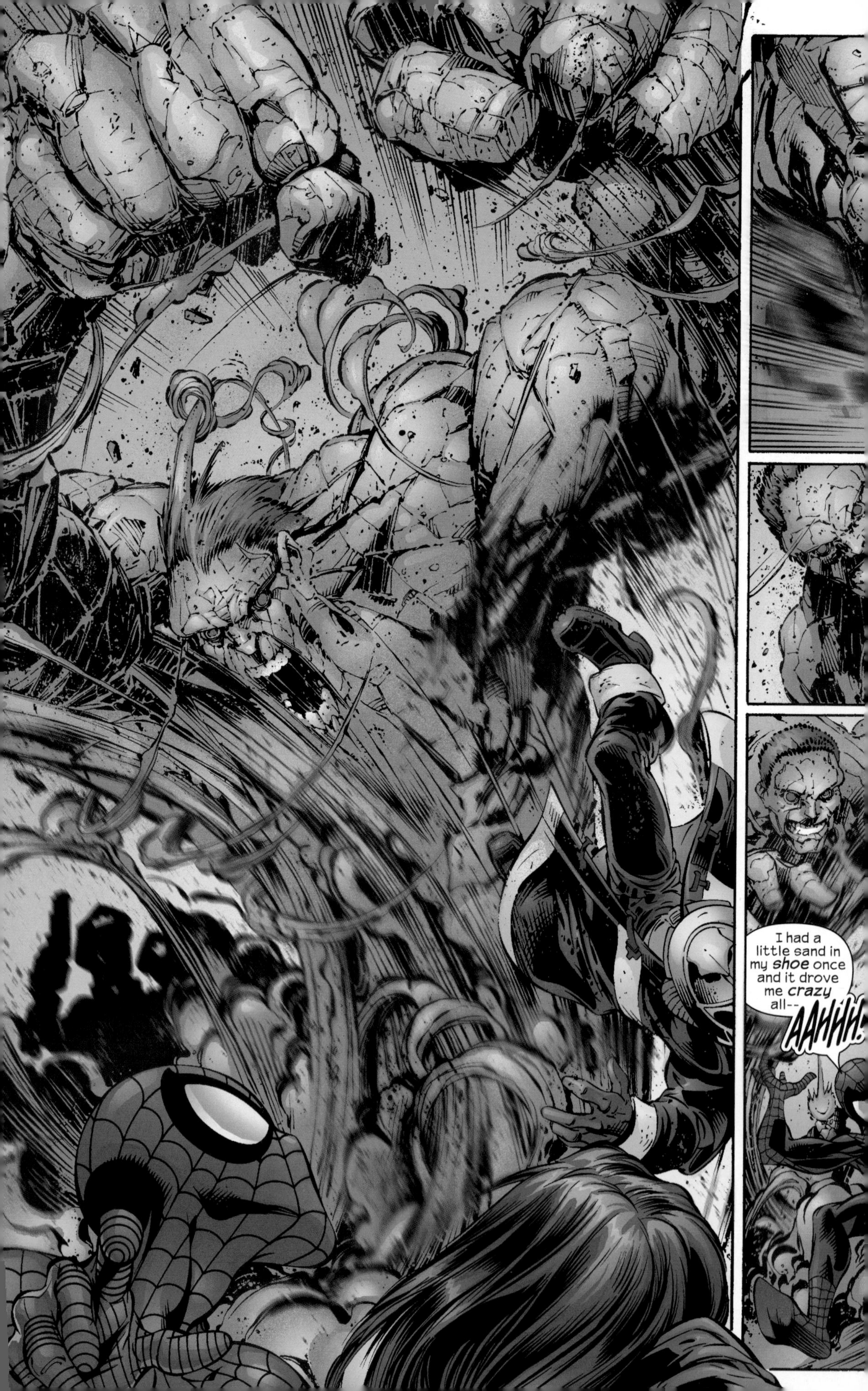
I had a little sand in my *shoe* once and it drove me *crazy* all--
AAHHH!

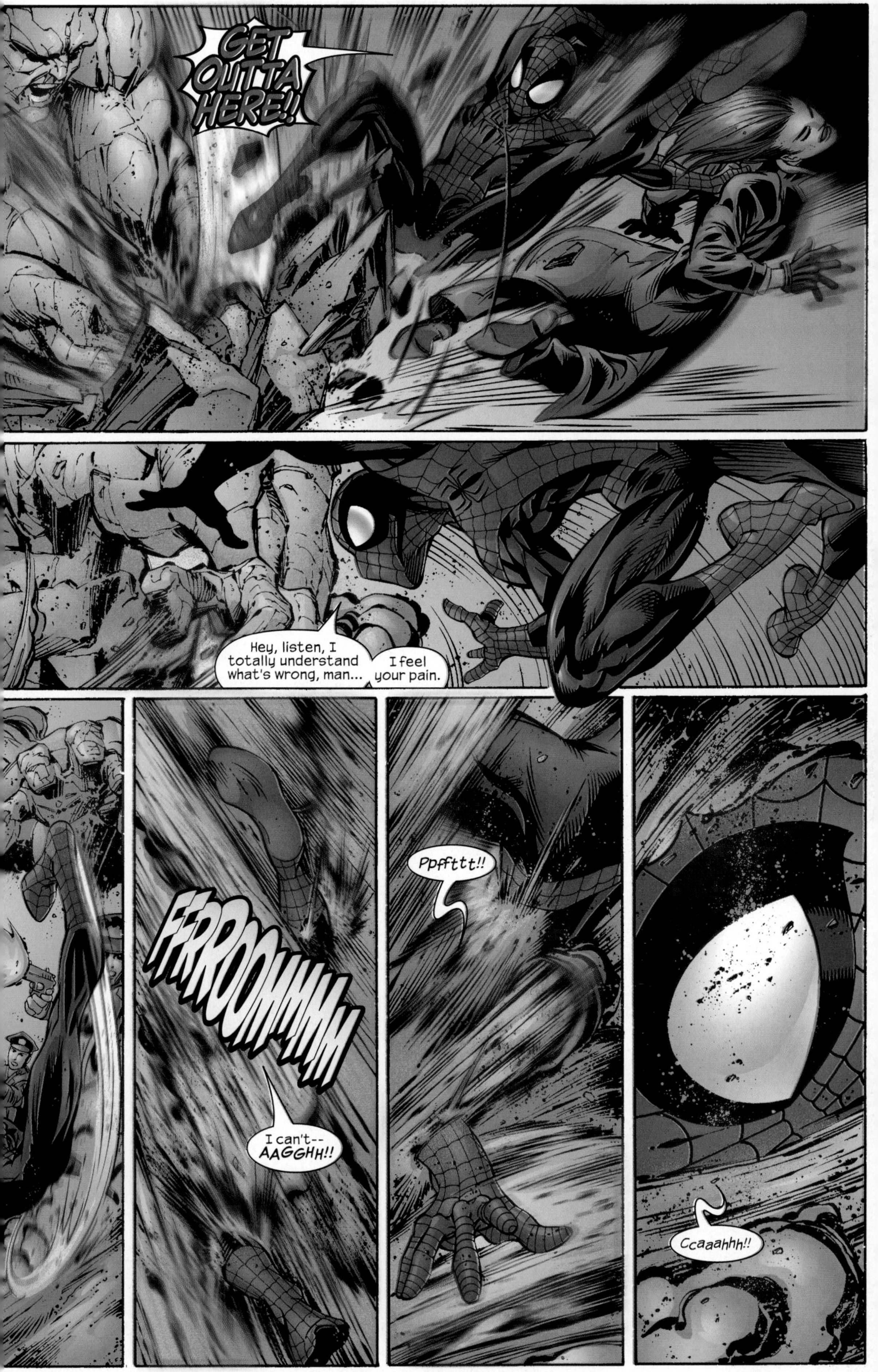
GET OUTTA HERE!!
Hey, listen, I totally understand what's wrong, man...
I feel your pain.
FFRROOMMMM
I can't-- AAGGHH!!
Ppffttt!!
Ccaaahhh!!

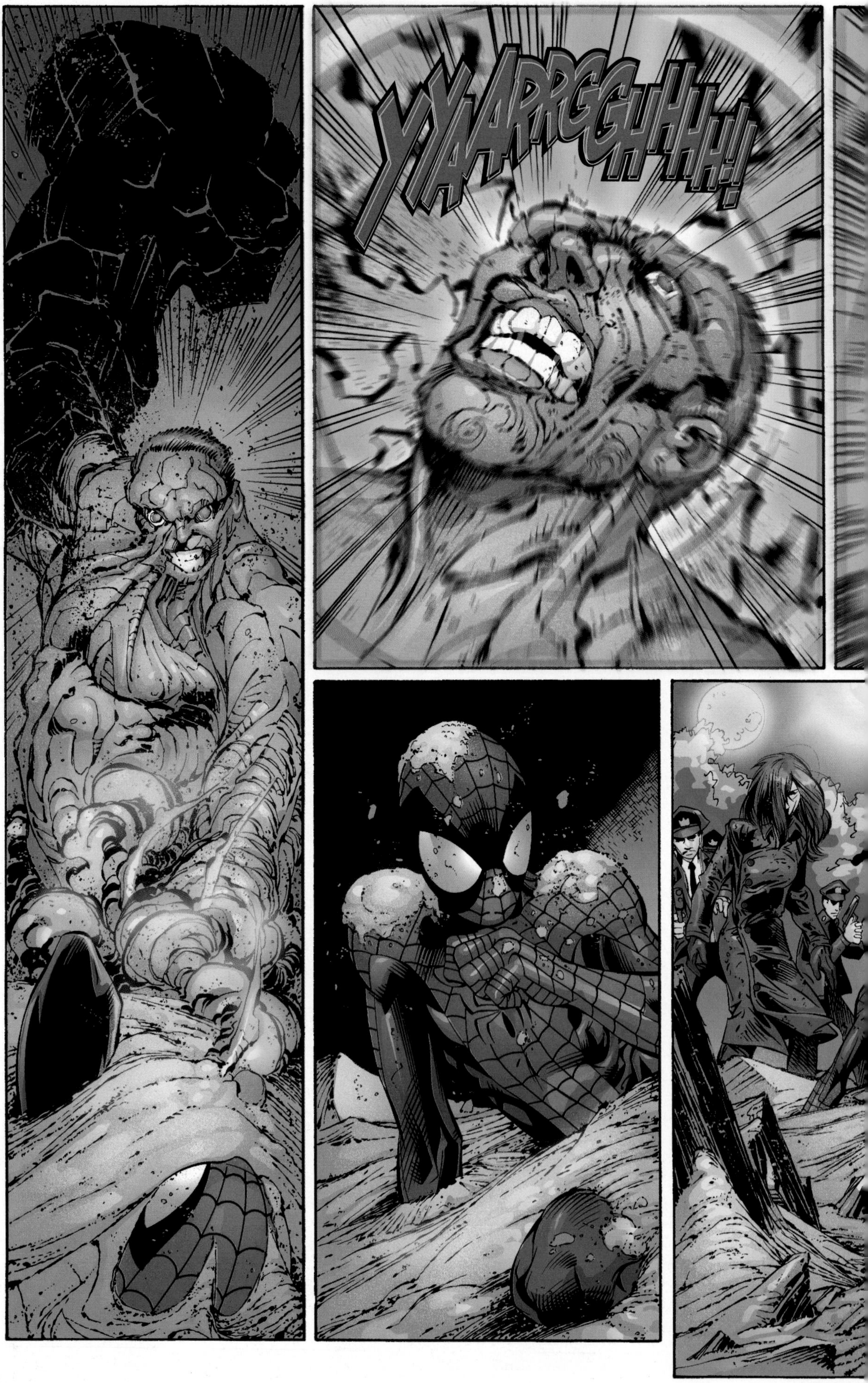
YYAARRGGHHHH!!

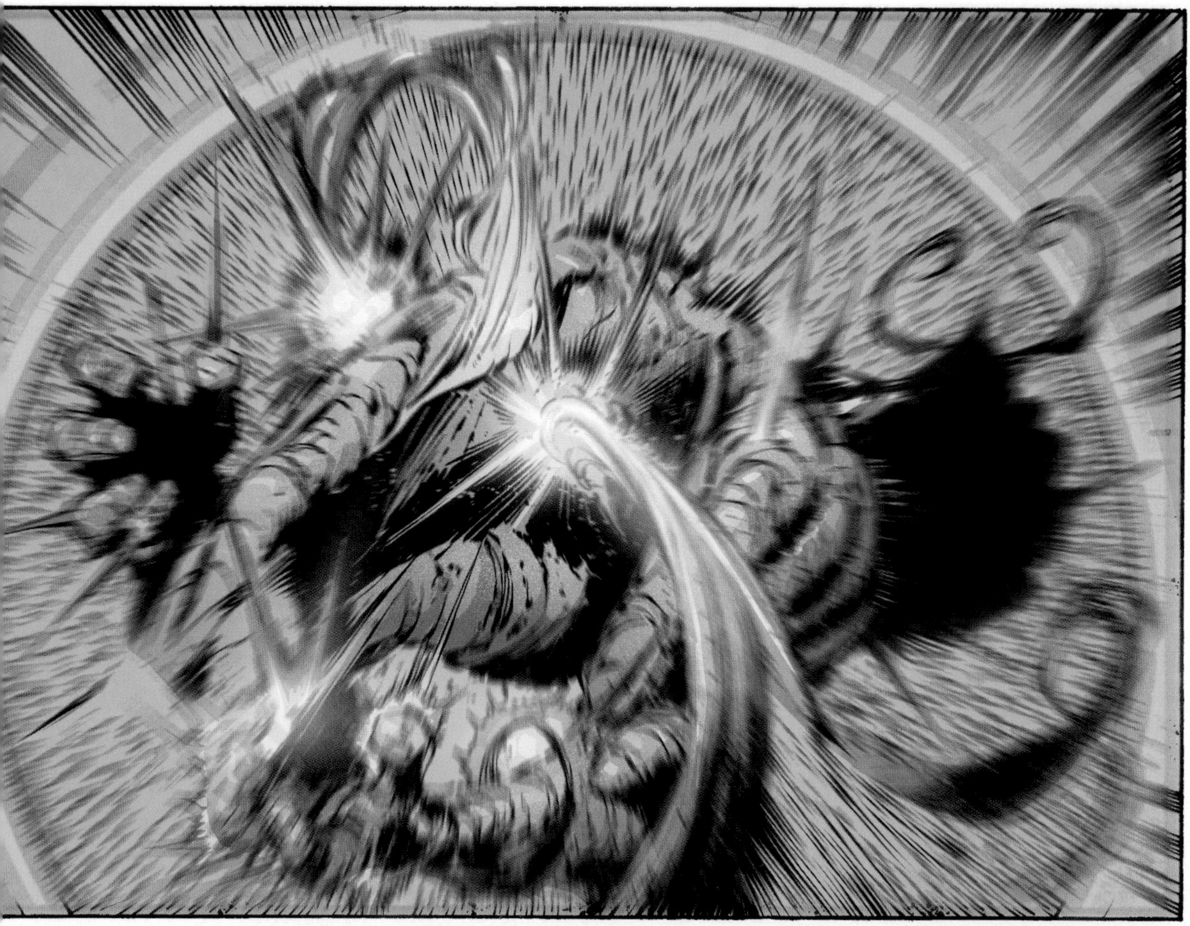

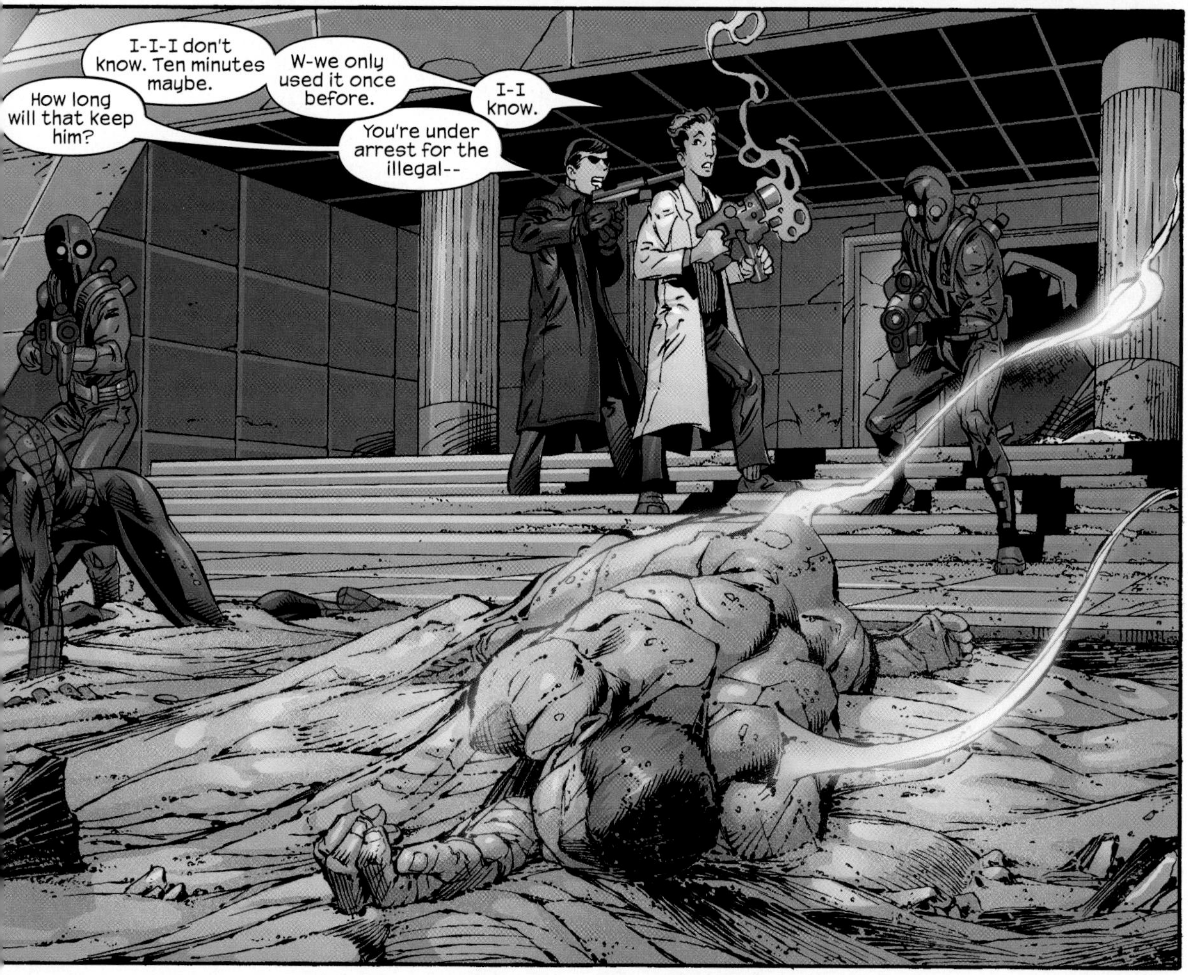
How long will that keep him?
I-I-I don't know. Ten minutes maybe.
W-we only used it once before.
I-I know.
You're under arrest for the illegal--

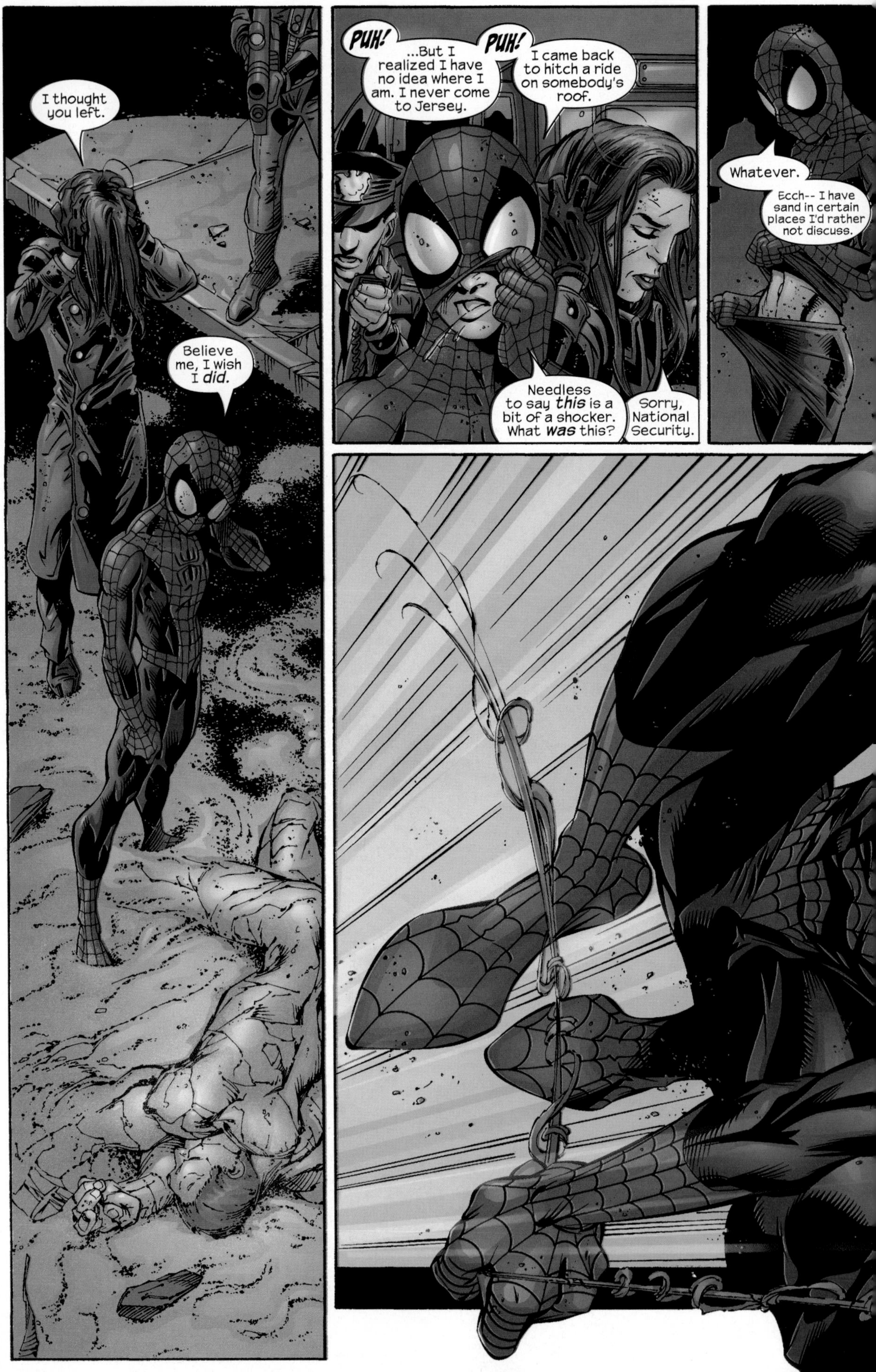
I thought you left.
Believe me, I wish I *did.*
PUH!
...But I realized I have no idea where I am. I never come to Jersey.
PUH!
I came back to hitch a ride on somebody's roof.
Needless to say *this* is a bit of a shocker. What *was* this?
Sorry, National Security.
Whatever.
Ecch-- I have sand in certain places I'd rather not discuss.

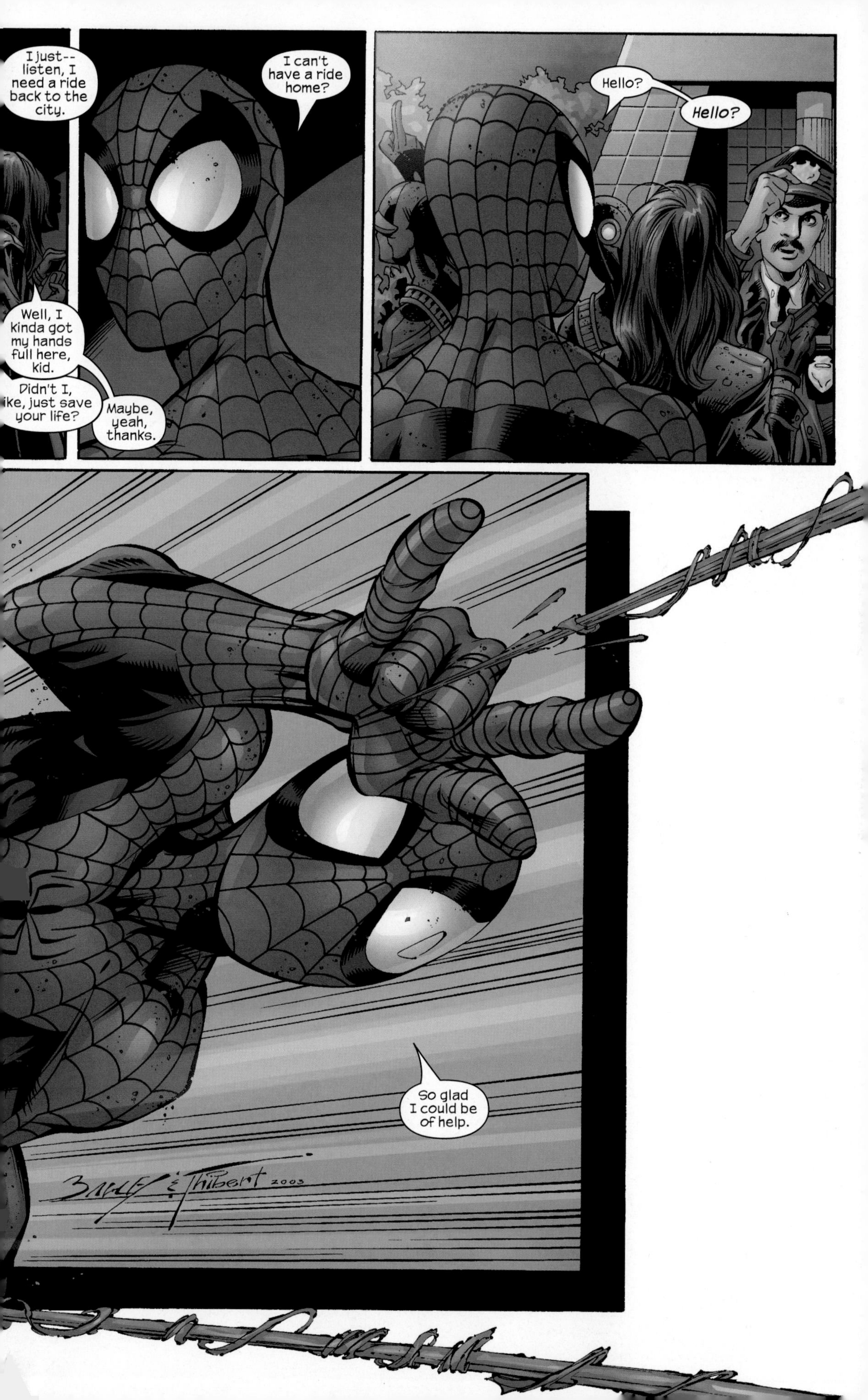

I just-- listen, I need a ride back to the city.
Well, I kinda got my hands full here, kid.
Didn't I, like, just save your life?
Maybe, yeah, thanks.
I can't have a ride home?
Hello?
Hello?
So glad I could be of help.
BAGLEY & Thibert 2003

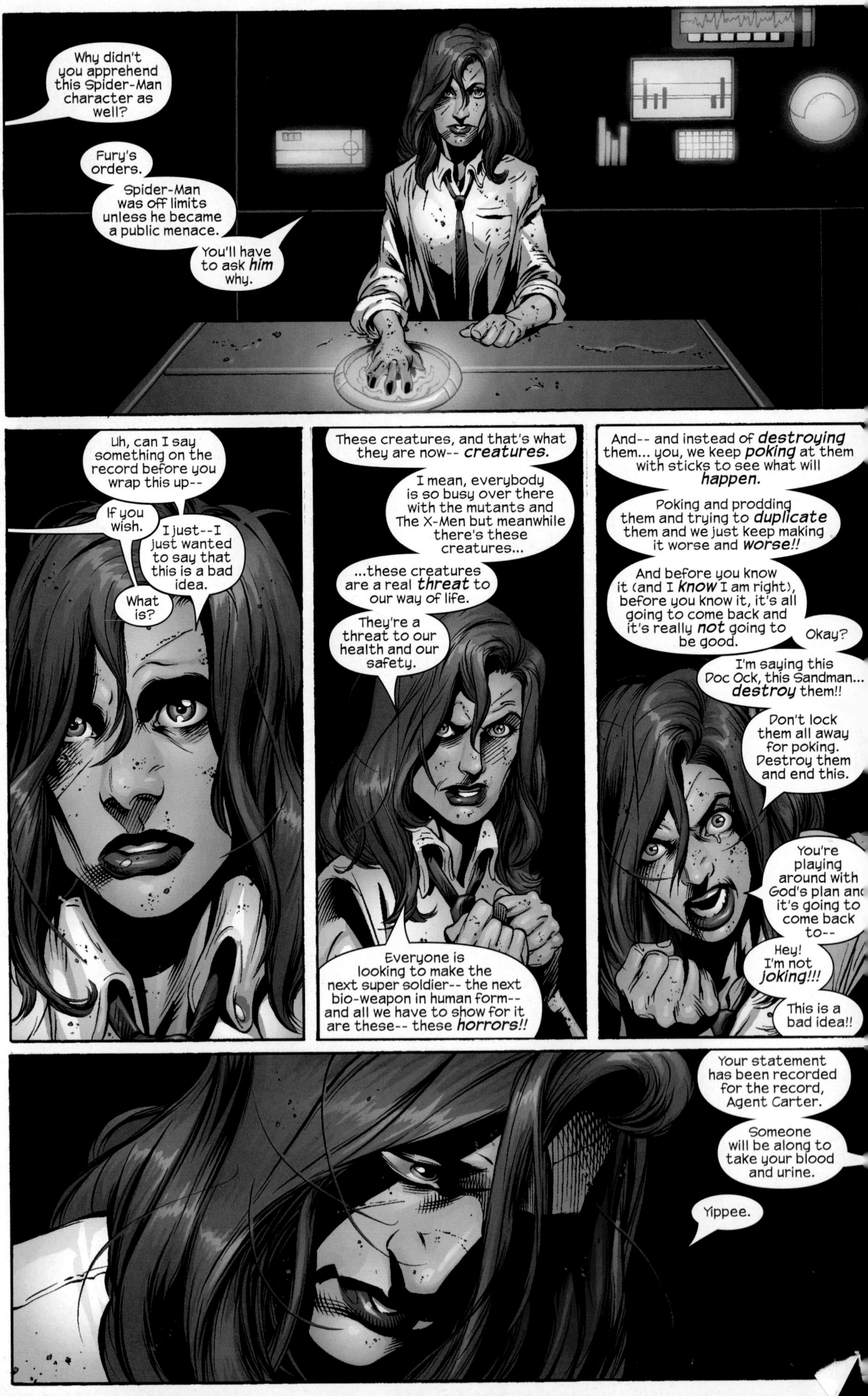
Why didn't you apprehend this Spider-Man character as well?
Fury's orders.
Spider-Man was off limits unless he became a public menace.
You'll have to ask *him* why.
Uh, can I say something on the record before you wrap this up--
If you wish.
I just--I just wanted to say that this is a bad idea.
What is?
These creatures, and that's what they are now-- *creatures.*
I mean, everybody is so busy over there with the mutants and The X-Men but meanwhile there's these creatures...
...these creatures are a real *threat* to our way of life.
They're a threat to our health and our safety.
Everyone is looking to make the next super soldier-- the next bio-weapon in human form-- and all we have to show for it are these-- these *horrors!!*
And-- and instead of *destroying* them... you, we keep *poking* at them with sticks to see what will *happen.*
Poking and prodding them and trying to *duplicate* them and we just keep making it worse and *worse!!*
And before you know it (and I *know* I am right), before you know it, it's all going to come back and it's really *not* going to be good.
Okay?
I'm saying this Doc Ock, this Sandman... *destroy* them!!
Don't lock them all away for poking. Destroy them and end this.
You're playing around with God's plan and it's going to come back to--
Hey! I'm not *joking!!!*
This is a bad idea!!
Your statement has been recorded for the record, Agent Carter.
Someone will be along to take your blood and urine.
Yippee.

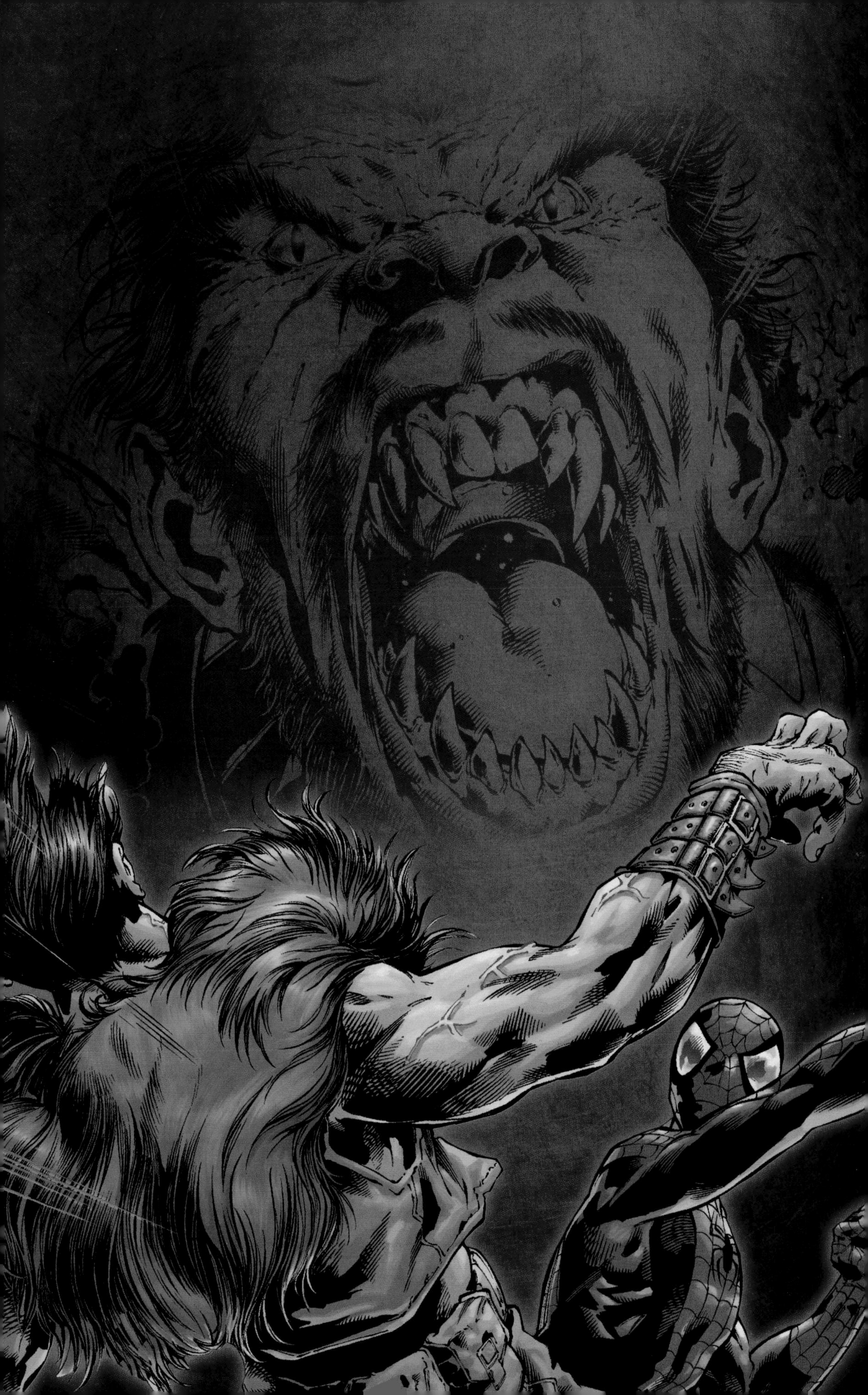

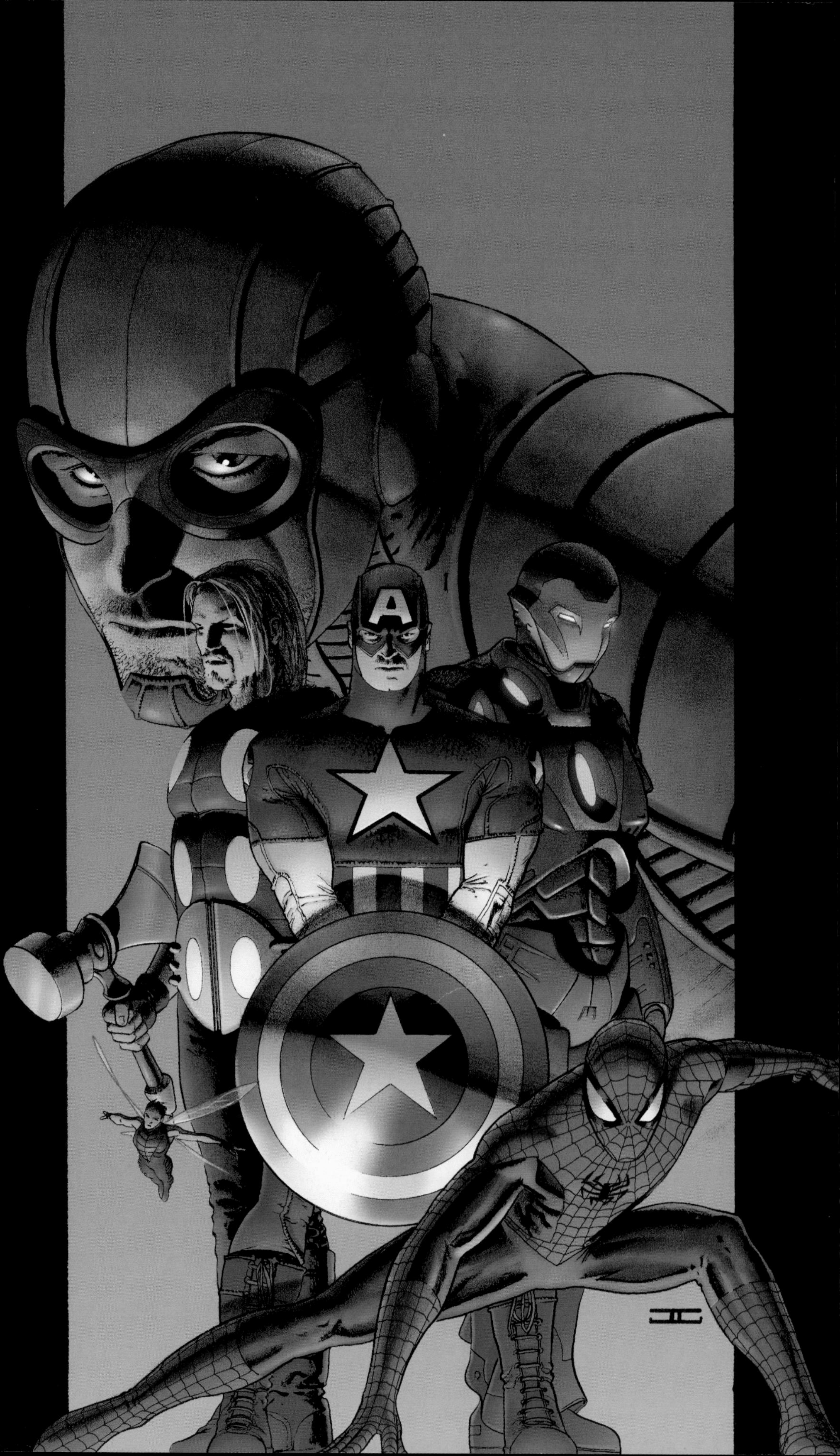

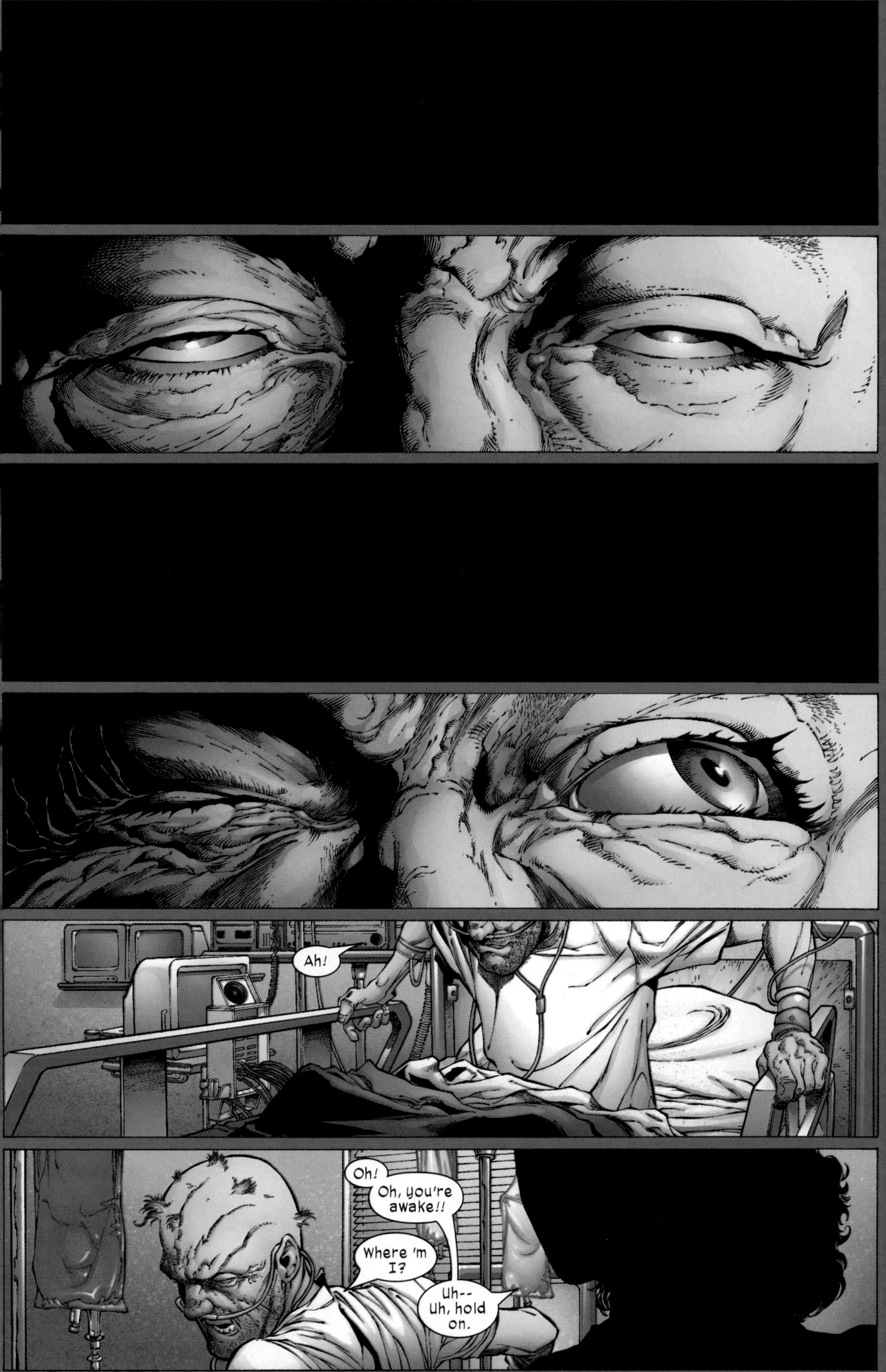
Ah!
Oh!
Oh, you're awake!!
Where 'm I?
Uh--
Uh, hold on.

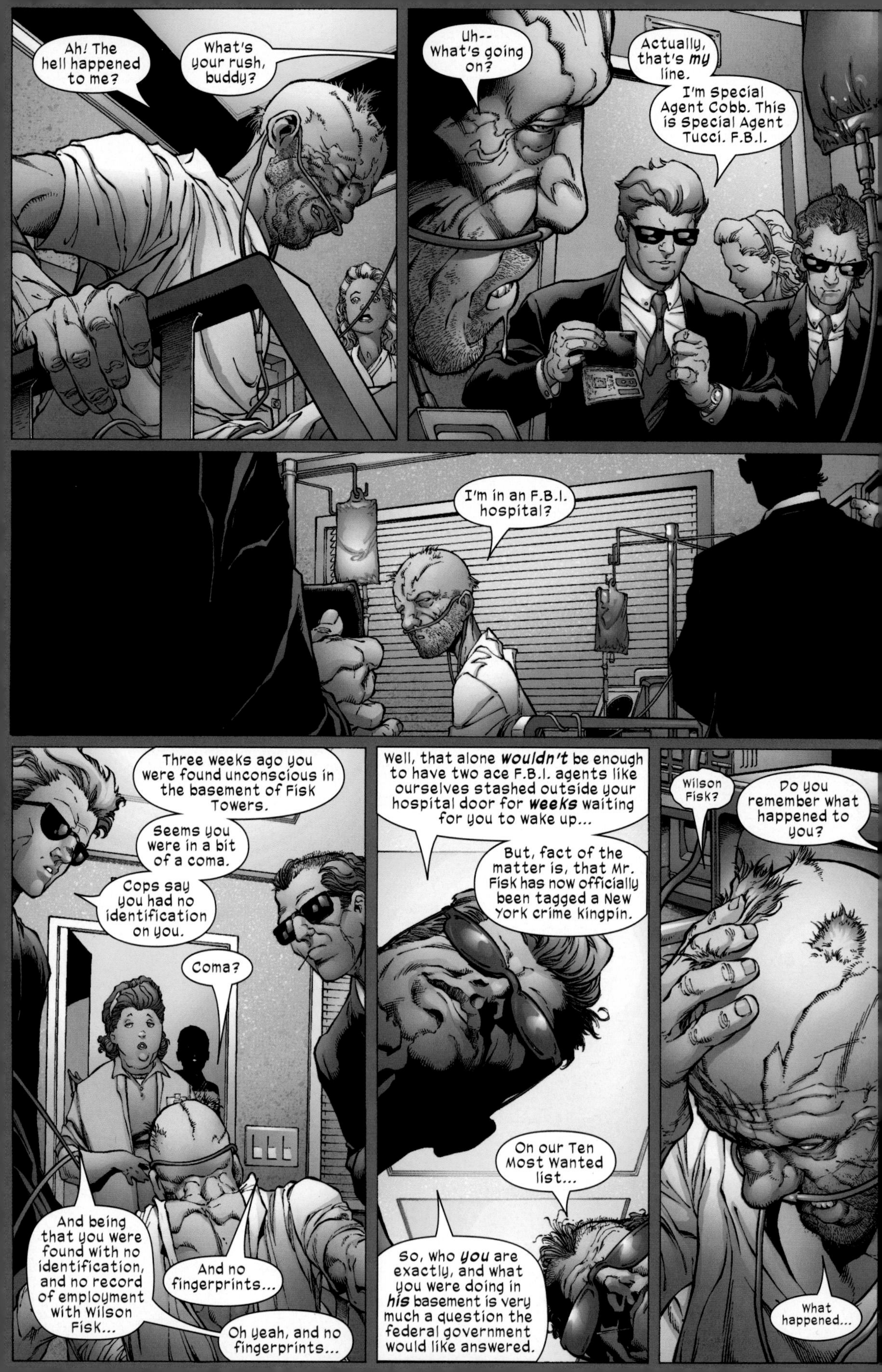

Ah! The hell happened to me?
What's your rush, buddy?
Uh-- What's going on?
Actually, that's *my* line.
I'm Special Agent Cobb. This is Special Agent Tucci. F.B.I.
I'm in an F.B.I. hospital?
Three weeks ago you were found unconscious in the basement of Fisk Towers.
Seems you were in a bit of a coma.
Cops say you had no identification on you.
Coma?
And being that you were found with no identification, and no record of employment with Wilson Fisk...
And no fingerprints...
Oh yeah, and no fingerprints...
Well, that alone *wouldn't* be enough to have two ace F.B.I. agents like ourselves stashed outside your hospital door for *weeks* waiting for you to wake up...
But, fact of the matter is, that Mr. Fisk has now officially been tagged a New York crime kingpin.
On our Ten Most Wanted list...
So, who *you* are exactly, and what you were doing in *his* basement is very much a question the federal government would like answered.
Wilson Fisk?
Do you remember what happened to you?
What happened...

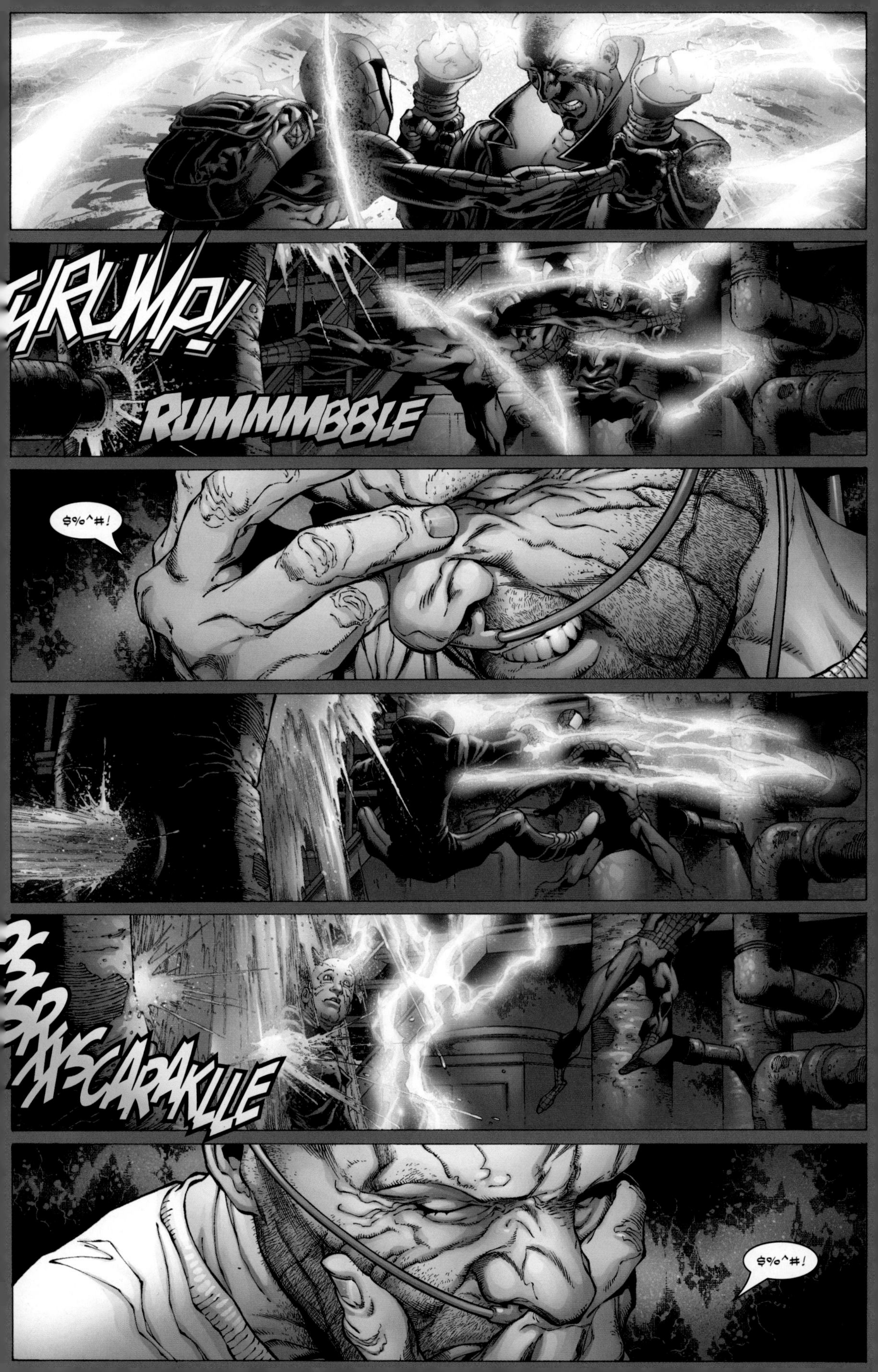
KRUMP!
RUMMMMBBLE
$%^#!
$%^#!

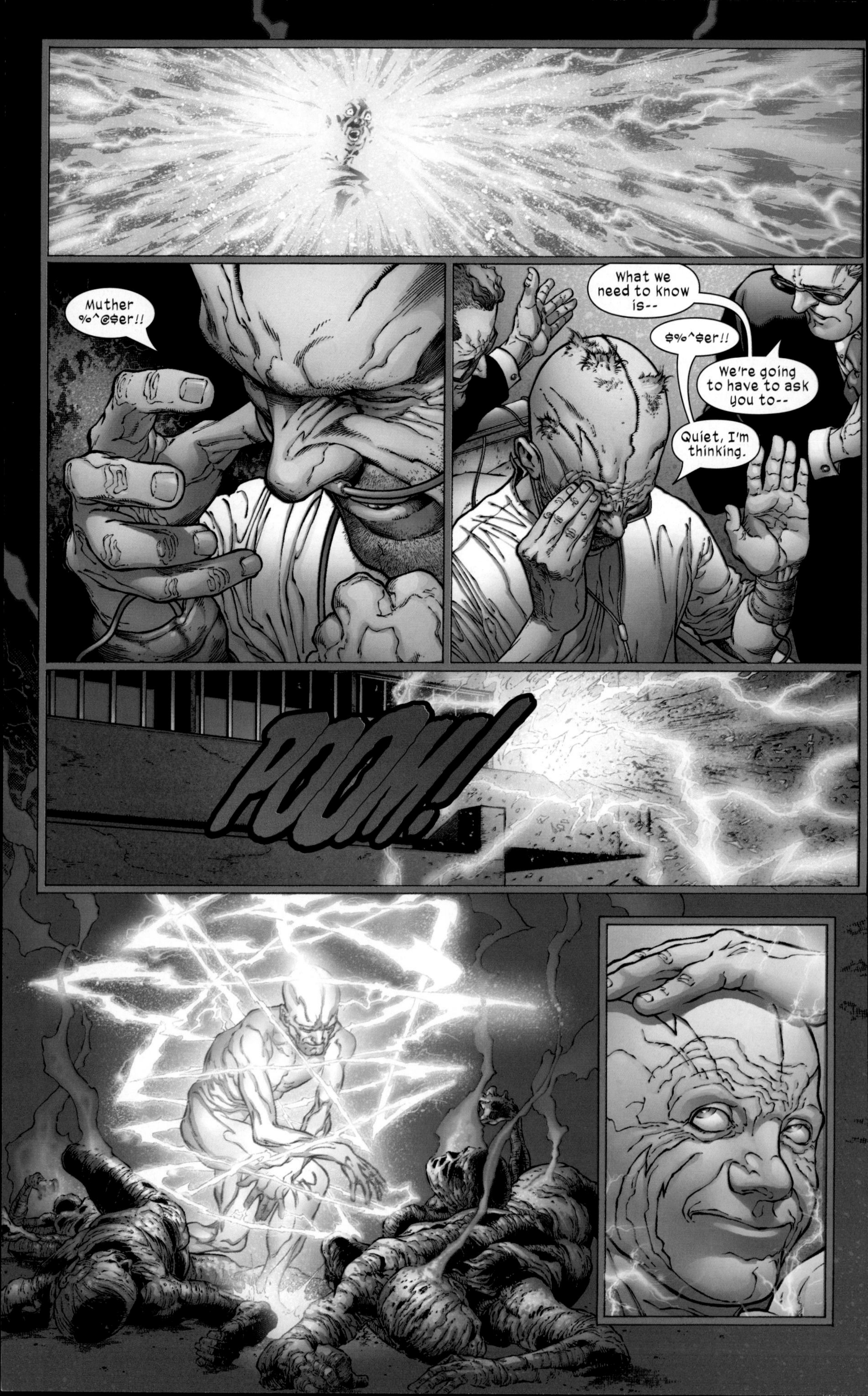
Muther %^@$er!!
What we need to know is--
$%^$er!!
We're going to have to ask you to--
Quiet, I'm thinking.
POOM!

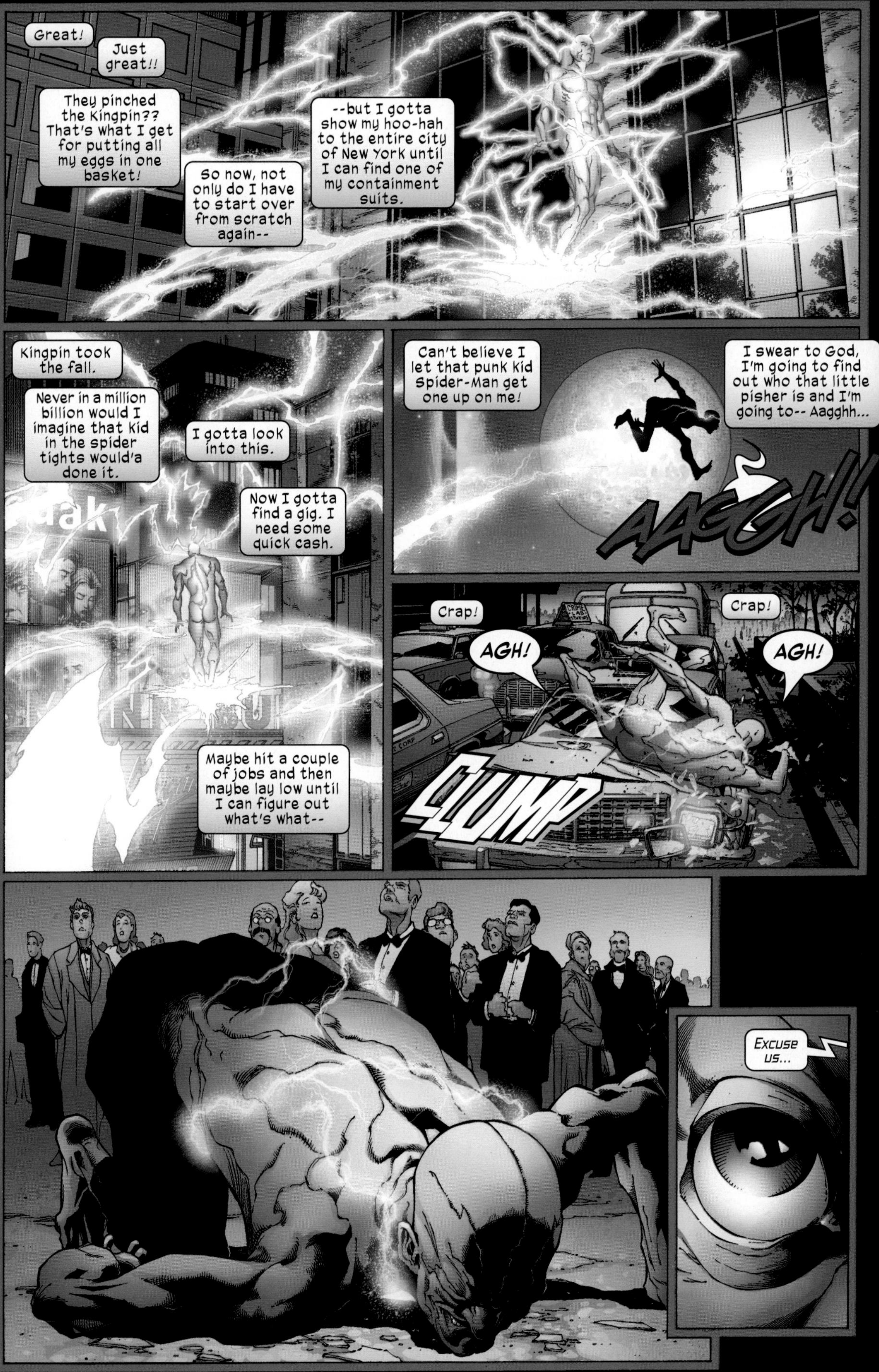
Great!
Just great!!
They pinched the Kingpin?? That's what I get for putting all my eggs in one basket!
So now, not only do I have to start over from scratch again--
--but I gotta show my hoo-hah to the entire city of New York until I can find one of my containment suits.
Kingpin took the fall.
Never in a million billion would I imagine that kid in the spider tights would'a done it.
I gotta look into this.
Now I gotta find a gig. I need some quick cash.
Maybe hit a couple of jobs and then maybe lay low until I can figure out what's what--
Can't believe I let that punk kid Spider-Man get one up on me!
I swear to God, I'm going to find out who that little pisher is and I'm going to-- Aagghh...
AAGGH!
Crap!
AGH!
Crap!
AGH!
CLUMP
Excuse us...

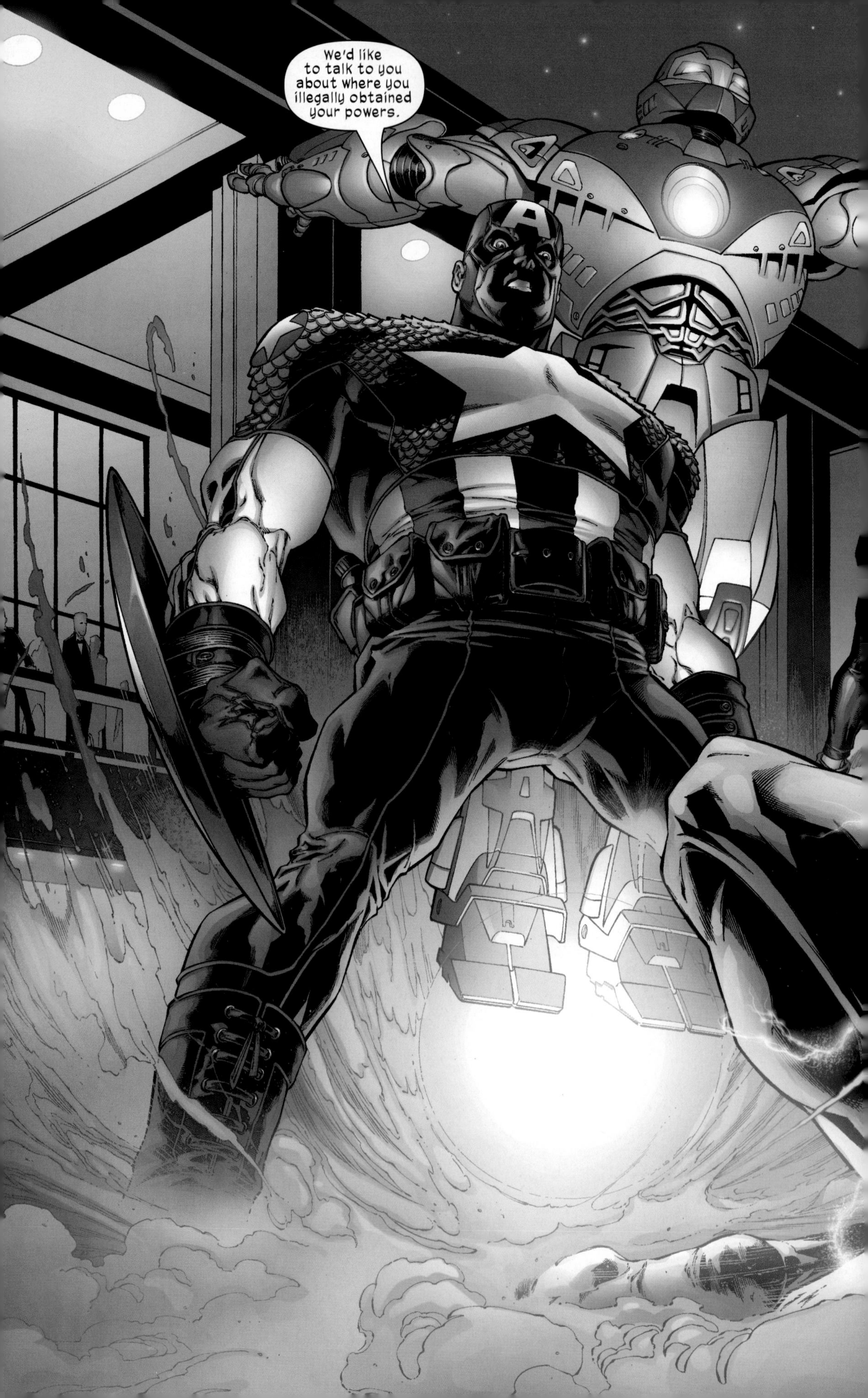
We'd like to talk to you about where you illegally obtained your powers.

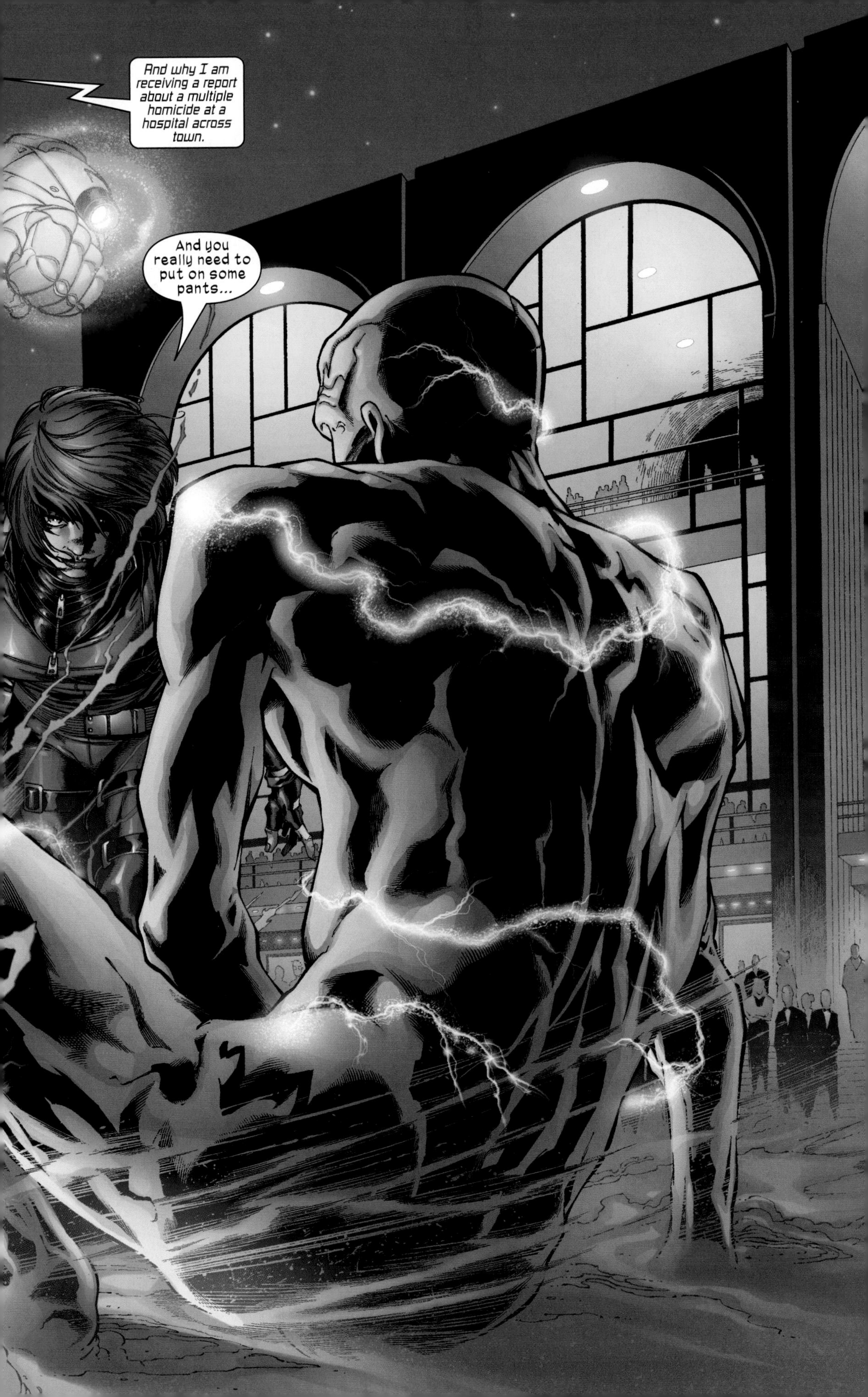
And why I am receiving a report about a multiple homicide at a hospital across town.
And you really need to put on some pants...

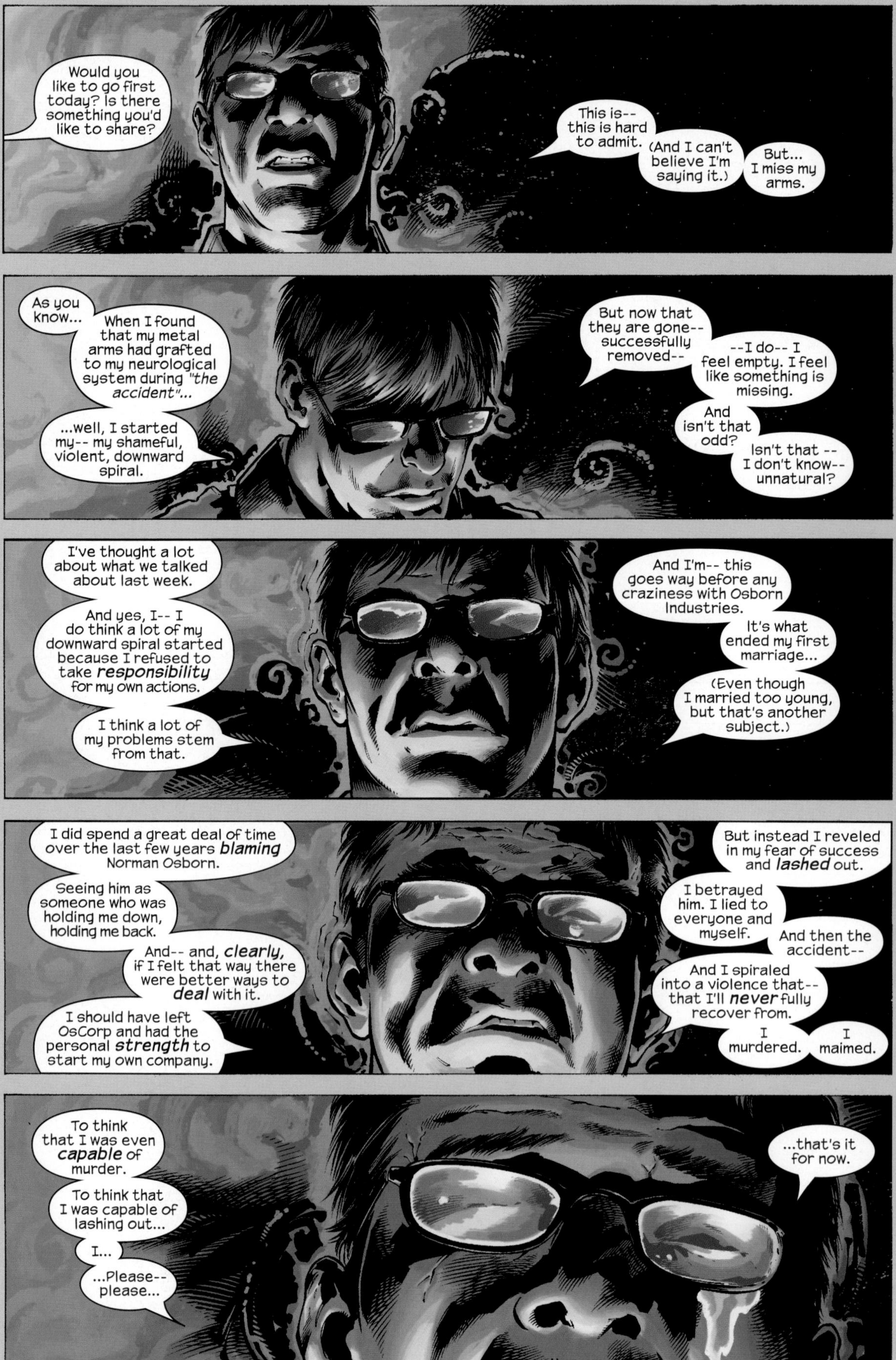
Would you like to go first today? Is there something you'd like to share?
This is-- this is hard to admit.
(And I can't believe I'm saying it.)
But... I miss my arms.
As you know...
When I found that my metal arms had grafted to my neurological system during "the accident"...
...well, I started my-- my shameful, violent, downward spiral.
But now that they are gone-- successfully removed--
--I do-- I feel empty. I feel like something is missing.
And isn't that odd?
Isn't that -- I don't know-- unnatural?
I've thought a lot about what we talked about last week.
And yes, I-- I do think a lot of my downward spiral started because I refused to take responsibility for my own actions.
I think a lot of my problems stem from that.
And I'm-- this goes way before any craziness with Osborn Industries.
It's what ended my first marriage...
(Even though I married too young, but that's another subject.)
I did spend a great deal of time over the last few years blaming Norman Osborn.
Seeing him as someone who was holding me down, holding me back.
And-- and, clearly, if I felt that way there were better ways to deal with it.
I should have left OsCorp and had the personal strength to start my own company.
But instead I reveled in my fear of success and lashed out.
I betrayed him. I lied to everyone and myself.
And then the accident--
And I spiraled into a violence that-- that I'll never fully recover from.
I murdered.
I maimed.
To think that I was even capable of murder.
To think that I was capable of lashing out...
I...
...Please-- please...
...that's it for now.

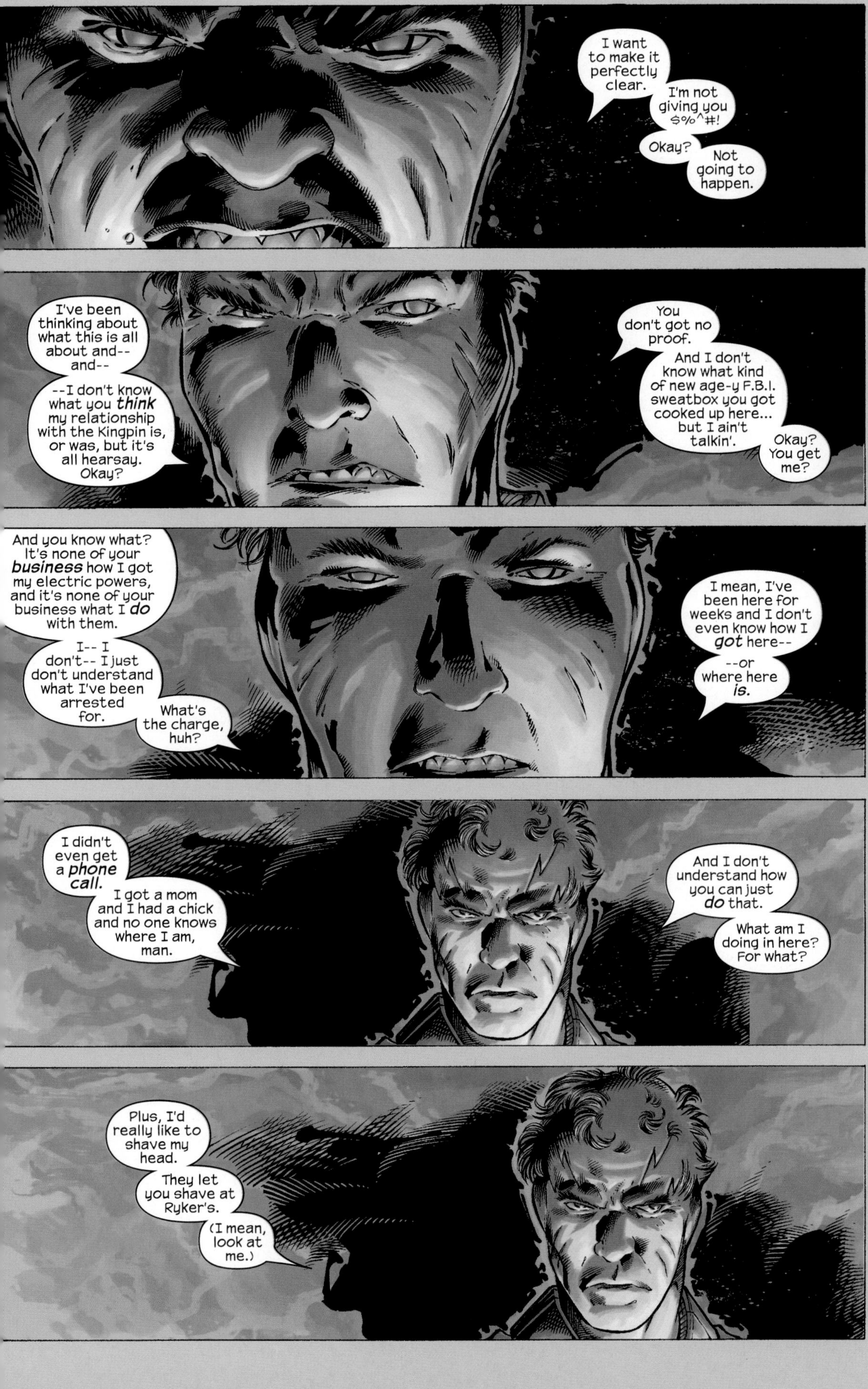

I want to make it perfectly clear.
I'm not giving you $%^#!
Okay?
Not going to happen.
I've been thinking about what this is all about and-- and--
--I don't know what you think my relationship with the Kingpin is, or was, but it's all hearsay. Okay?
You don't got no proof.
And I don't know what kind of new age-y F.B.I. sweatbox you got cooked up here... but I ain't talkin'.
Okay? You get me?
And you know what? It's none of your business how I got my electric powers, and it's none of your business what I do with them.
I-- I don't-- I just don't understand what I've been arrested for.
What's the charge, huh?
I mean, I've been here for weeks and I don't even know how I got here--
--or where here is.
I didn't even get a phone call.
I got a mom and I had a chick and no one knows where I am, man.
And I don't understand how you can just do that.
What am I doing in here? For what?
Plus, I'd really like to shave my head.
They let you shave at Ryker's.
(I mean, look at me.)

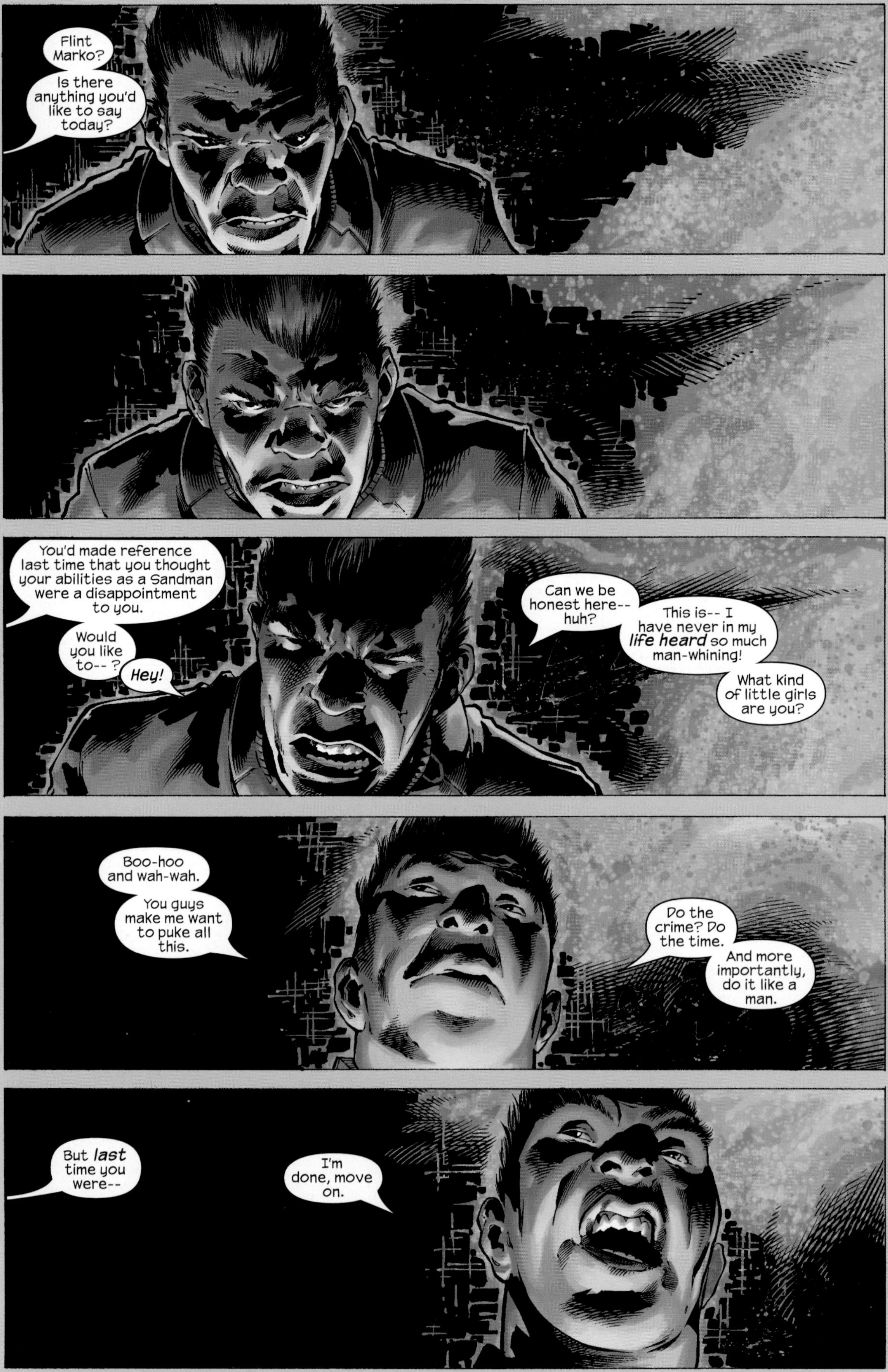
Flint Marko?
Is there anything you'd like to say today?
You'd made reference last time that you thought your abilities as a Sandman were a disappointment to you.
Would you like to-- ?
Hey!
Can we be honest here-- huh?
This is-- I have never in my life heard so much man-whining!
What kind of little girls are you?
Boo-hoo and wah-wah.
You guys make me want to puke all this.
Do the crime? Do the time.
And more importantly, do it like a man.
But last time you were--
I'm done, move on.

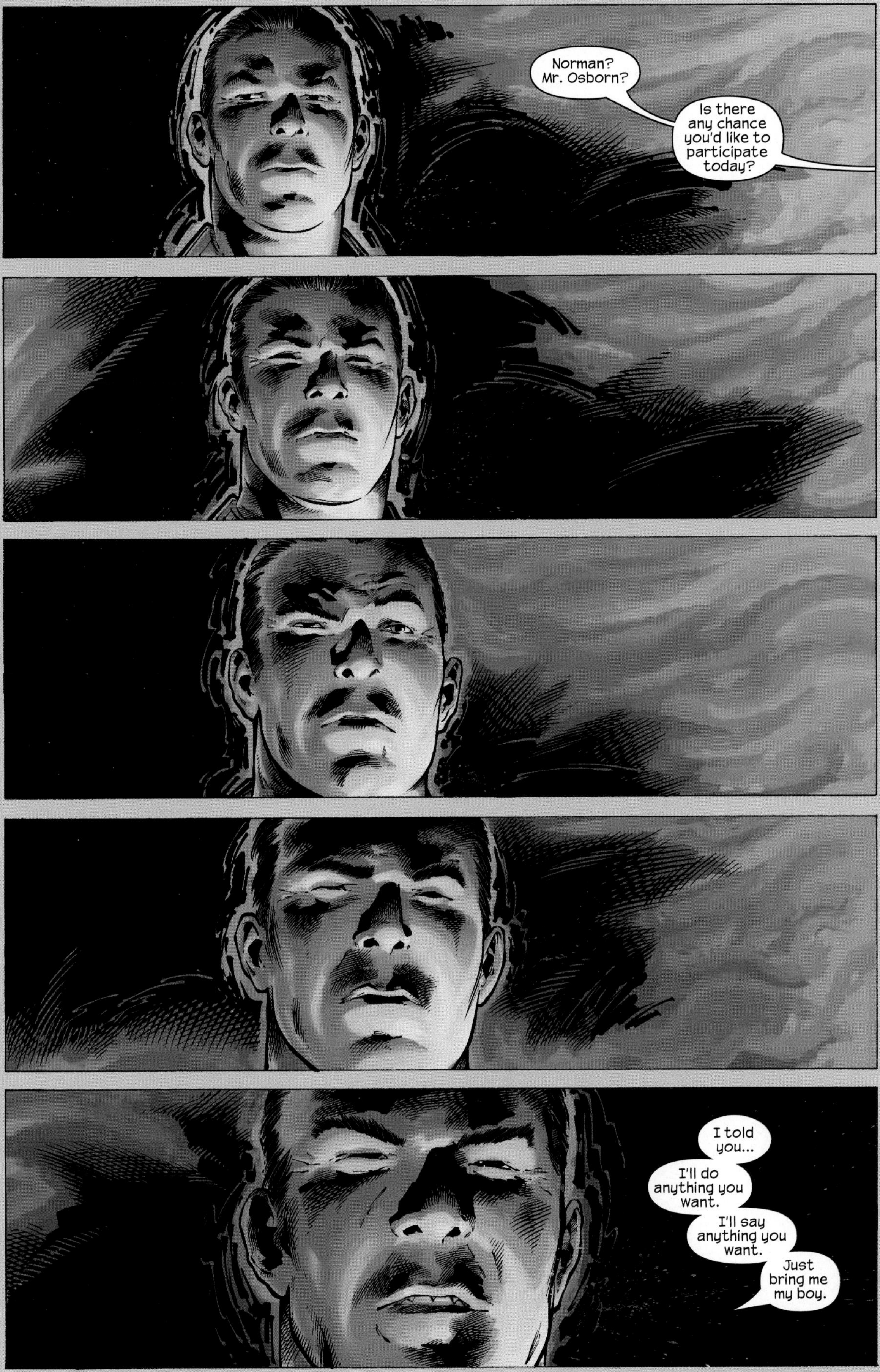
Norman? Mr. Osborn?
Is there any chance you'd like to participate today?
I told you...
I'll do anything you want.
I'll say anything you want.
Just bring me my boy.

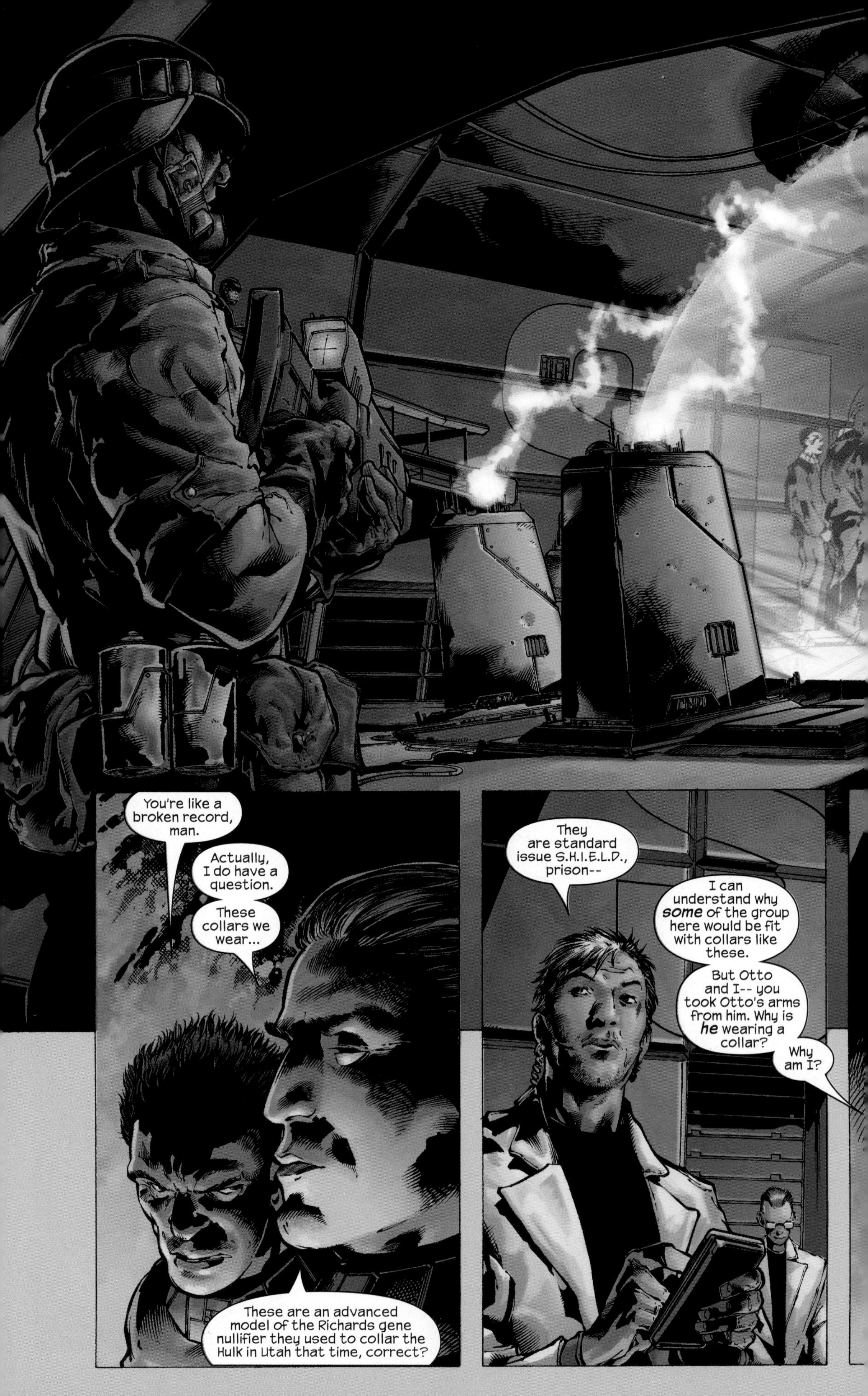

You're like a broken record, man.
Actually, I do have a question.
These collars we wear...
These are an advanced model of the Richards gene nullifier they used to collar the Hulk in Utah that time, correct?
They are standard issue S.H.I.E.L.D., prison--
I can understand why *some* of the group here would be fit with collars like these.
But Otto and I-- you took Otto's arms from him. Why is *he* wearing a collar?
Why am I?

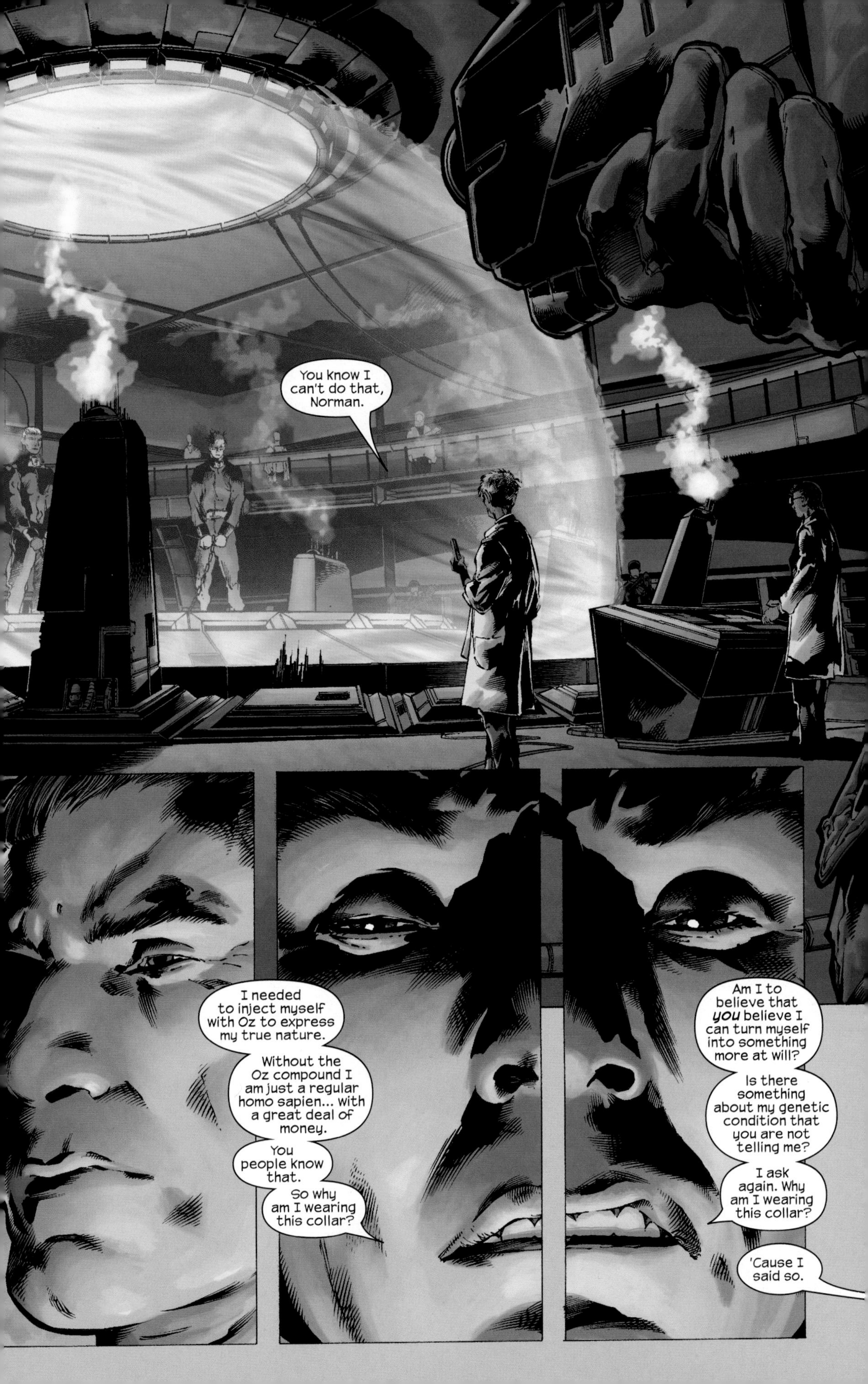

You know I can't do that, Norman.
I needed to inject myself with Oz to express my true nature.
Without the Oz compound I am just a regular homo sapien... with a great deal of money.
You people know that.
So why am I wearing this collar?
Am I to believe that *you* believe I can turn myself into something more at will?
Is there something about my genetic condition that you are not telling me?
I ask again. Why am I wearing this collar?
'Cause I said so.

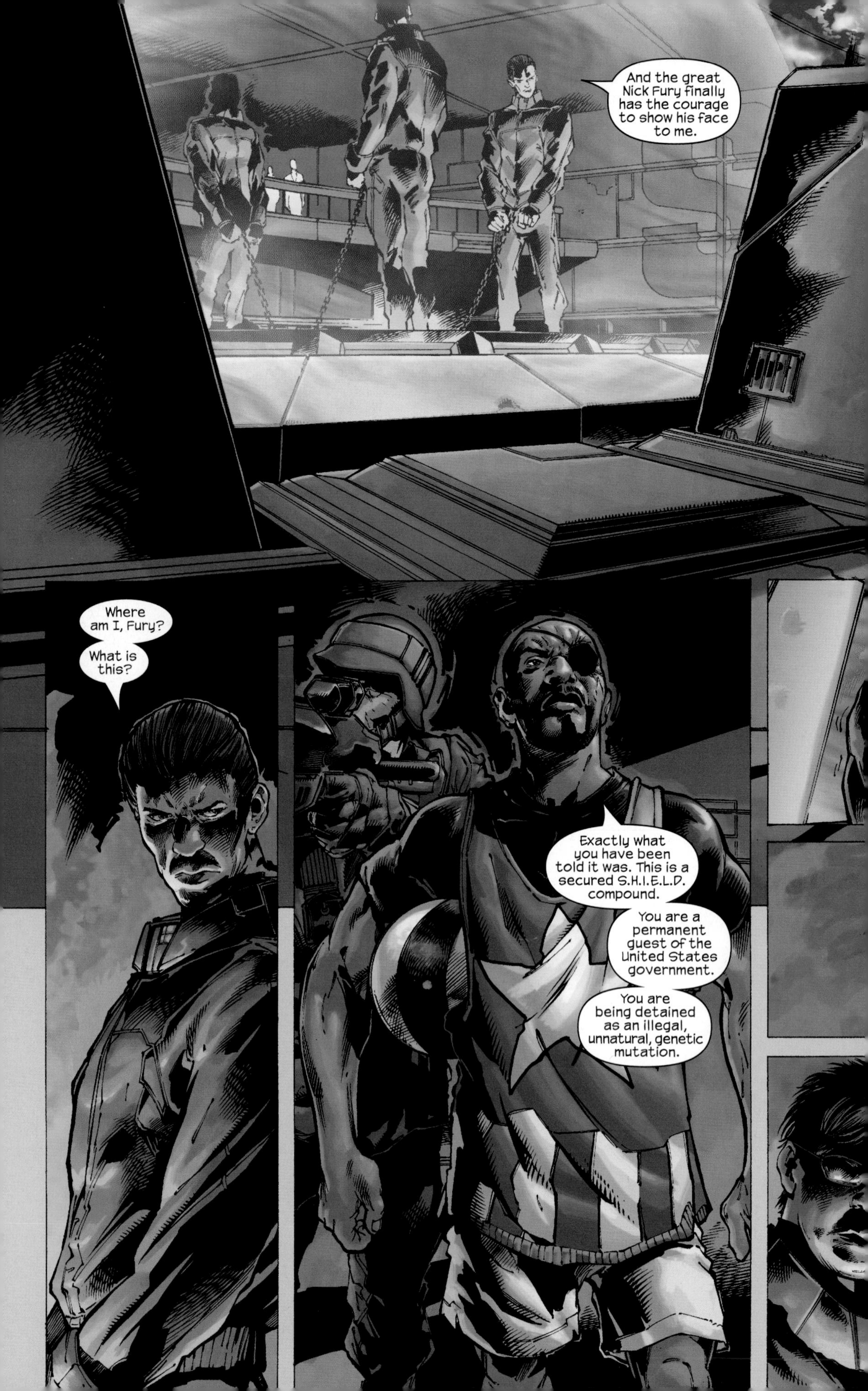

And the great Nick Fury finally has the courage to show his face to me.
Where am I, Fury?
What is this?
Exactly what you have been told it was. This is a secured S.H.I.E.L.D. compound.
You are a permanent guest of the United States government.
You are being detained as an illegal, unnatural, genetic mutation.

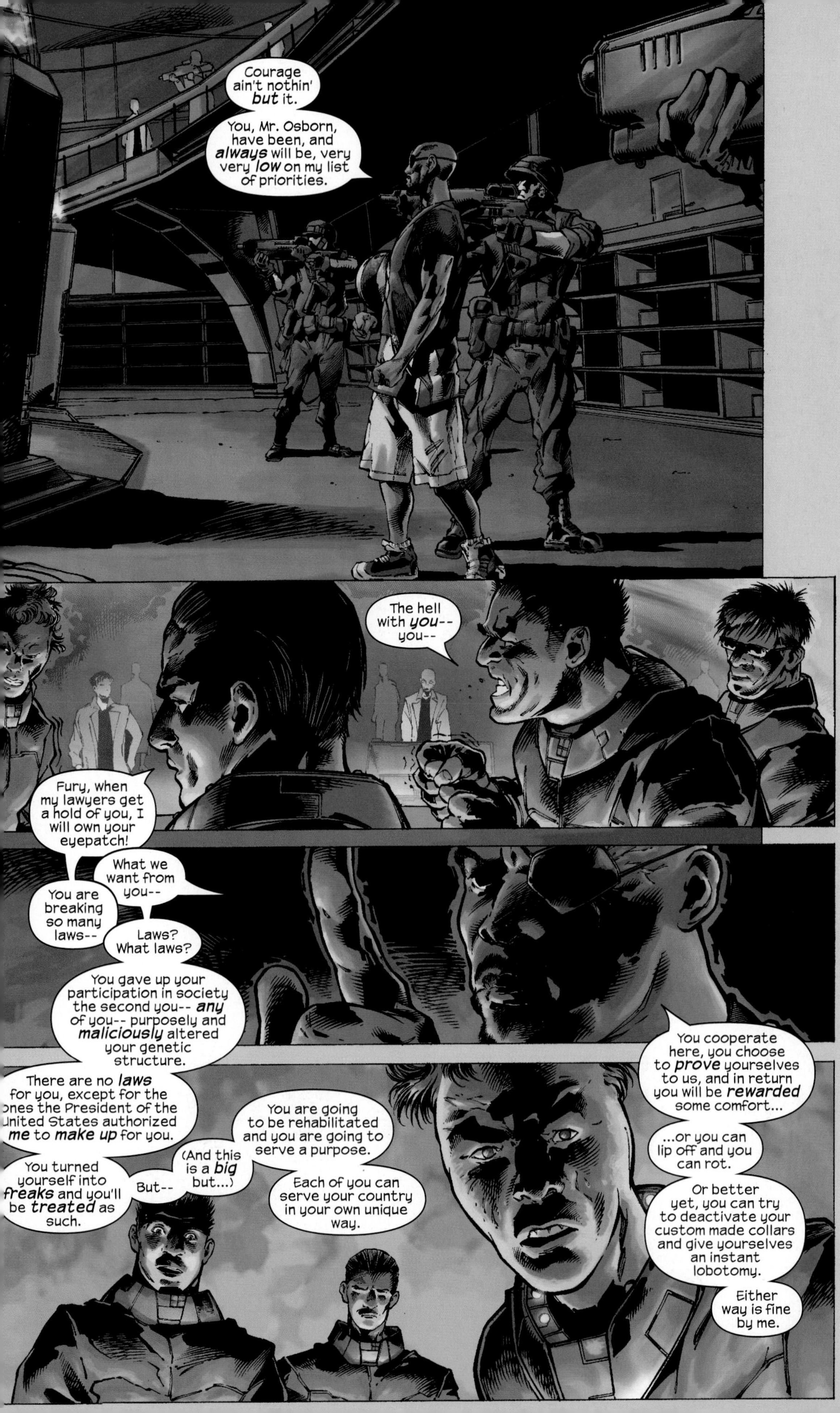
Courage ain't nothin' *but* it.
You, Mr. Osborn, have been, and *always* will be, very very *low* on my list of priorities.
The hell with *you*-- you--
Fury, when my lawyers get a hold of you, I will own your eyepatch!
What we want from you--
You are breaking so many laws--
Laws? What laws?
You gave up your participation in society the second you-- *any* of you-- purposely and *maliciously* altered your genetic structure.
There are no *laws* for you, except for the ones the President of the United States authorized *me* to *make up* for you.
You turned yourself into *freaks* and you'll be *treated* as such.
But--
(And this is a *big* but...)
You are going to be rehabilitated and you are going to serve a purpose.
Each of you can serve your country in your own unique way.
You cooperate here, you choose to *prove* yourselves to us, and in return you will be *rewarded* some comfort...
...or you can lip off and you can rot.
Or better yet, you can try to deactivate your custom made collars and give yourselves an instant lobotomy.
Either way is fine by me.

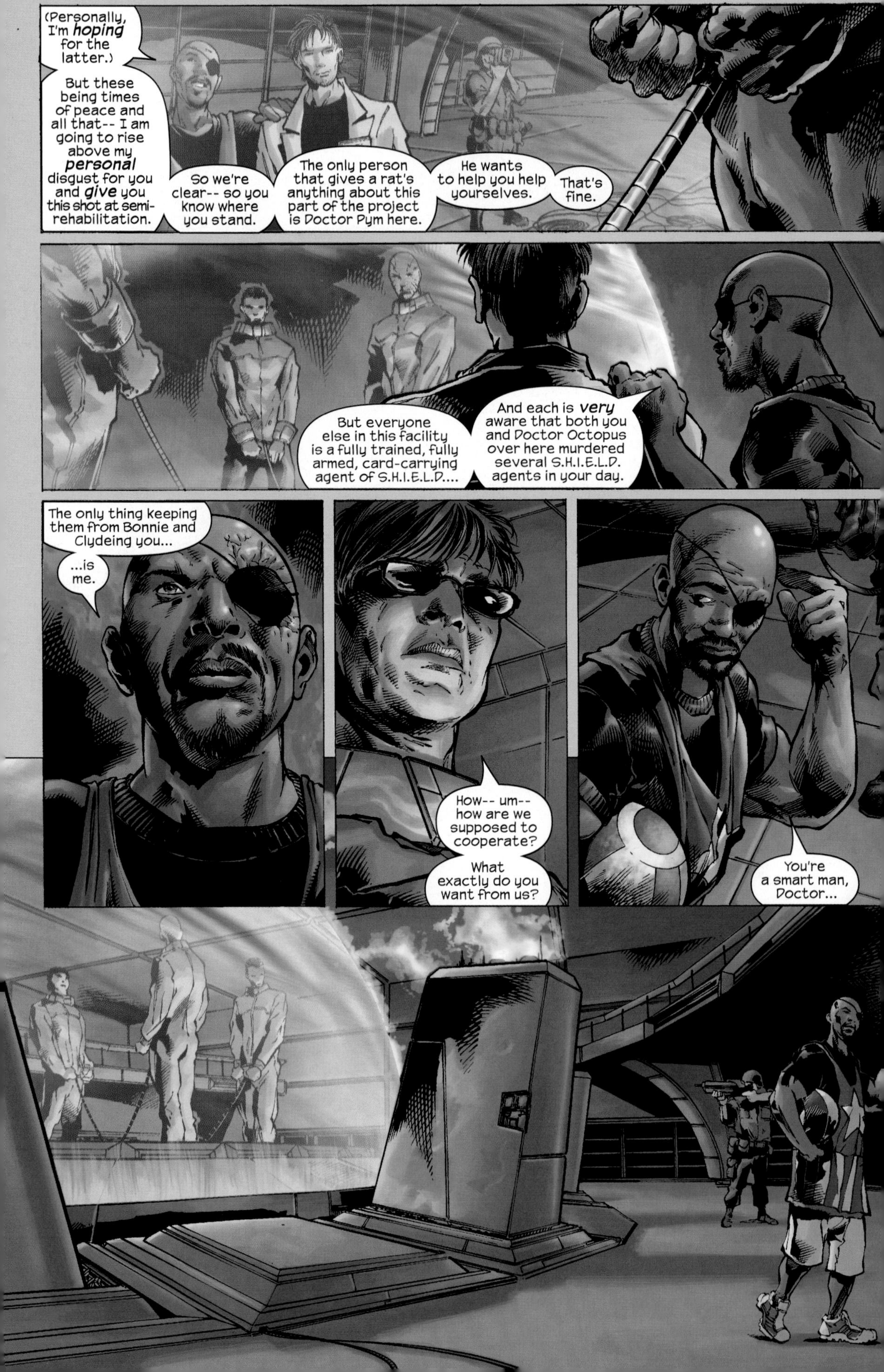
(Personally, I'm hoping for the latter.)
But these being times of peace and all that-- I am going to rise above my personal disgust for you and give you this shot at semi-rehabilitation.
So we're clear-- so you know where you stand.
The only person that gives a rat's anything about this part of the project is Doctor Pym here.
He wants to help you help yourselves.
That's fine.
But everyone else in this facility is a fully trained, fully armed, card-carrying agent of S.H.I.E.L.D....
And each is very aware that both you and Doctor Octopus over here murdered several S.H.I.E.L.D. agents in your day.
The only thing keeping them from Bonnie and Clydeing you...
...is me.
How-- um-- how are we supposed to cooperate?
What exactly do you want from us?
You're a smart man, Doctor...

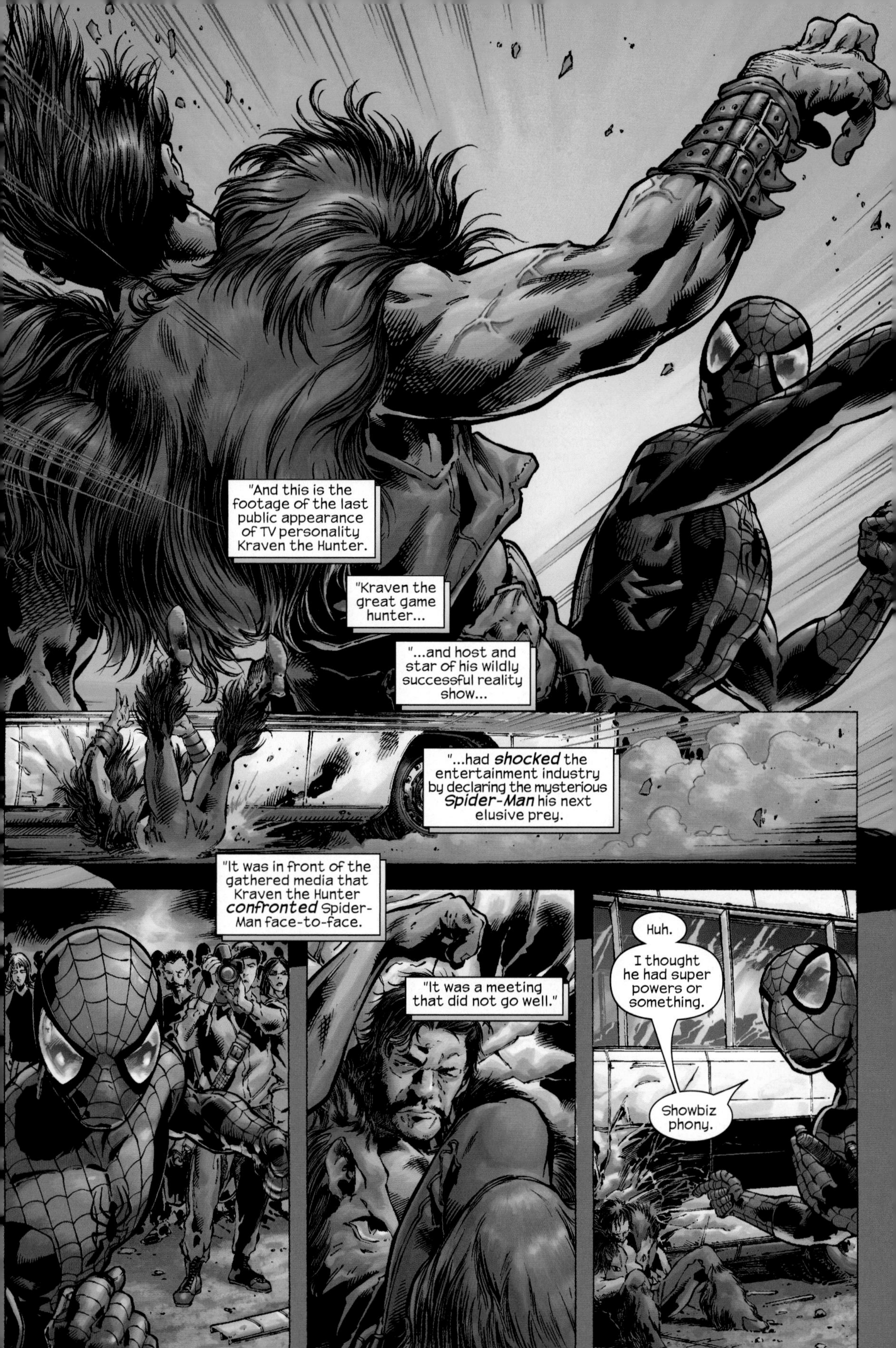
"And this is the footage of the last public appearance of TV personality Kraven the Hunter.
"Kraven the great game hunter...
"...and host and star of his wildly successful reality show...
"...had shocked the entertainment industry by declaring the mysterious Spider-Man his next elusive prey.
"It was in front of the gathered media that Kraven the Hunter confronted Spider-Man face-to-face.
"It was a meeting that did not go well."
Huh.
I thought he had super powers or something.
Showbiz phony.

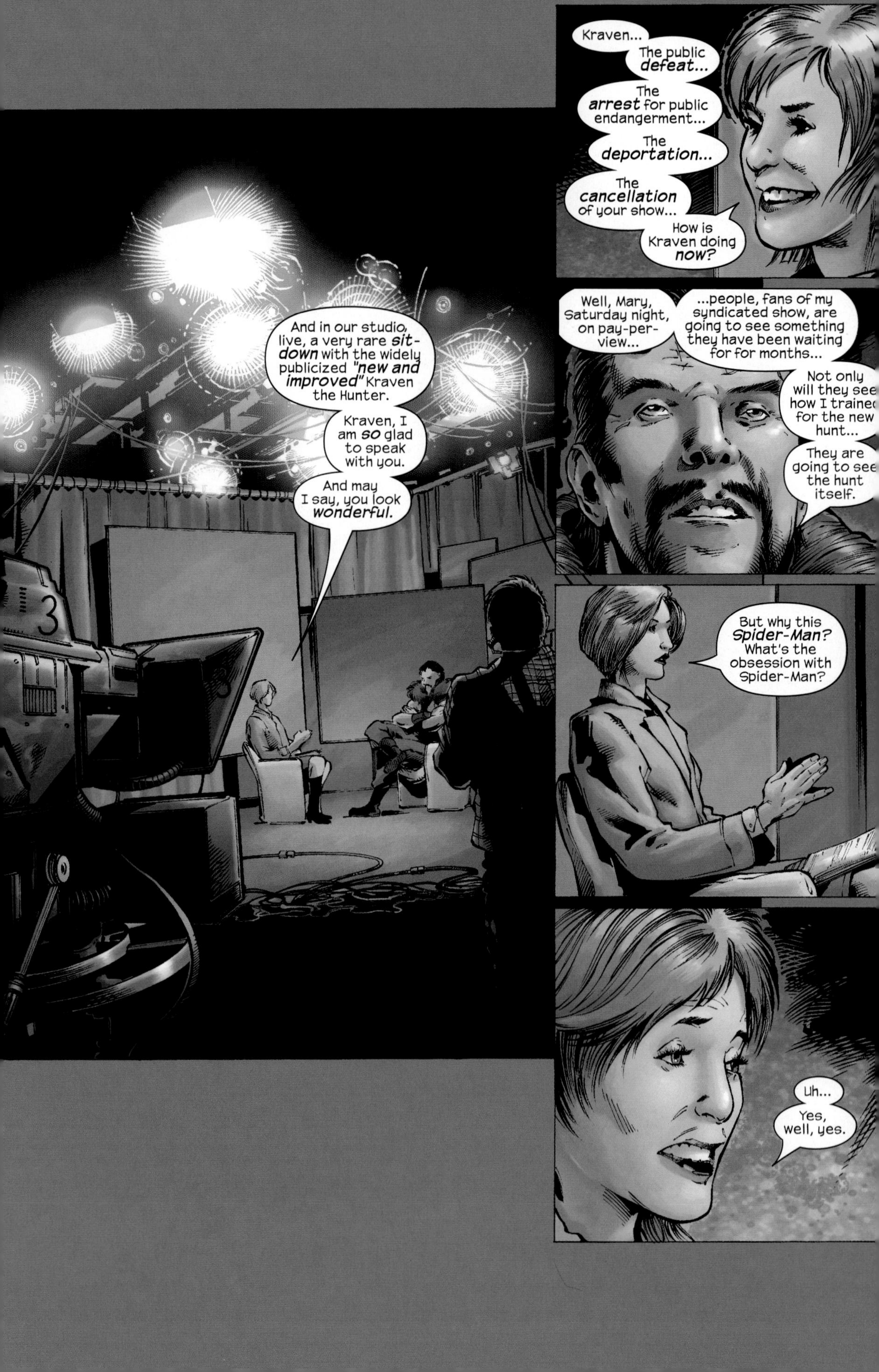

And in our studio, live, a very rare *sit-down* with the widely publicized *"new and improved"* Kraven the Hunter.
Kraven, I am *so* glad to speak with you.
And may I say, you look *wonderful.*
Kraven...
The public *defeat...*
The *arrest* for public endangerment...
The *deportation...*
The *cancellation* of your show...
How is Kraven doing *now?*
Well, Mary, Saturday night, on pay-per-view...
...people, fans of my syndicated show, are going to see something they have been waiting for for months...
Not only will they see how I traine for the new hunt...
They are going to see the hunt itself.
But why this *Spider-Man?* What's the obsession with Spider-Man?
Uh...
Yes, well, yes.

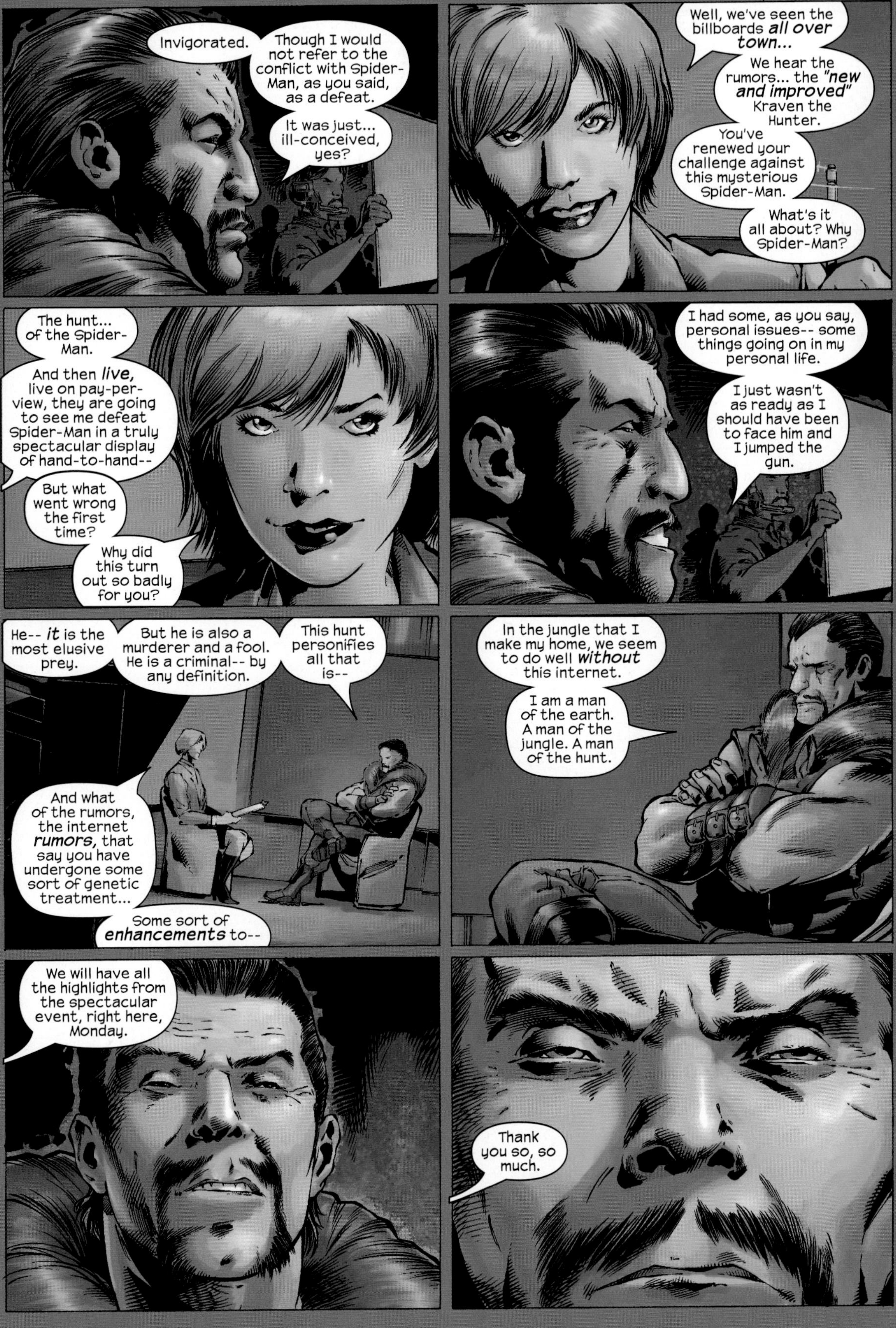
Invigorated.
Though I would not refer to the conflict with Spider-Man, as you said, as a defeat.
It was just... ill-conceived, yes?
Well, we've seen the billboards *all over town...*
We hear the rumors... the *"new and improved"* Kraven the Hunter.
You've renewed your challenge against this mysterious Spider-Man.
What's it all about? Why Spider-Man?
The hunt... of the Spider-Man.
And then *live,* live on pay-per-view, they are going to see me defeat Spider-Man in a truly spectacular display of hand-to-hand--
But what went wrong the first time?
Why did this turn out so badly for you?
I had some, as you say, personal issues-- some things going on in my personal life.
I just wasn't as ready as I should have been to face him and I jumped the gun.
He-- *it* is the most elusive prey.
But he is also a murderer and a fool. He is a criminal-- by any definition.
This hunt personifies all that is--
And what of the rumors, the internet *rumors,* that say you have undergone some sort of genetic treatment...
Some sort of *enhancements* to--
In the jungle that I make my home, we seem to do well *without* this internet.
I am a man of the earth. A man of the jungle. A man of the hunt.
We will have all the highlights from the spectacular event, right here, Monday.
Thank you so, so much.

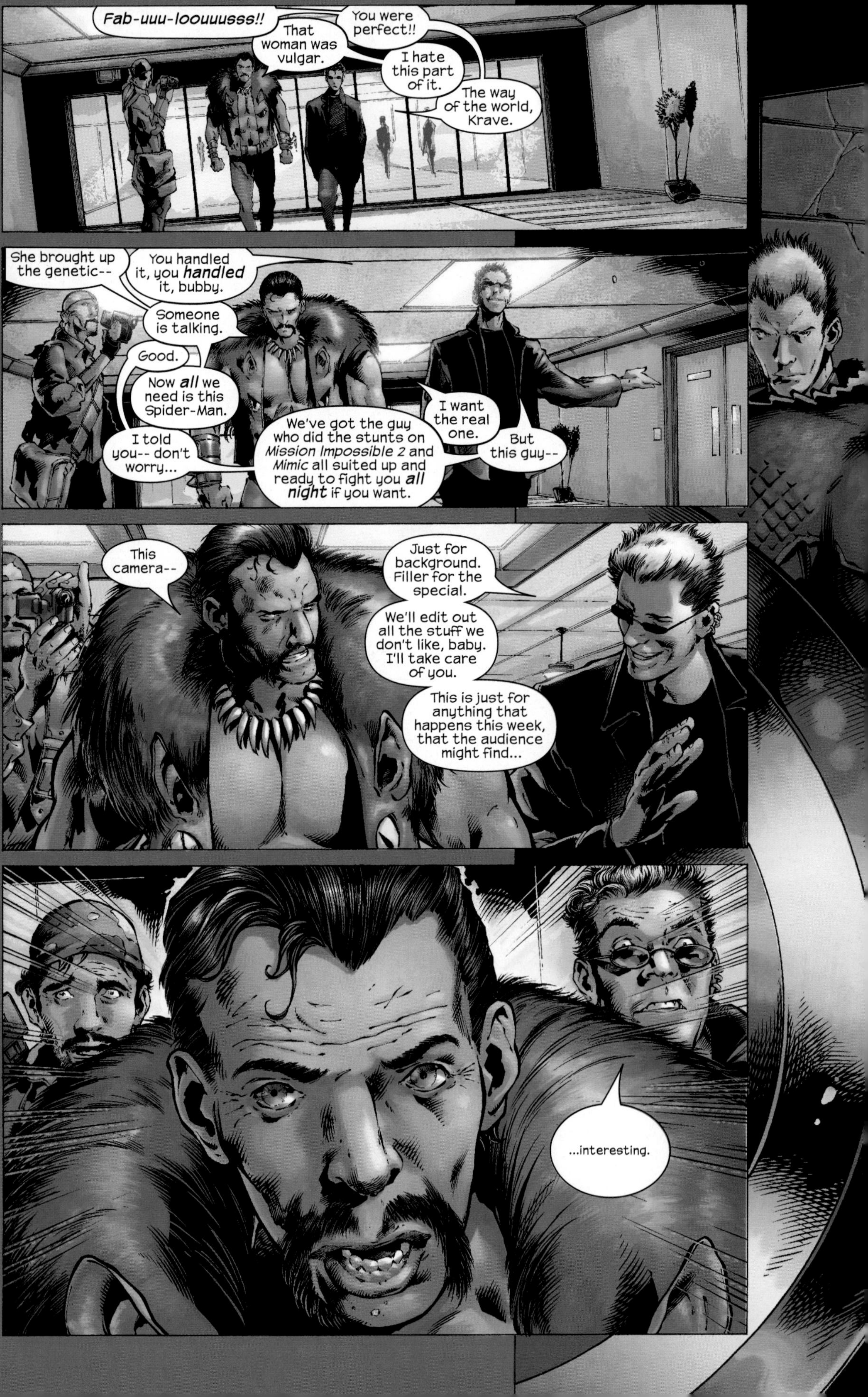
Fab-uuu-loouuusss!!
You were perfect!!
That woman was vulgar.
I hate this part of it.
The way of the world, Krave.
She brought up the genetic--
You handled it, you *handled* it, bubby.
Someone is talking.
Good.
Now *all* we need is this Spider-Man.
I told you-- don't worry...
We've got the guy who did the stunts on *Mission Impossible 2* and *Mimic* all suited up and ready to fight you *all night* if you want.
I want the real one.
But this guy--
This camera--
Just for background. Filler for the special.
We'll edit out all the stuff we don't like, baby. I'll take care of you.
This is just for anything that happens this week, that the audience might find...
...interesting.

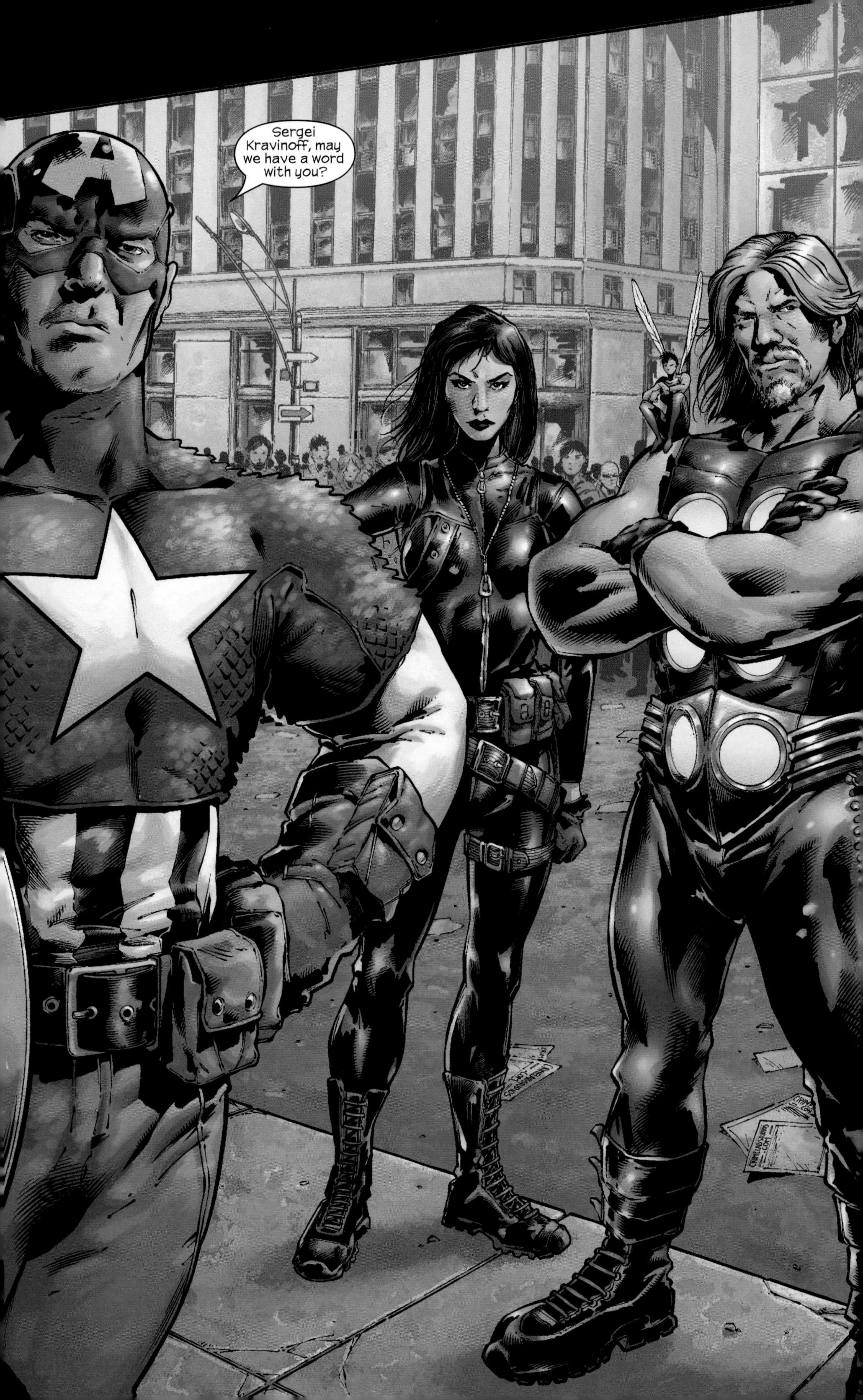
Sergei Kravinoff, may we have a word with you?

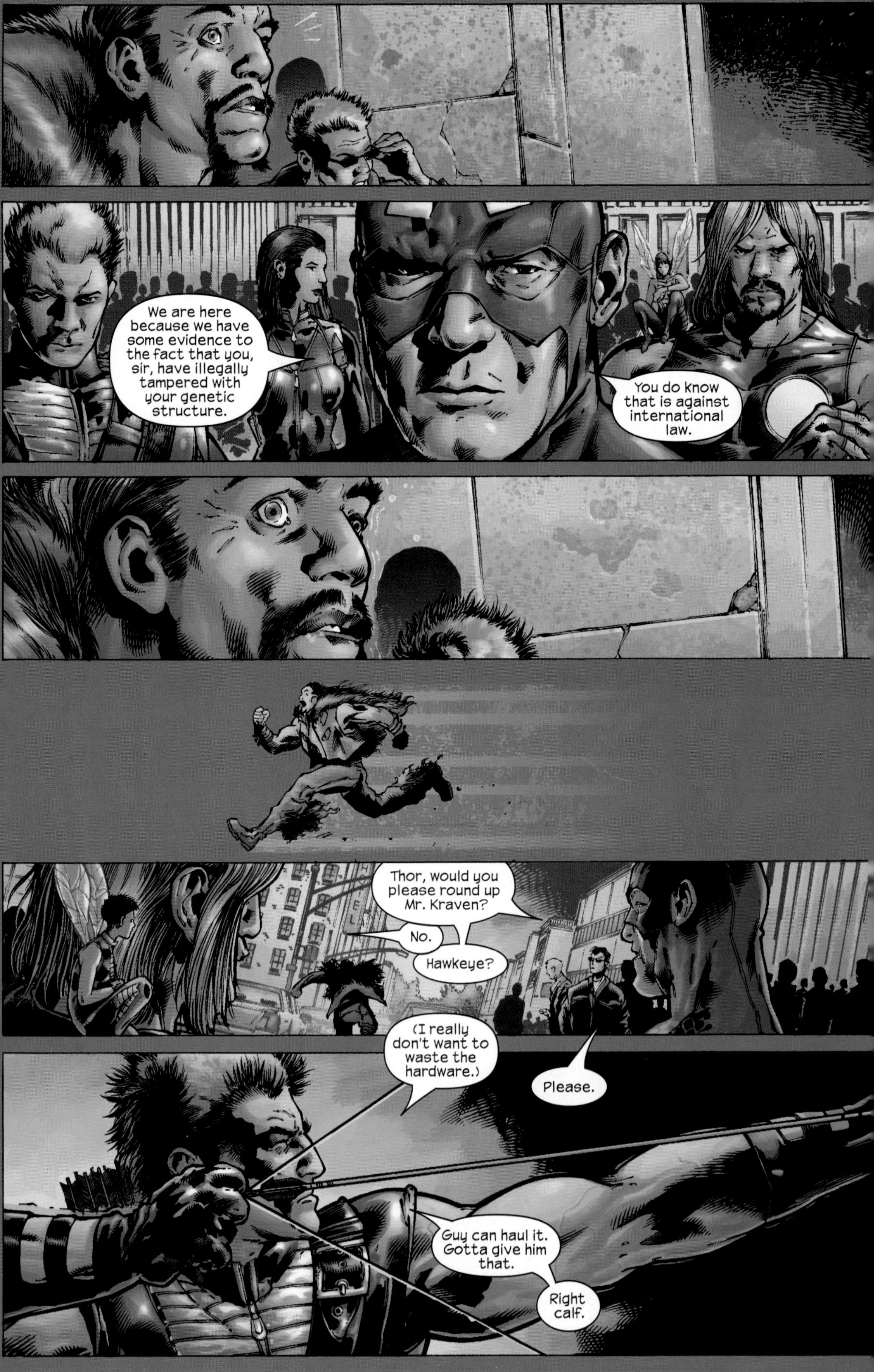

We are here because we have some evidence to the fact that you, sir, have illegally tampered with your genetic structure.
You do know that is against international law.
Thor, would you please round up Mr. Kraven?
No.
Hawkeye?
(I really don't want to waste the hardware.)
Please.
Guy can haul it. Gotta give him that.
Right calf.

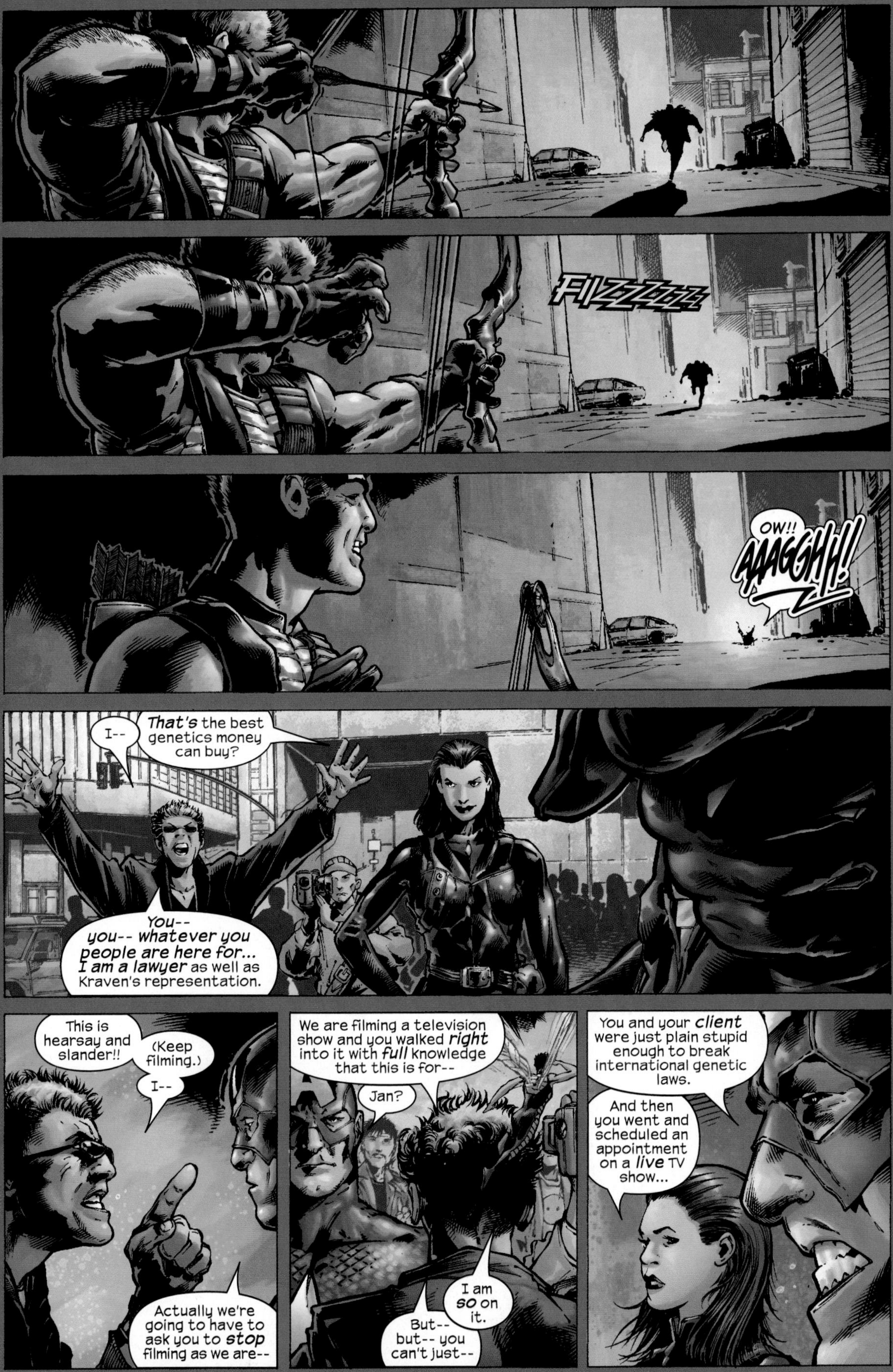
FIZZZZZZ
OW!!
AAAGGHH!
I--
That's the best genetics money can buy?
You-- you-- whatever you people are here for... I am a lawyer as well as Kraven's representation.
This is hearsay and slander!!
(Keep filming.)
I--
Actually we're going to have to ask you to stop filming as we are--
We are filming a television show and you walked right into it with full knowledge that this is for--
Jan?
I am so on it.
But-- but-- you can't just--
You and your client were just plain stupid enough to break international genetic laws.
And then you went and scheduled an appointment on a live TV show...

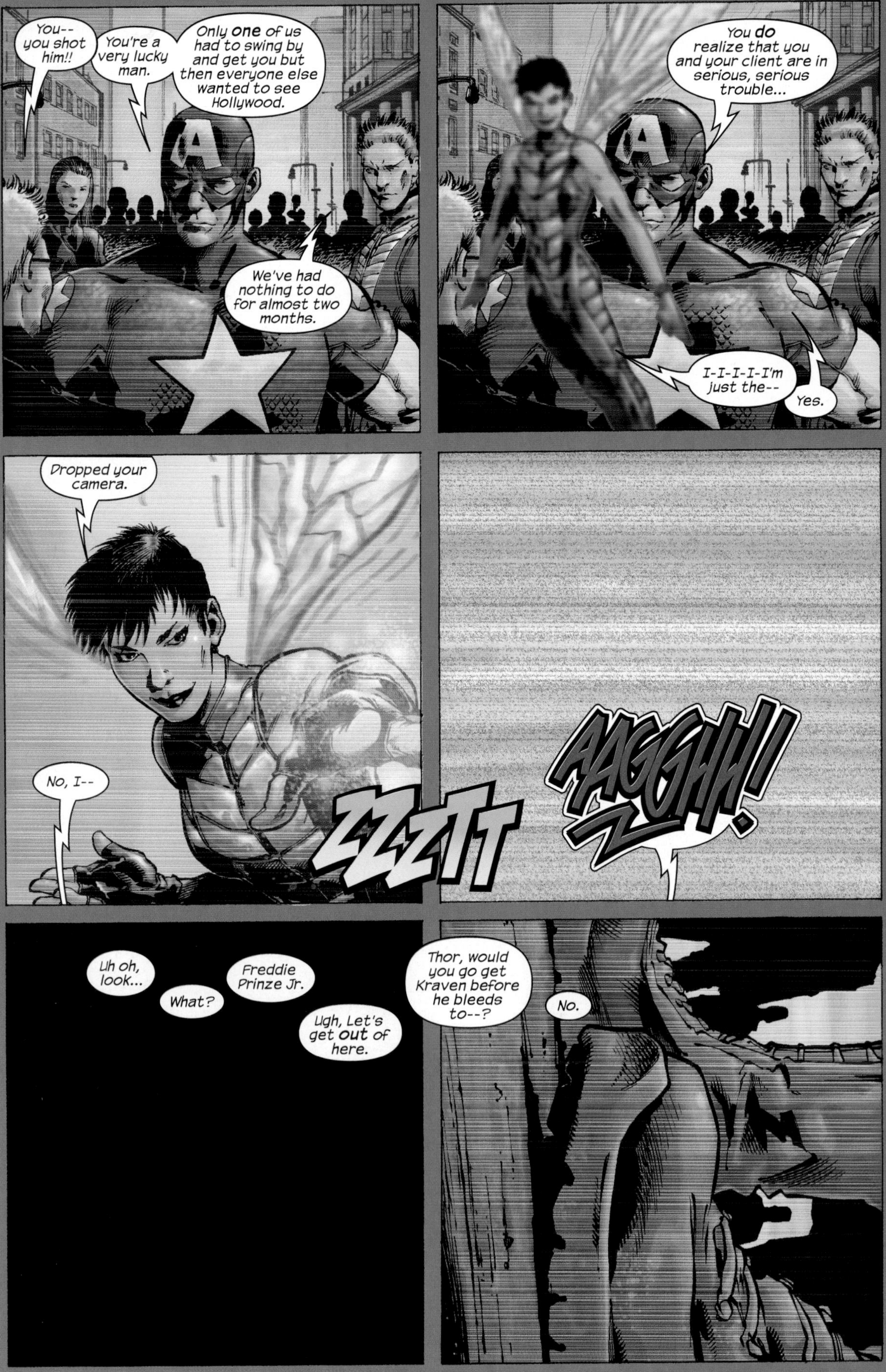
You-- you shot him!!
You're a very lucky man.
Only one of us had to swing by and get you but then everyone else wanted to see Hollywood.
We've had nothing to do for almost two months.
You do realize that you and your client are in serious, serious trouble...
I-I-I-I-I'm just the--
Yes.
Dropped your camera.
No, I--
ZZZTT
AAGGHH!!
Uh oh, look...
What?
Freddie Prinze Jr.
Ugh, Let's get out of here.
Thor, would you go get Kraven before he bleeds to--?
No.

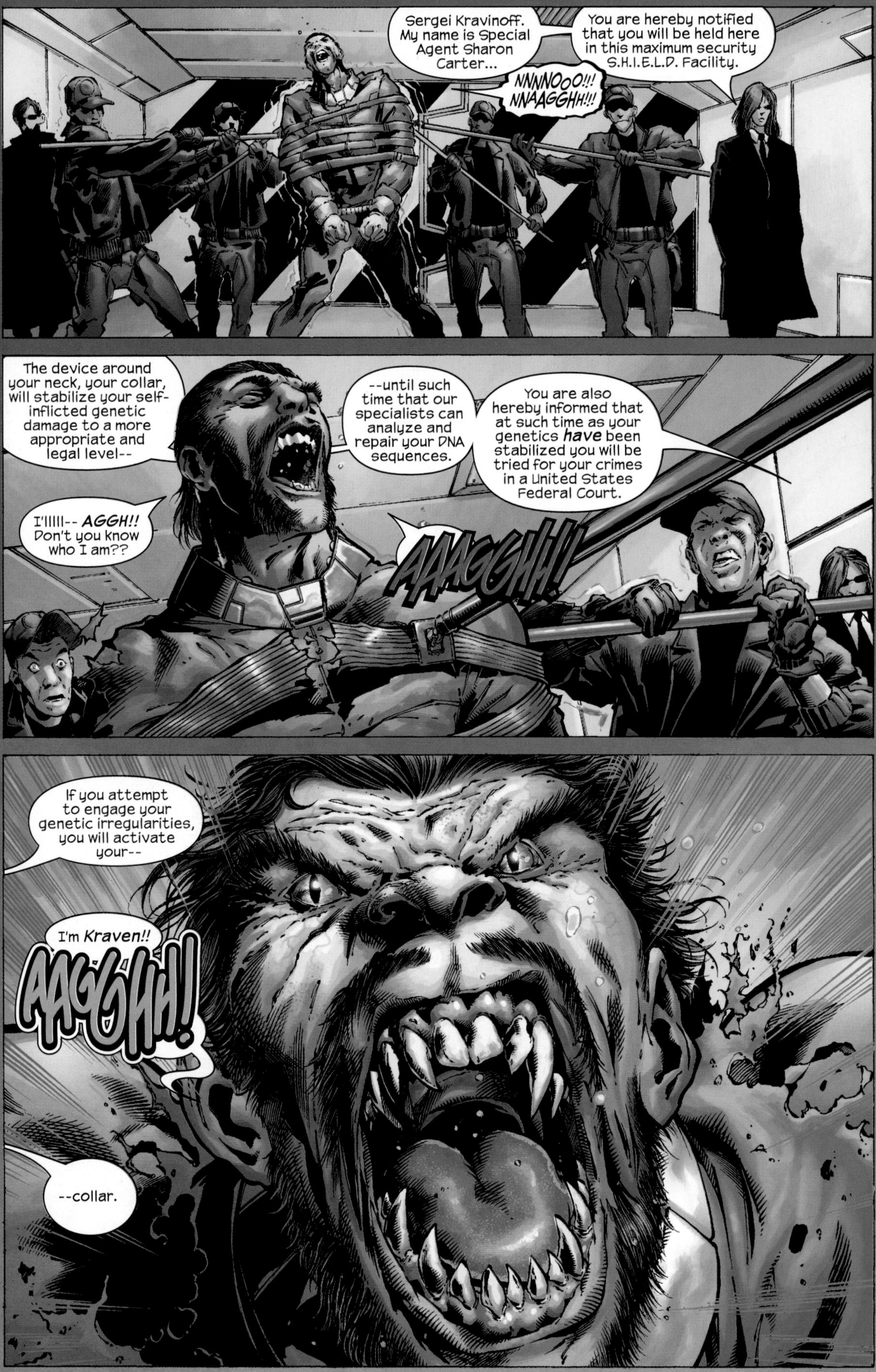
Sergei Kravinoff. My name is Special Agent Sharon Carter...
You are hereby notified that you will be held here in this maximum security S.H.I.E.L.D. Facility.
NNNNOOO!!! NNAAGGHH!!!
The device around your neck, your collar, will stabilize your self-inflicted genetic damage to a more appropriate and legal level--
--until such time that our specialists can analyze and repair your DNA sequences.
You are also hereby informed that at such time as your genetics *have* been stabilized you will be tried for your crimes in a United States Federal Court.
I'lllll-- **AGGH!!** Don't you know who I am??
AAAGGHH!
If you attempt to engage your genetic irregularities, you will activate your--
I'm *Kraven*!!
AAGGHH!
--collar.

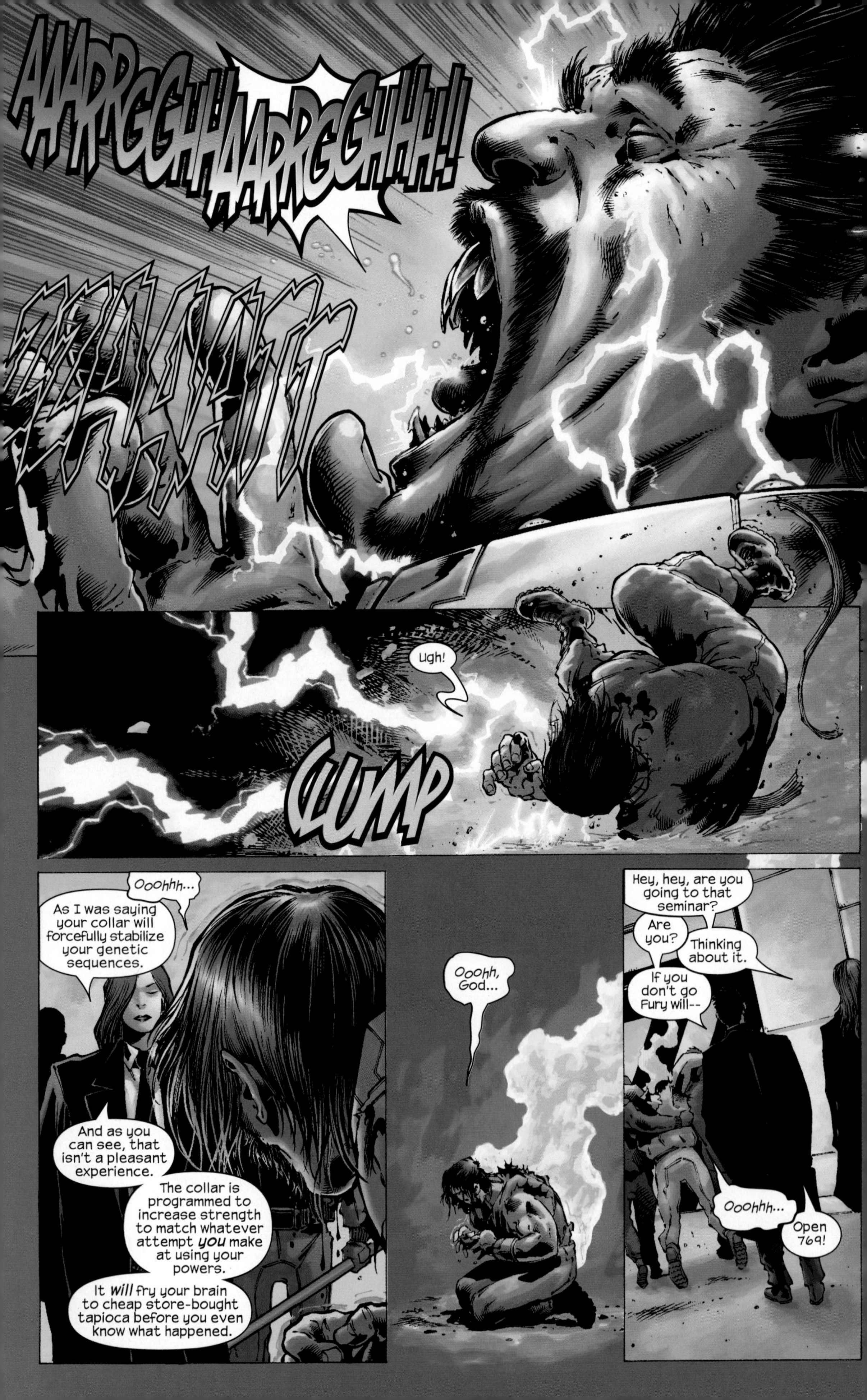
AAARRGGHHAARRGGHHH!!
ZZZAAAAACK
Ugh!
CLUMP
Ooohhh...
As I was saying your collar will forcefully stabilize your genetic sequences.
And as you can see, that isn't a pleasant experience.
The collar is programmed to increase strength to match whatever attempt *you* make at using your powers.
It *will* fry your brain to cheap store-bought tapioca before you even know what happened.
Ooohh, God...
Hey, hey, are you going to that seminar?
Are you?
Thinking about it.
If you don't go Fury will--
Ooohhh...
Open 769!

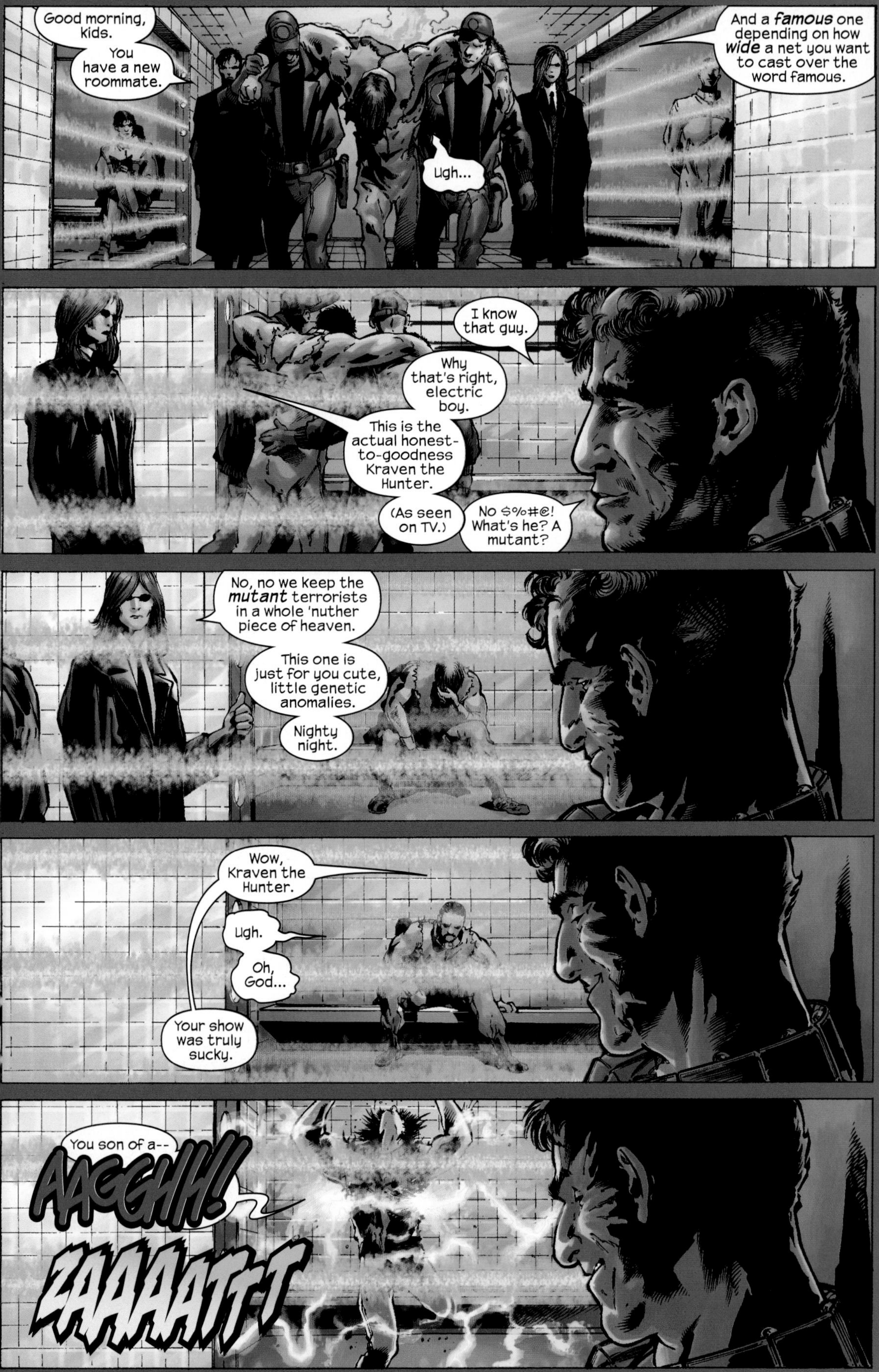

Good morning, kids.
You have a new roommate.
And a *famous* one depending on how *wide* a net you want to cast over the word famous.
Ugh...
I know that guy.
Why that's right, electric boy.
This is the actual honest-to-goodness Kraven the Hunter.
(As seen on TV.)
No $%#@! What's he? A mutant?
No, no we keep the *mutant* terrorists in a whole 'nuther piece of heaven.
This one is just for you cute, little genetic anomalies.
Nighty night.
Wow, Kraven the Hunter.
Ugh.
Oh, God...
Your show was truly sucky.
You son of a--
AAGGHH!
ZAAAATT T

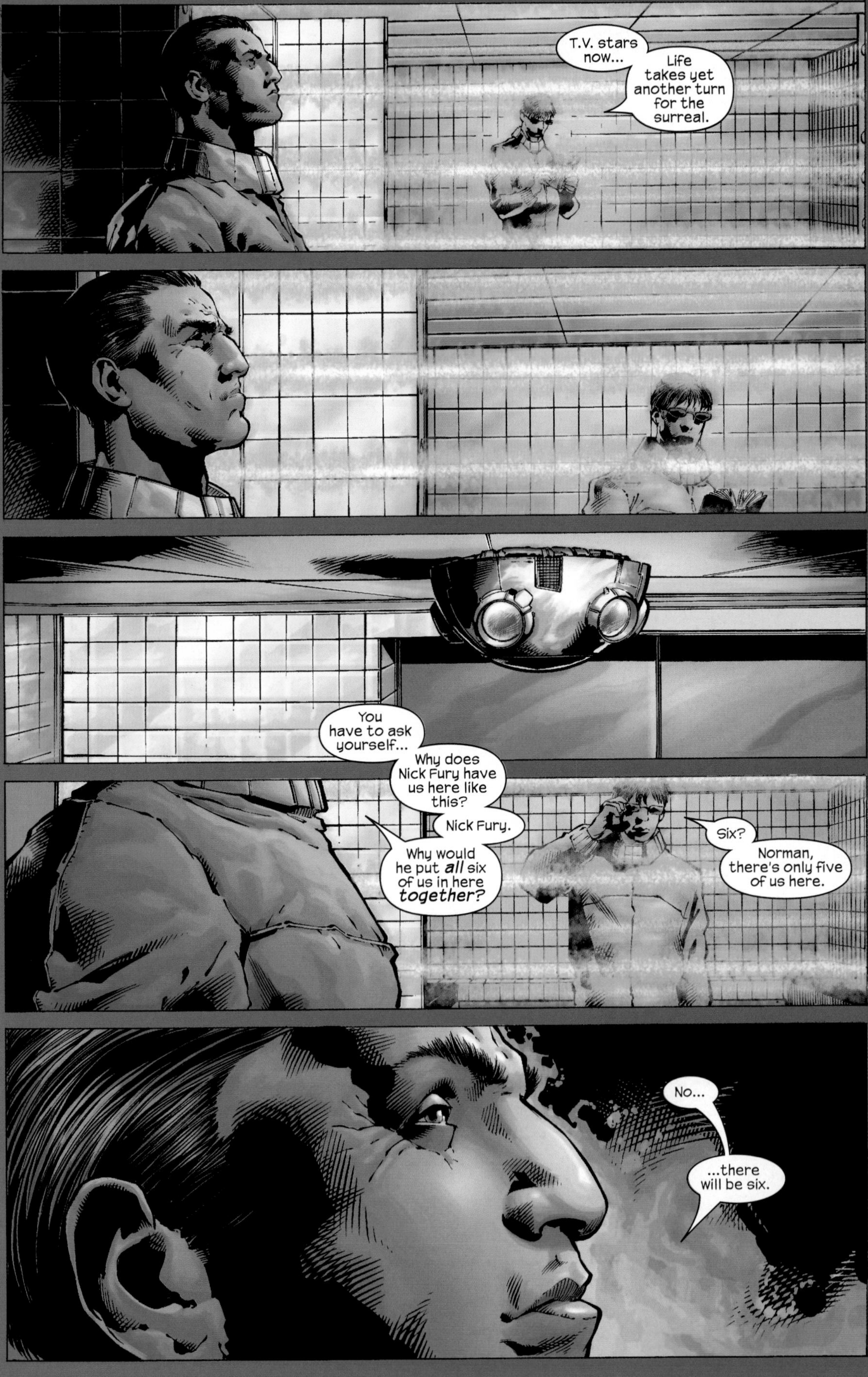
T.V. stars now...
Life takes yet another turn for the surreal.
You have to ask yourself...
Why does Nick Fury have us here like this?
Nick Fury.
Why would he put *all* six of us in here *together*?
Six?
Norman, there's only five of us here.
No...
...there will be six.

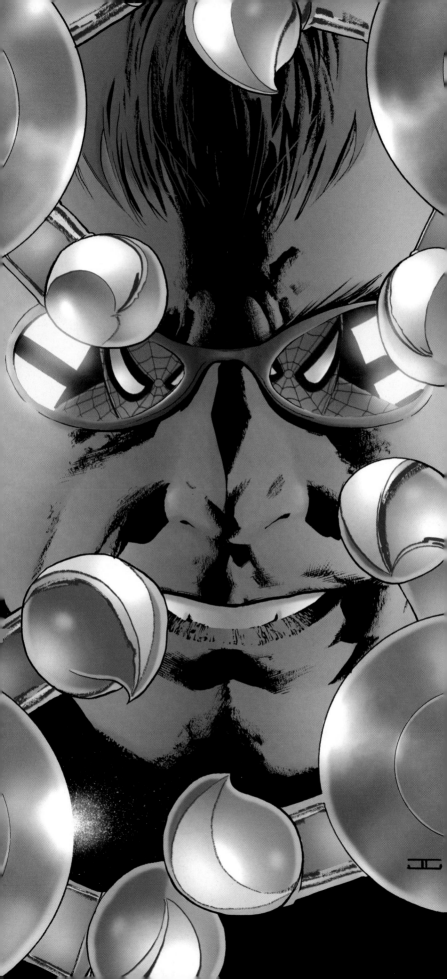

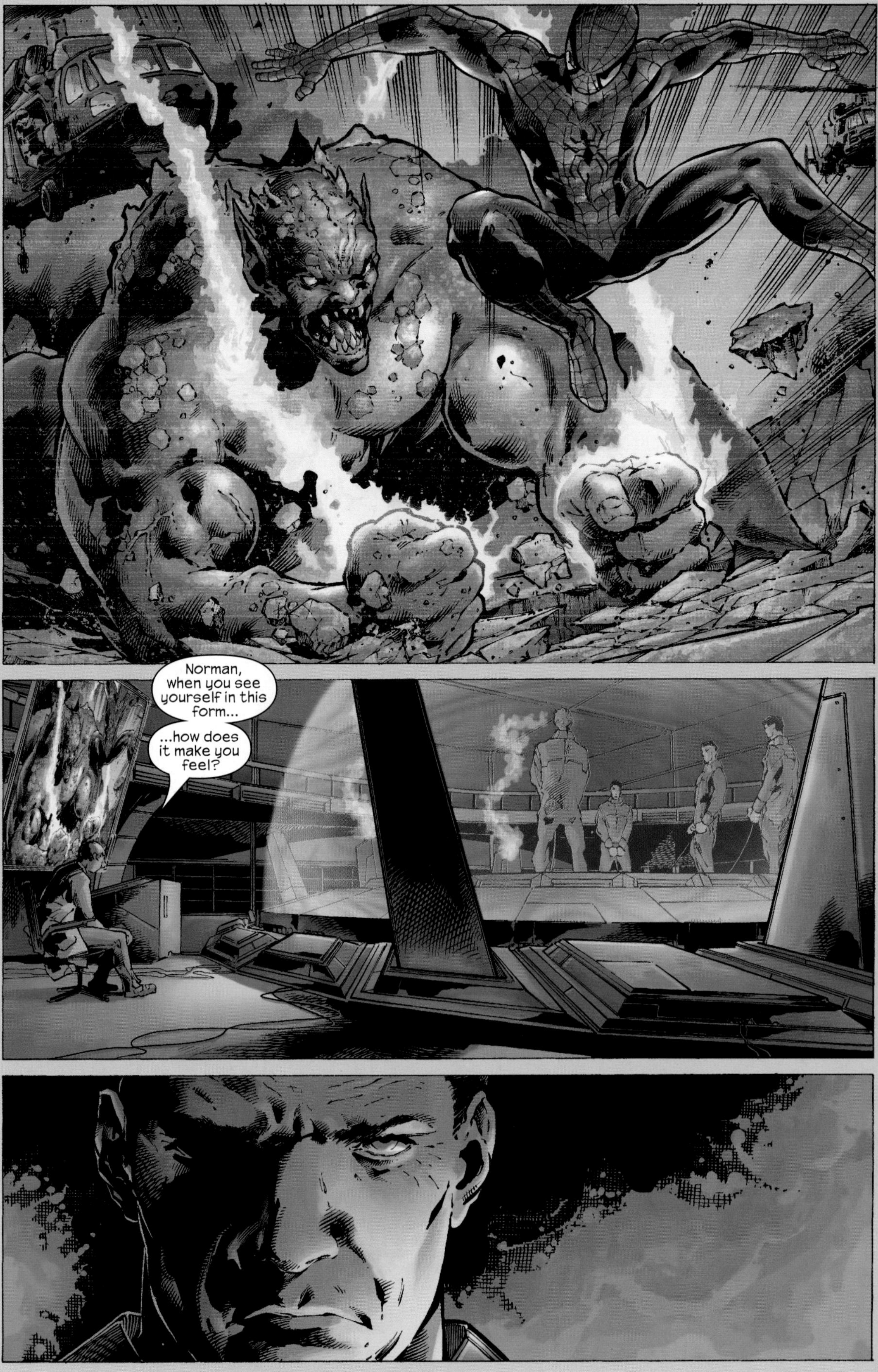
Norman, when you see yourself in this form...
...how does it make you feel?

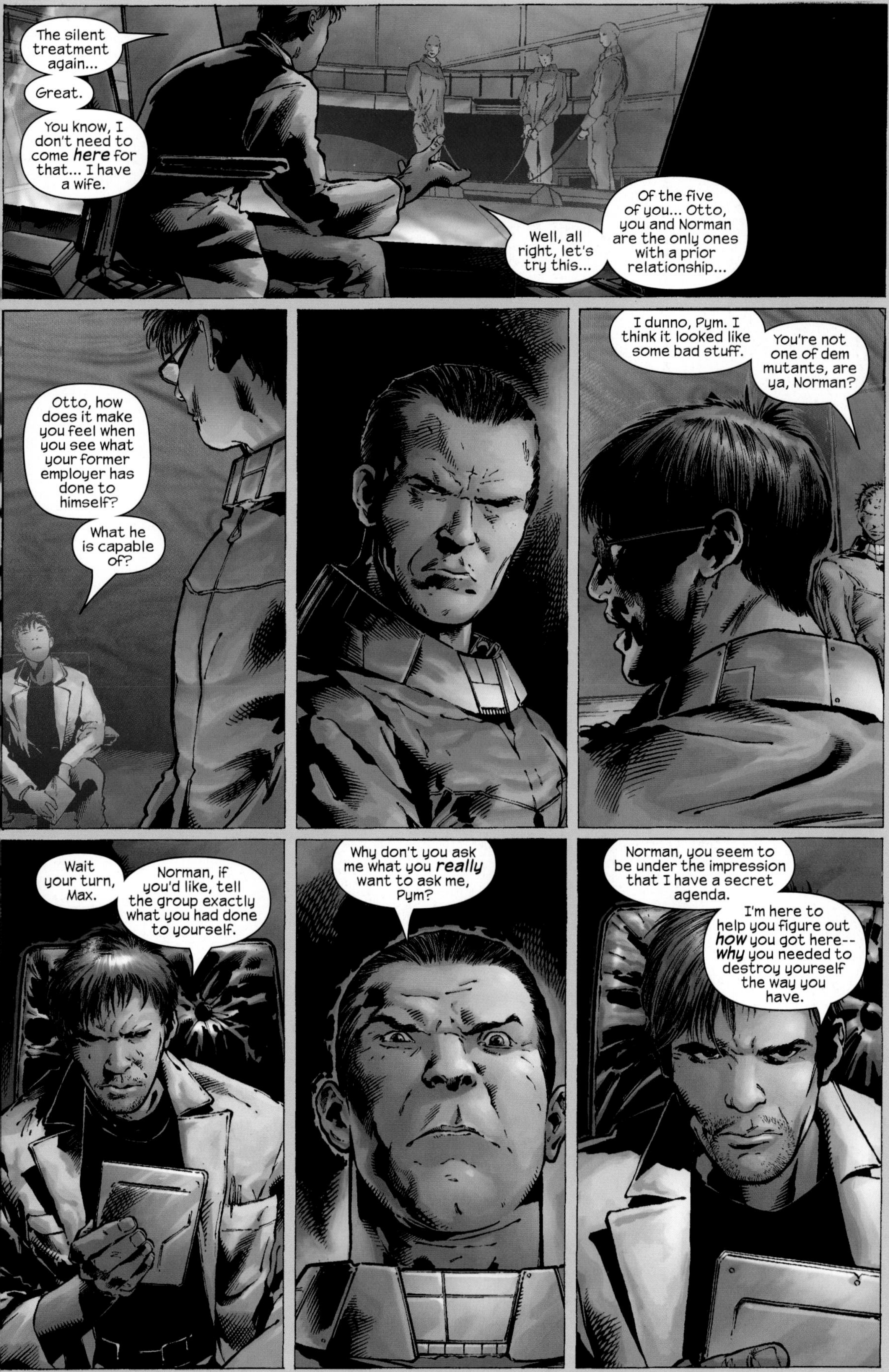
The silent treatment again...
Great.
You know, I don't need to come *here* for that... I have a wife.
Well, all right, let's try this...
Of the five of you... Otto, you and Norman are the only ones with a prior relationship...
Otto, how does it make you feel when you see what your former employer has done to himself?
What he is capable of?
I dunno, Pym. I think it looked like some bad stuff.
You're not one of dem mutants, are ya, Norman?
Wait your turn, Max.
Norman, if you'd like, tell the group exactly what you had done to yourself.
Why don't you ask me what you *really* want to ask me, Pym?
Norman, you seem to be under the impression that I have a secret agenda.
I'm here to help you figure out *how* you got here-- *why* you needed to destroy yourself the way you have.

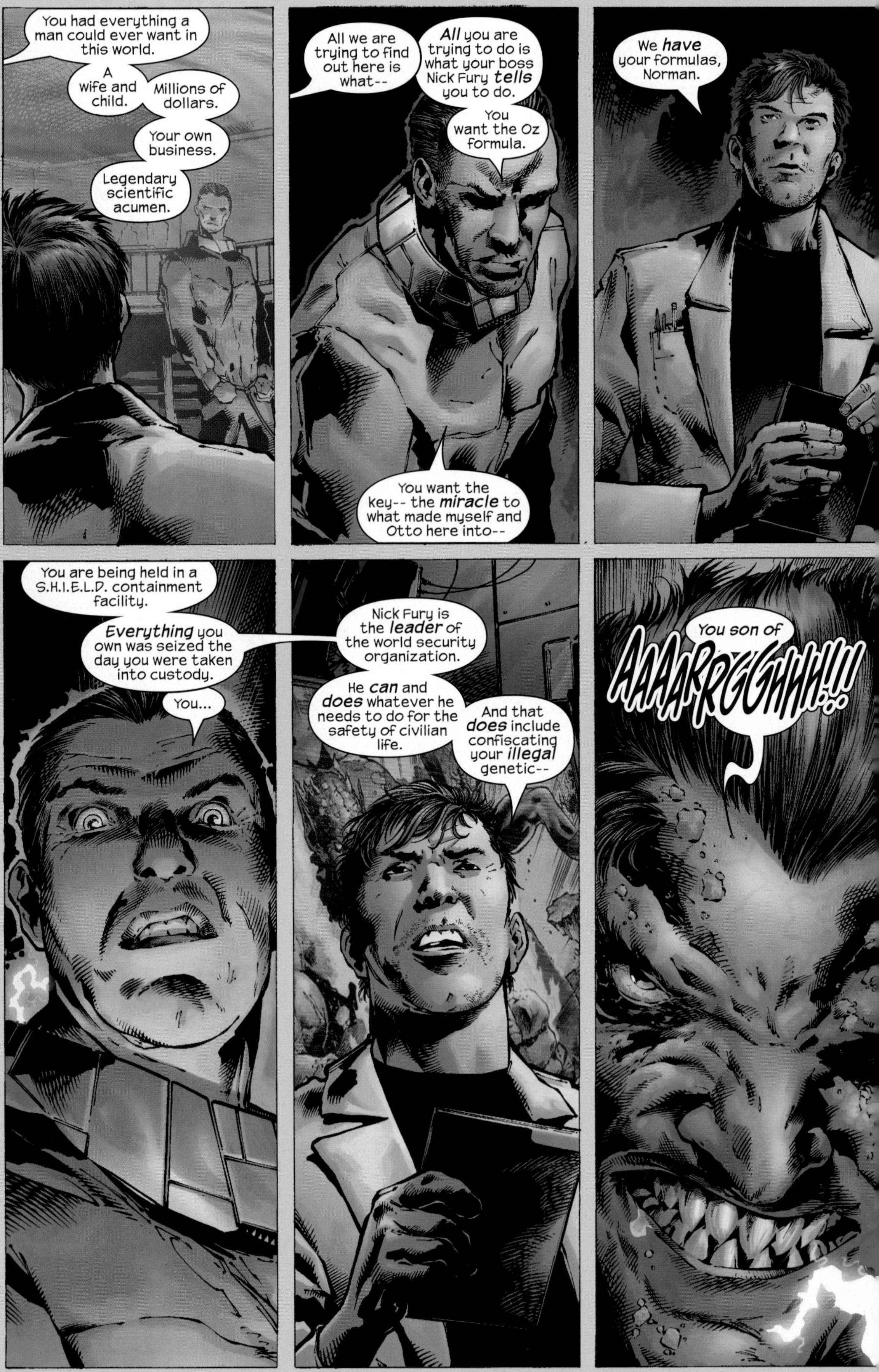
You had everything a man could ever want in this world.
A wife and child.
Millions of dollars.
Your own business.
Legendary scientific acumen.
All we are trying to find out here is what--
All you are trying to do is what your boss Nick Fury *tells* you to do.
You want the Oz formula.
You want the key-- the *miracle* to what made myself and Otto here into--
We *have* your formulas, Norman.
You are being held in a S.H.I.E.L.D. containment facility.
Everything you own was seized the day you were taken into custody.
You...
Nick Fury is the *leader* of the world security organization.
He *can* and *does* whatever he needs to do for the safety of civilian life.
And that *does* include confiscating your *illegal* genetic--
You son of
AAAARRGGHHH!!!

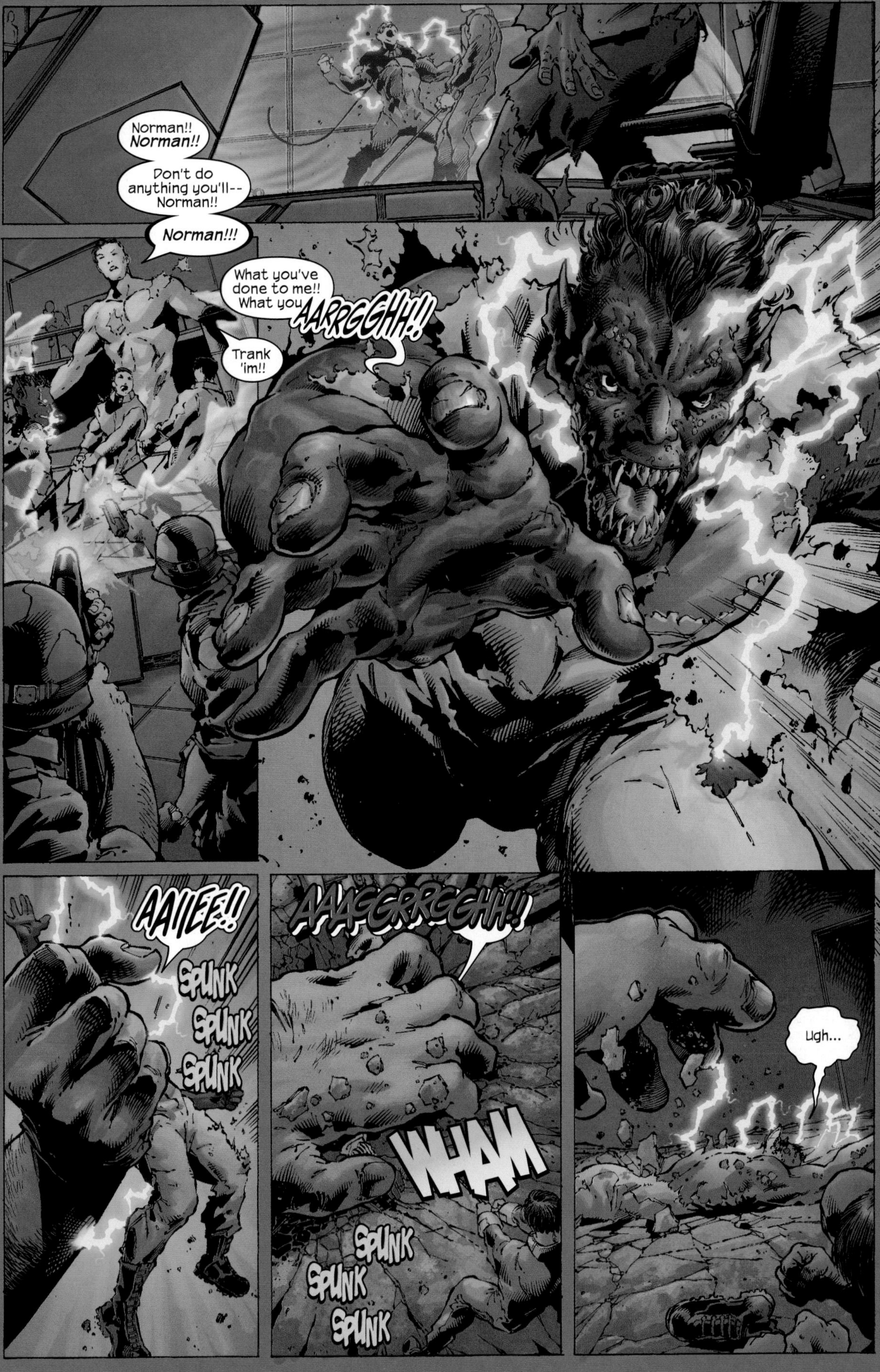
Norman!! Norman!!
Don't do anything you'll-- Norman!!
Norman!!!
What you've done to me!! What you
AARRGGHH!!
Trank 'im!!
AAIIEE!!
SPUNK
SPUNK
SPUNK
AAAGGRRGGHH!!
WHAM
SPUNK
SPUNK
SPUNK
Ugh...

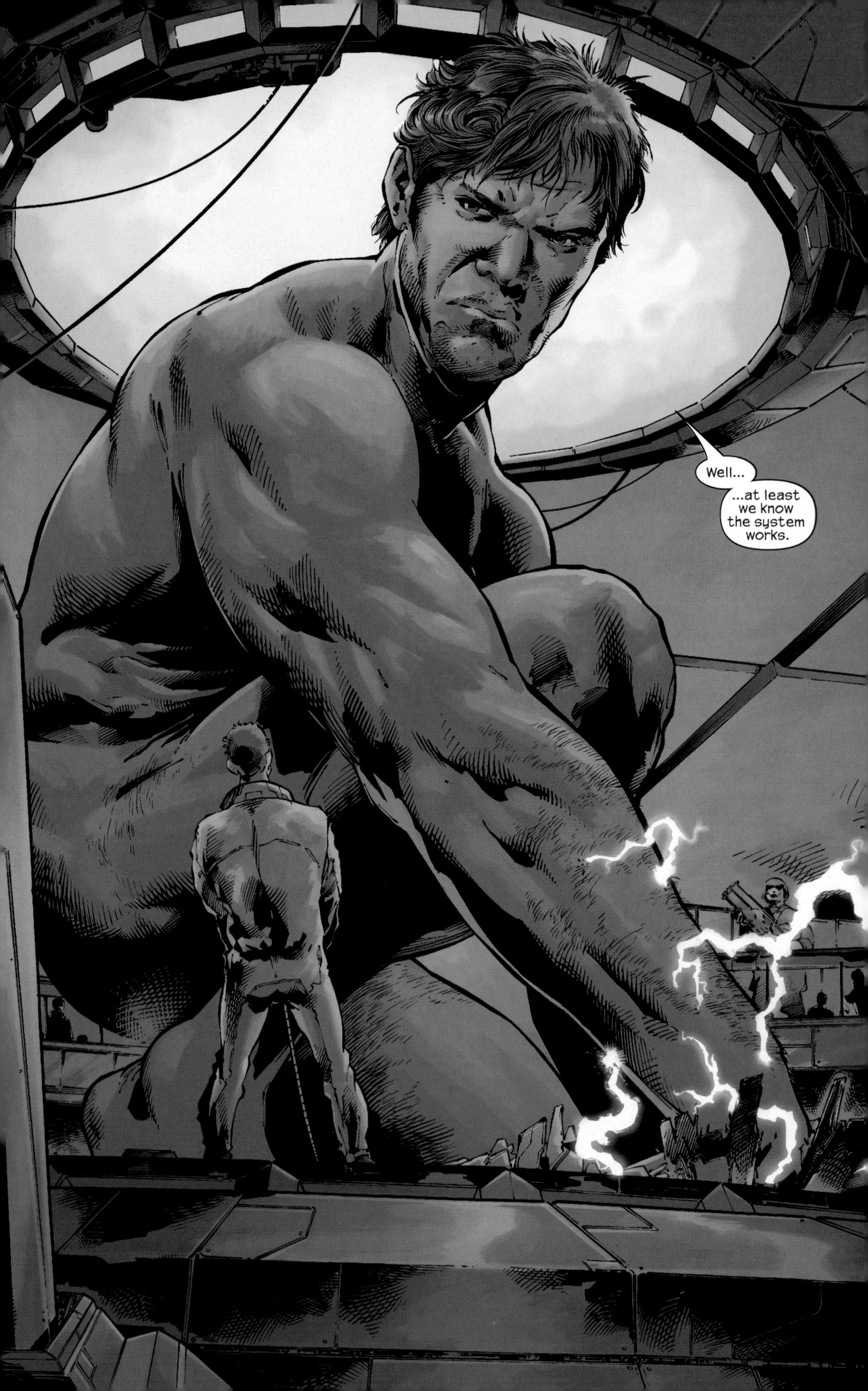
Well...
...at least we know the system works.

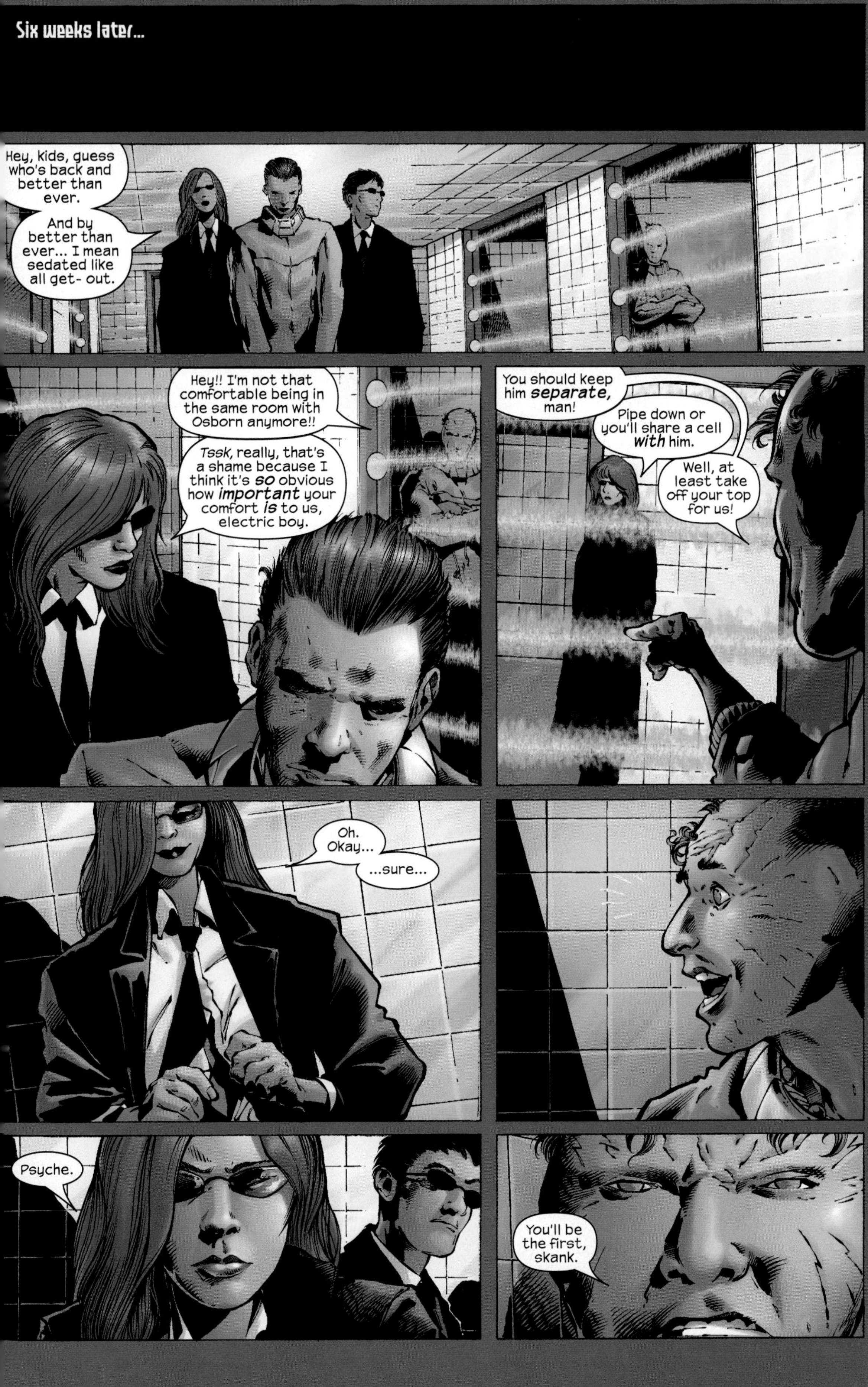
Six weeks later...
Hey, kids, guess who's back and better than ever.
And by better than ever... I mean sedated like all get- out.
Hey!! I'm not that comfortable being in the same room with Osborn anymore!!
Tssk, really, that's a shame because I think it's so obvious how important your comfort is to us, electric boy.
You should keep him separate, man!
Pipe down or you'll share a cell with him.
Well, at least take off your top for us!
Oh. Okay...
...sure...
Psyche.
You'll be the first, skank.

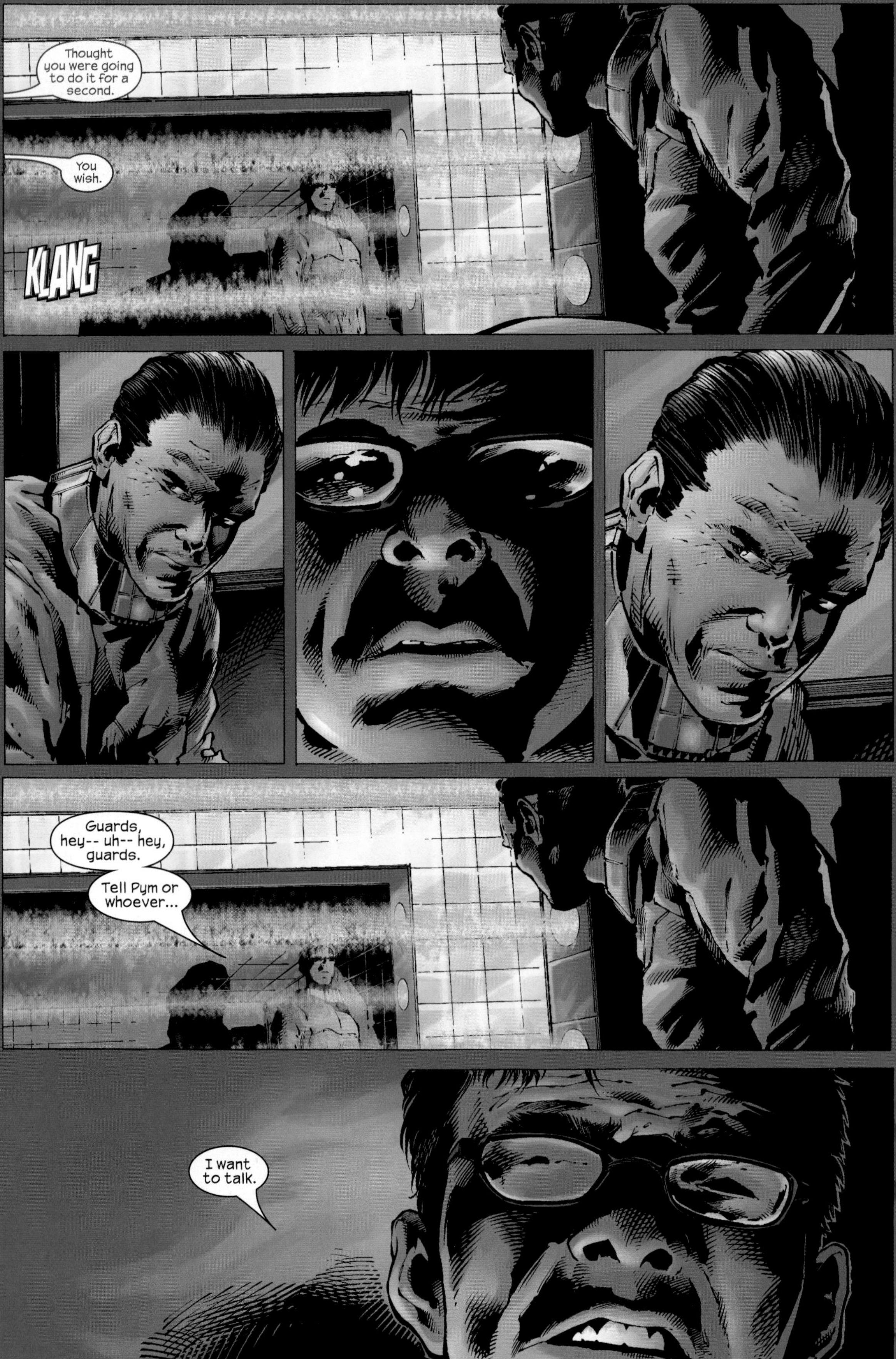
Thought you were going to do it for a second.
You wish.
KLANG
Guards, hey-- uh-- hey, guards.
Tell Pym or whoever...
I want to talk.

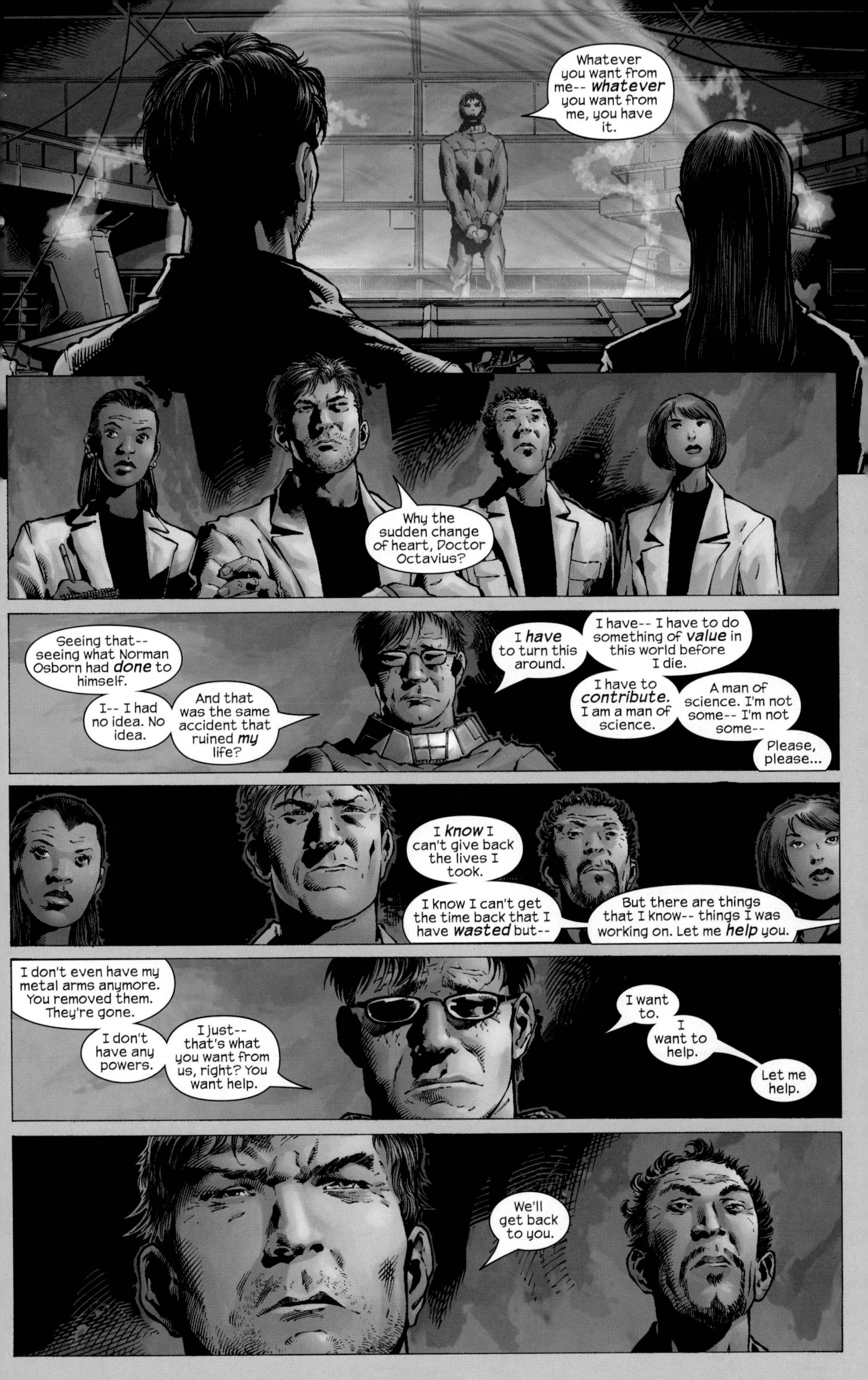
Whatever you want from me-- whatever you want from me, you have it.
Why the sudden change of heart, Doctor Octavius?
Seeing that-- seeing what Norman Osborn had done to himself.
I-- I had no idea. No idea.
And that was the same accident that ruined my life?
I have to turn this around.
I have-- I have to do something of value in this world before I die.
I have to contribute. I am a man of science.
A man of science. I'm not some-- I'm not some--
Please, please...
I know I can't give back the lives I took.
I know I can't get the time back that I have wasted but--
But there are things that I know-- things I was working on. Let me help you.
I don't even have my metal arms anymore. You removed them. They're gone.
I don't have any powers.
I just-- that's what you want from us, right? You want help.
I want to.
I want to help.
Let me help.
We'll get back to you.

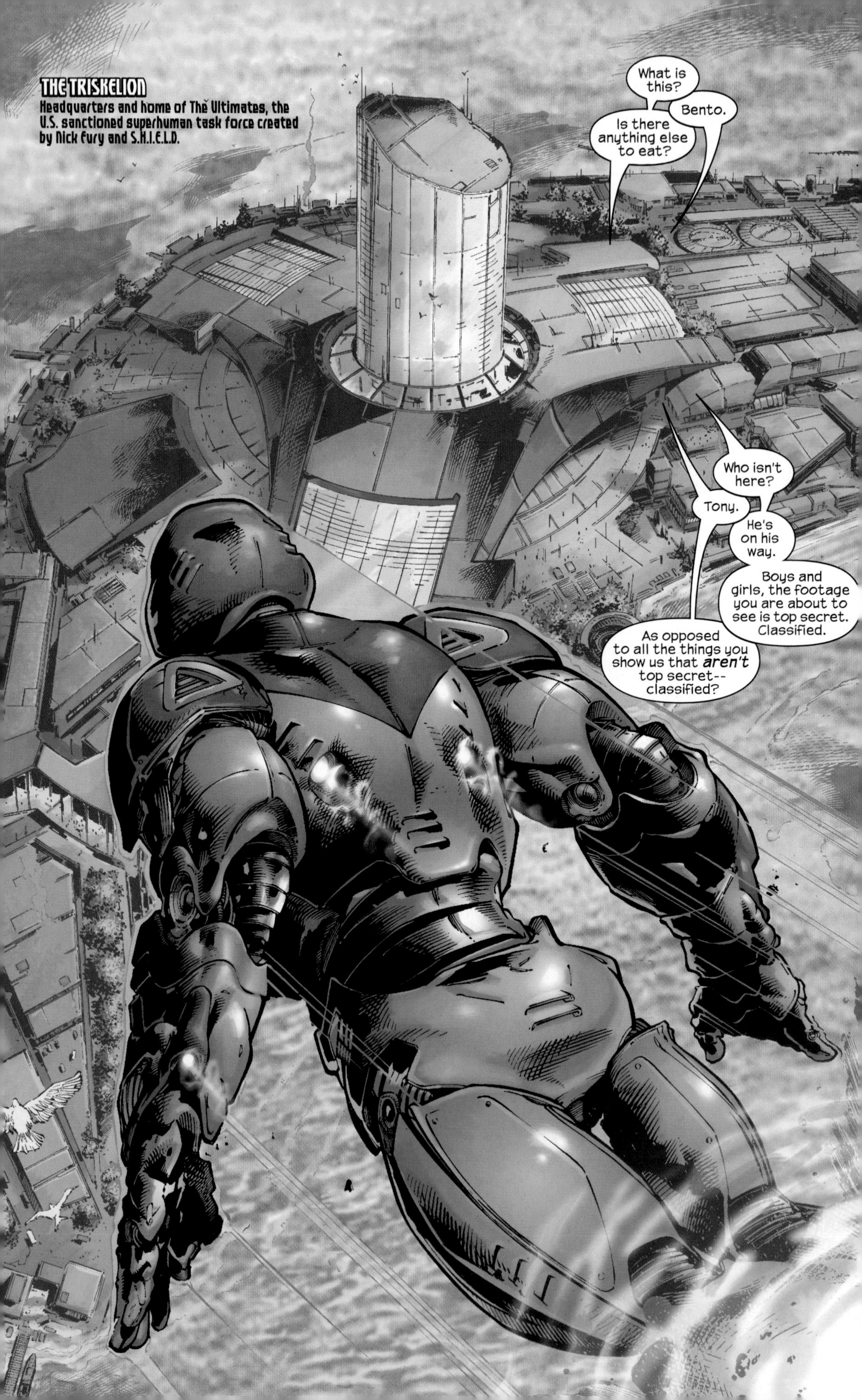
THE TRISKELION
Headquarters and home of The Ultimates, the U.S. sanctioned superhuman task force created by Nick Fury and S.H.I.E.L.D.
What is this?
Bento.
Is there anything else to eat?
Who isn't here?
Tony.
He's on his way.
Boys and girls, the footage you are about to see is top secret. Classified.
As opposed to all the things you show us that *aren't* top secret--classified?

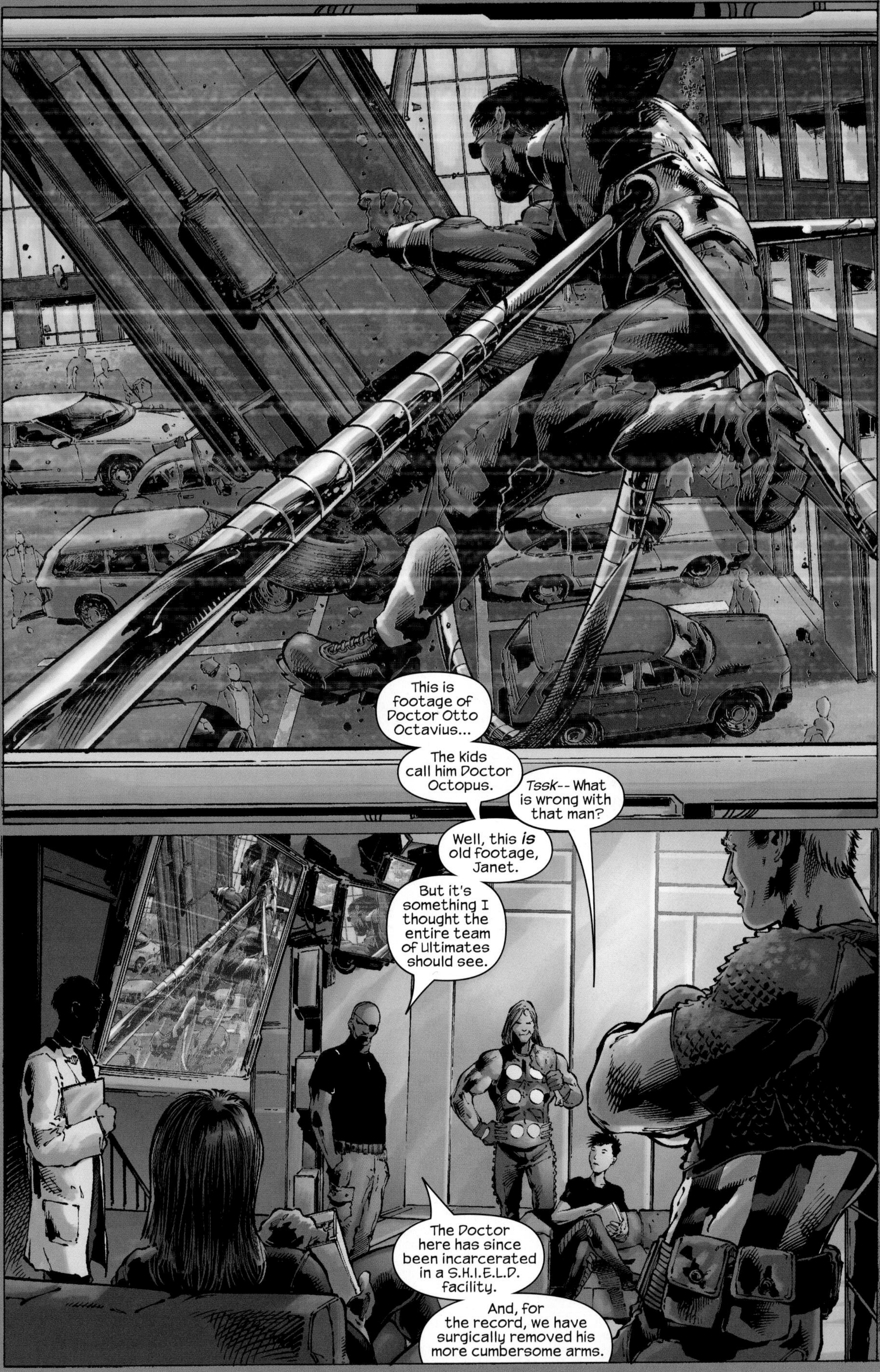
This is footage of Doctor Otto Octavius...
The kids call him Doctor Octopus.
Tssk-- What is wrong with that man?
Well, this *is* old footage, Janet.
But it's something I thought the entire team of Ultimates should see.
The Doctor here has since been incarcerated in a S.H.I.E.L.D. facility.
And, for the record, we have surgically removed his more cumbersome arms.

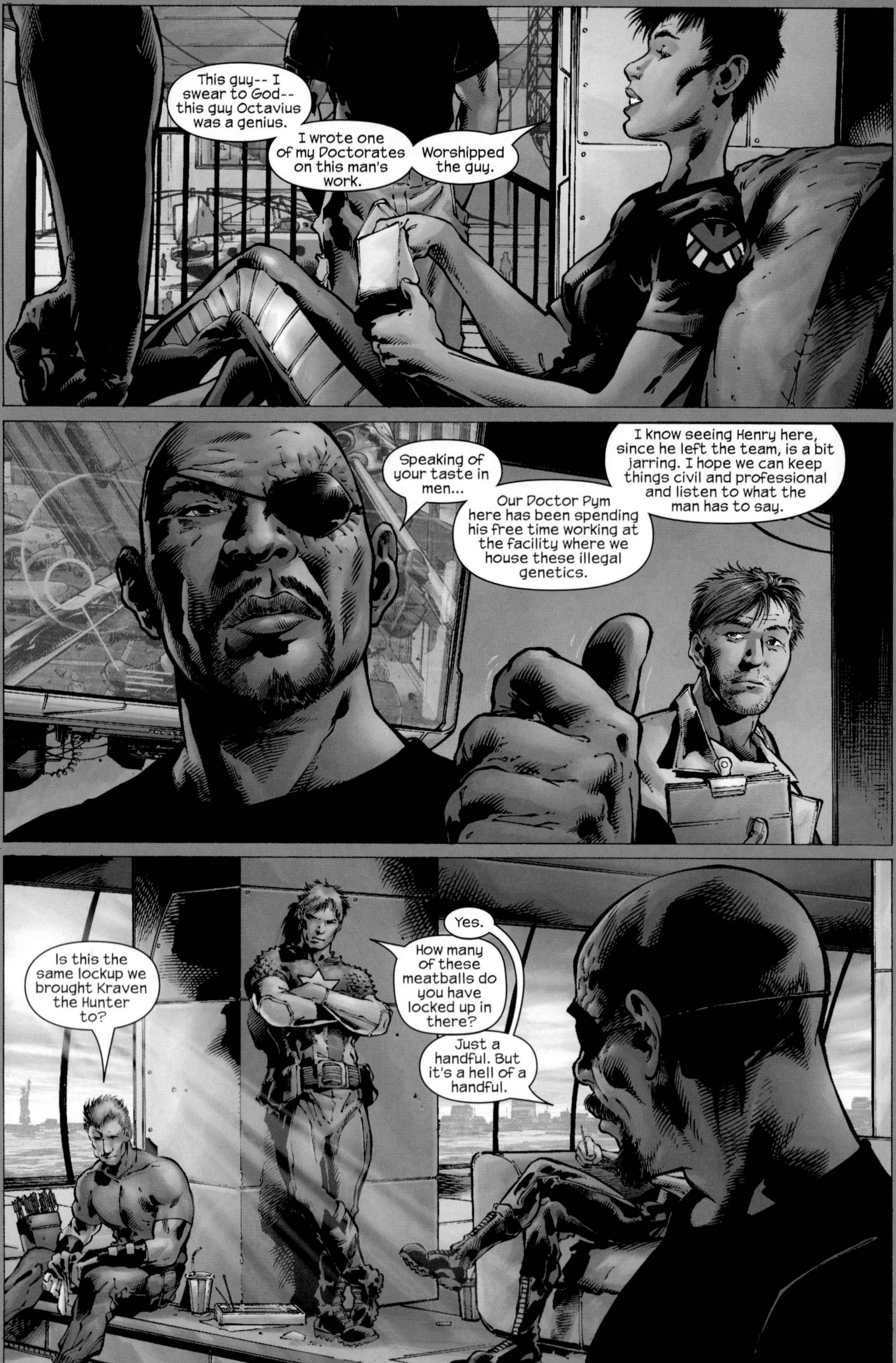

This guy-- I swear to God-- this guy Octavius was a genius.
I wrote one of my Doctorates on this man's work.
Worshipped the guy.
Speaking of your taste in men...
Our Doctor Pym here has been spending his free time working at the facility where we house these illegal genetics.
I know seeing Henry here, since he left the team, is a bit jarring. I hope we can keep things civil and professional and listen to what the man has to say.
Is this the same lockup we brought Kraven the Hunter to?
Yes.
How many of these meatballs do you have locked up in there?
Just a handful. But it's a hell of a handful.

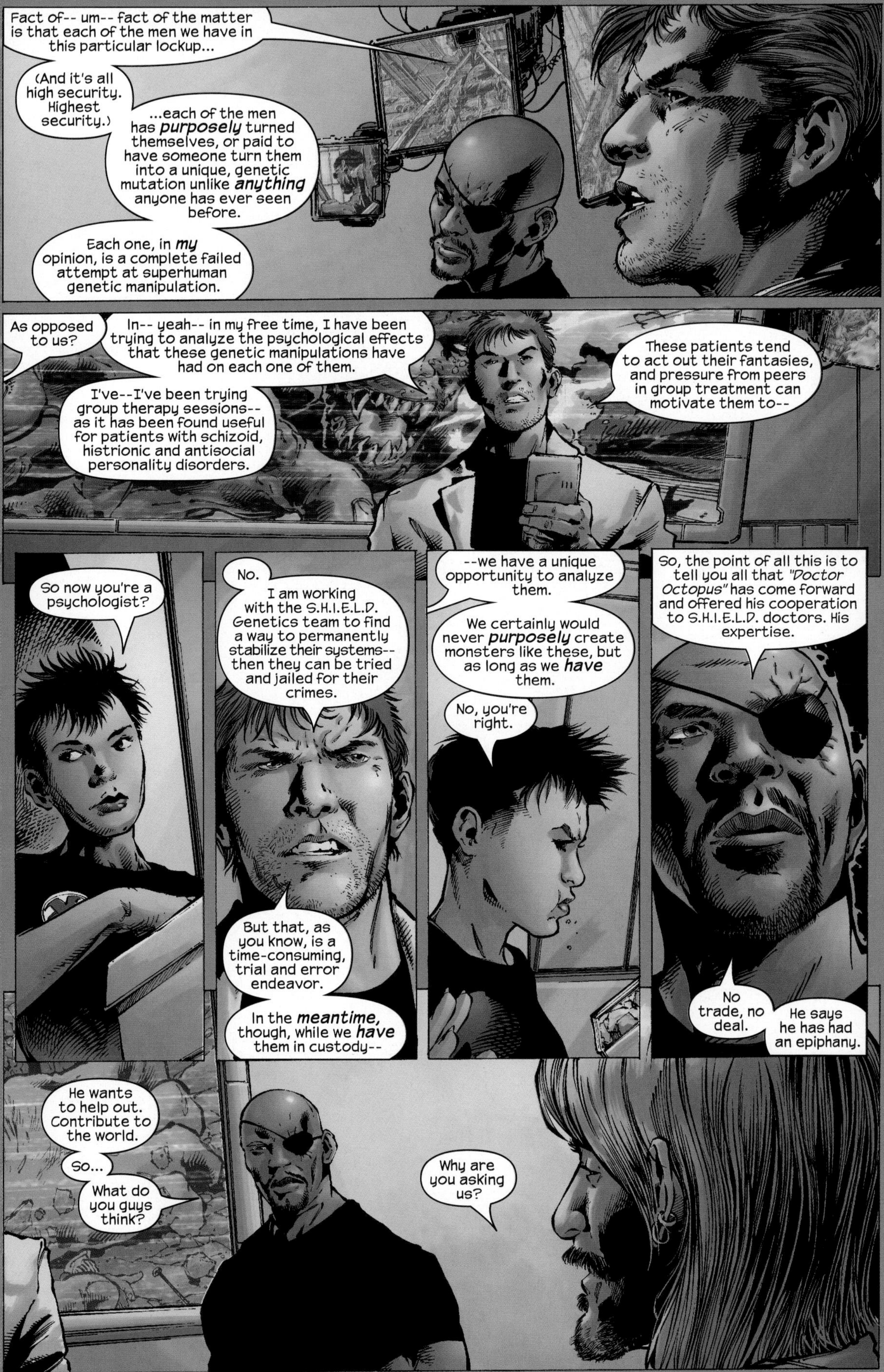
Fact of-- um-- fact of the matter is that each of the men we have in this particular lockup...
(And it's all high security. Highest security.)
...each of the men has purposely turned themselves, or paid to have someone turn them into a unique, genetic mutation unlike anything anyone has ever seen before.
Each one, in my opinion, is a complete failed attempt at superhuman genetic manipulation.
As opposed to us?
In-- yeah-- in my free time, I have been trying to analyze the psychological effects that these genetic manipulations have had on each one of them.
I've--I've been trying group therapy sessions--as it has been found useful for patients with schizoid, histrionic and antisocial personality disorders.
These patients tend to act out their fantasies, and pressure from peers in group treatment can motivate them to--
So now you're a psychologist?
No.
I am working with the S.H.I.E.L.D. Genetics team to find a way to permanently stabilize their systems--then they can be tried and jailed for their crimes.
But that, as you know, is a time-consuming, trial and error endeavor.
In the meantime, though, while we have them in custody--
--we have a unique opportunity to analyze them.
We certainly would never purposely create monsters like these, but as long as we have them.
No, you're right.
So, the point of all this is to tell you all that "Doctor Octopus" has come forward and offered his cooperation to S.H.I.E.L.D. doctors. His expertise.
No trade, no deal.
He says he has had an epiphany.
He wants to help out. Contribute to the world.
So...
What do you guys think?
Why are you asking us?

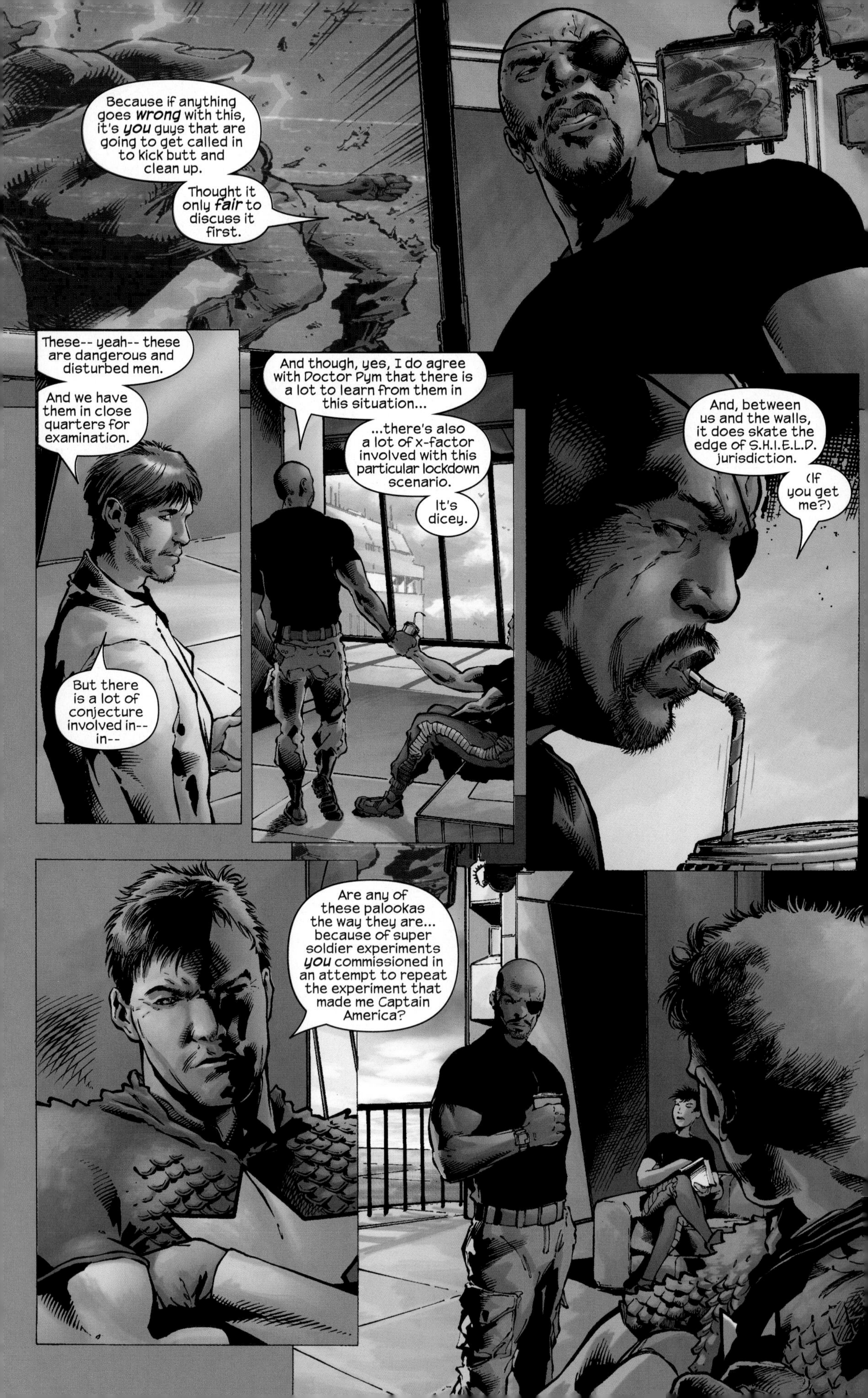
Because if anything goes *wrong* with this, it's *you* guys that are going to get called in to kick butt and clean up.
Thought it only *fair* to discuss it first.
These-- yeah-- these are dangerous and disturbed men.
And we have them in close quarters for examination.
But there is a lot of conjecture involved in-- in--
And though, yes, I do agree with Doctor Pym that there is a lot to learn from them in this situation...
...there's also a lot of x-factor involved with this particular lockdown scenario.
It's dicey.
And, between us and the walls, it does skate the edge of S.H.I.E.L.D. jurisdiction.
(If you get me?)
Are any of these palookas the way they are... because of super soldier experiments *you* commissioned in an attempt to repeat the experiment that made me Captain America?

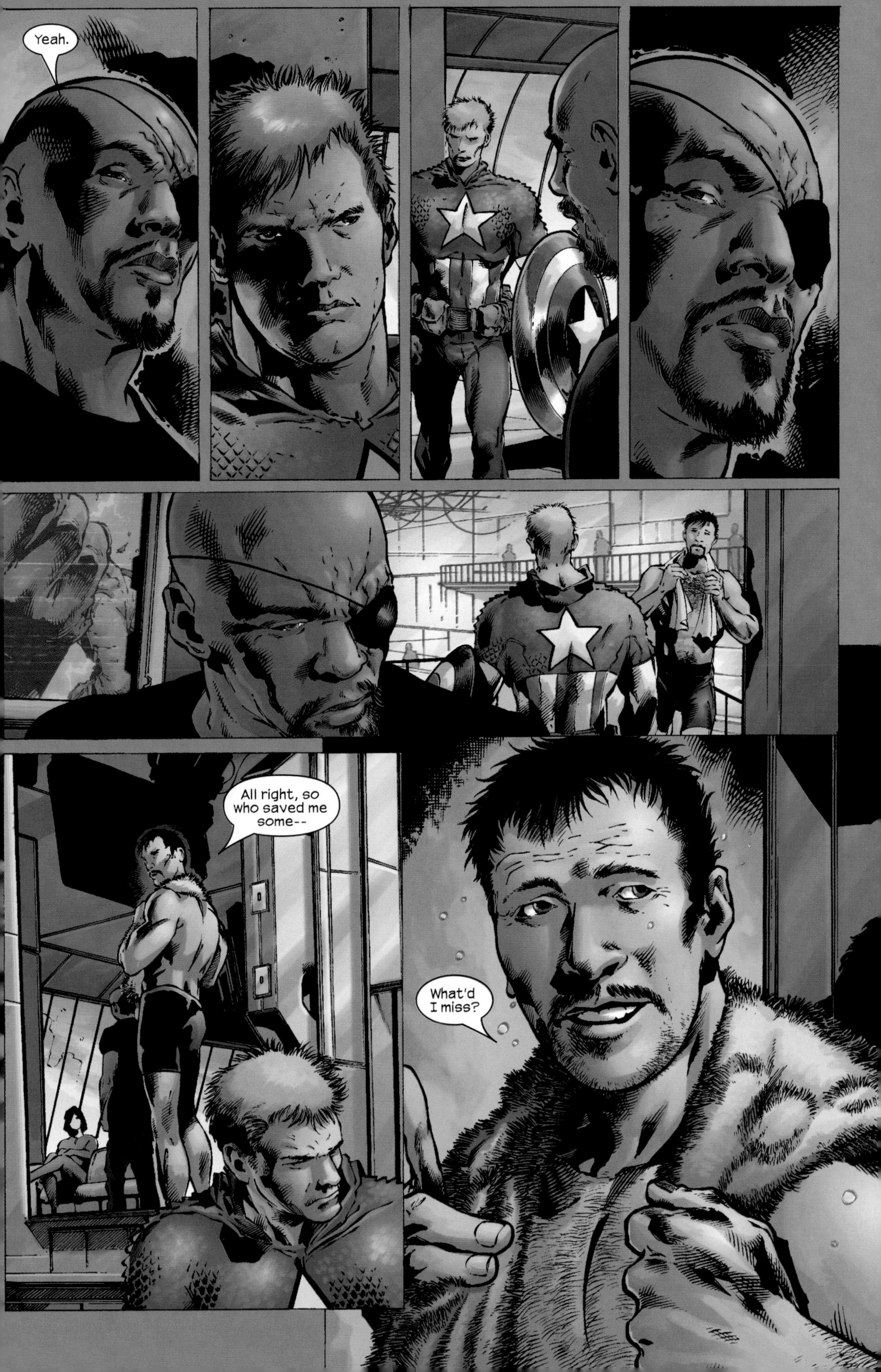
Yeah.
All right, so who saved me some--
What'd I miss?

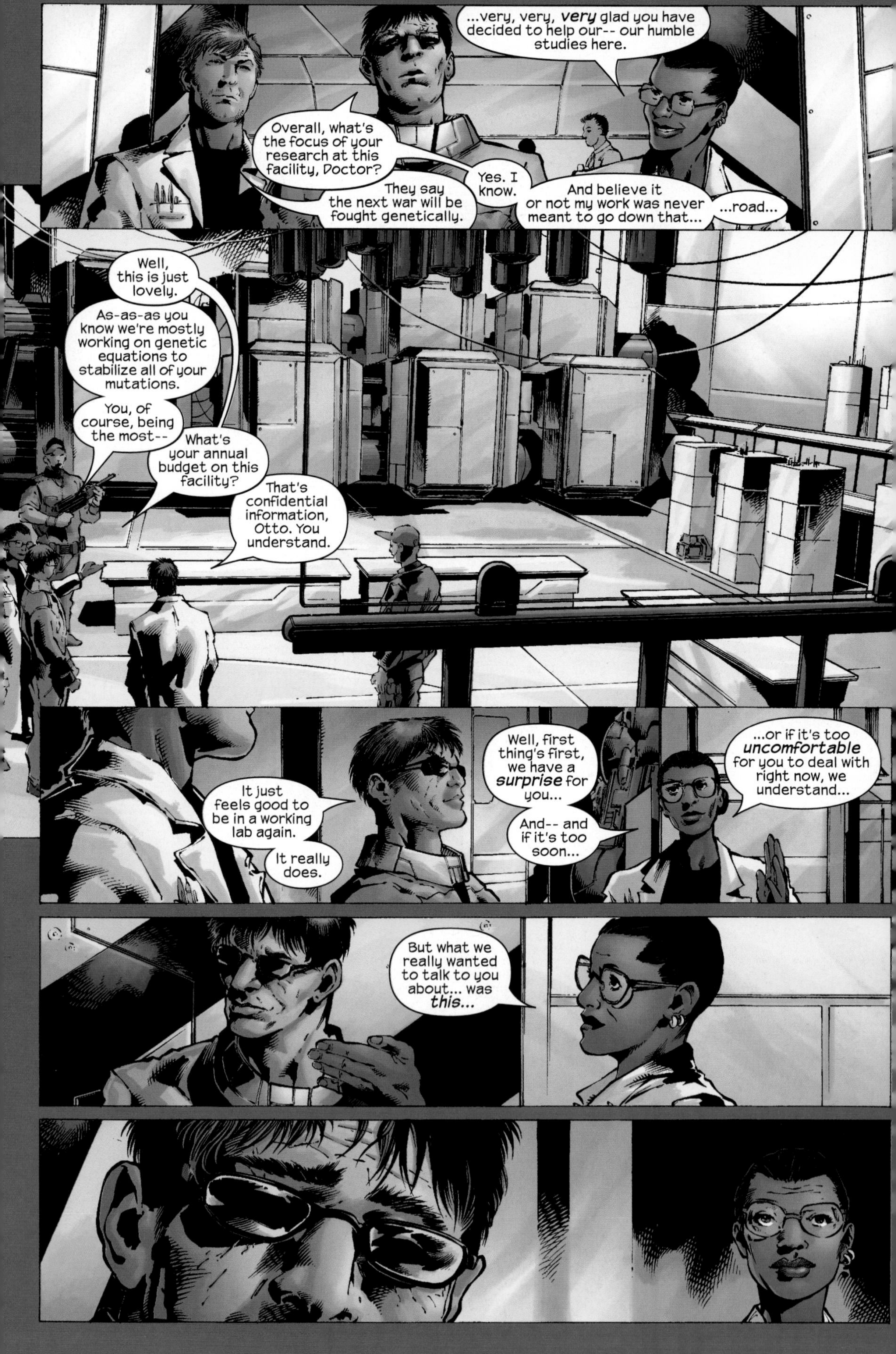
...very, very, very glad you have decided to help our-- our humble studies here.
Overall, what's the focus of your research at this facility, Doctor?
They say the next war will be fought genetically.
Yes. I know.
And believe it or not my work was never meant to go down that...
...road...
Well, this is just lovely.
As-as-as you know we're mostly working on genetic equations to stabilize all of your mutations.
You, of course, being the most--
What's your annual budget on this facility?
That's confidential information, Otto. You understand.
It just feels good to be in a working lab again.
It really does.
Well, first thing's first, we have a surprise for you...
And-- and if it's too soon...
...or if it's too uncomfortable for you to deal with right now, we understand...
But what we really wanted to talk to you about... was this...

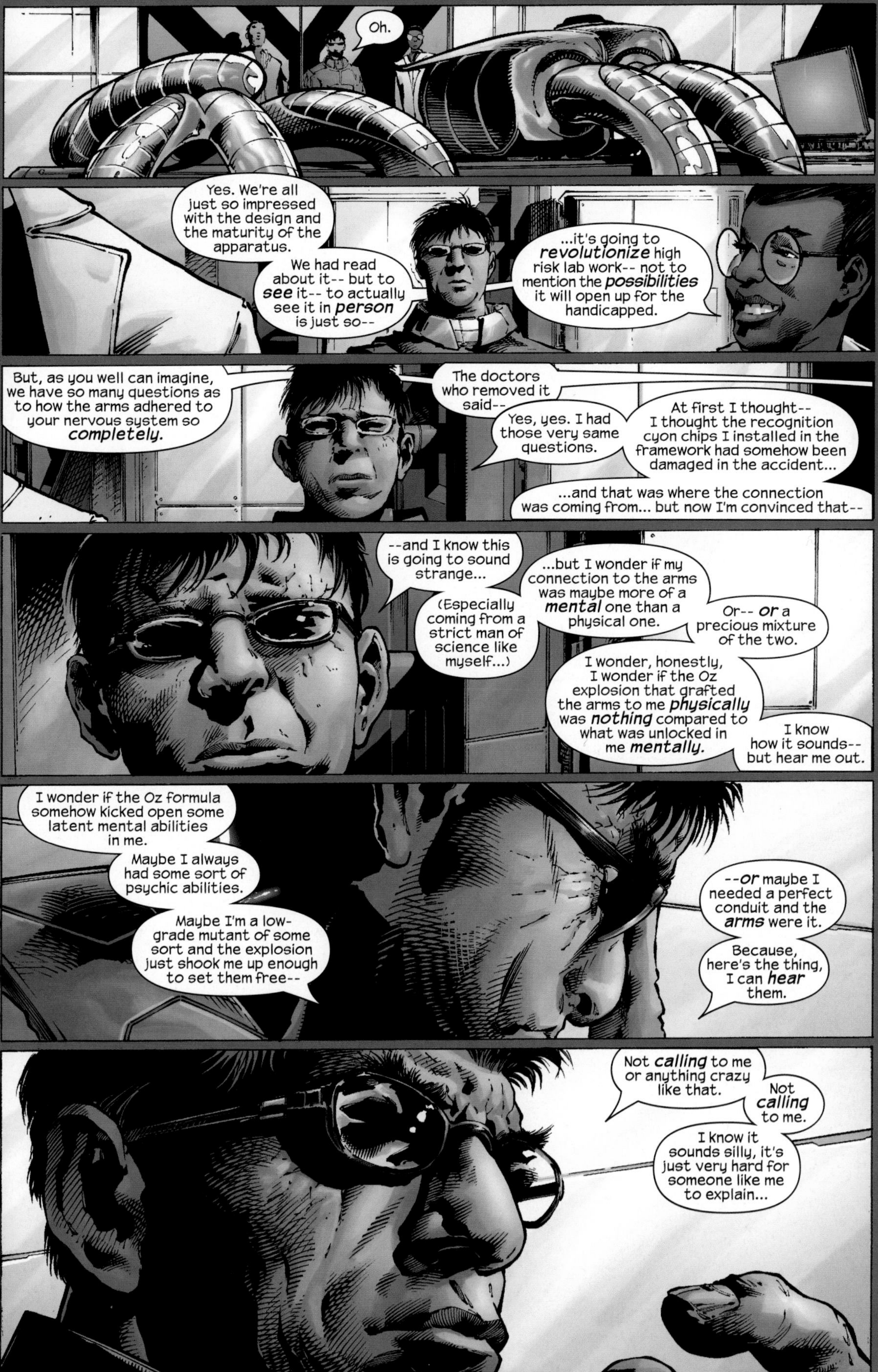
Oh.
Yes. We're all just so impressed with the design and the maturity of the apparatus.
We had read about it-- but to see it-- to actually see it in person is just so--
...it's going to revolutionize high risk lab work-- not to mention the possibilities it will open up for the handicapped.
But, as you well can imagine, we have so many questions as to how the arms adhered to your nervous system so completely.
The doctors who removed it said--
Yes, yes. I had those very same questions.
At first I thought-- I thought the recognition cyon chips I installed in the framework had somehow been damaged in the accident...
...and that was where the connection was coming from... but now I'm convinced that--
--and I know this is going to sound strange...
(Especially coming from a strict man of science like myself...)
...but I wonder if my connection to the arms was maybe more of a mental one than a physical one.
Or-- or a precious mixture of the two.
I wonder, honestly, I wonder if the Oz explosion that grafted the arms to me physically was nothing compared to what was unlocked in me mentally.
I know how it sounds-- but hear me out.
I wonder if the Oz formula somehow kicked open some latent mental abilities in me.
Maybe I always had some sort of psychic abilities.
Maybe I'm a low-grade mutant of some sort and the explosion just shook me up enough to set them free--
--or maybe I needed a perfect conduit and the arms were it.
Because, here's the thing, I can hear them.
Not calling to me or anything crazy like that.
Not calling to me.
I know it sounds silly, it's just very hard for someone like me to explain...

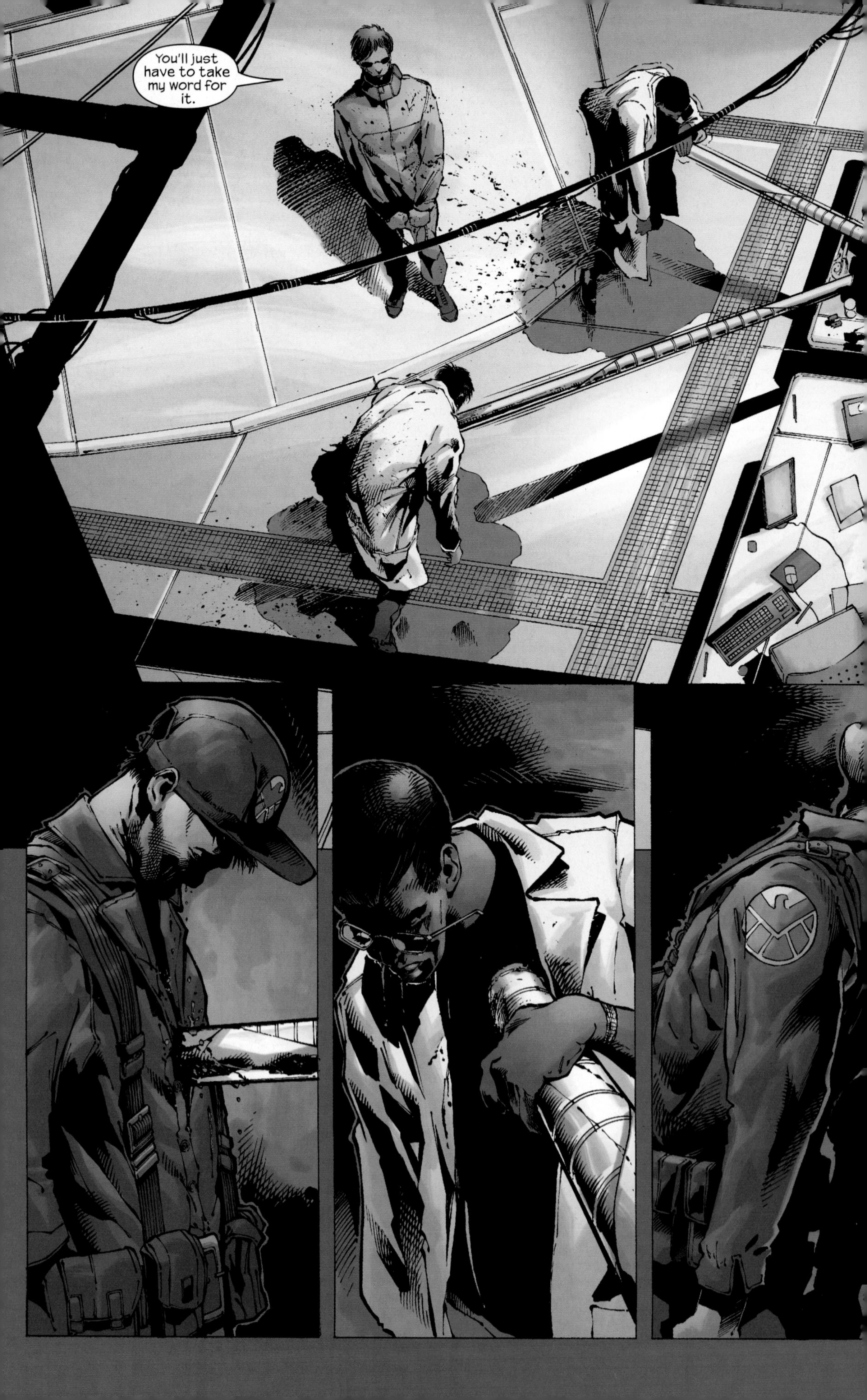
You'll just have to take my word for it.

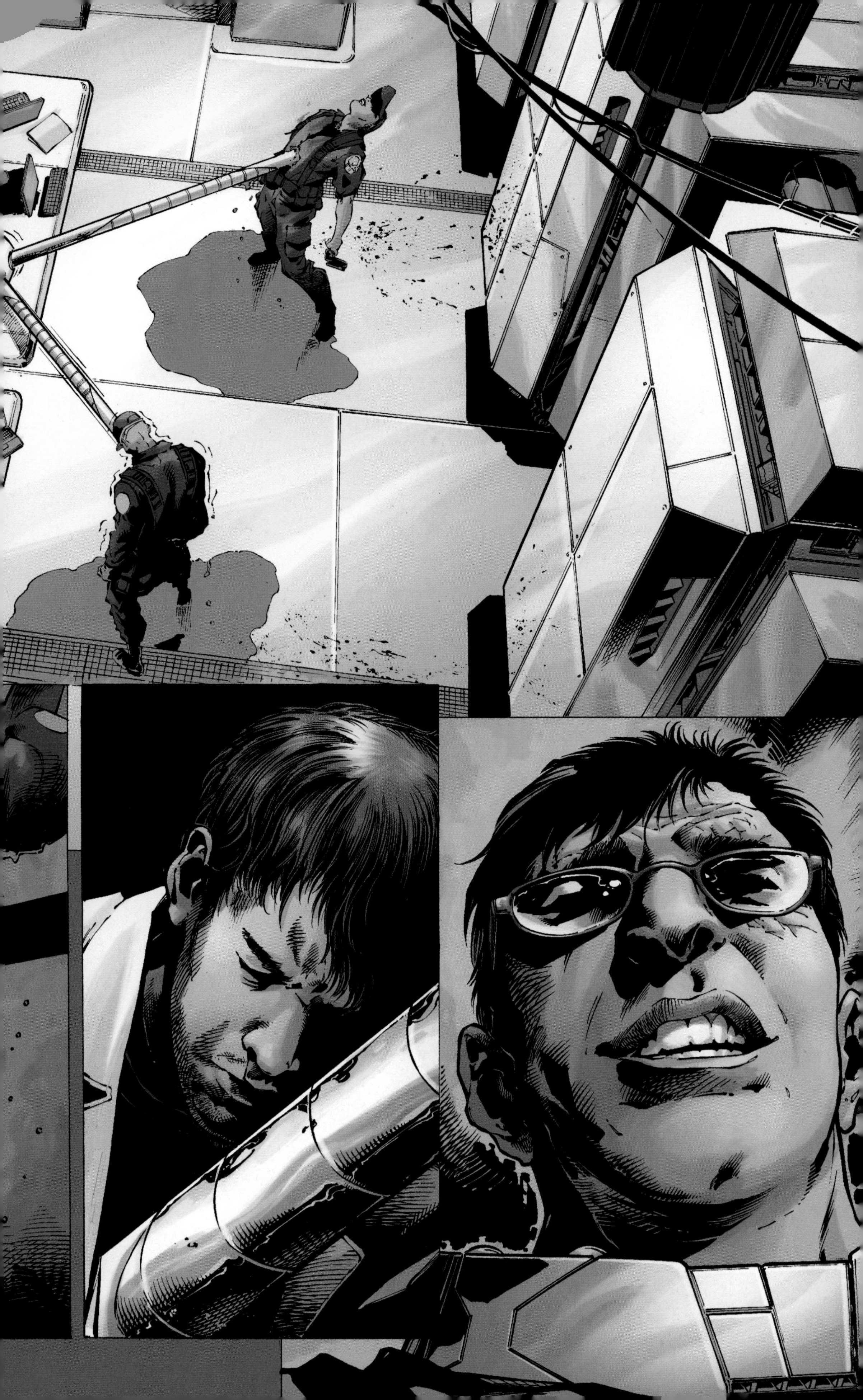

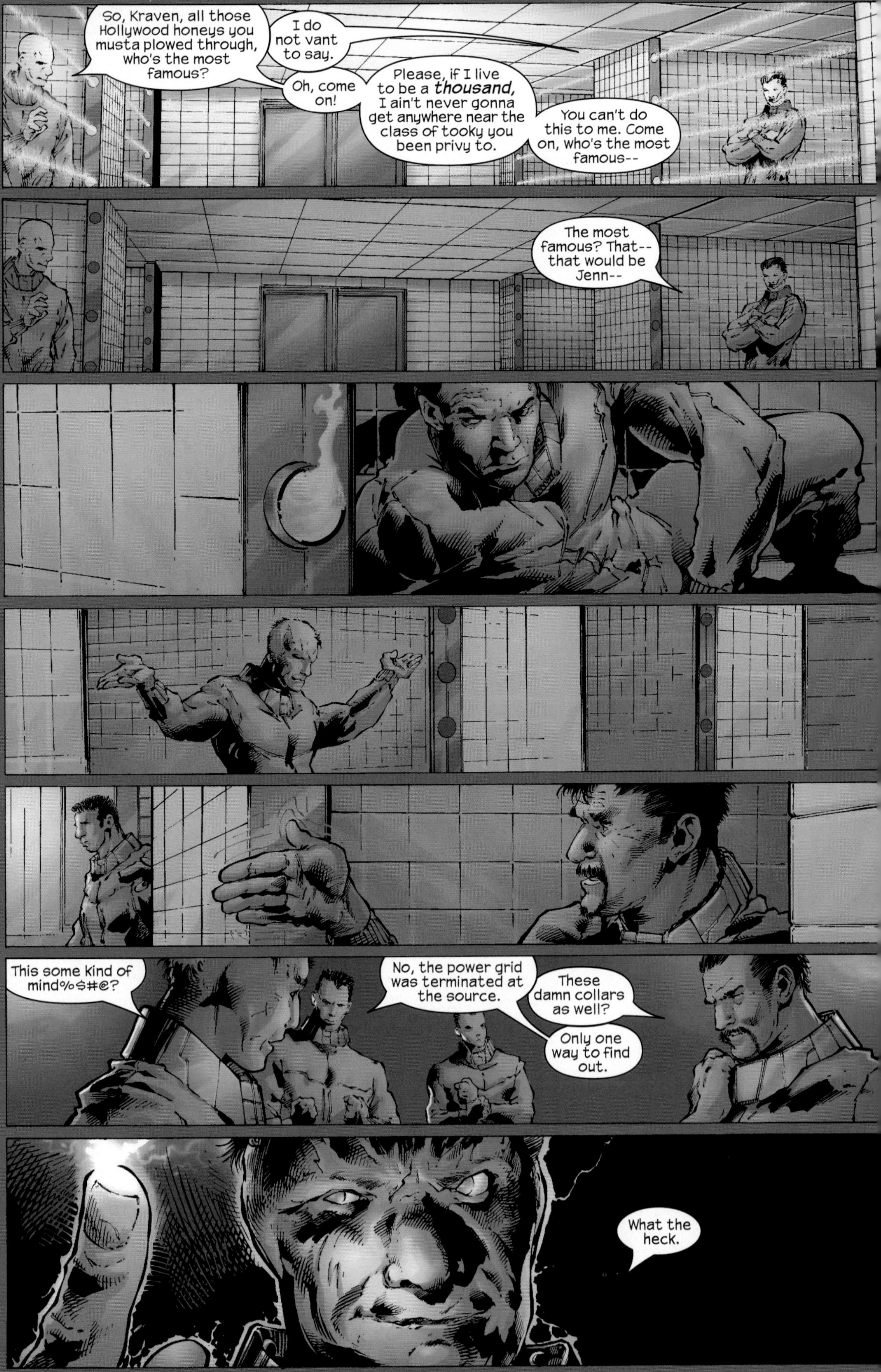
So, Kraven, all those Hollywood honeys you musta plowed through, who's the most famous?
I do not vant to say.
Oh, come on!
Please, if I live to be a thousand, I ain't never gonna get anywhere near the class of tooky you been privy to.
You can't do this to me. Come on, who's the most famous--
The most famous? That--that would be Jenn--
This some kind of mind%$#@?
No, the power grid was terminated at the source.
These damn collars as well?
Only one way to find out.
What the heck.

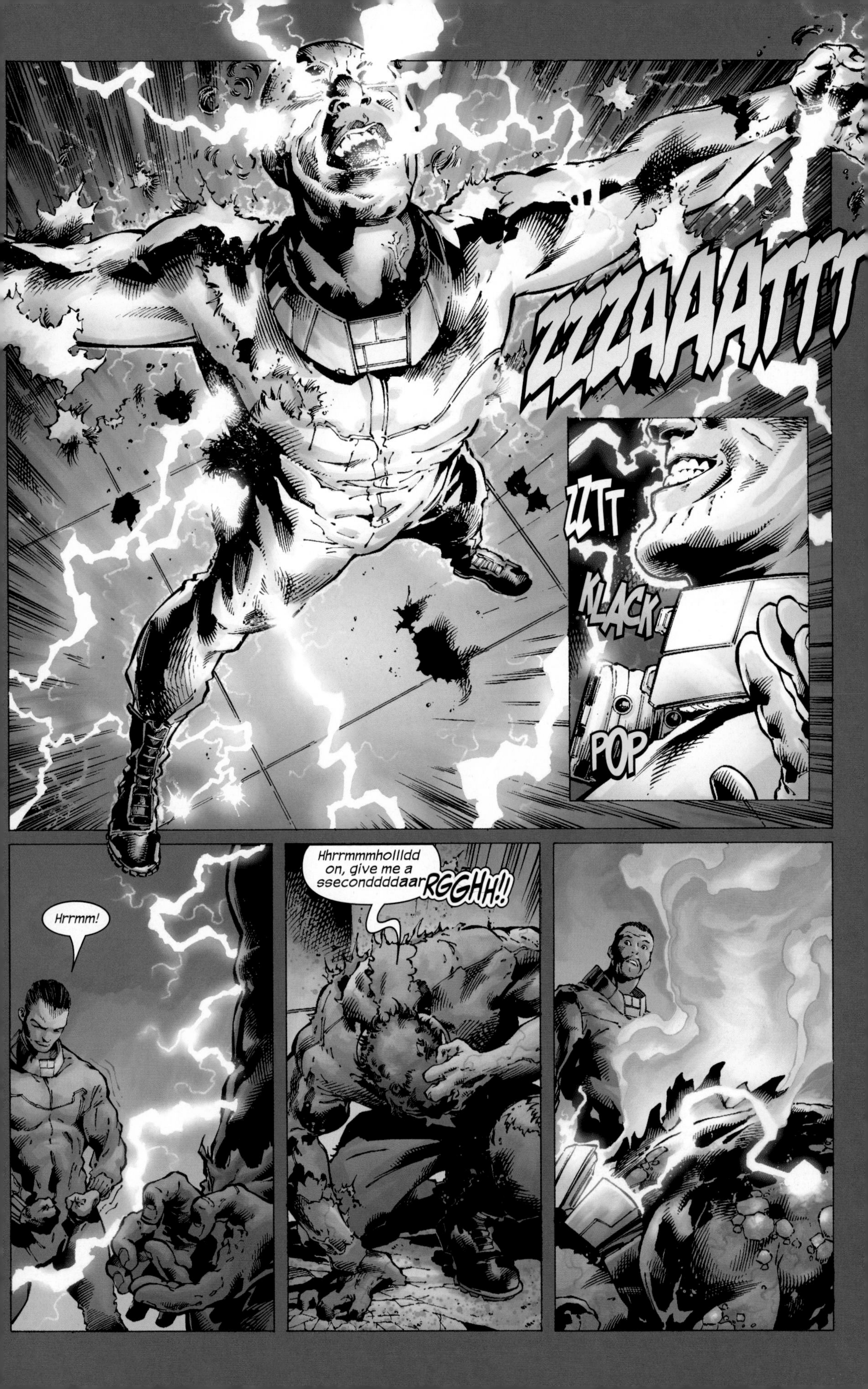
ZZZAAATTT
ZZTT
KLACK
POP
Hrrmm!
Hhrrmmmhollldd on, give me a sseconddddaarRGGHH!!

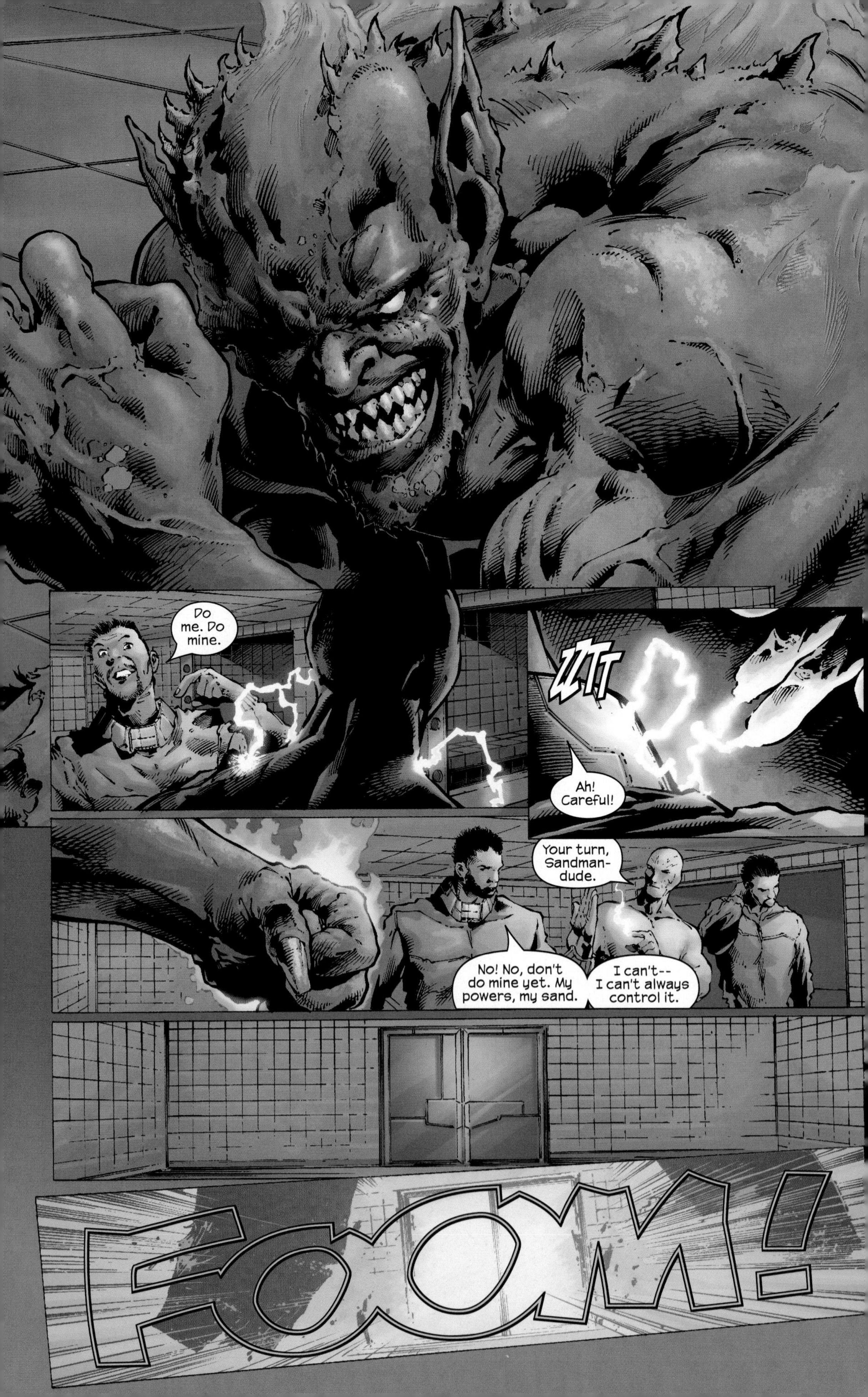

Do me. Do mine.
ZZTT
Ah! Careful!
Your turn, Sandman-dude.
No! No, don't do mine yet. My powers, my sand.
I can't-- I can't always control it.
FOOM!

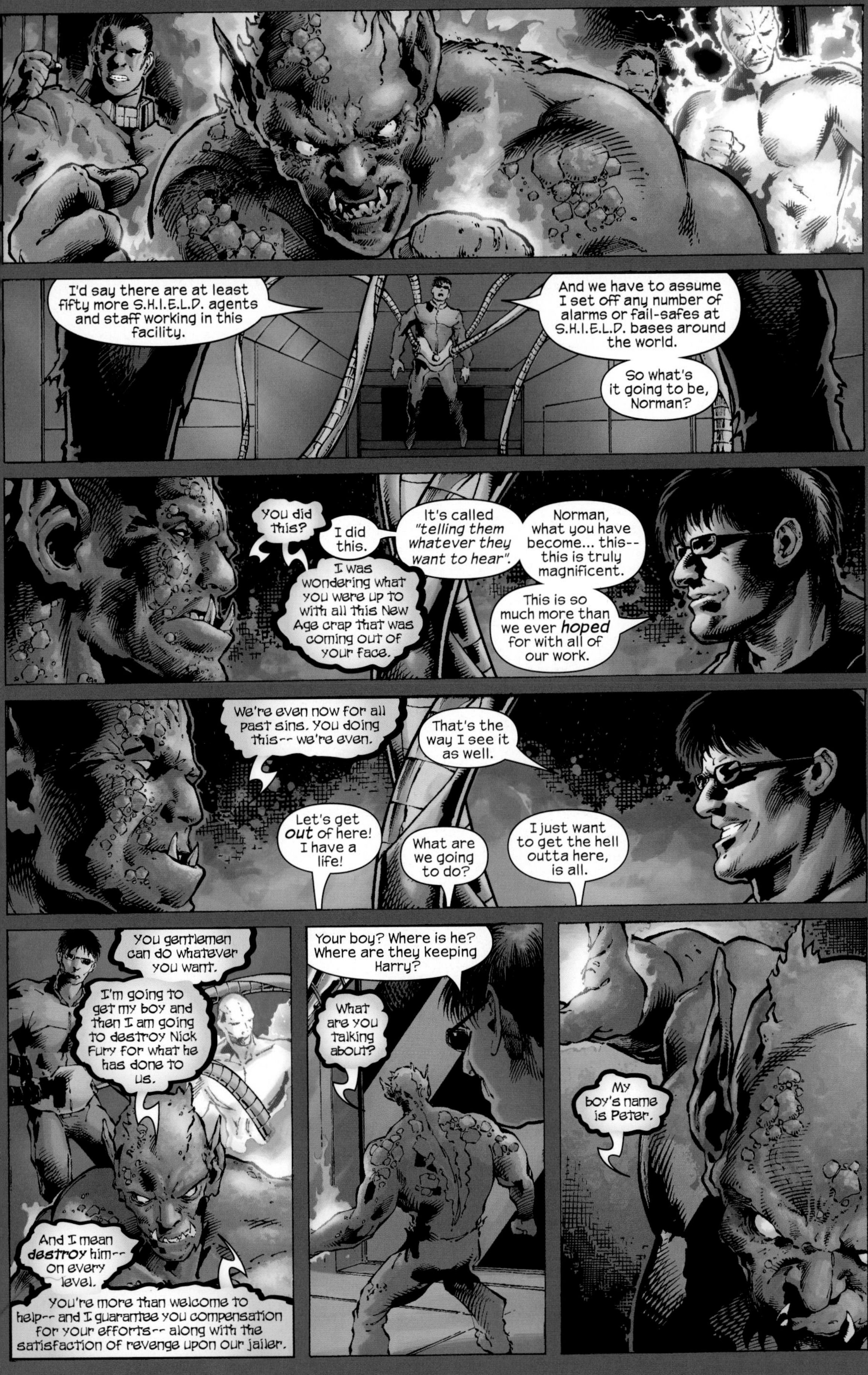
I'd say there are at least fifty more S.H.I.E.L.D. agents and staff working in this facility.
And we have to assume I set off any number of alarms or fail-safes at S.H.I.E.L.D. bases around the world.
So what's it going to be, Norman?
You did this?
I did this.
I was wondering what you were up to with all this New Age crap that was coming out of your face.
It's called "telling them whatever they want to hear".
Norman, what you have become... this-- this is truly magnificent.
This is so much more than we ever hoped for with all of our work.
We're even now for all past sins. You doing this-- we're even.
That's the way I see it as well.
Let's get out of here! I have a life!
What are we going to do?
I just want to get the hell outta here, is all.
You gentlemen can do whatever you want.
I'm going to get my boy and then I am going to destroy Nick Fury for what he has done to us.
And I mean destroy him-- on every level.
You're more than welcome to help-- and I guarantee you compensation for your efforts-- along with the satisfaction of revenge upon our jailer.
Your boy? Where is he? Where are they keeping Harry?
What are you talking about?
My boy's name is Peter.

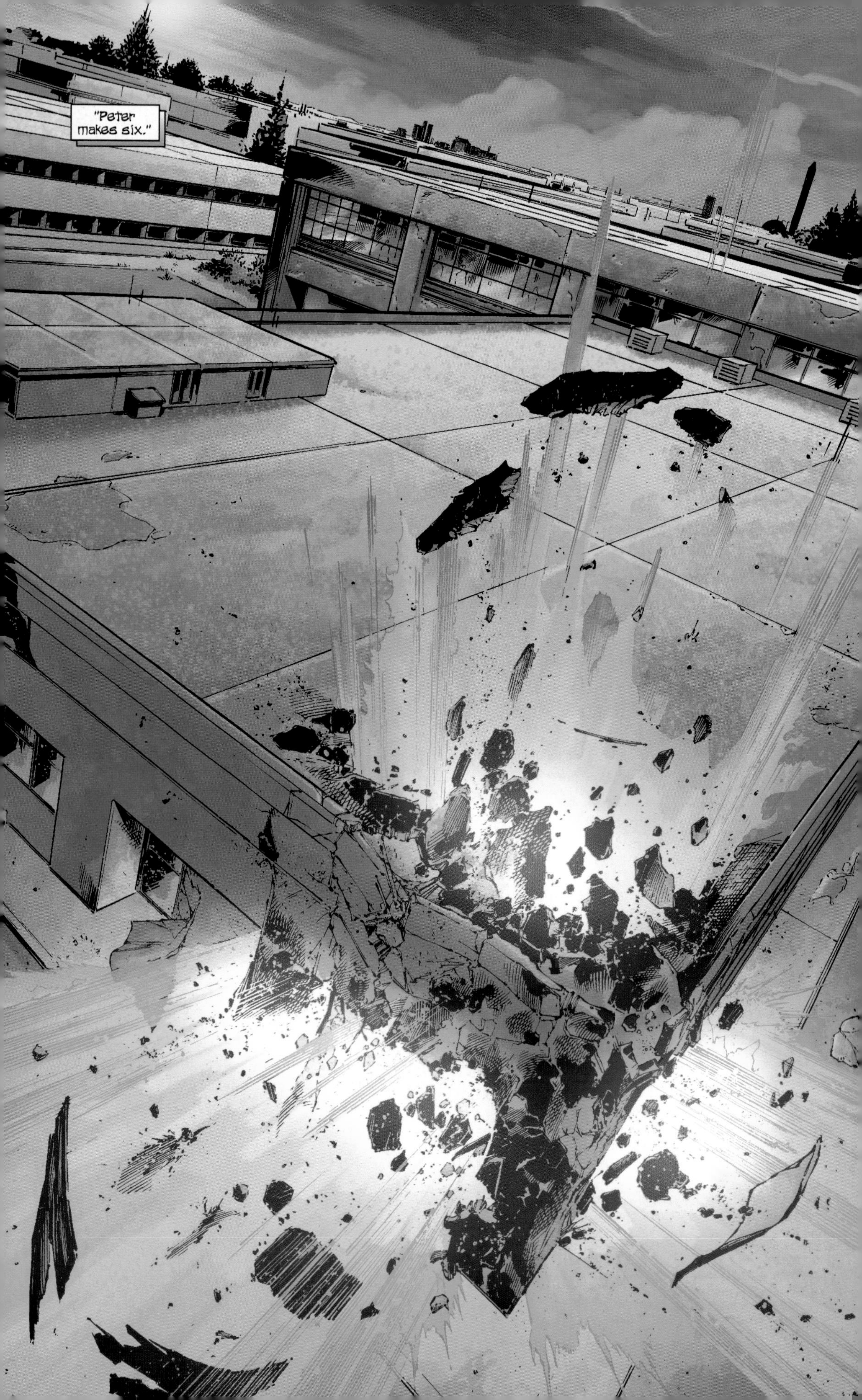
"Peter makes six."

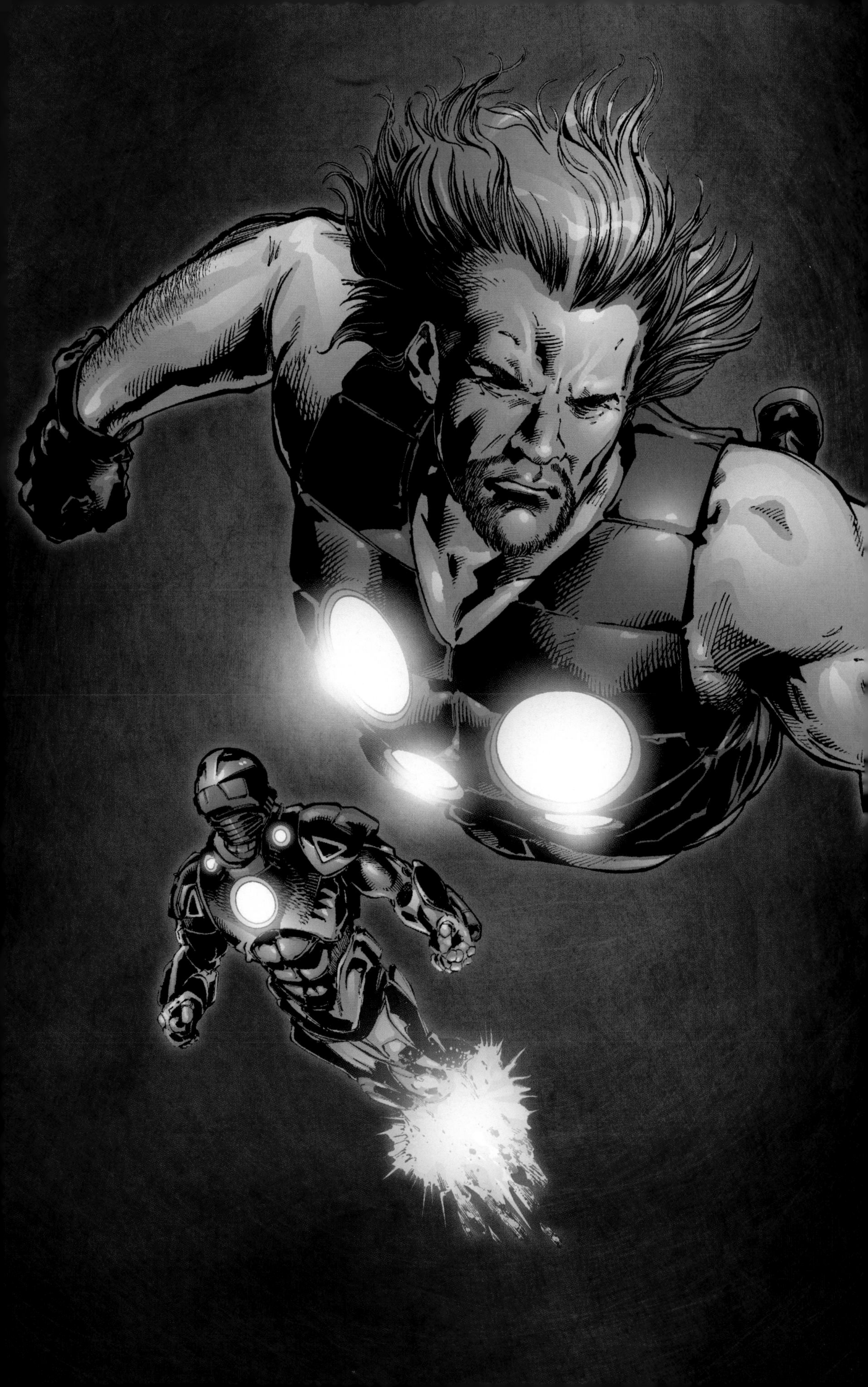

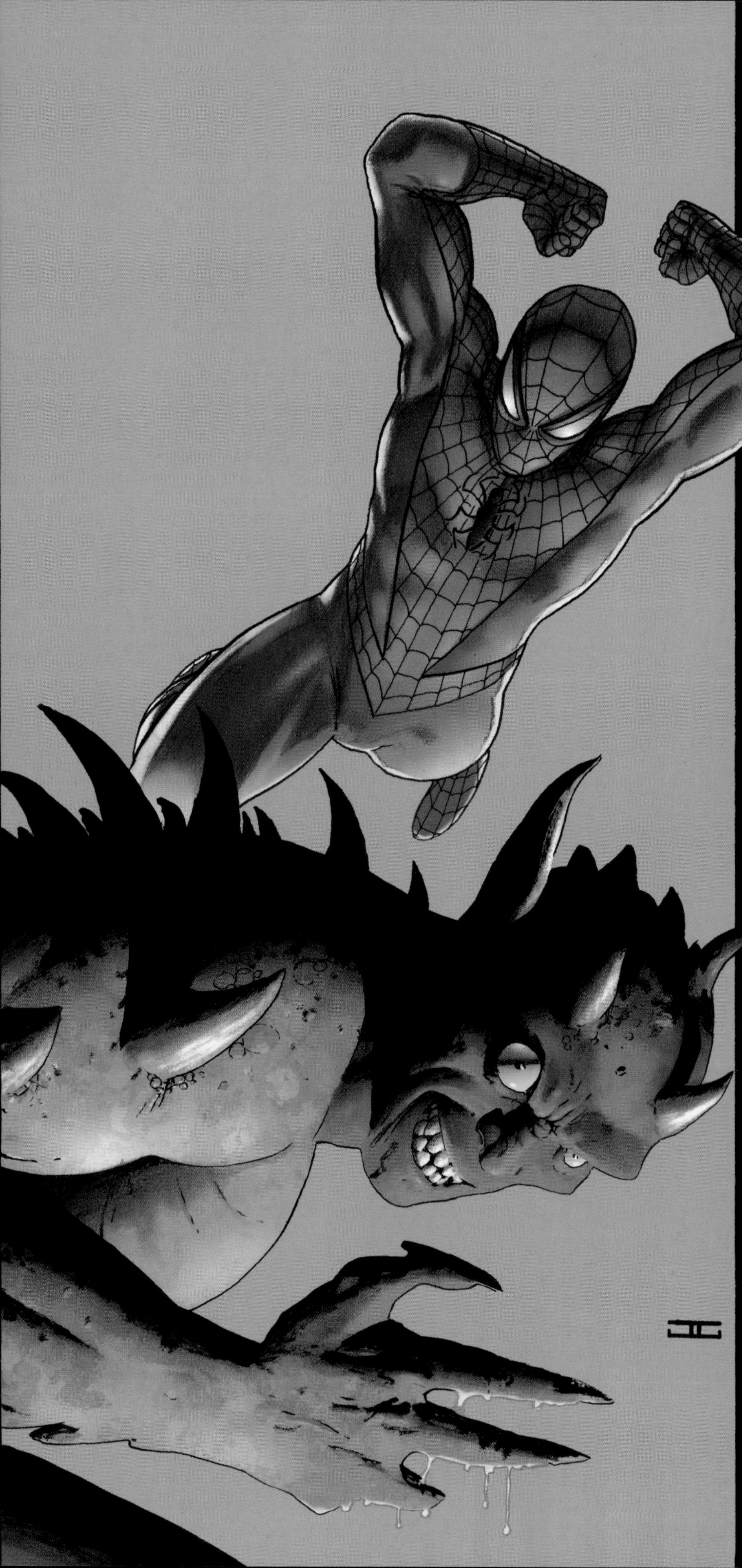

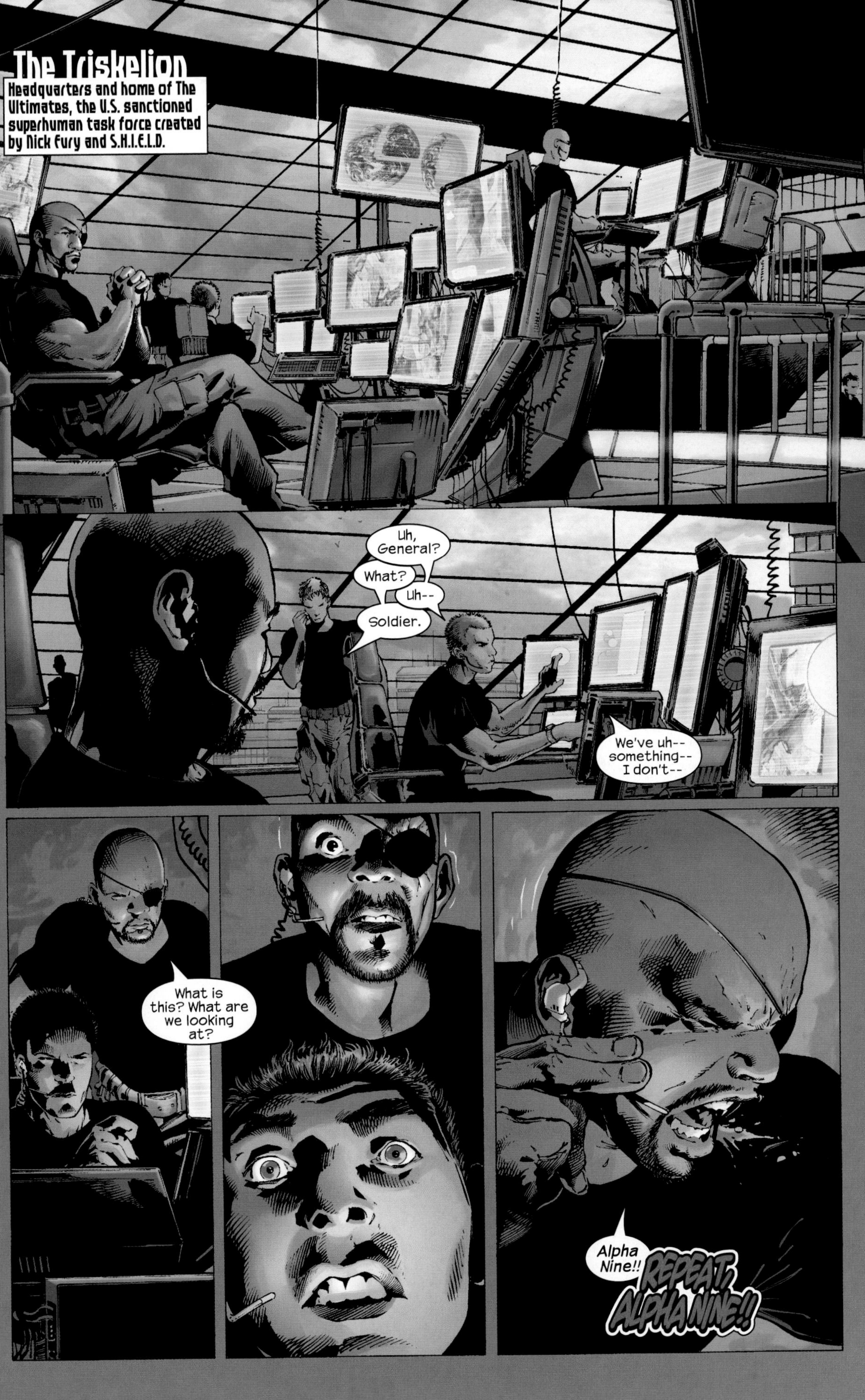
The Triskelion
Headquarters and home of The Ultimates, the U.S. sanctioned superhuman task force created by Nick Fury and S.H.I.E.L.D.
Uh, General?
What?
Uh--
Soldier.
We've uh-- something-- I don't--
What is this? What are we looking at?
Alpha Nine!!
REPEAT, ALPHA NINE!!

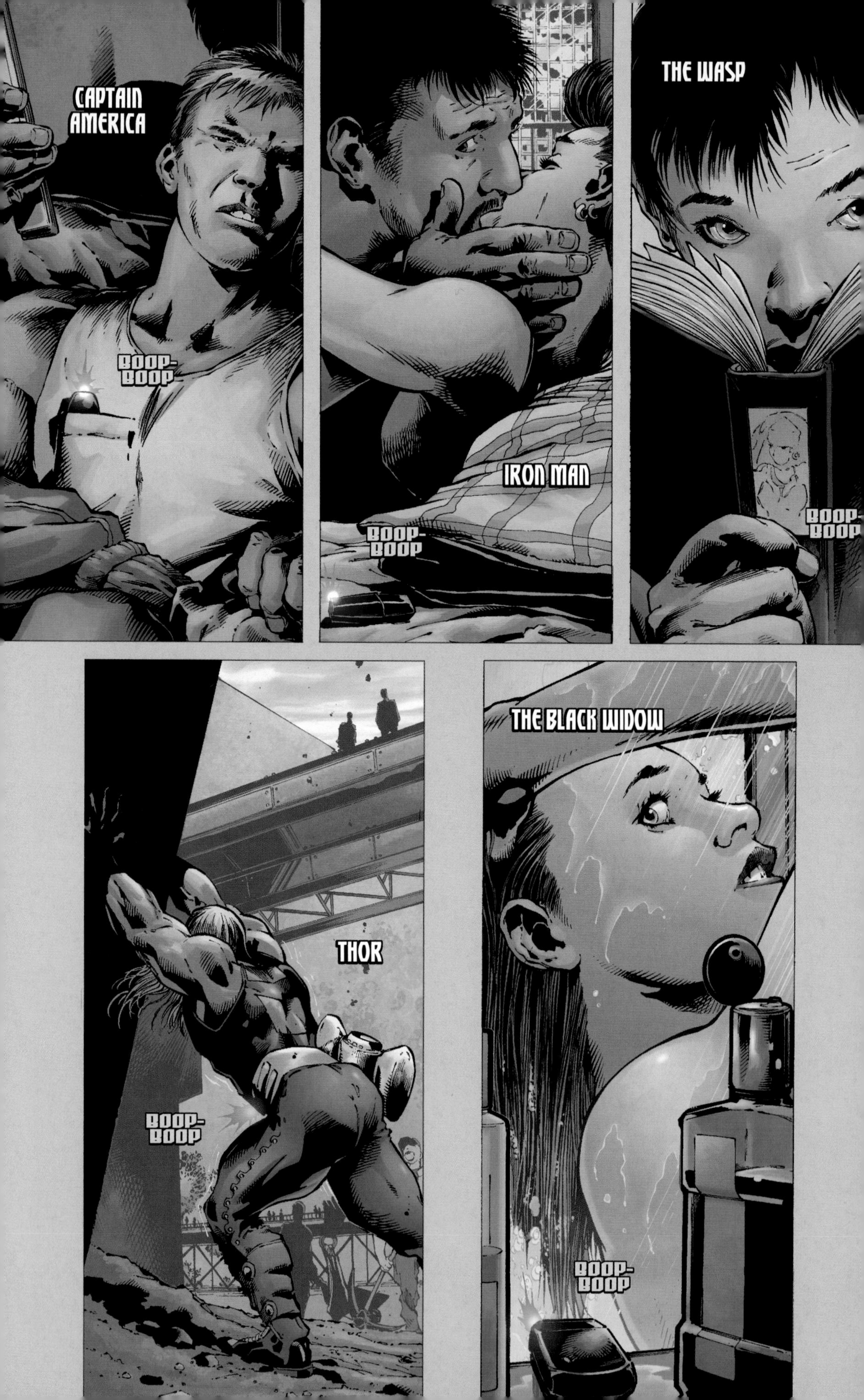
CAPTAIN AMERICA
BOOP-BOOP
IRON MAN
BOOP-BOOP
THE WASP
BOOP-BOOP
THOR
BOOP-BOOP
THE BLACK WIDOW
BOOP-BOOP

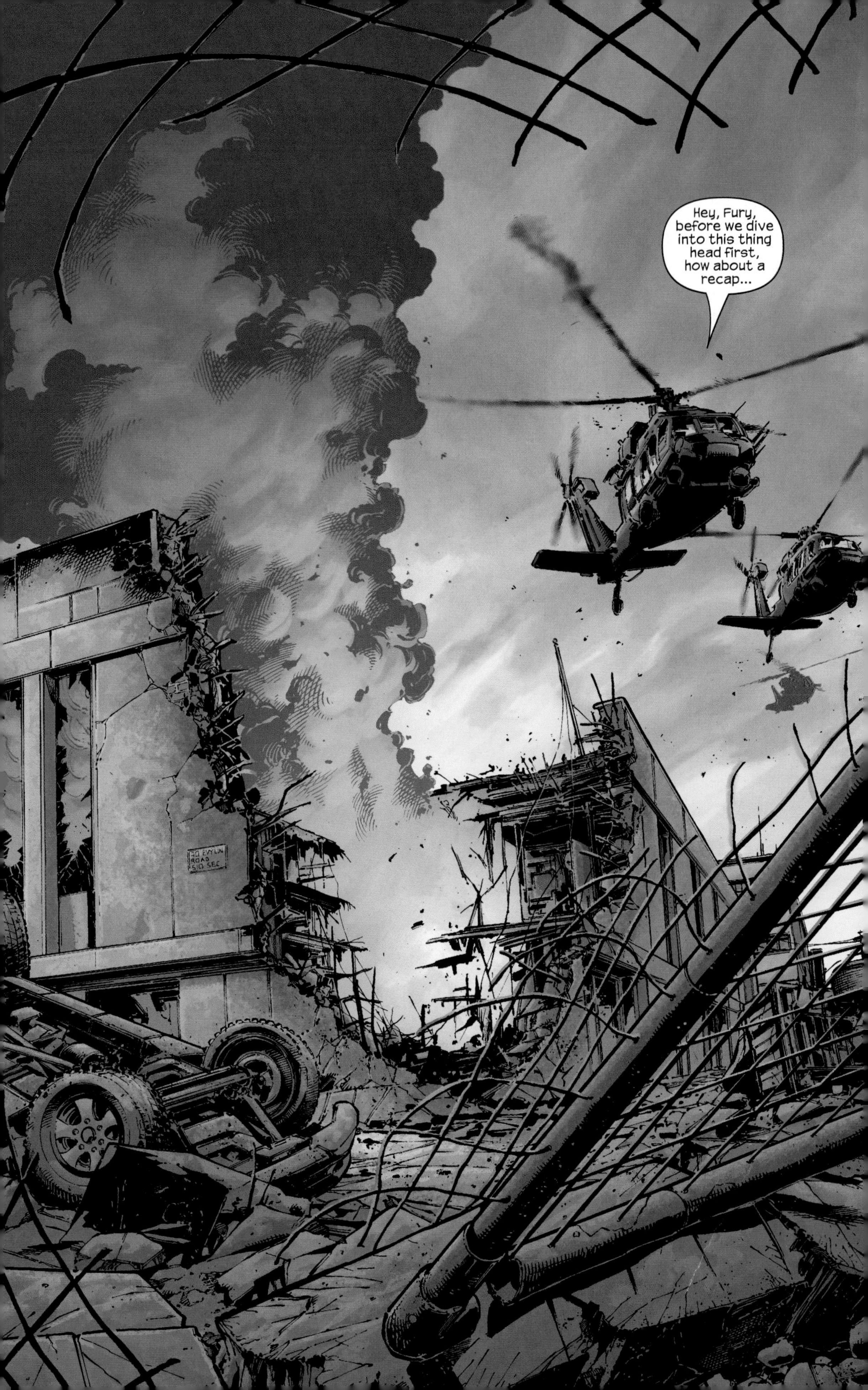
Hey, Fury, before we dive into this thing head first, how about a recap...

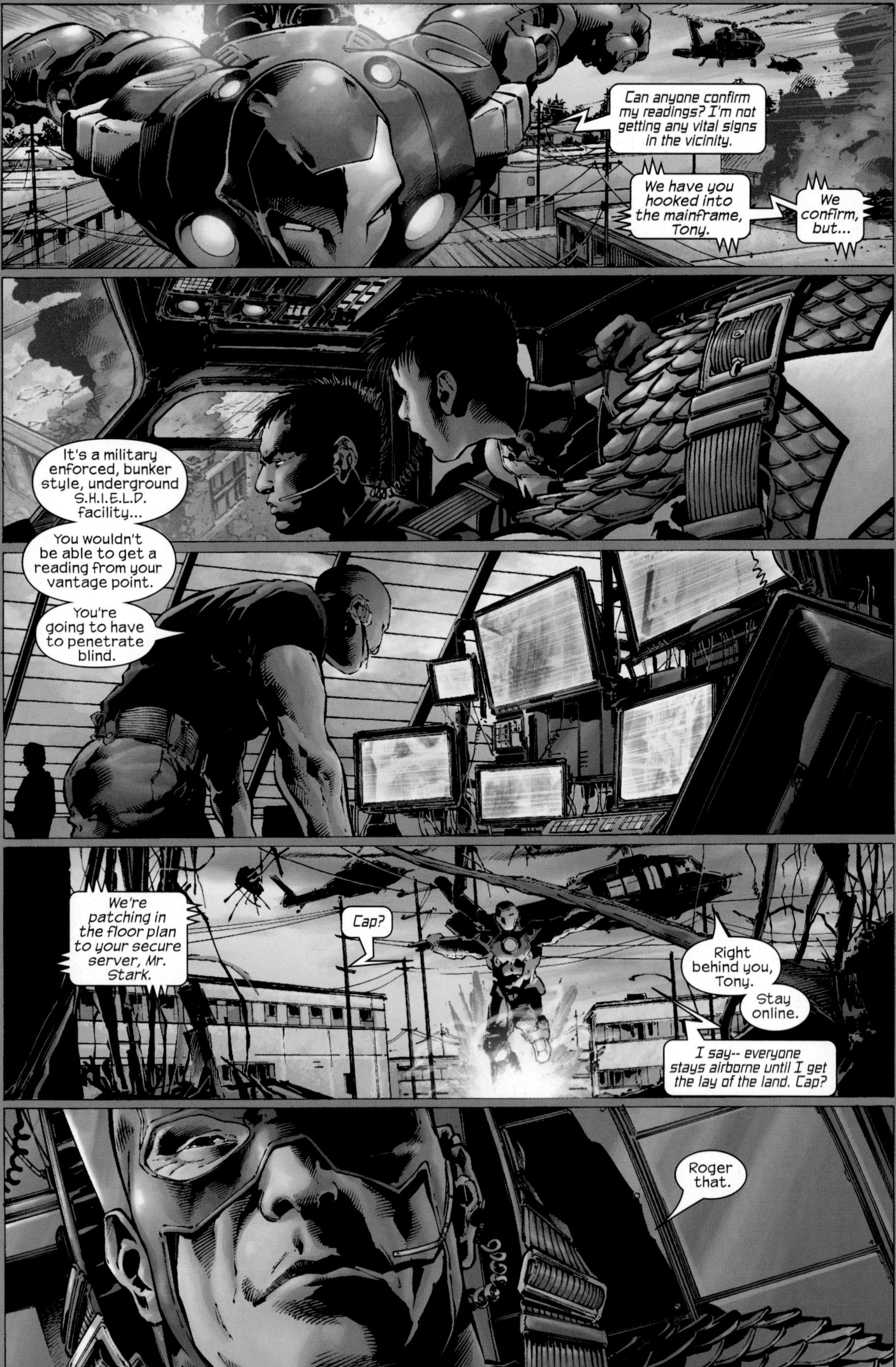
Can anyone confirm my readings? I'm not getting any vital signs in the vicinity.
We have you hooked into the mainframe, Tony.
We confirm, but...
It's a military enforced, bunker style, underground S.H.I.E.L.D. facility...
You wouldn't be able to get a reading from your vantage point.
You're going to have to penetrate blind.
We're patching in the floor plan to your secure server, Mr. Stark.
Cap?
Right behind you, Tony.
Stay online.
I say-- everyone stays airborne until I get the lay of the land. Cap?
Roger that.

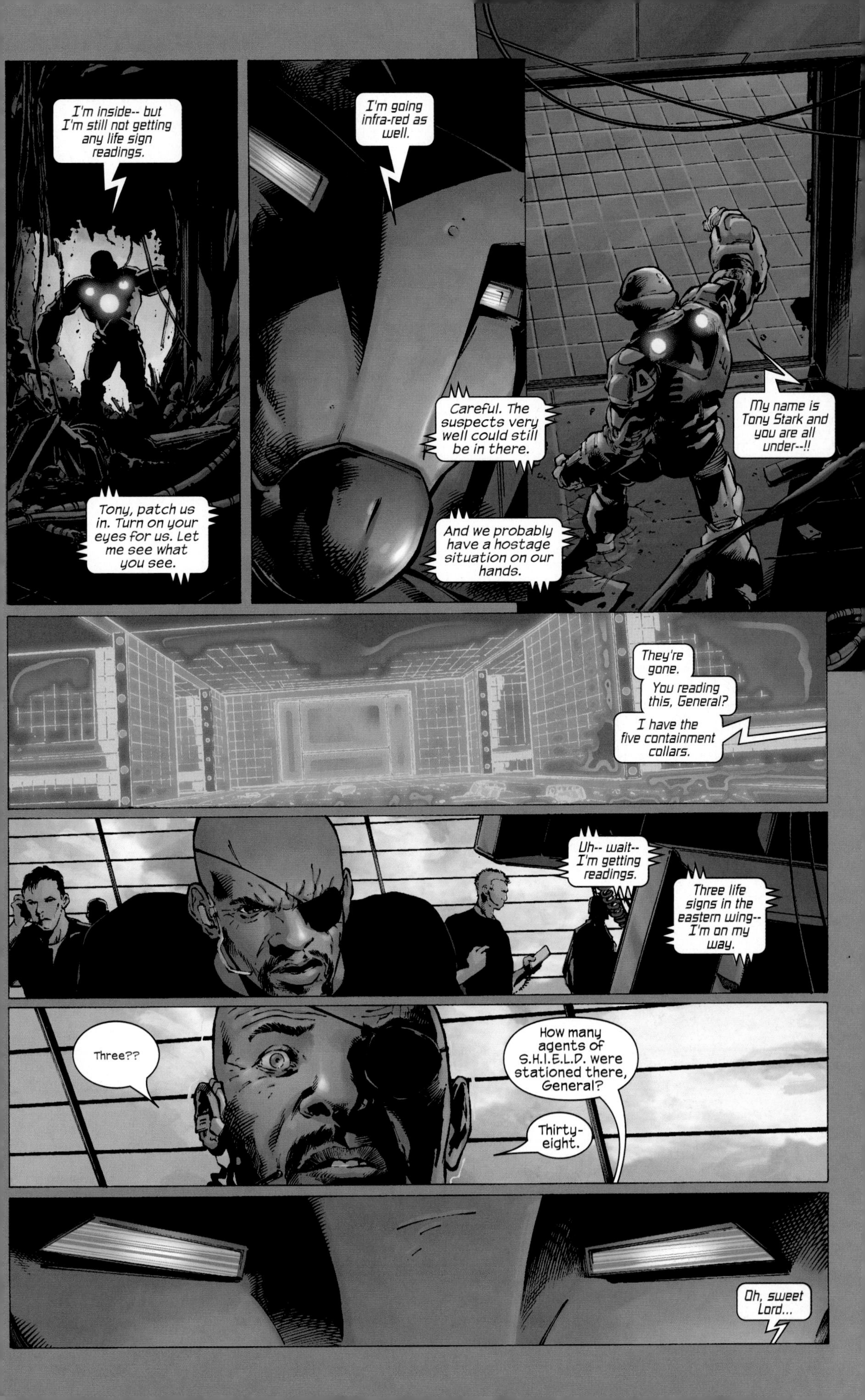

I'm inside-- but I'm still not getting any life sign readings.
Tony, patch us in. Turn on your eyes for us. Let me see what you see.
I'm going infra-red as well.
Careful. The suspects very well could still be in there.
And we probably have a hostage situation on our hands.
My name is Tony Stark and you are all under--!!
They're gone.
You reading this, General?
I have the five containment collars.
Uh-- wait-- I'm getting readings.
Three life signs in the eastern wing-- I'm on my way.
Three??
How many agents of S.H.I.E.L.D. were stationed there, General?
Thirty-eight.
Oh, sweet Lord...

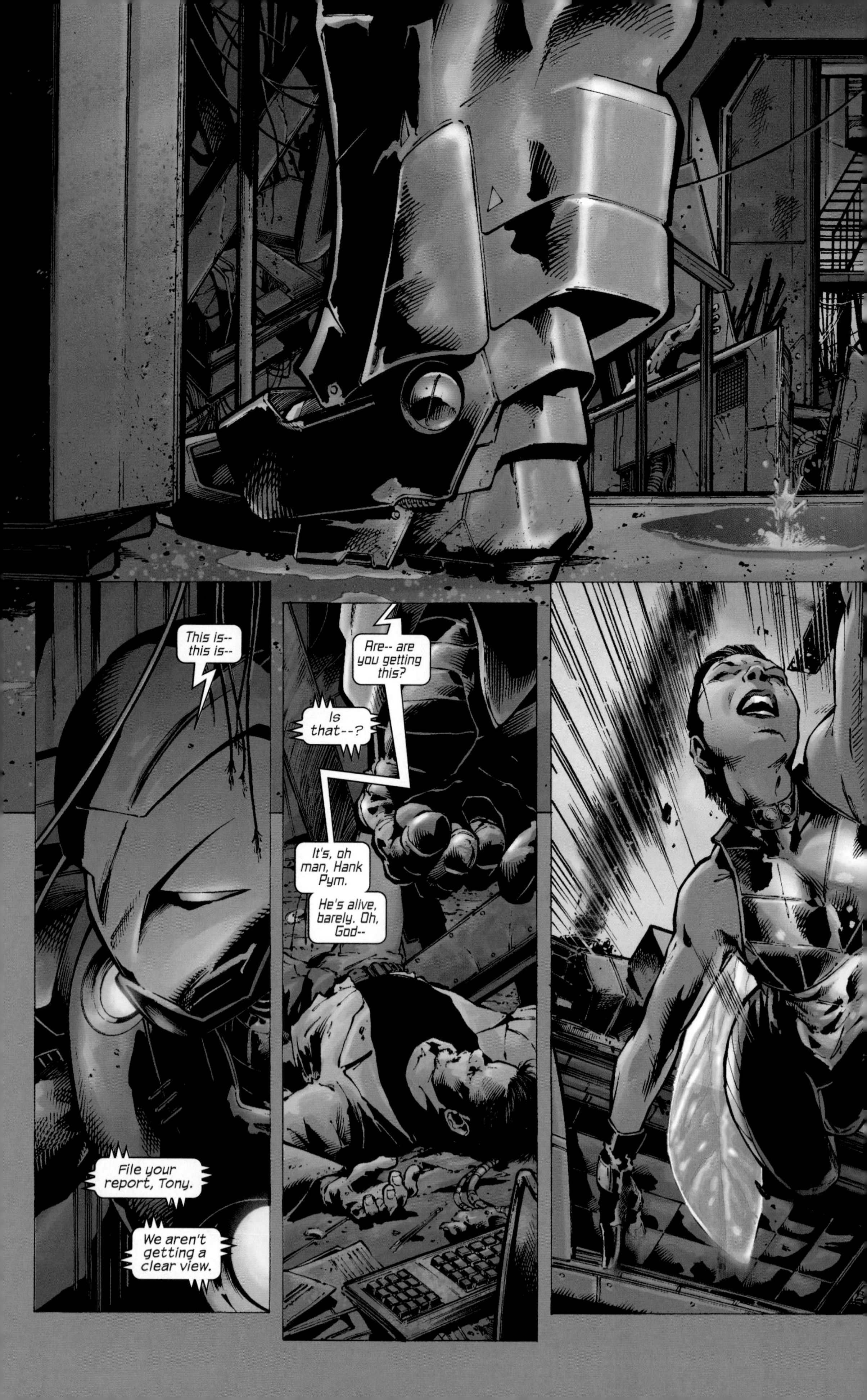
This is--
this is--
Are-- are
you getting
this?
Is
that--?
It's, oh
man, Hank
Pym.
He's alive,
barely. Oh,
God--
File your
report, Tony.
We aren't
getting a
clear view.

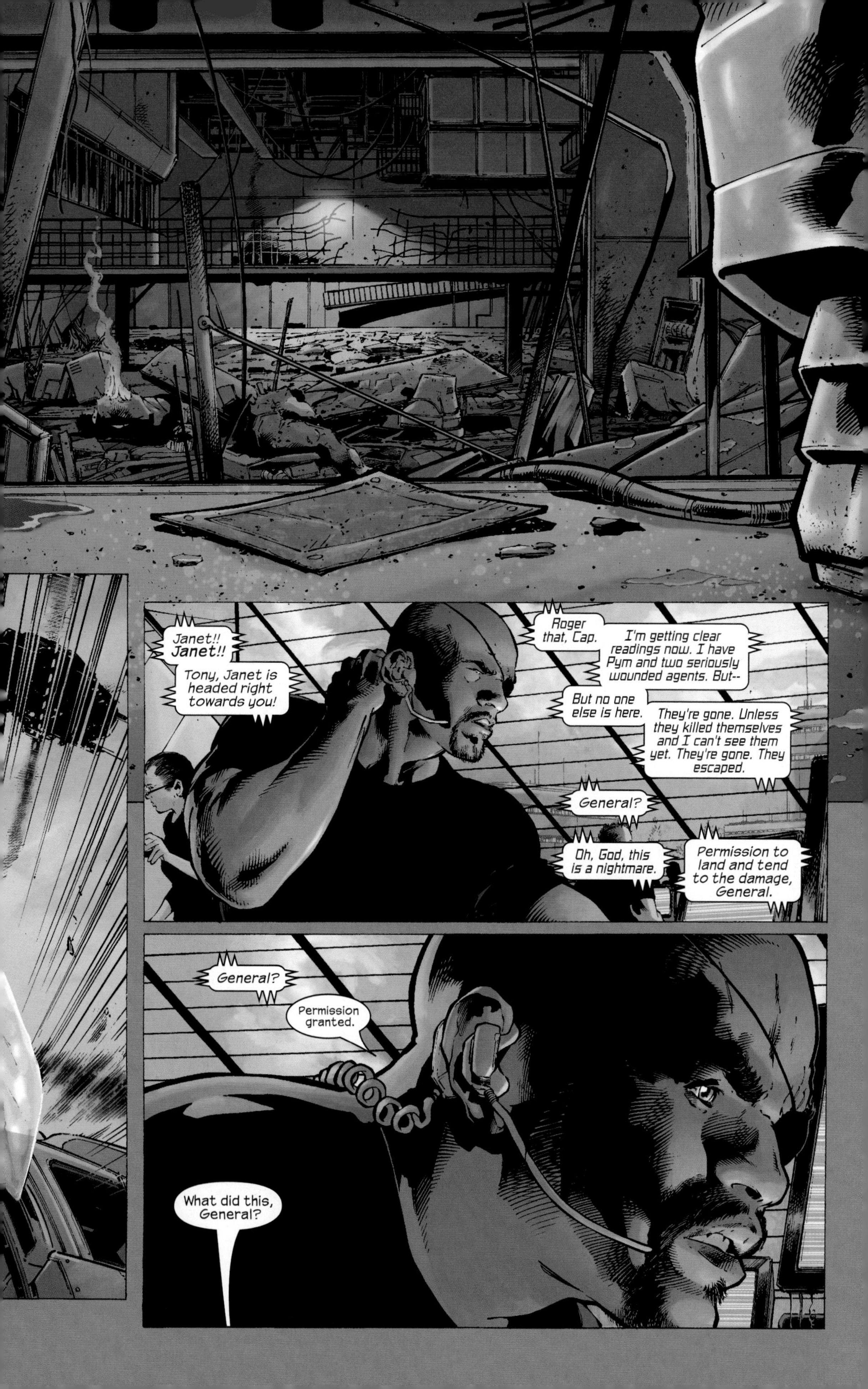
Janet!! Janet!!
Tony, Janet is headed right towards you!
Roger that, Cap.
I'm getting clear readings now. I have Pym and two seriously wounded agents. But--
But no one else is here.
They're gone. Unless they killed themselves and I can't see them yet. They're gone. They escaped.
General?
Oh, God, this is a nightmare.
Permission to land and tend to the damage, General.
General?
Permission granted.
What did this, General?

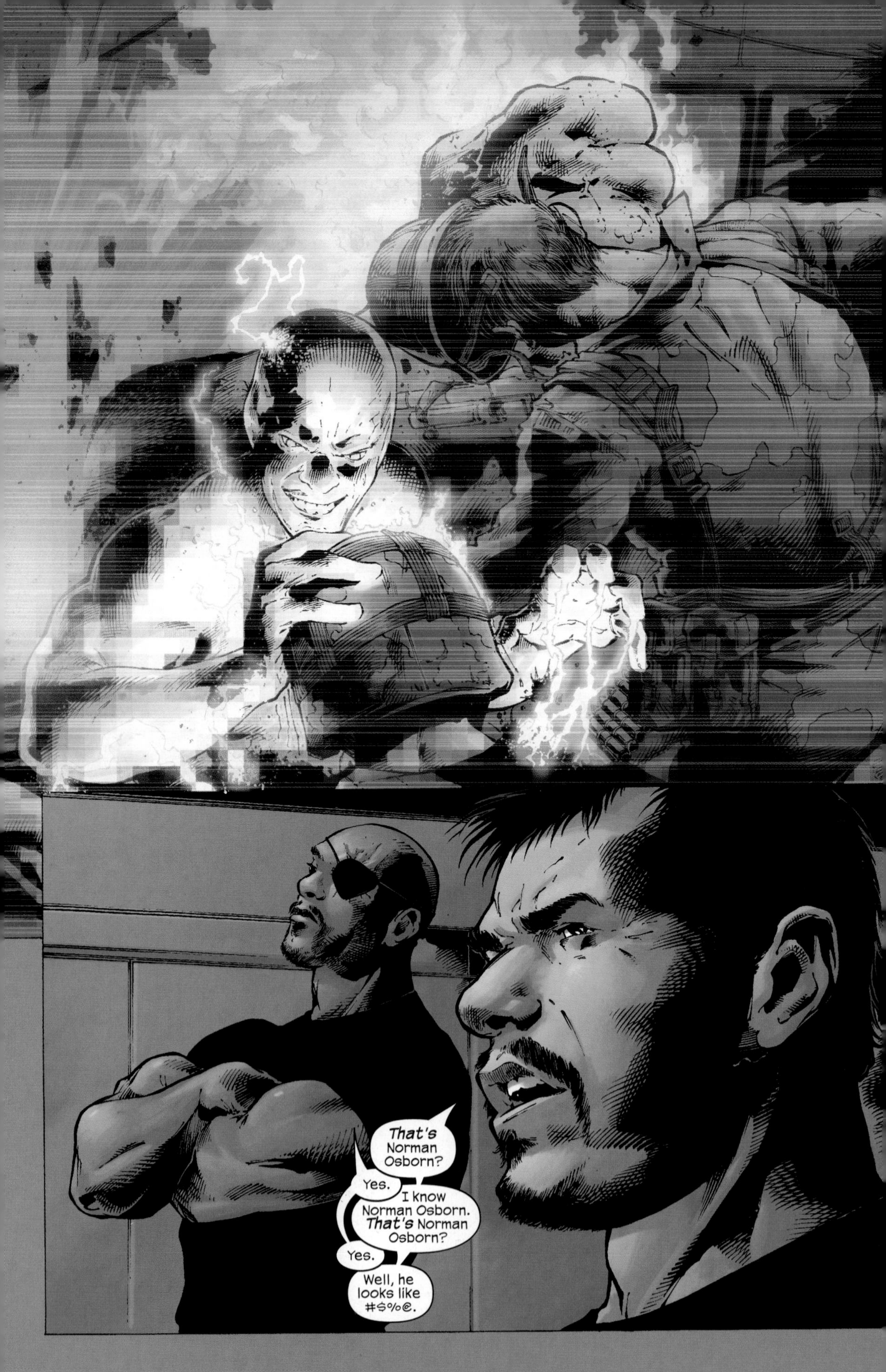
That's Norman Osborn?
Yes.
I know Norman Osborn. That's Norman Osborn?
Yes.
Well, he looks like #$%@.

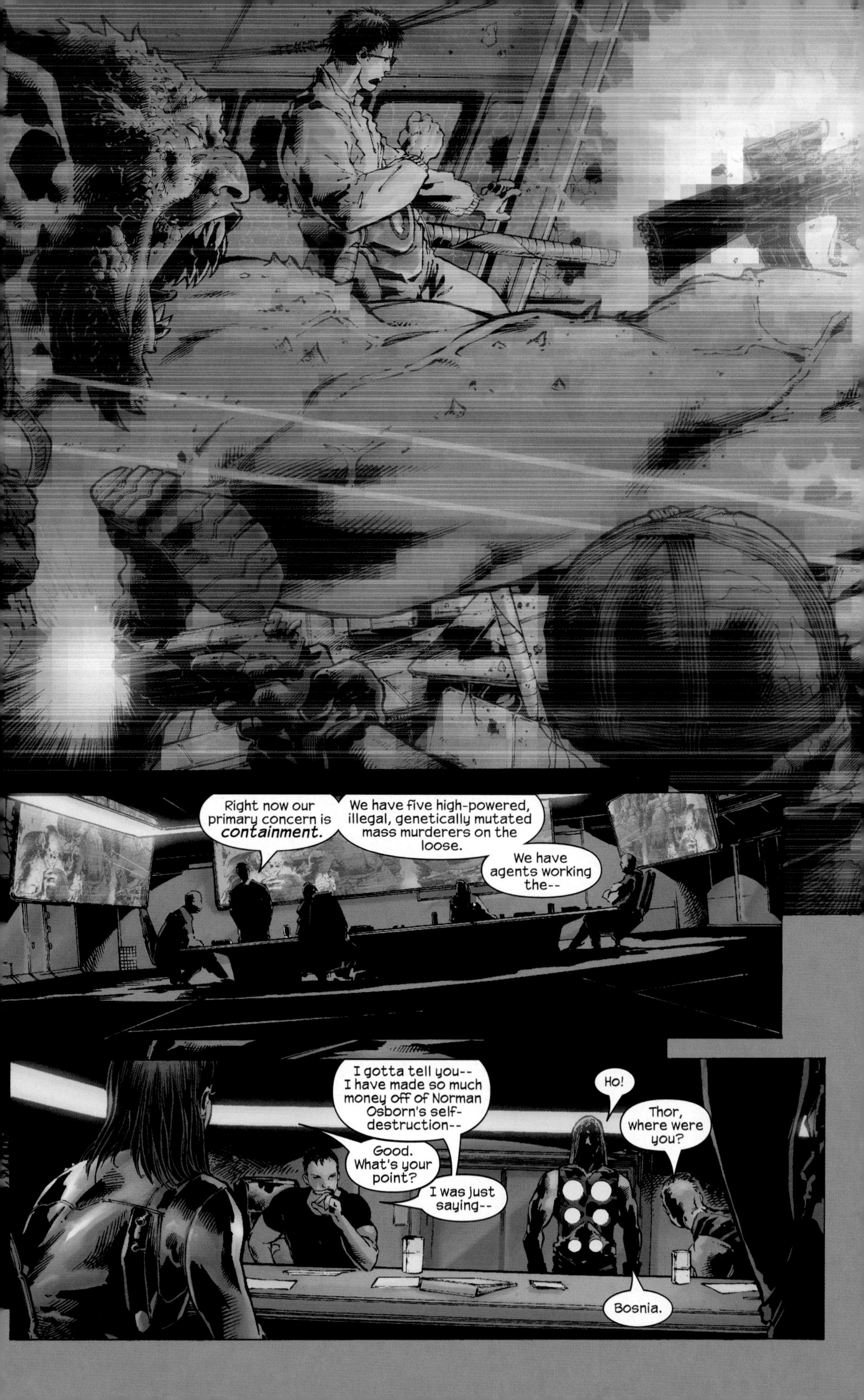
Right now our primary concern is *containment.*
We have five high-powered, illegal, genetically mutated mass murderers on the loose.
We have agents working the--
I gotta tell you-- I have made so much money off of Norman Osborn's self-destruction--
Good. What's your point?
I was just saying--
Ho!
Thor, where were you?
Bosnia.

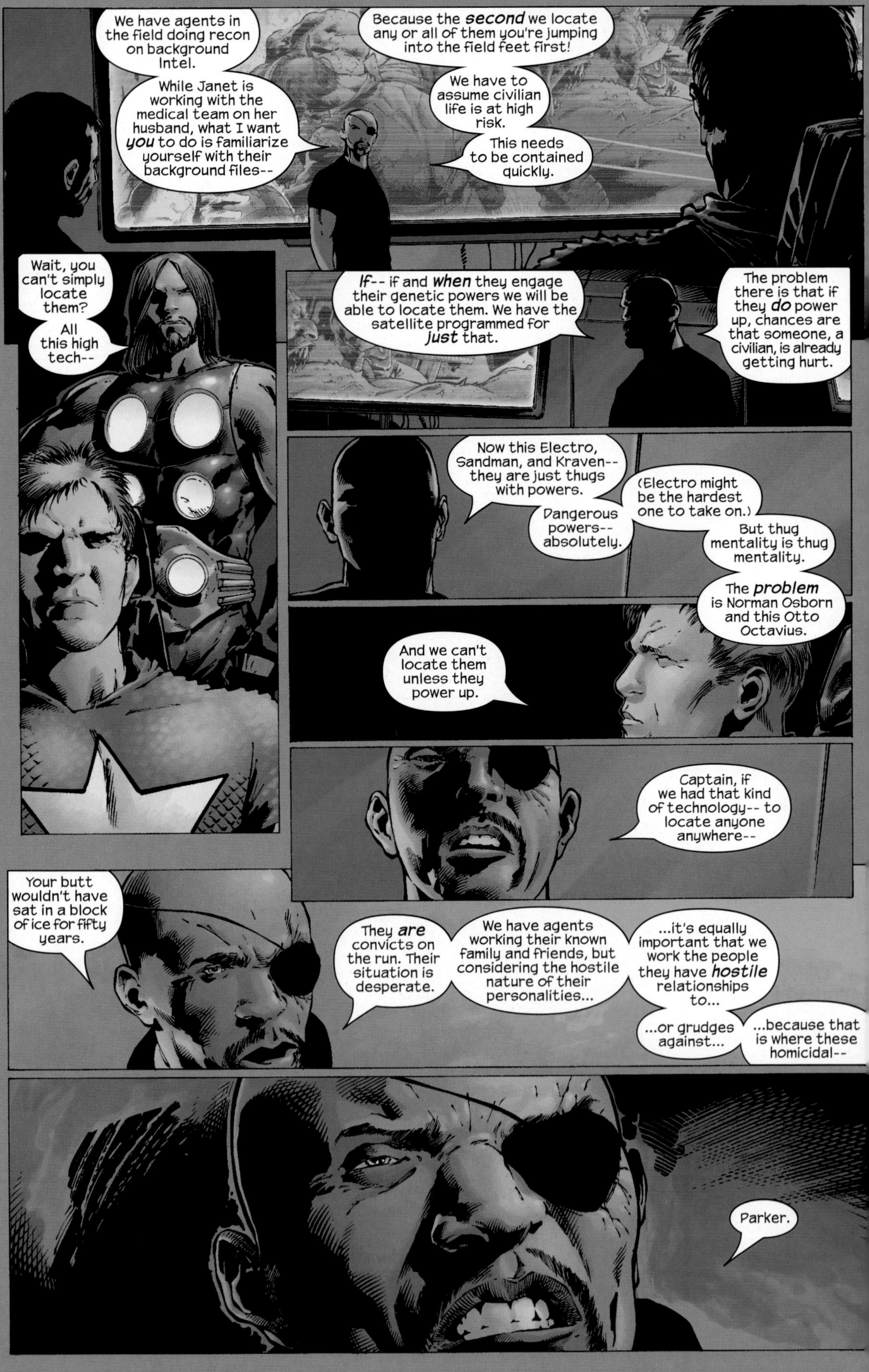

We have agents in the field doing recon on background Intel.
While Janet is working with the medical team on her husband, what I want *you* to do is familiarize yourself with their background files--
Because the *second* we locate any or all of them you're jumping into the field feet first!
We have to assume civilian life is at high risk.
This needs to be contained quickly.
Wait, you can't simply locate them?
All this high tech--
If-- if and *when* they engage their genetic powers we will be able to locate them. We have the satellite programmed for *just* that.
The problem there is that if they *do* power up, chances are that someone, a civilian, is already getting hurt.
Now this Electro, Sandman, and Kraven-- they are just thugs with powers.
Dangerous powers-- absolutely.
(Electro might be the hardest one to take on.)
But thug mentality is thug mentality.
The *problem* is Norman Osborn and this Otto Octavius.
And we can't locate them unless they power up.
Captain, if we had that kind of technology-- to locate anyone anywhere--
Your butt wouldn't have sat in a block of ice for fifty years.
They *are* convicts on the run. Their situation is desperate.
We have agents working their known family and friends, but considering the hostile nature of their personalities...
...it's equally important that we work the people they have *hostile* relationships to...
...or grudges against...
...because that is where these homicidal--
Parker.

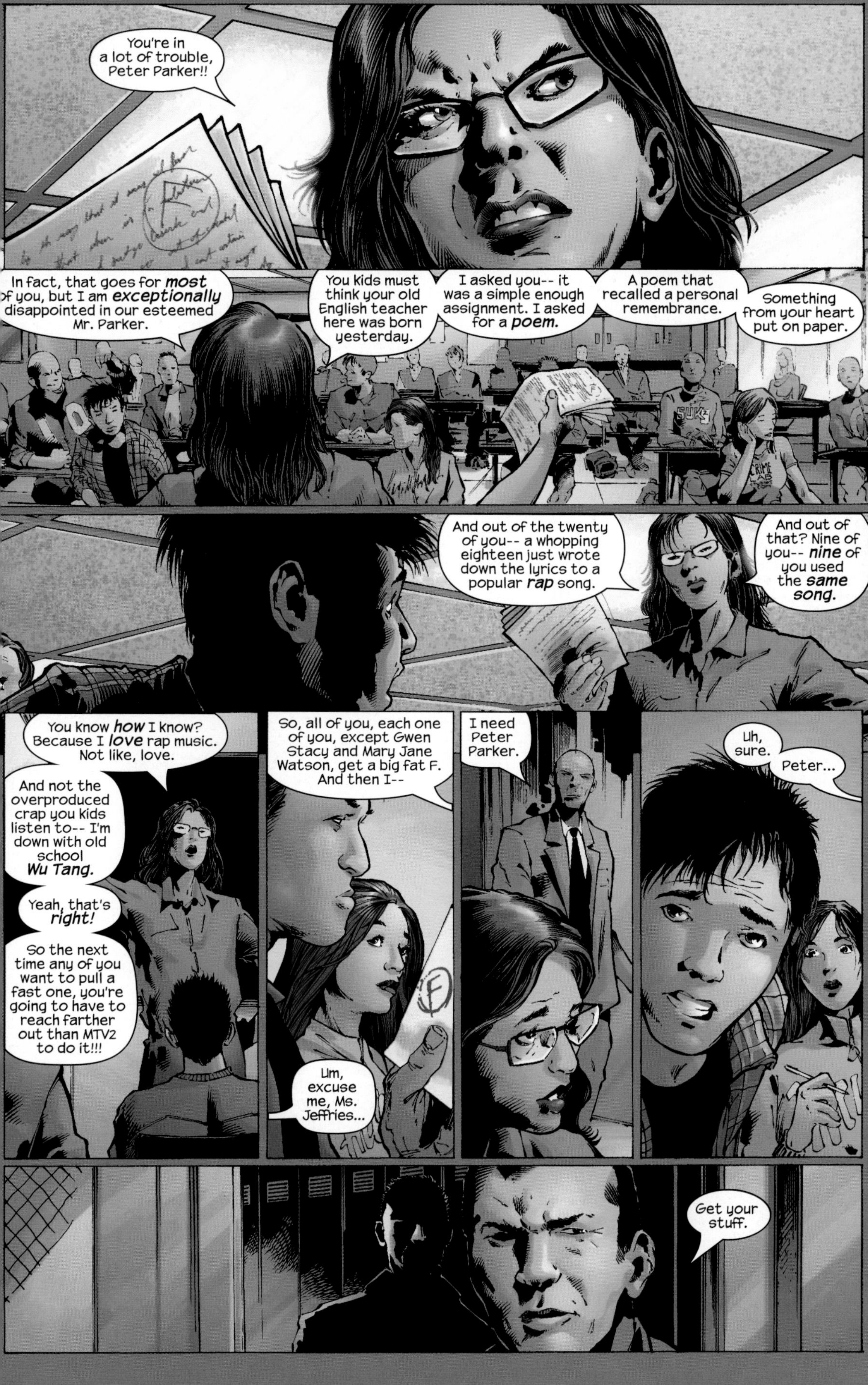
You're in a lot of trouble, Peter Parker!!
In fact, that goes for most of you, but I am exceptionally disappointed in our esteemed Mr. Parker.
You kids must think your old English teacher here was born yesterday.
I asked you-- it was a simple enough assignment. I asked for a poem.
A poem that recalled a personal remembrance.
Something from your heart put on paper.
And out of the twenty of you-- a whopping eighteen just wrote down the lyrics to a popular rap song.
And out of that? Nine of you-- nine of you used the same song.
You know how I know? Because I love rap music. Not like, love.
And not the overproduced crap you kids listen to-- I'm down with old school Wu Tang.
Yeah, that's right!
So the next time any of you want to pull a fast one, you're going to have to reach farther out than MTV2 to do it!!!
So, all of you, each one of you, except Gwen Stacy and Mary Jane Watson, get a big fat F. And then I--
Um, excuse me, Ms. Jeffries...
I need Peter Parker.
Uh, sure.
Peter...
Get your stuff.

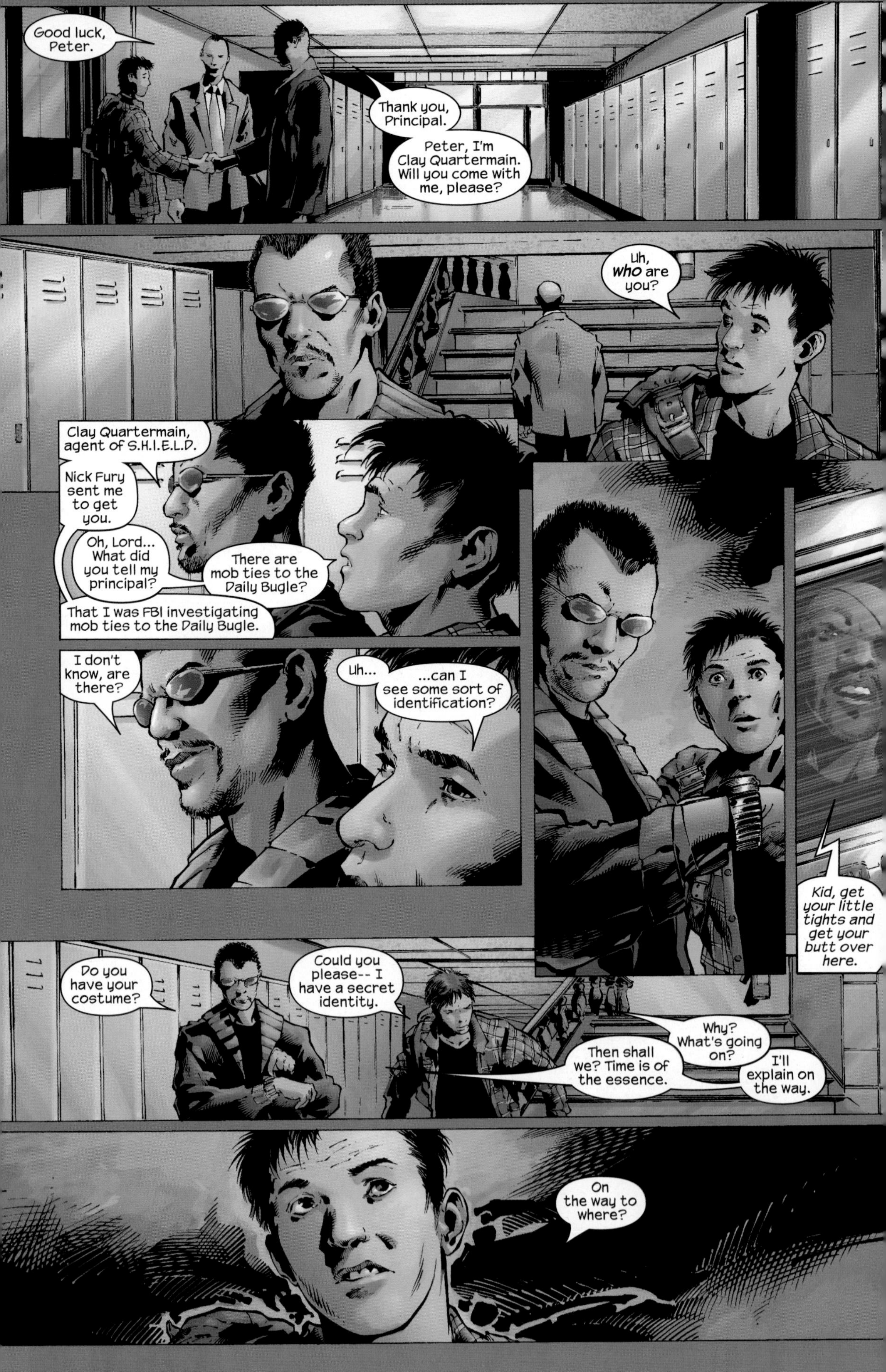
Good luck, Peter.
Thank you, Principal.
Peter, I'm Clay Quartermain. Will you come with me, please?
Uh, *who* are you?
Clay Quartermain, agent of S.H.I.E.L.D.
Nick Fury sent me to get you.
Oh, Lord... What did you tell my principal?
That I was FBI investigating mob ties to the Daily Bugle.
There are mob ties to the Daily Bugle?
I don't know, are there?
Uh...
...can I see some sort of identification?
Kid, get your little tights and get your butt over here.
Do you have your costume?
Could you please-- I have a secret identity.
Why? What's going on?
I'll explain on the way.
Then shall we? Time is of the essence.
On the way to where?

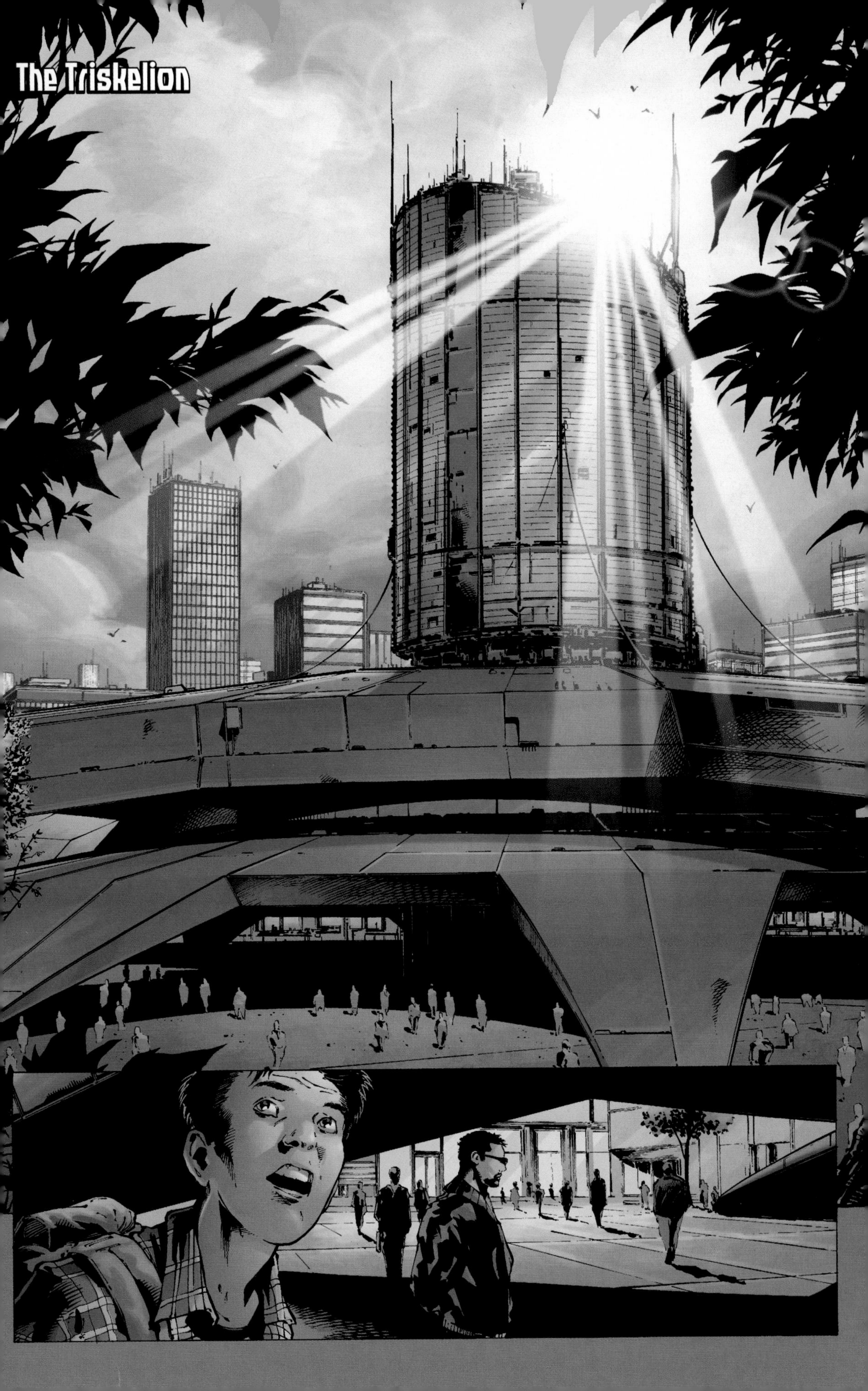
The Triskelion

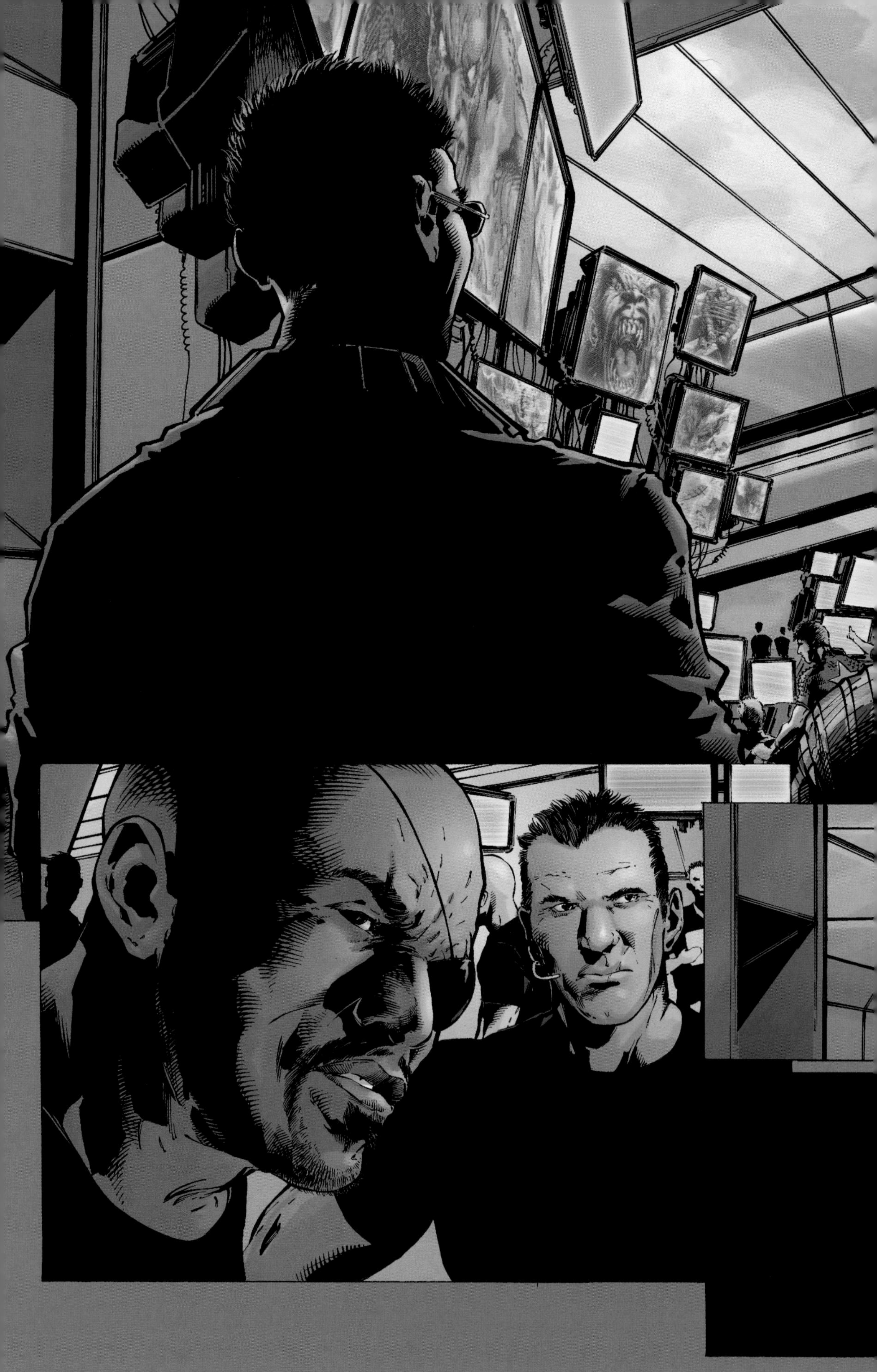

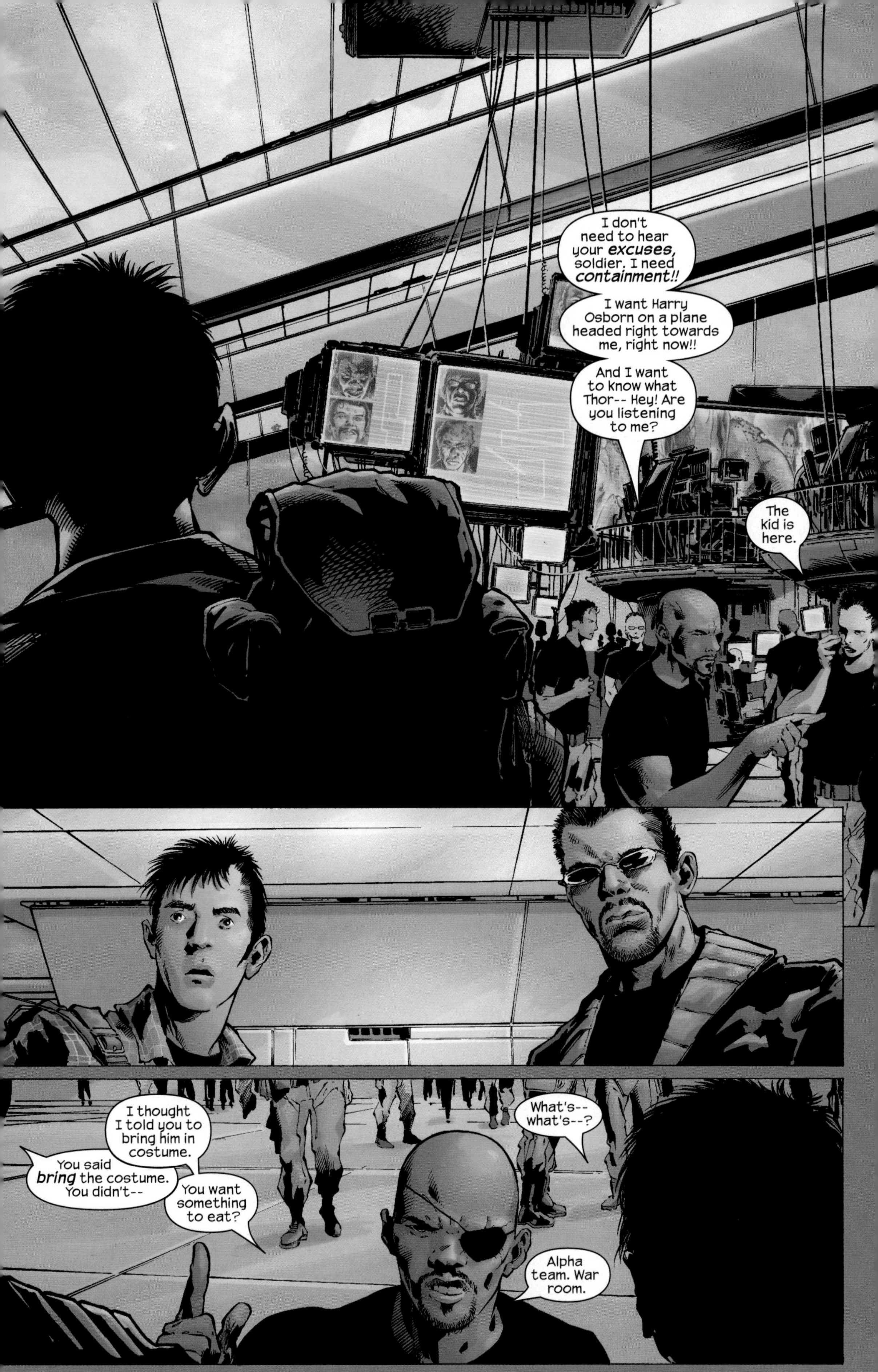

I don't need to hear your *excuses,* soldier. I need *containment!!*
I want Harry Osborn on a plane headed right towards me, right now!!
And I want to know what Thor-- Hey! Are you listening to me?
The kid is here.
I thought I told you to bring him in costume.
You said *bring* the costume. You didn't--
You want something to eat?
What's-- what's--?
Alpha team. War room.

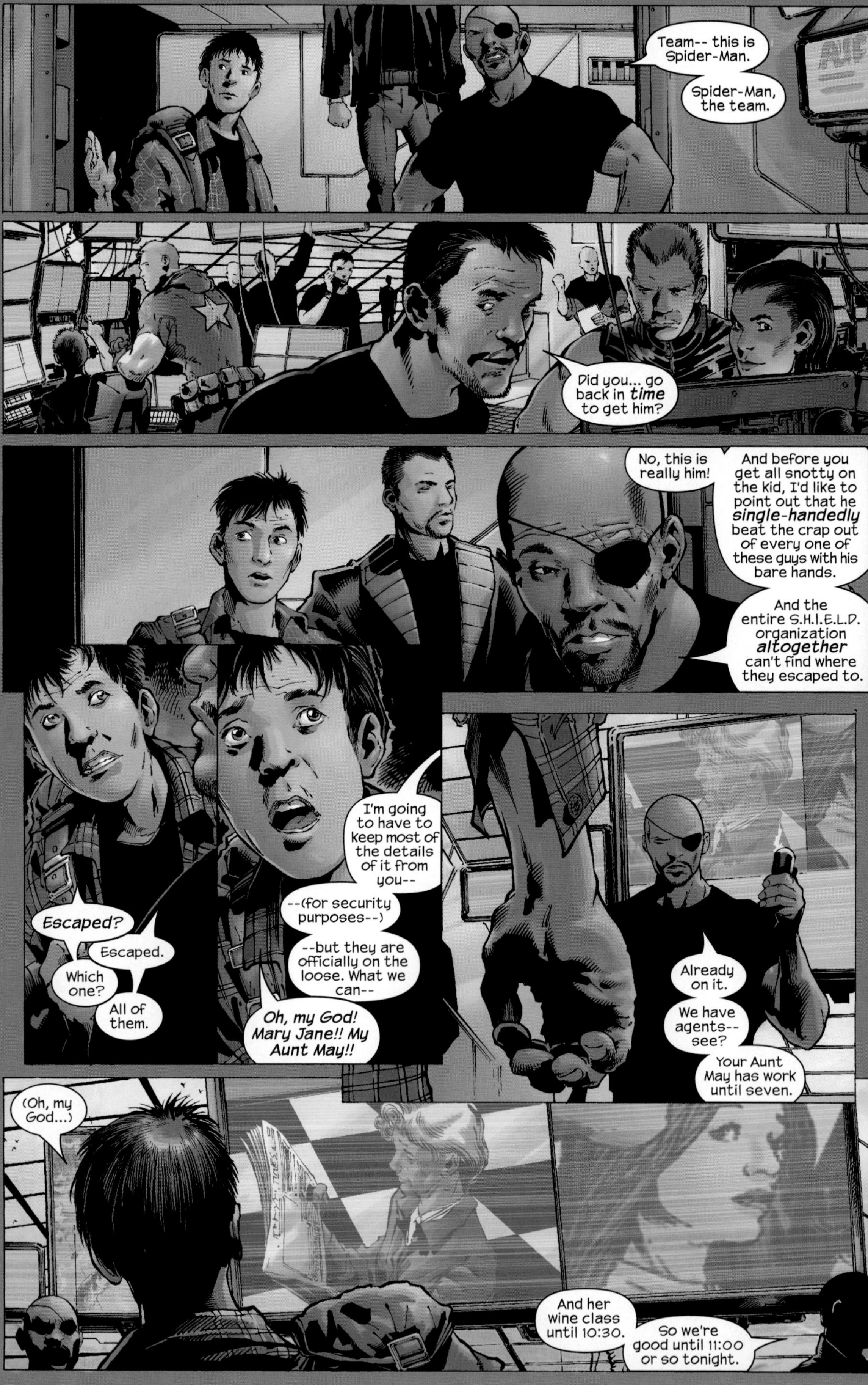

Team-- this is Spider-Man.
Spider-Man, the team.
Did you... go back in *time* to get him?
No, this is really him!
And before you get all snotty on the kid, I'd like to point out that he *single-handedly* beat the crap out of every one of these guys with his bare hands.
And the entire S.H.I.E.L.D. organization *altogether* can't find where they escaped to.
Escaped?
Escaped.
Which one?
All of them.
I'm going to have to keep most of the details of it from you--
--(for security purposes--)
--but they are officially on the loose. What we can--
Oh, my God! Mary Jane!! My Aunt May!!
Already on it.
We have agents-- see?
Your Aunt May has work until seven.
(Oh, my God...)
And her wine class until 10:30.
So we're good until 11:00 or so tonight.

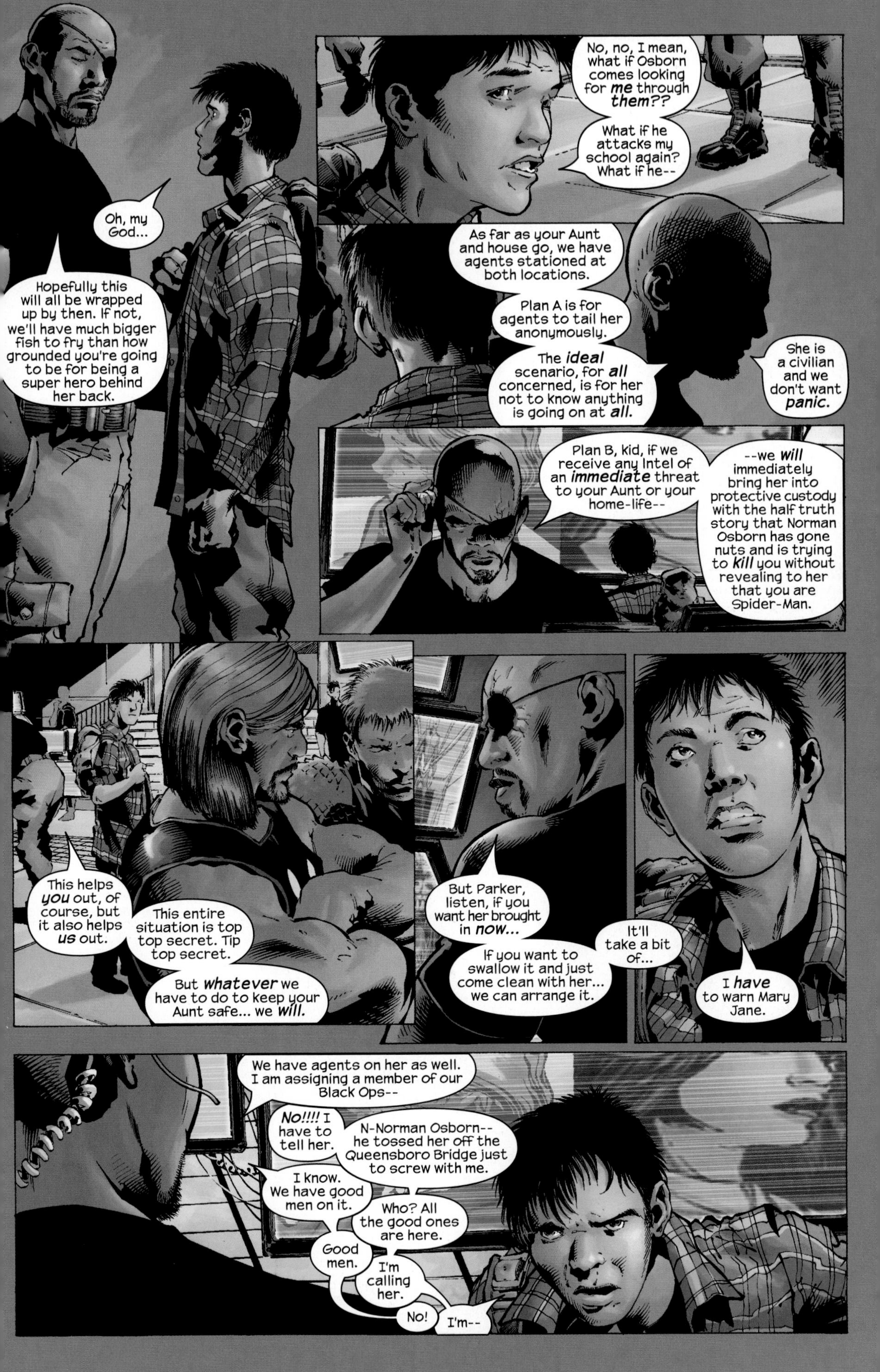
No, no, I mean, what if Osborn comes looking for me through them??
What if he attacks my school again? What if he--
Oh, my God...
Hopefully this will all be wrapped up by then. If not, we'll have much bigger fish to fry than how grounded you're going to be for being a super hero behind her back.
As far as your Aunt and house go, we have agents stationed at both locations.
Plan A is for agents to tail her anonymously.
The ideal scenario, for all concerned, is for her not to know anything is going on at all.
She is a civilian and we don't want panic.
Plan B, kid, if we receive any Intel of an immediate threat to your Aunt or your home-life--
--we will immediately bring her into protective custody with the half truth story that Norman Osborn has gone nuts and is trying to kill you without revealing to her that you are Spider-Man.
This helps you out, of course, but it also helps us out.
This entire situation is top top secret. Tip top secret.
But whatever we have to do to keep your Aunt safe... we will.
But Parker, listen, if you want her brought in now...
If you want to swallow it and just come clean with her... we can arrange it.
It'll take a bit of...
I have to warn Mary Jane.
We have agents on her as well. I am assigning a member of our Black Ops--
No!!!! I have to tell her.
N-Norman Osborn-- he tossed her off the Queensboro Bridge just to screw with me.
I know. We have good men on it.
Who? All the good ones are here.
Good men.
I'm calling her.
No!
I'm--

KID! I LOST THIRTY-FIVE PEOPLE TODAY!!

That's more agents in a single day than I have lost since I took this job!!

Thirty-five families lost someone today-- and yet *still* I am bending over backwards for you--

But you keep bustin' my chops on this and you can go back to Queens and fend for yourself!!!

I don't-- I don't understand.

What's-- what do you think they are going to do?

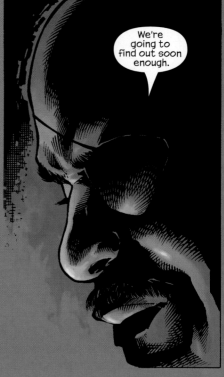

We're going to find out soon enough.

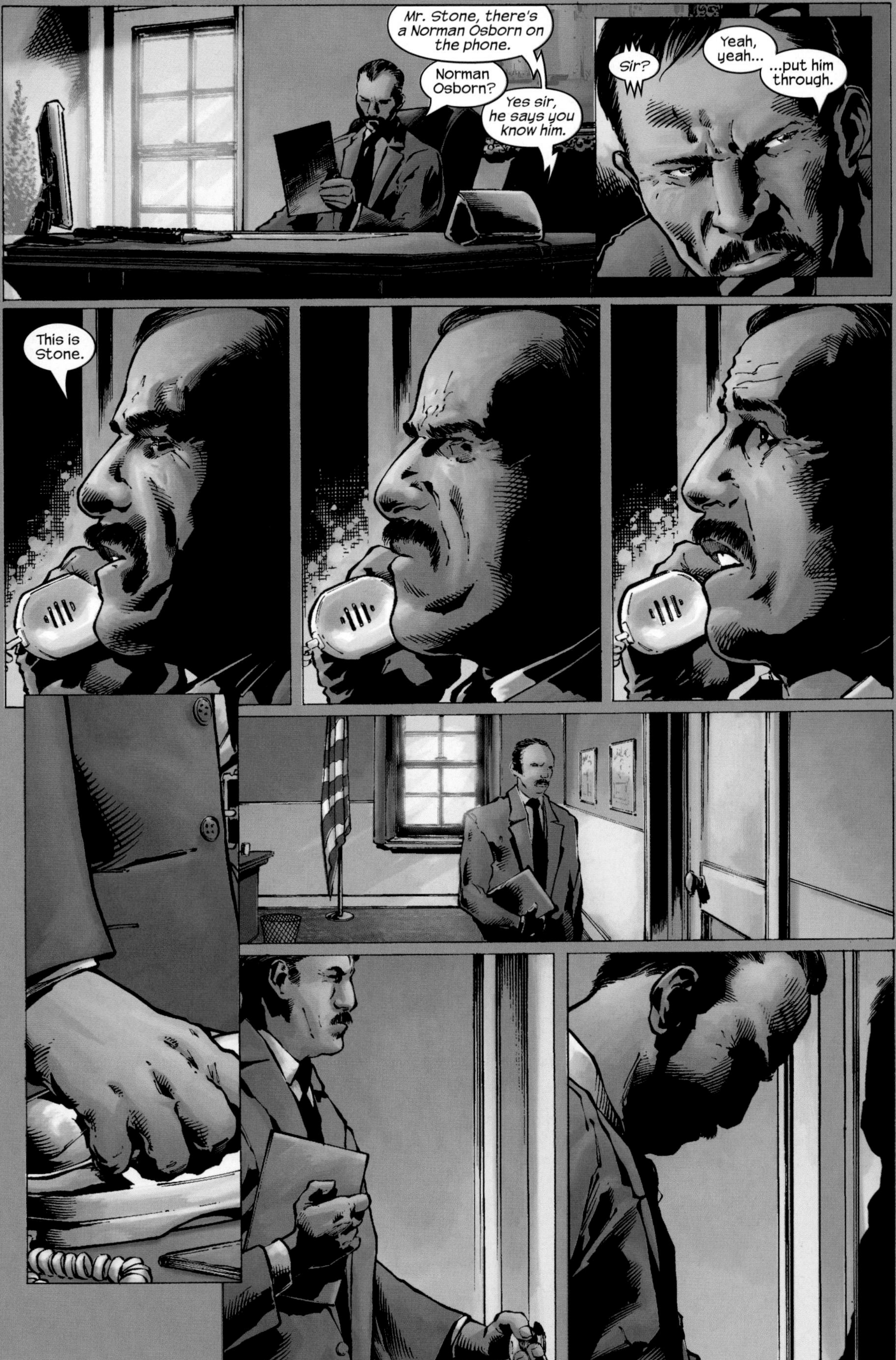
Mr. Stone, there's a Norman Osborn on the phone.
Norman Osborn?
Yes sir, he says you know him.
Sir?
Yeah, yeah...
...put him through.
This is Stone.

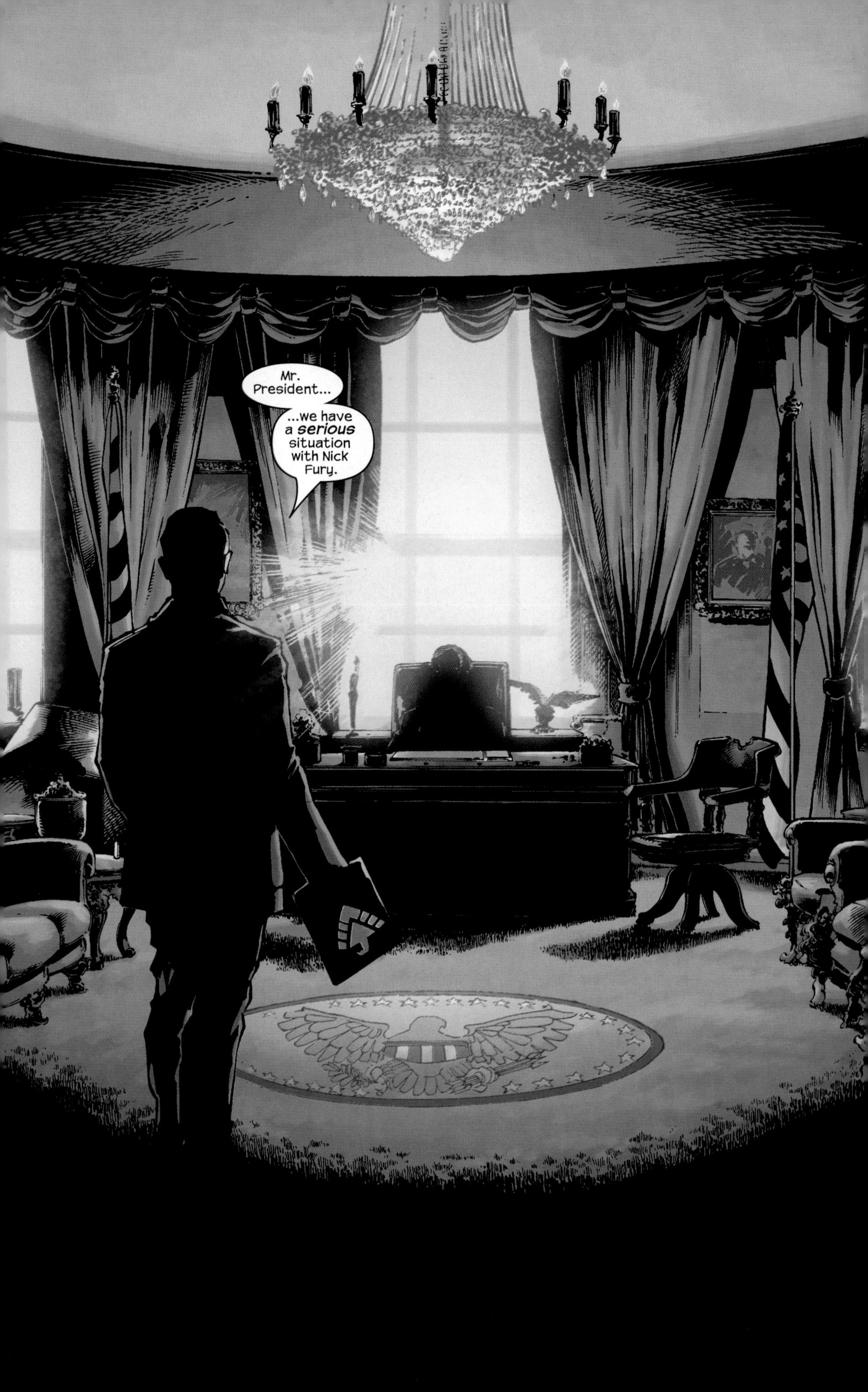
Mr. President...
...we have a *serious* situation with Nick Fury.

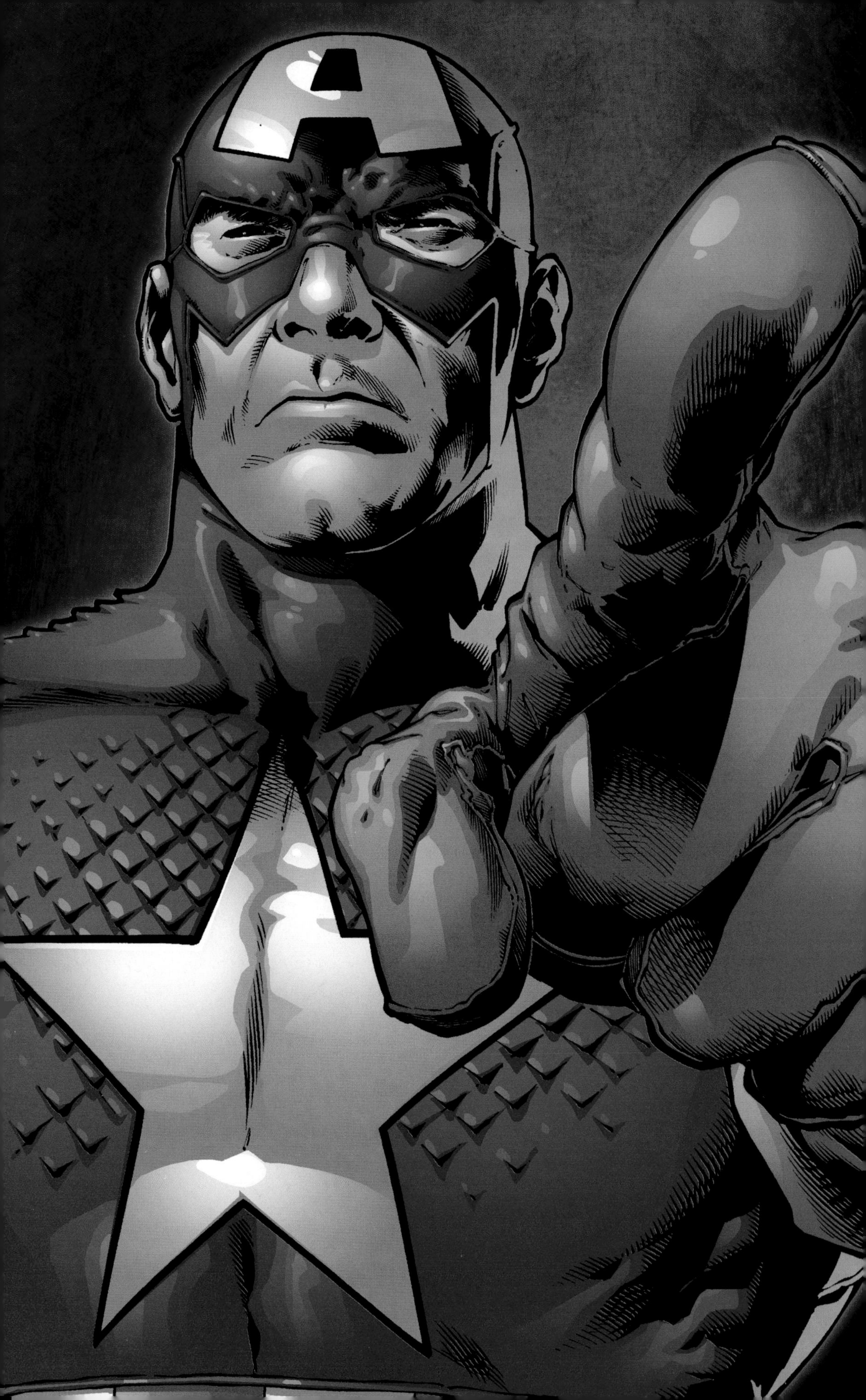

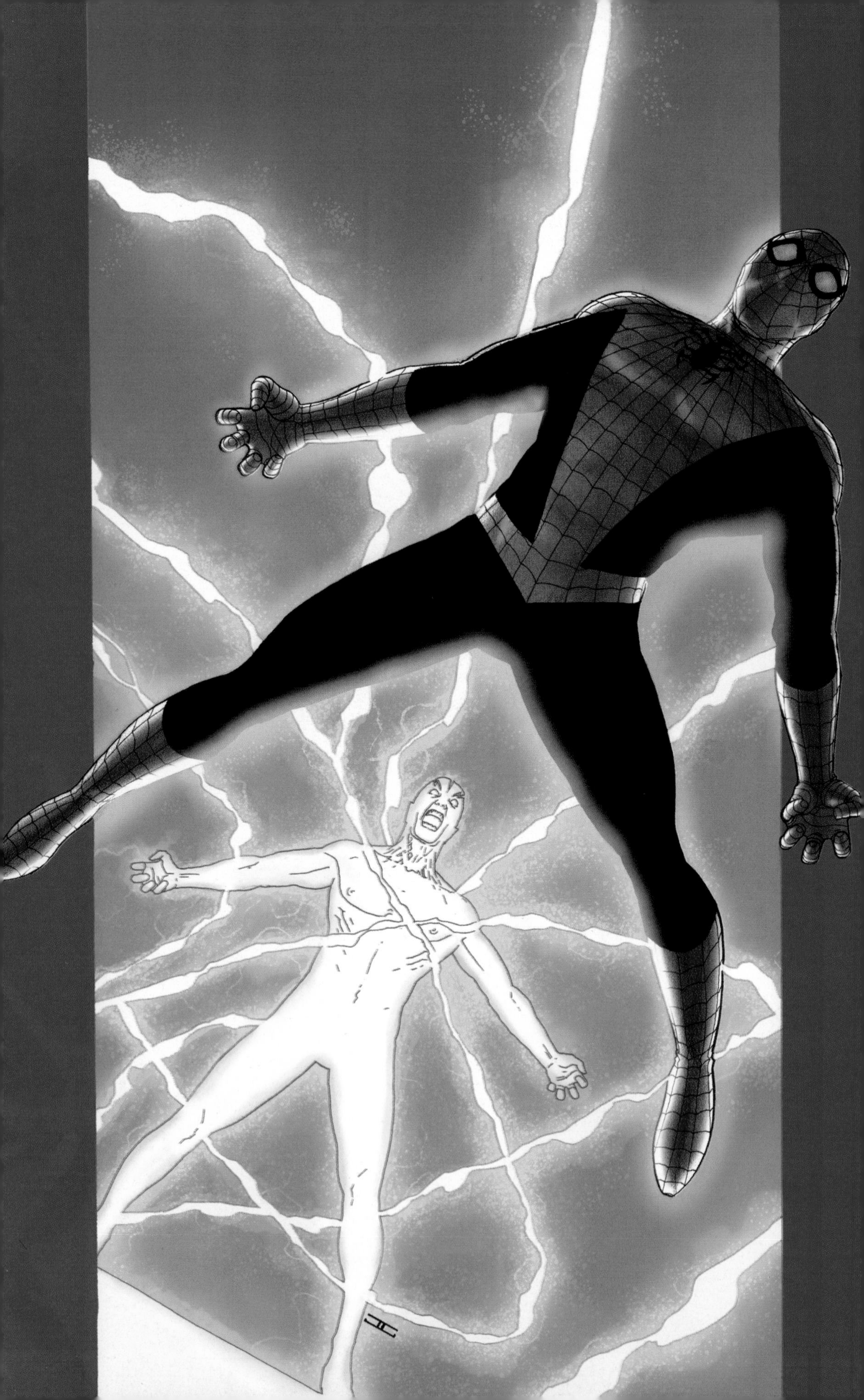

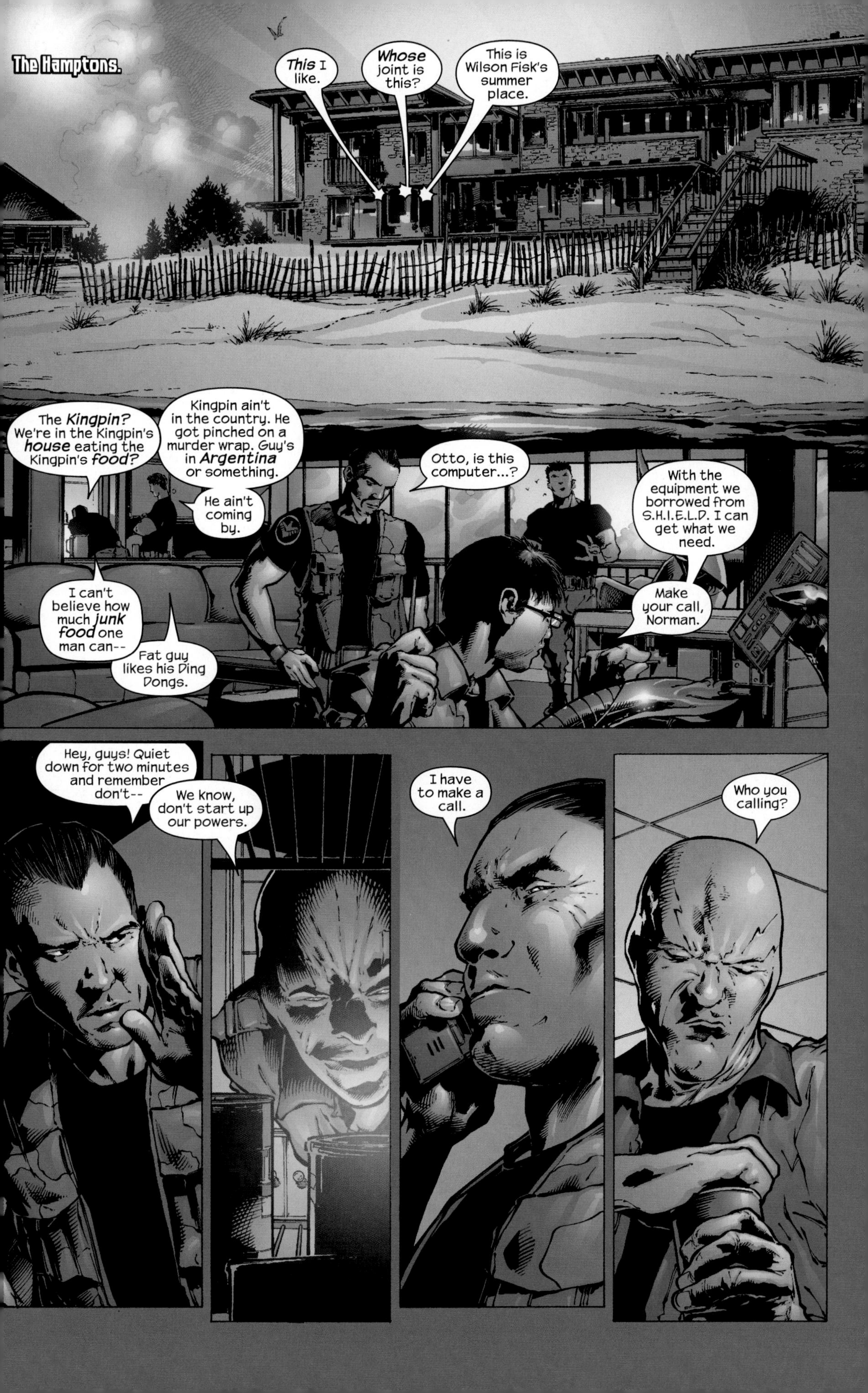
The Hamptons.
This I like.
Whose joint is this?
This is Wilson Fisk's summer place.
The Kingpin? We're in the Kingpin's house eating the Kingpin's food?
Kingpin ain't in the country. He got pinched on a murder wrap. Guy's in Argentina or something.
He ain't coming by.
Otto, is this computer...?
With the equipment we borrowed from S.H.I.E.L.D. I can get what we need.
Make your call, Norman.
I can't believe how much junk food one man can--
Fat guy likes his Ding Dongs.
Hey, guys! Quiet down for two minutes and remember don't--
We know, don't start up our powers.
I have to make a call.
Who you calling?

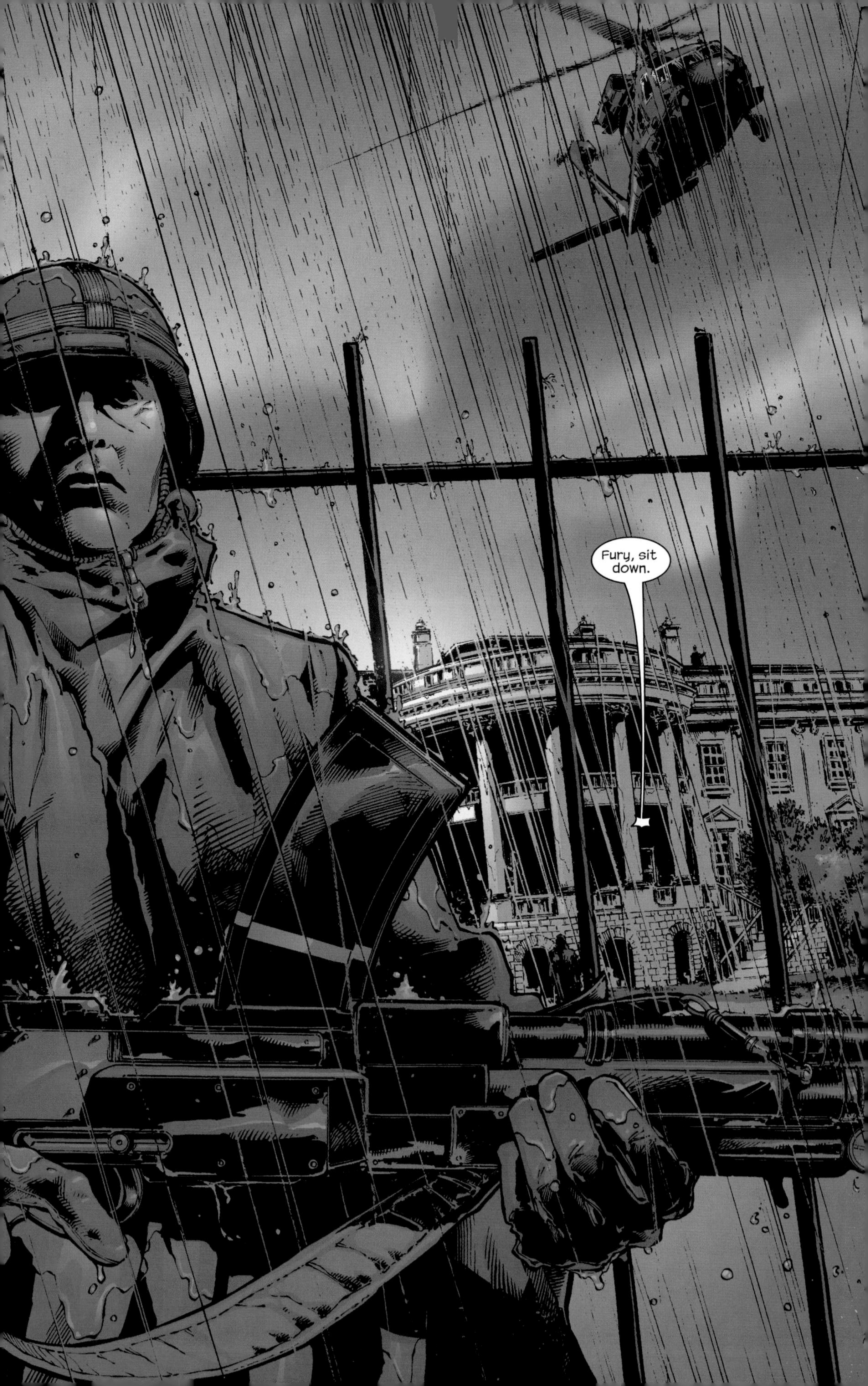
Fury, sit down.

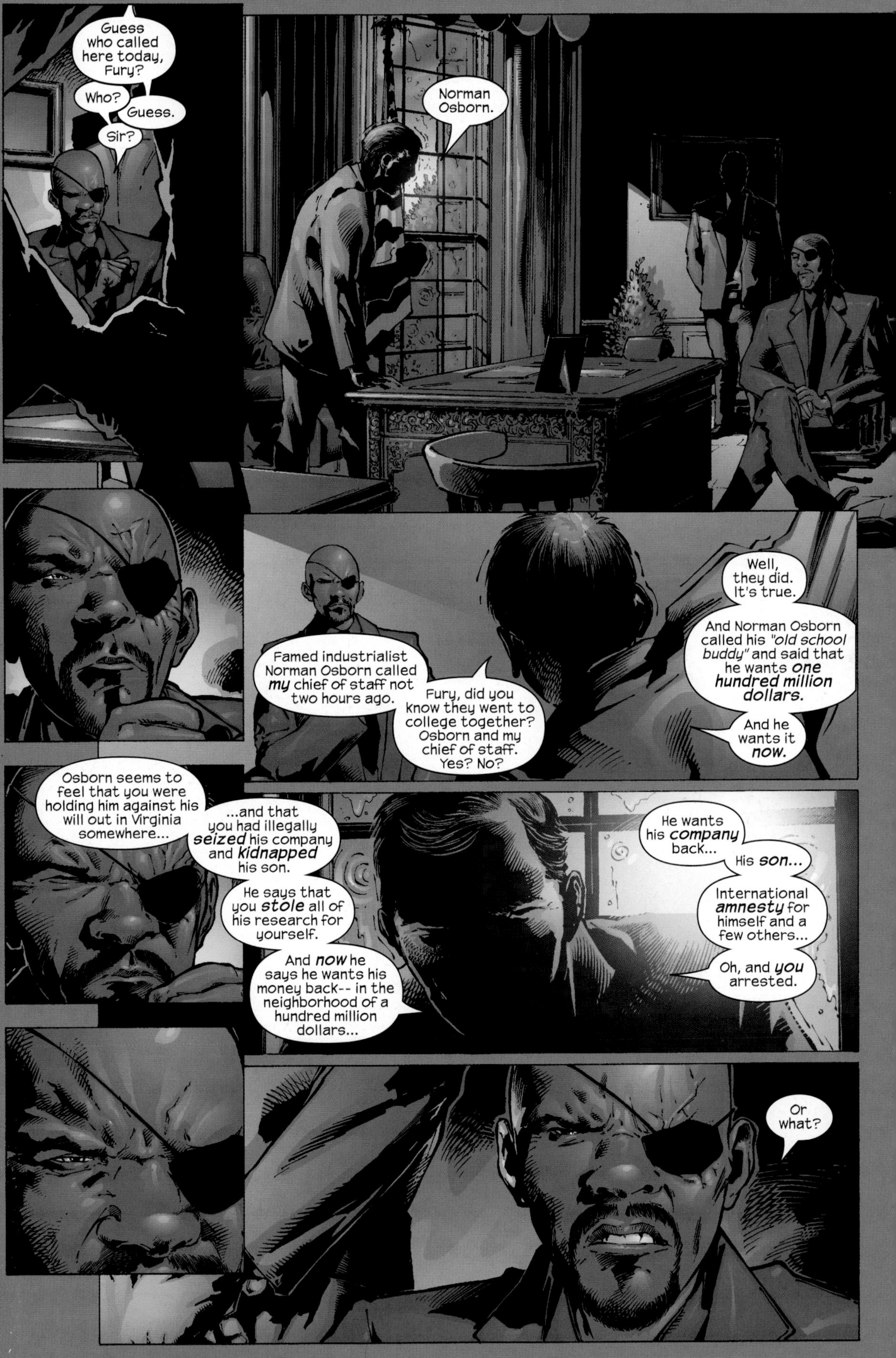
Guess who called here today, Fury?
Who?
Guess.
Sir?
Norman Osborn.
Famed industrialist Norman Osborn called *my* chief of staff not two hours ago.
Fury, did you know they went to college together? Osborn and my chief of staff. Yes? No?
Well, they did. It's true.
And Norman Osborn called his *"old school buddy"* and said that he wants ***one hundred million dollars.***
And he wants it ***now.***
Osborn seems to feel that you were holding him against his will out in Virginia somewhere...
...and that you had illegally ***seized*** his company and ***kidnapped*** his son.
He says that you ***stole*** all of his research for yourself.
And ***now*** he says he wants his money back-- in the neighborhood of a hundred million dollars...
He wants his ***company*** back...
His ***son...***
International ***amnesty*** for himself and a few others...
Oh, and ***you*** arrested.
Or what?

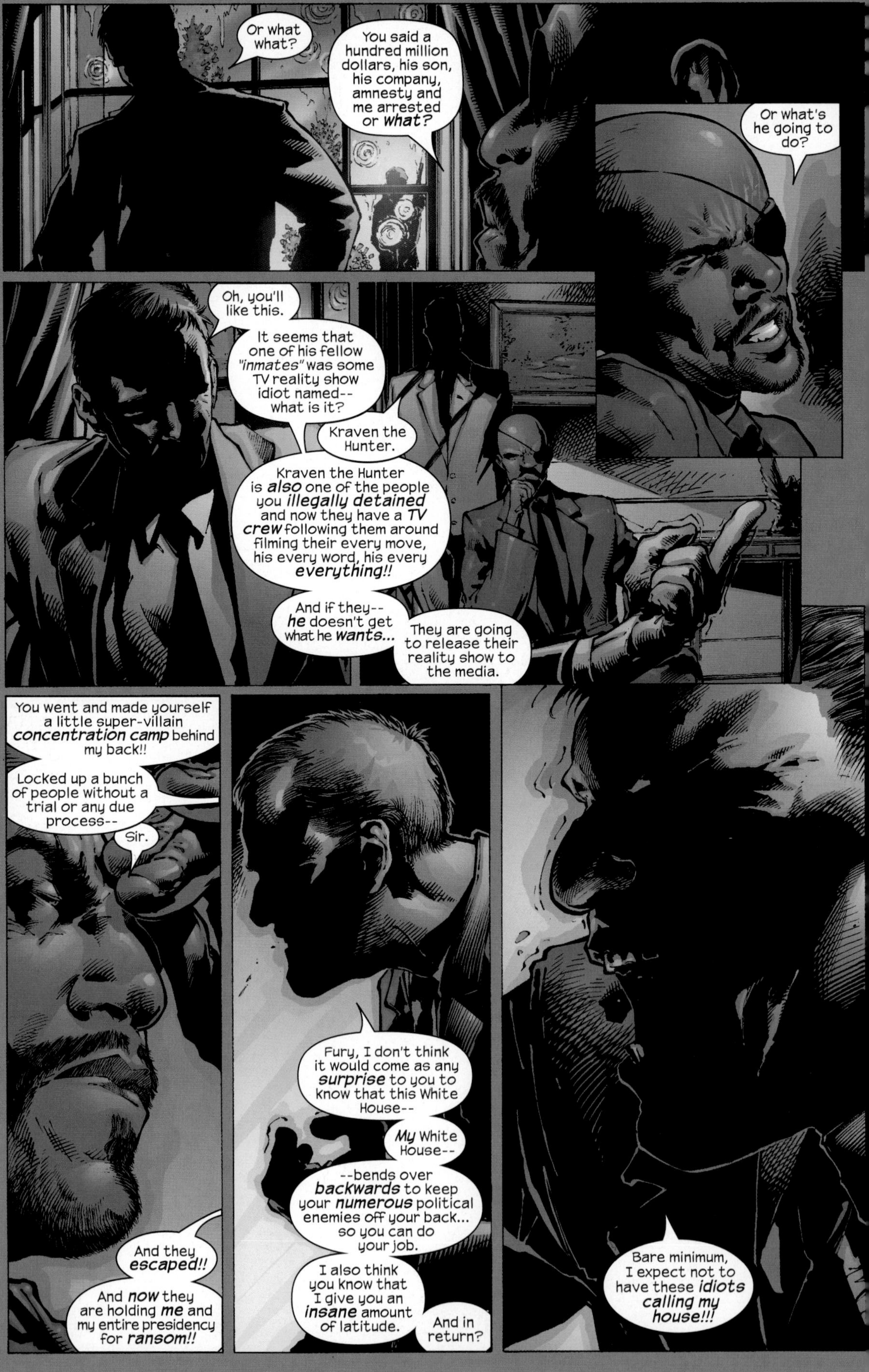
Or what what?
You said a hundred million dollars, his son, his company, amnesty and me arrested or what?
Or what's he going to do?
Oh, you'll like this.
It seems that one of his fellow "inmates" was some TV reality show idiot named-- what is it?
Kraven the Hunter.
Kraven the Hunter is also one of the people you illegally detained and now they have a TV crew following them around filming their every move, his every word, his every everything!!
And if they-- he doesn't get what he wants...
They are going to release their reality show to the media.
You went and made yourself a little super-villain concentration camp behind my back!!
Locked up a bunch of people without a trial or any due process--
Sir.
And they escaped!!
And now they are holding me and my entire presidency for ransom!!
Fury, I don't think it would come as any surprise to you to know that this White House--
My White House--
--bends over backwards to keep your numerous political enemies off your back... so you can do your job.
I also think you know that I give you an insane amount of latitude.
And in return?
Bare minimum, I expect not to have these idiots calling my house!!!

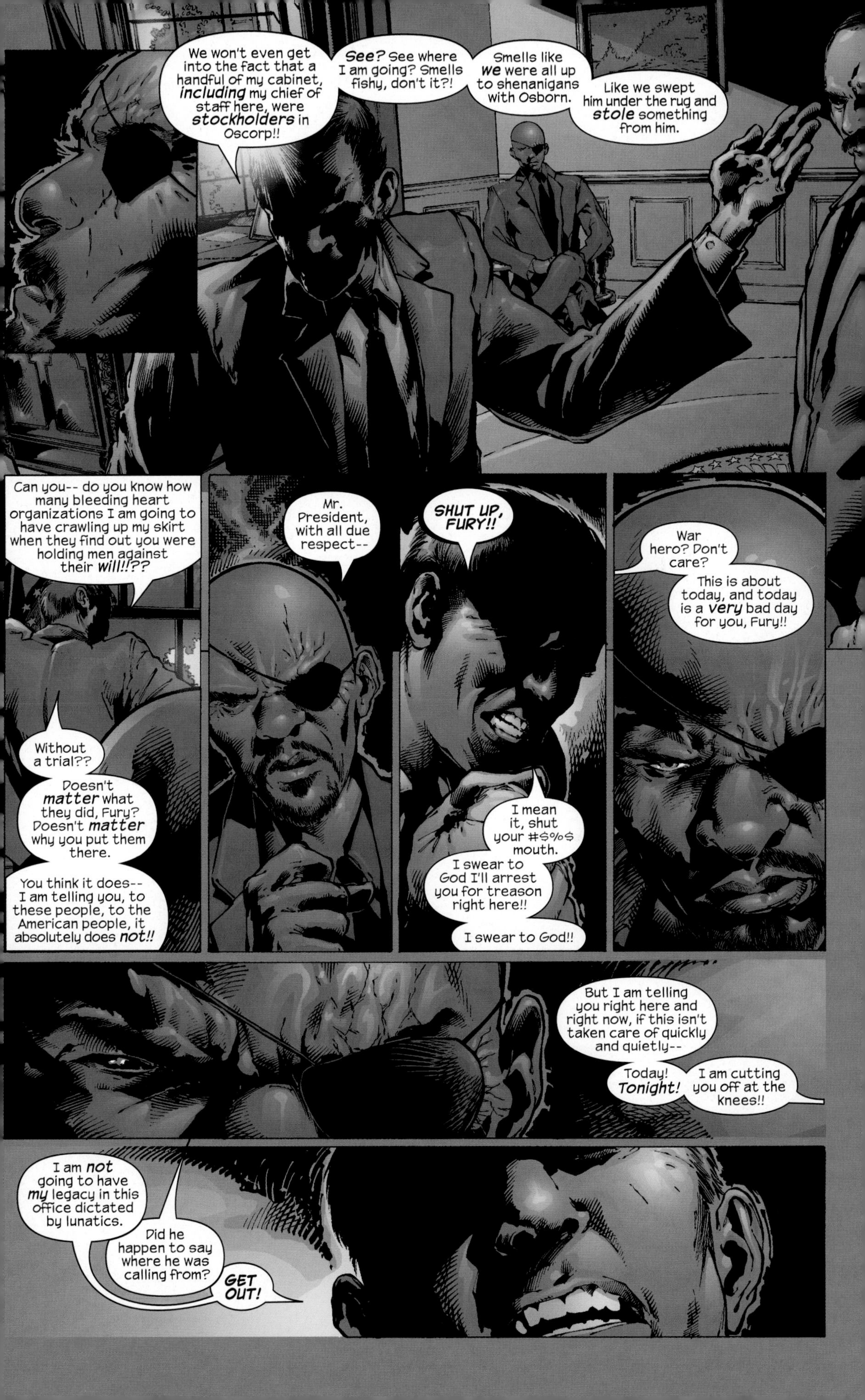

We won't even get into the fact that a handful of my cabinet, *including* my chief of staff here, were *stockholders* in Oscorp!!
See? See where I am going? Smells fishy, don't it?!
Smells like *we* were all up to shenanigans with Osborn.
Like we swept him under the rug and *stole* something from him.
Can you-- do you know how many bleeding heart organizations I am going to have crawling up my skirt when they find out you were holding men against their *will!!??*
Without a trial??
Doesn't *matter* what they did, Fury? Doesn't *matter* why you put them there.
You think it does-- I am telling you, to these people, to the American people, it absolutely does *not!!*
Mr. President, with all due respect--
SHUT UP, FURY!!
I mean it, shut your #$%$ mouth.
I swear to God I'll arrest you for treason right here!!
I swear to God!!
War hero? Don't care?
This is about today, and today is a *very* bad day for you, Fury!!
But I am telling you right here and right now, if this isn't taken care of quickly and quietly--
Today! *Tonight!*
I am cutting you off at the knees!!
I am *not* going to have *my* legacy in this office dictated by lunatics.
Did he happen to say where he was calling from?
GET OUT!

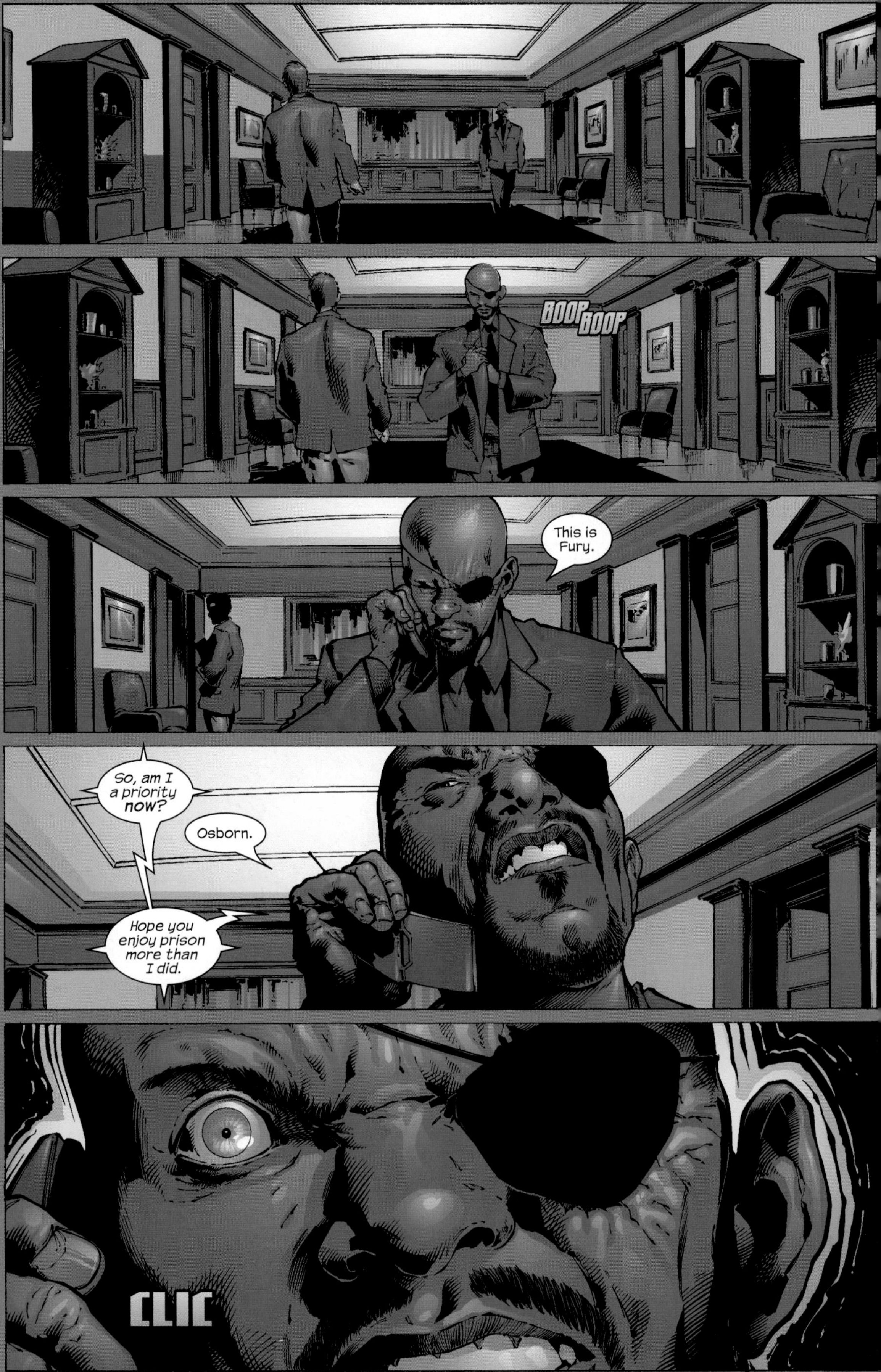
BOOP BOOP
This is Fury.
So, am I a priority now?
Osborn.
Hope you enjoy prison more than I did.
CLIC

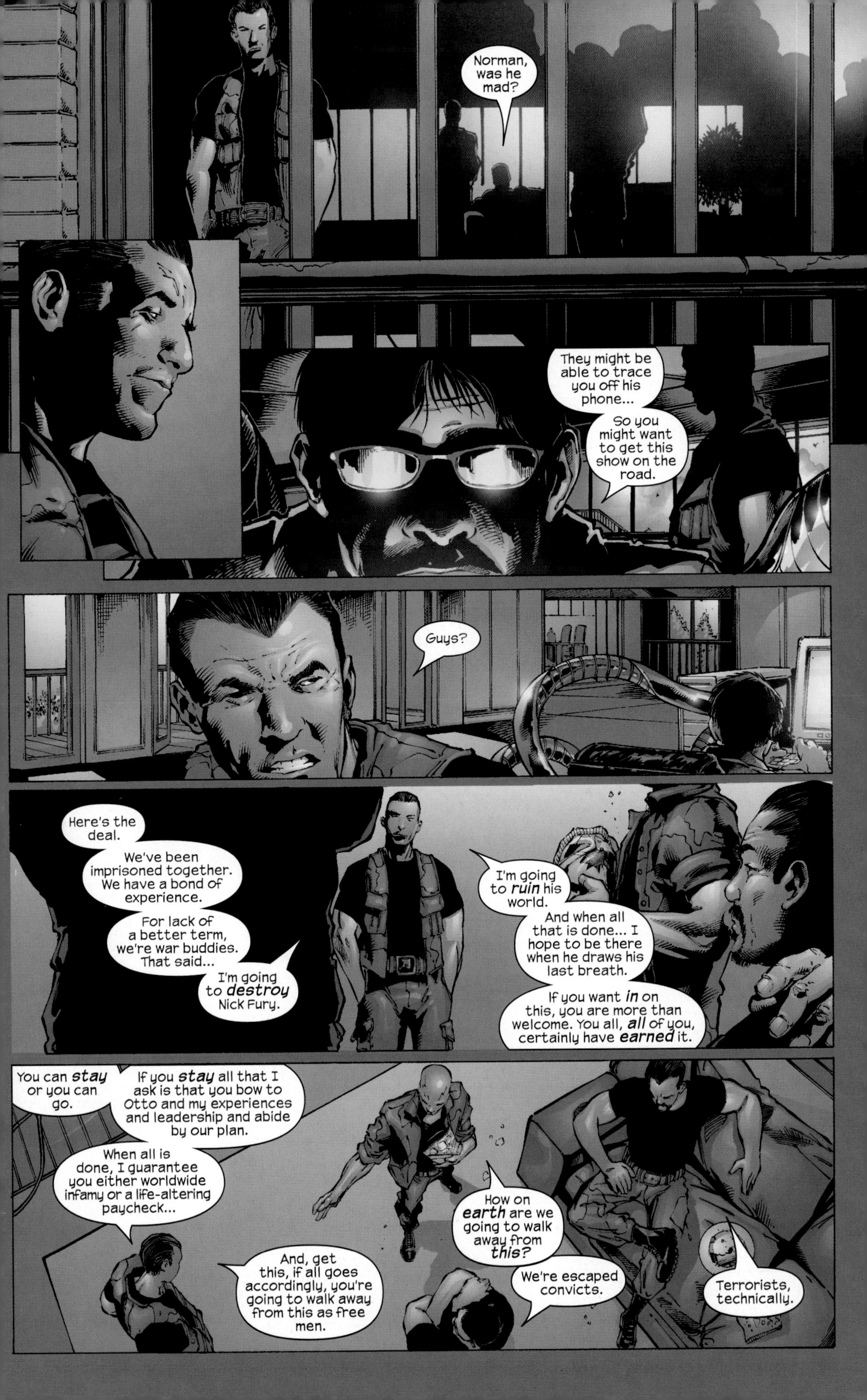
Norman, was he mad?
They might be able to trace you off his phone...
So you might want to get this show on the road.
Guys?
Here's the deal.
We've been imprisoned together. We have a bond of experience.
For lack of a better term, we're war buddies. That said...
I'm going to destroy Nick Fury.
I'm going to ruin his world.
And when all that is done... I hope to be there when he draws his last breath.
If you want in on this, you are more than welcome. You all, all of you, certainly have earned it.
You can stay or you can go.
If you stay all that I ask is that you bow to Otto and my experiences and leadership and abide by our plan.
When all is done, I guarantee you either worldwide infamy or a life-altering paycheck...
How on earth are we going to walk away from this?
And, get this, if all goes accordingly, you're going to walk away from this as free men.
We're escaped convicts.
Terrorists, technically.

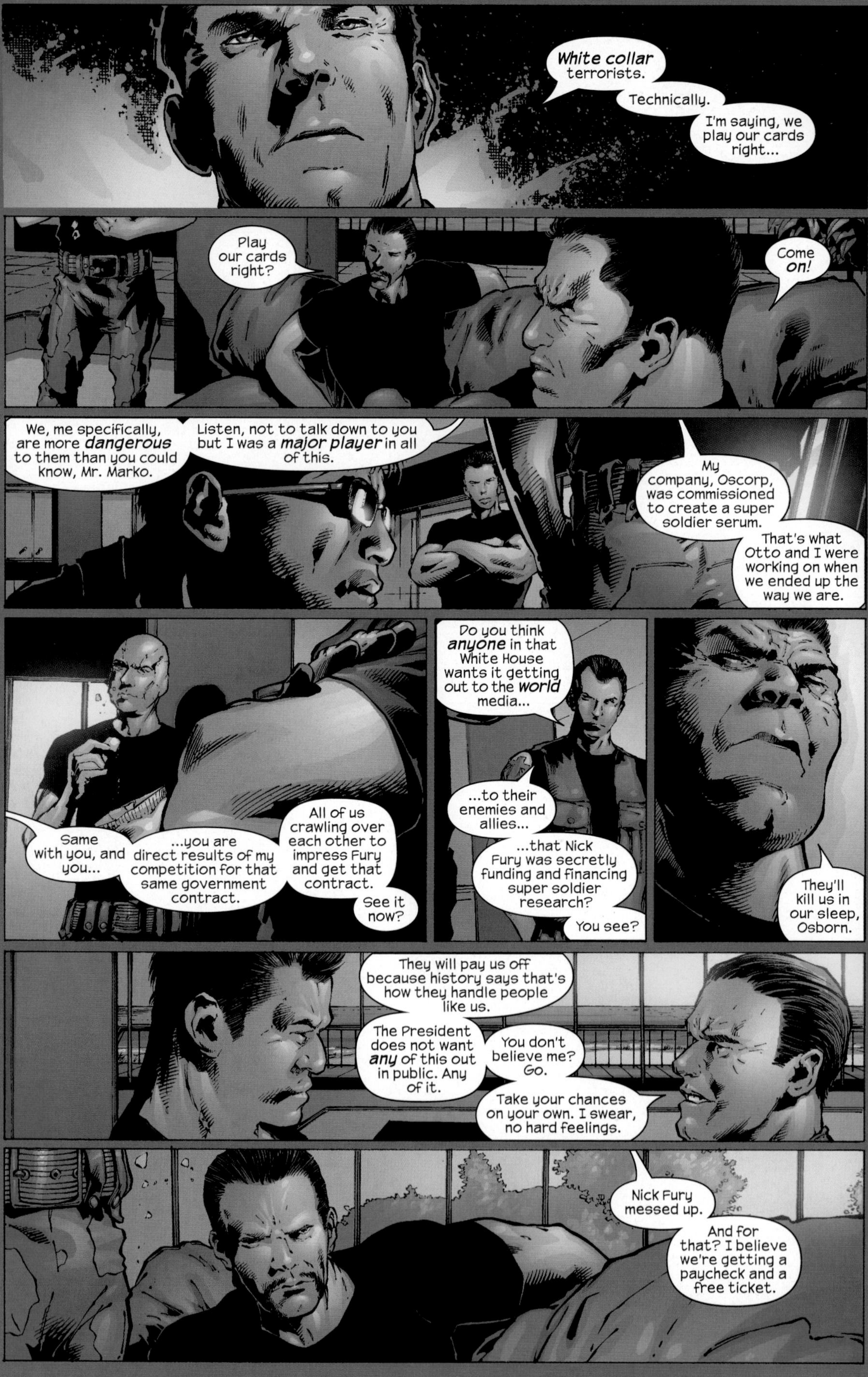
White collar terrorists.
Technically.
I'm saying, we play our cards right...
Play our cards right?
Come on!
We, me specifically, are more dangerous to them than you could know, Mr. Marko.
Listen, not to talk down to you but I was a major player in all of this.
My company, Oscorp, was commissioned to create a super soldier serum.
That's what Otto and I were working on when we ended up the way we are.
Same with you, and you...
...you are direct results of my competition for that same government contract.
All of us crawling over each other to impress Fury and get that contract.
See it now?
Do you think anyone in that White House wants it getting out to the world media...
...to their enemies and allies...
...that Nick Fury was secretly funding and financing super soldier research?
You see?
They'll kill us in our sleep, Osborn.
They will pay us off because history says that's how they handle people like us.
The President does not want any of this out in public. Any of it.
You don't believe me? Go.
Take your chances on your own. I swear, no hard feelings.
Nick Fury messed up.
And for that? I believe we're getting a paycheck and a free ticket.

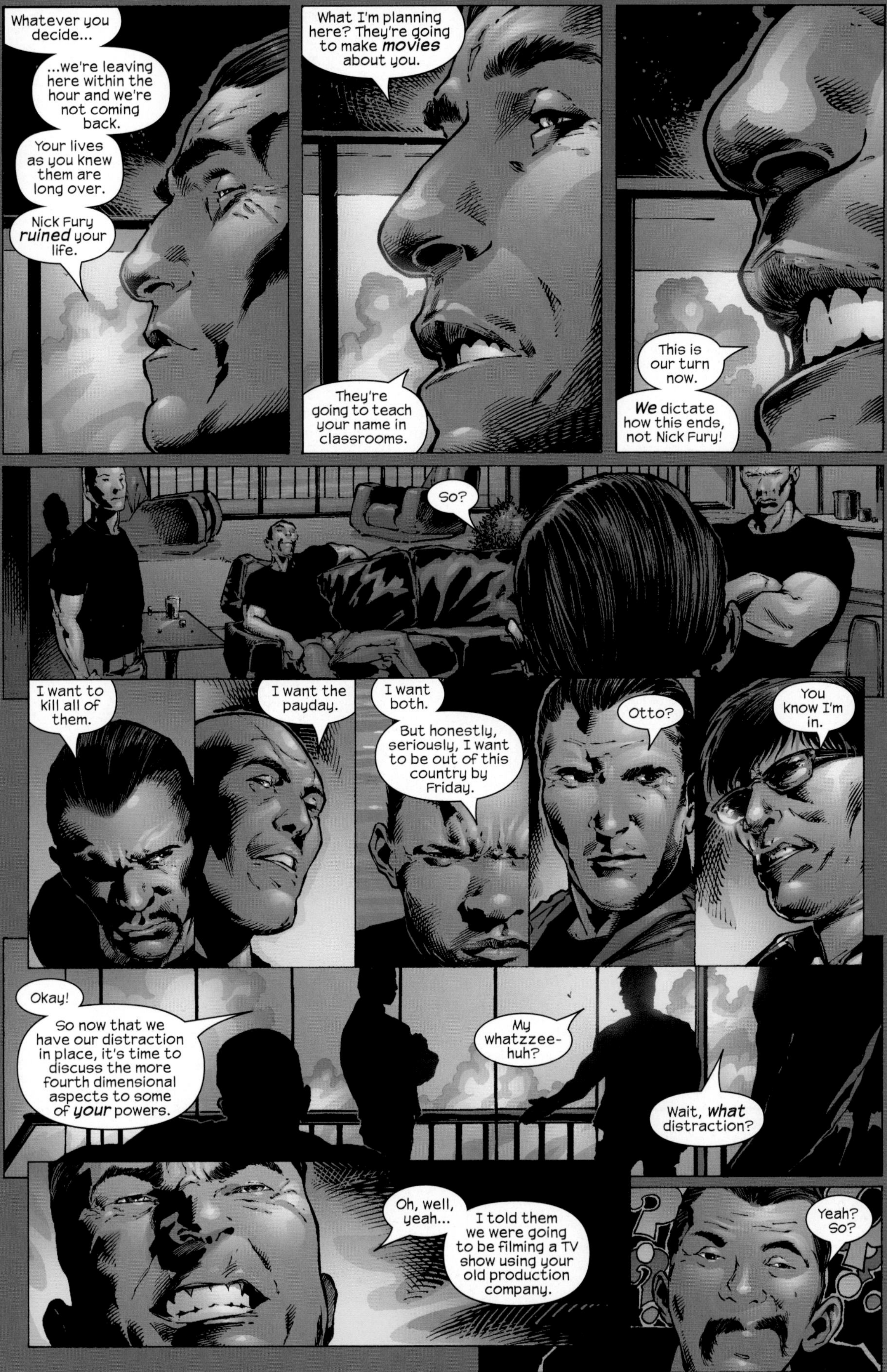
Whatever you decide...
...we're leaving here within the hour and we're not coming back.
Your lives as you knew them are long over.
Nick Fury ruined your life.
What I'm planning here? They're going to make movies about you.
They're going to teach your name in classrooms.
This is our turn now.
We dictate how this ends, not Nick Fury!
So?
I want to kill all of them.
I want the payday.
I want both.
But honestly, seriously, I want to be out of this country by Friday.
Otto?
You know I'm in.
Okay!
So now that we have our distraction in place, it's time to discuss the more fourth dimensional aspects to some of your powers.
My whatzzee-huh?
Wait, what distraction?
Oh, well, yeah...
I told them we were going to be filming a TV show using your old production company.
Yeah? So?

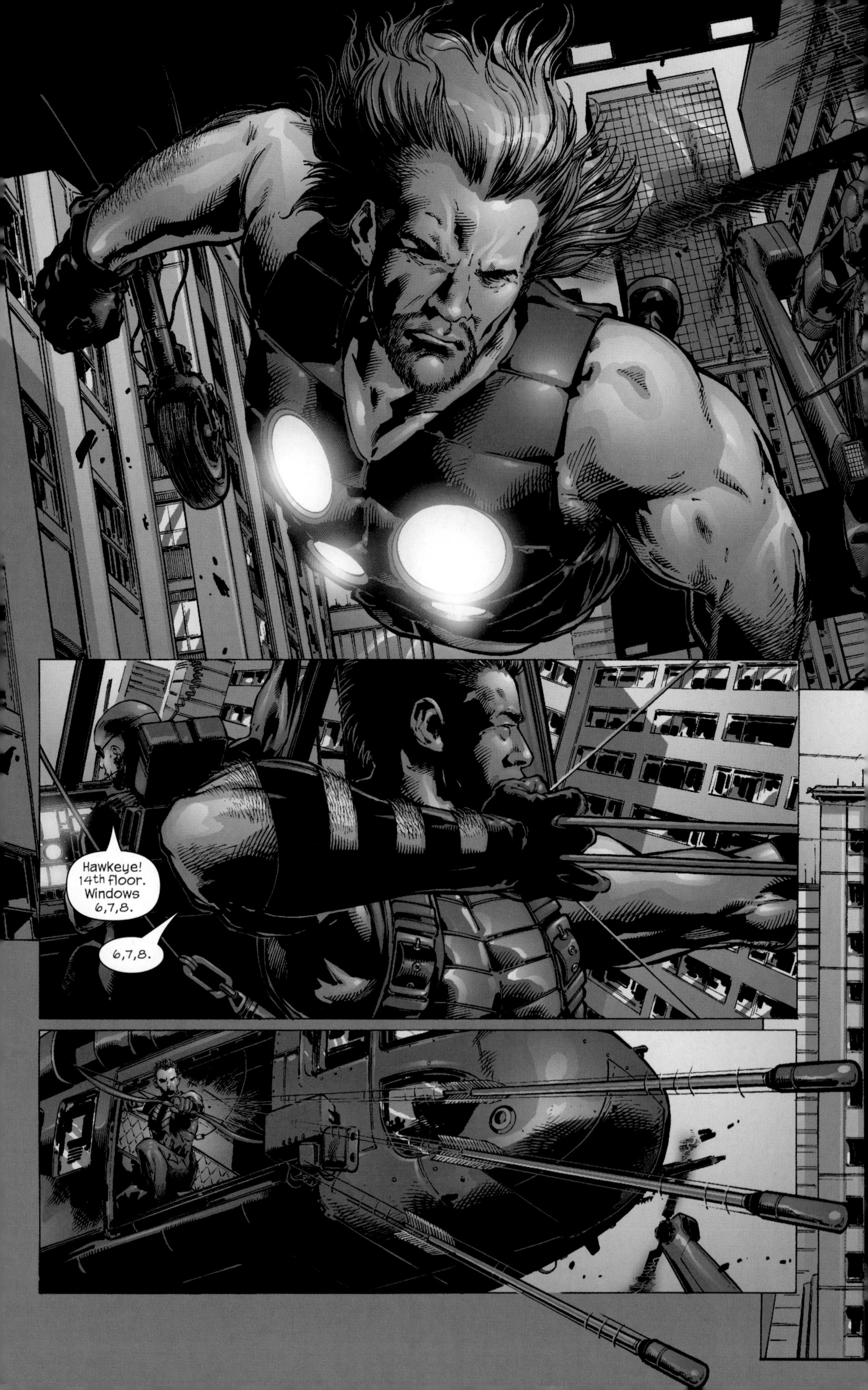
Hawkeye! 14th floor. Windows 6,7,8.
6,7,8.

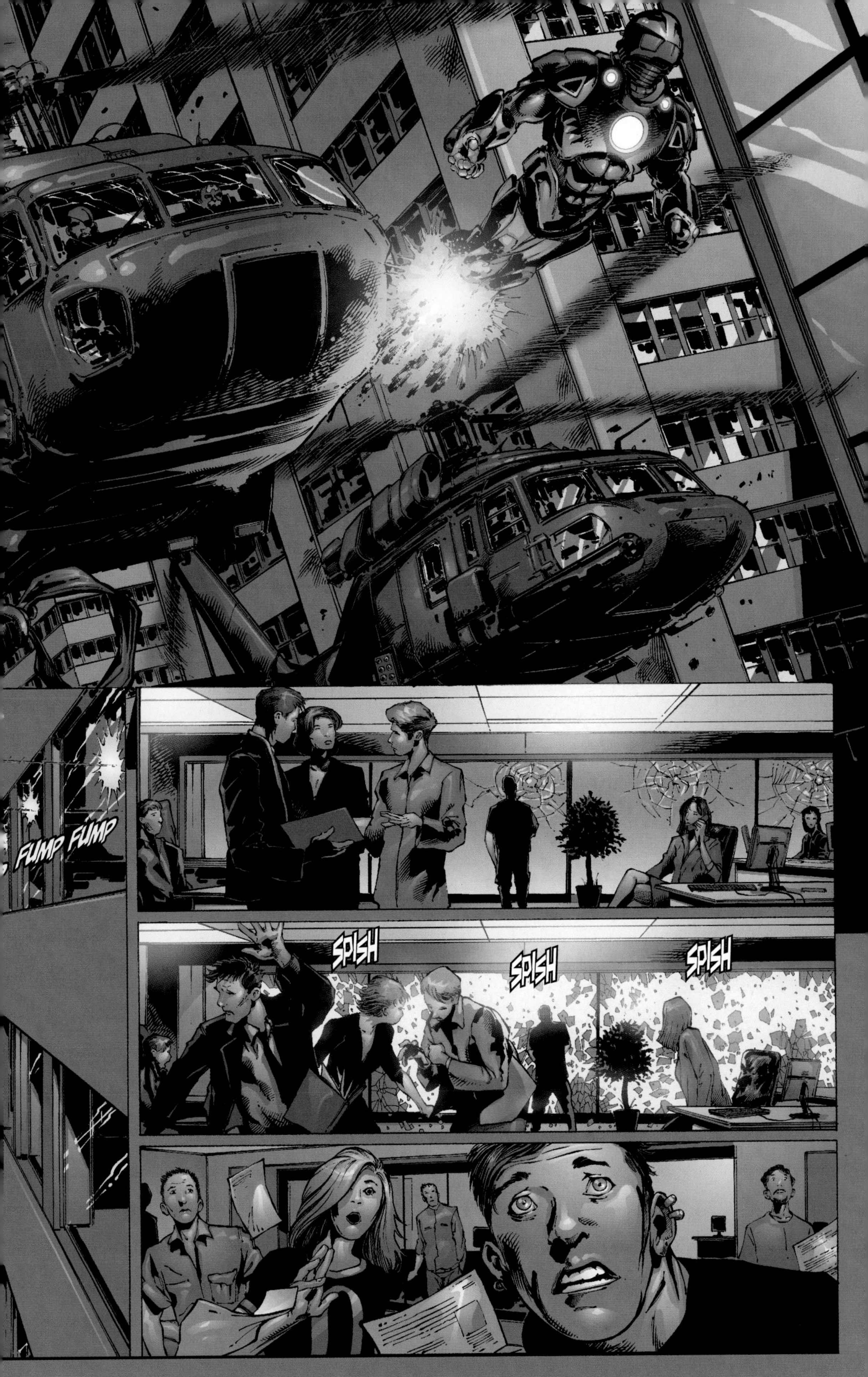
FUMP FUMP
SPISH
SPISH
SPISH

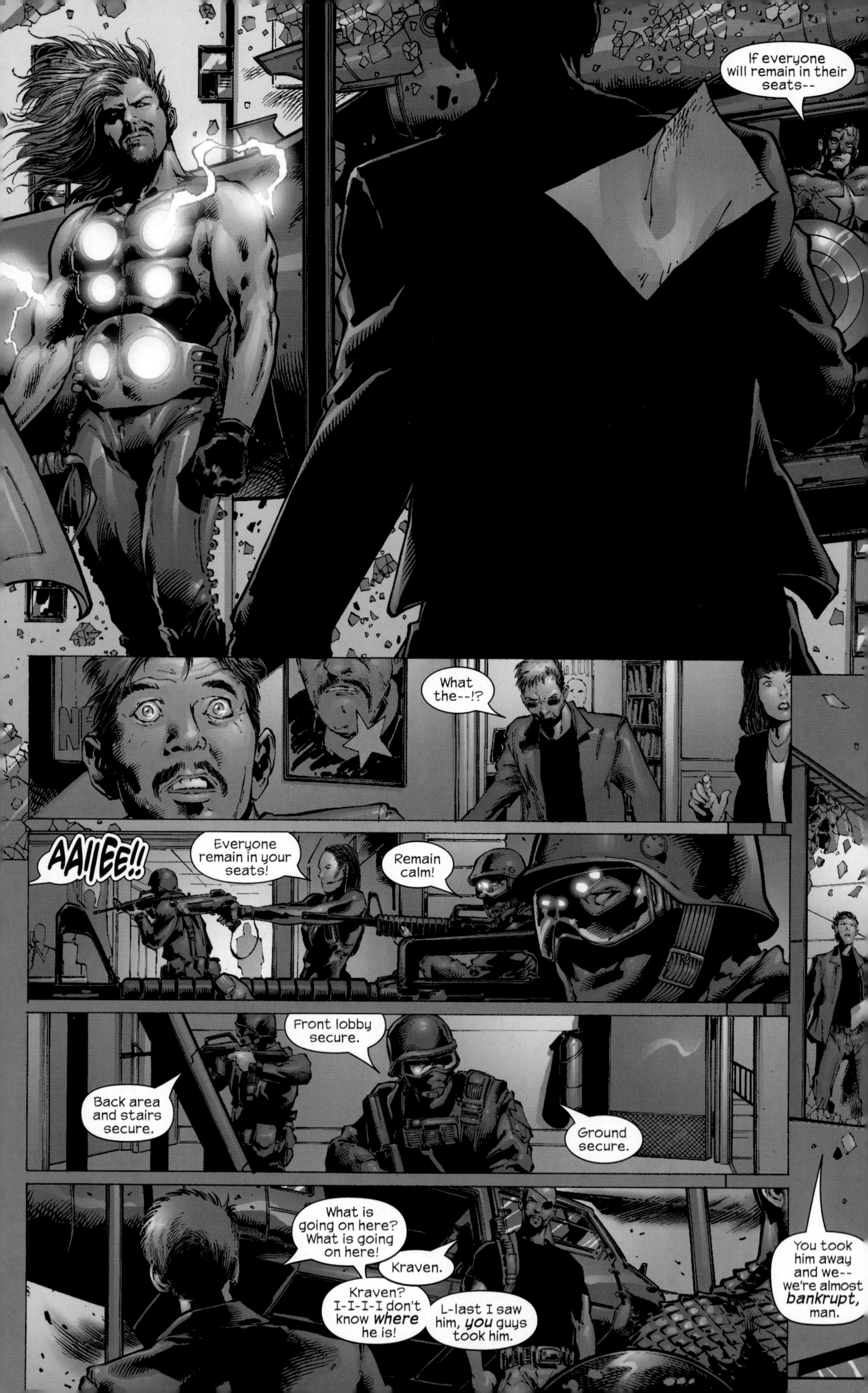

If everyone will remain in their seats--
What the--!?
AAIIEE!!
Everyone remain in your seats!
Remain calm!
Front lobby secure.
Back area and stairs secure.
Ground secure.
What is going on here? What is going on here!
Kraven.
Kraven? I-I-I-I don't know *where* he is!
L-last I saw him, *you* guys took him.
You took him away and we-- we're almost *bankrupt,* man.

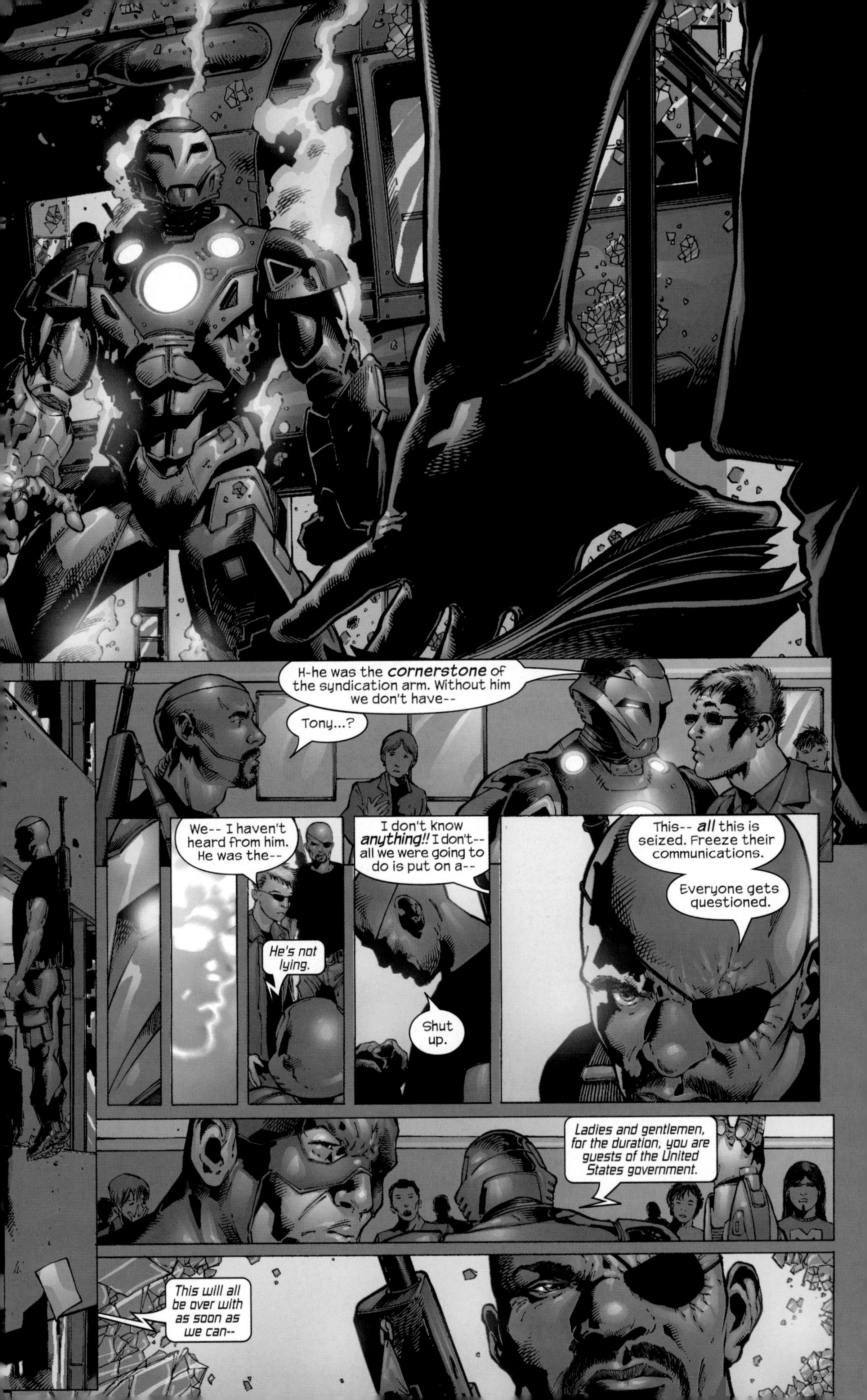
H-he was the *cornerstone* of the syndication arm. Without him we don't have--
Tony...?
We-- I haven't heard from him. He was the--
He's not lying.
I don't know *anything!!* I don't-- all we were going to do is put on a--
Shut up.
This-- *all* this is seized. Freeze their communications.
Everyone gets questioned.
Ladies and gentlemen, for the duration, you are guests of the United States government.
This will all be over with as soon as we can--

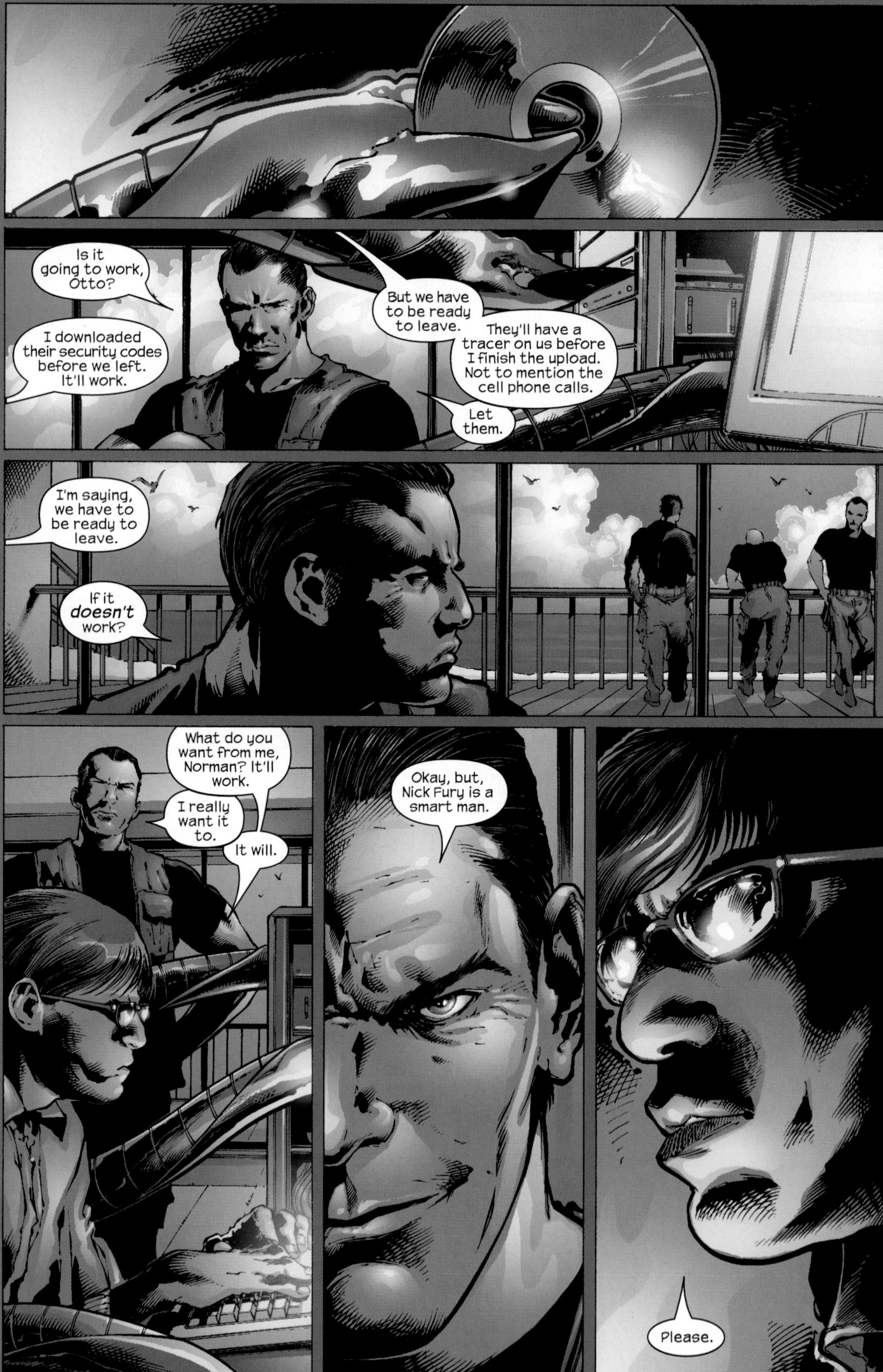
Is it going to work, Otto?
I downloaded their security codes before we left. It'll work.
But we have to be ready to leave.
They'll have a tracer on us before I finish the upload. Not to mention the cell phone calls.
Let them.
I'm saying, we have to be ready to leave.
If it *doesn't* work?
What do you want from me, Norman? It'll work.
I really want it to.
It will.
Okay, but, Nick Fury is a smart man.
Please.

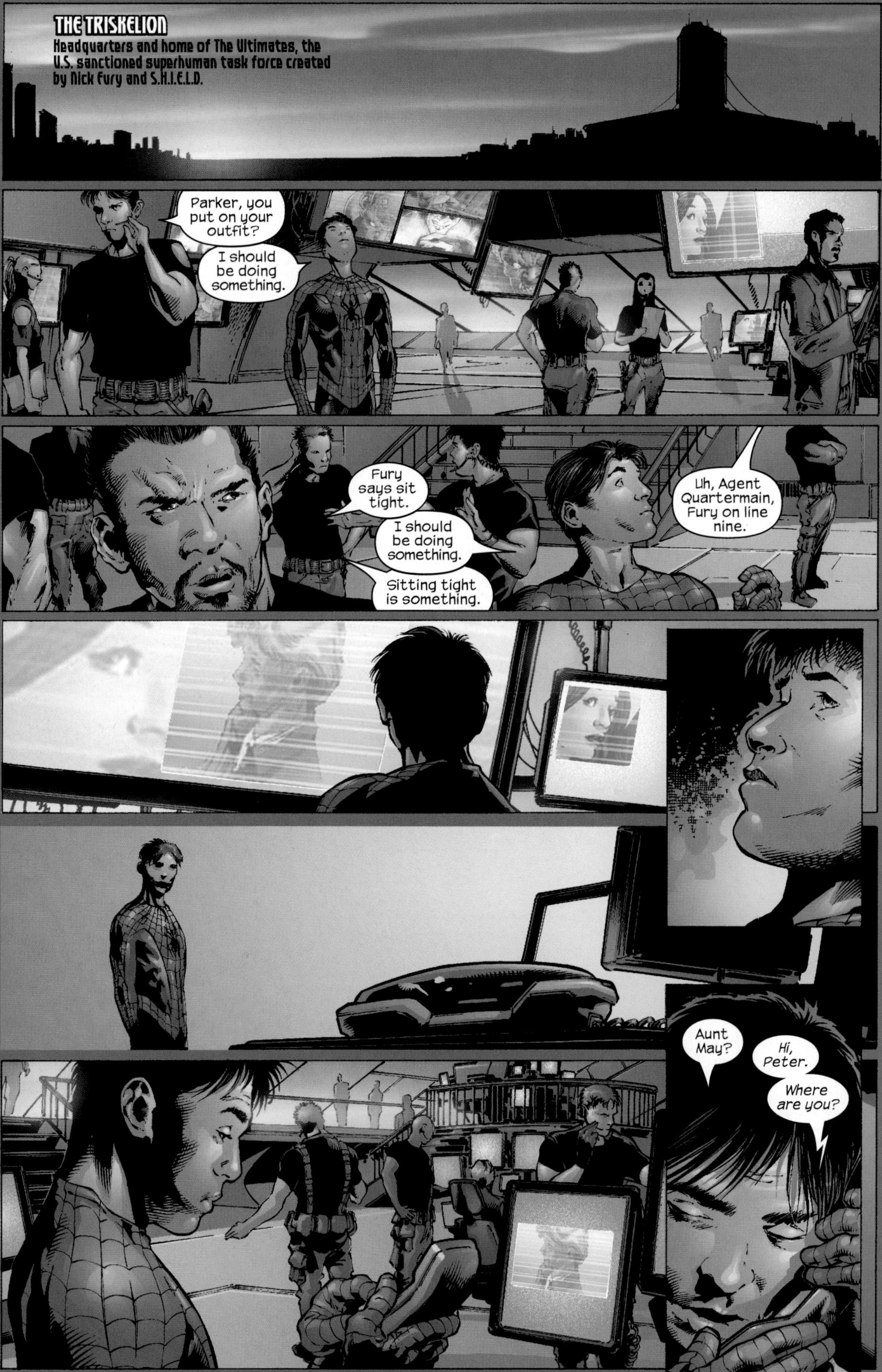
THE TRISKELION
Headquarters and home of The Ultimates, the U.S. sanctioned superhuman task force created by Nick Fury and S.H.I.E.L.D.
Parker, you put on your outfit?
I should be doing something.
Fury says sit tight.
I should be doing something.
Sitting tight is something.
Uh, Agent Quartermain, Fury on line nine.
Aunt May?
Hi, Peter.
Where are you?

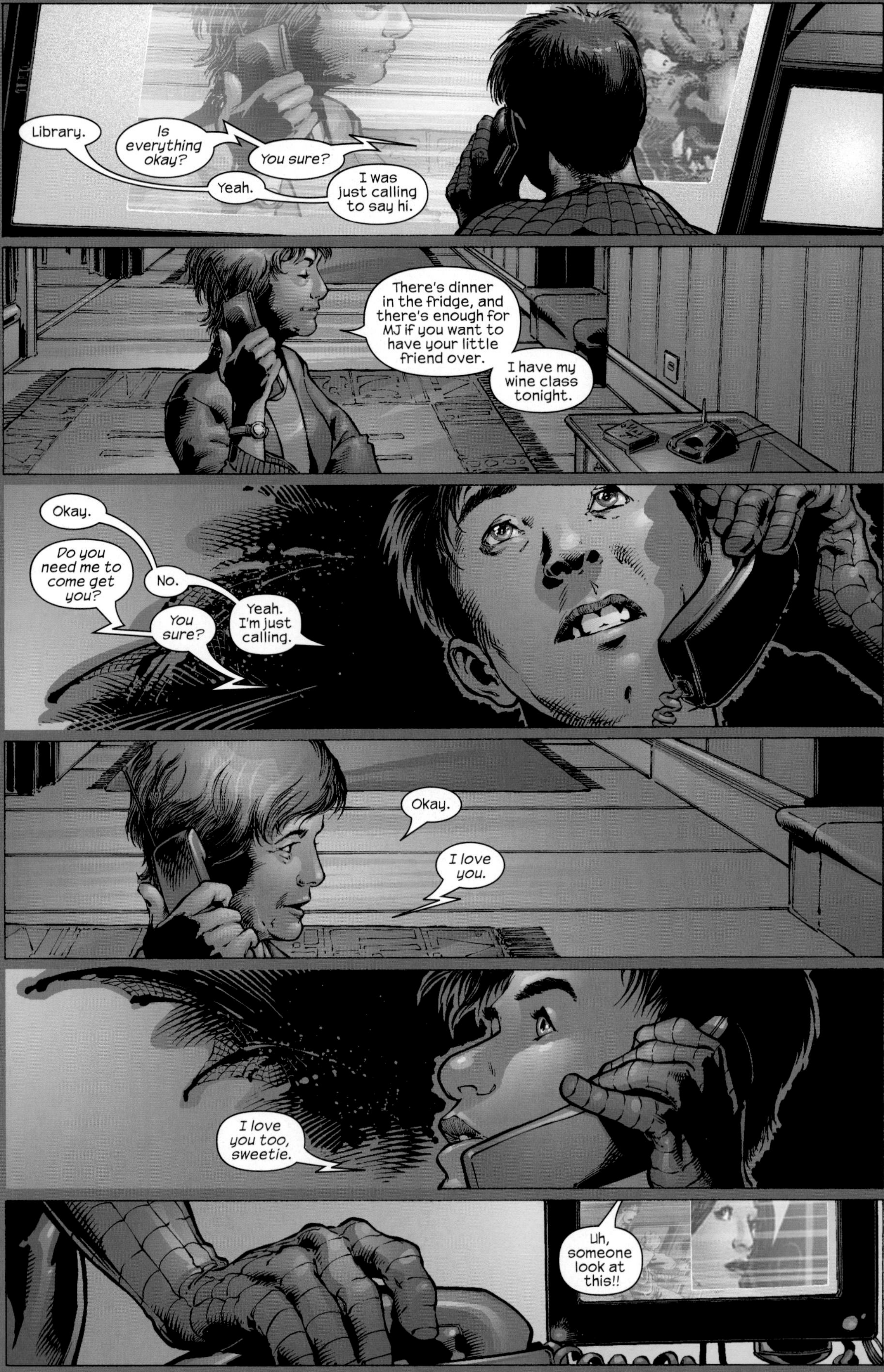
Library.
Is everything okay?
Yeah.
You sure?
I was just calling to say hi.
There's dinner in the fridge, and there's enough for MJ if you want to have your little friend over.
I have my wine class tonight.
Okay.
Do you need me to come get you?
No.
You sure?
Yeah. I'm just calling.
Okay.
I love you.
I love you too, sweetie.
Uh, someone look at this!!

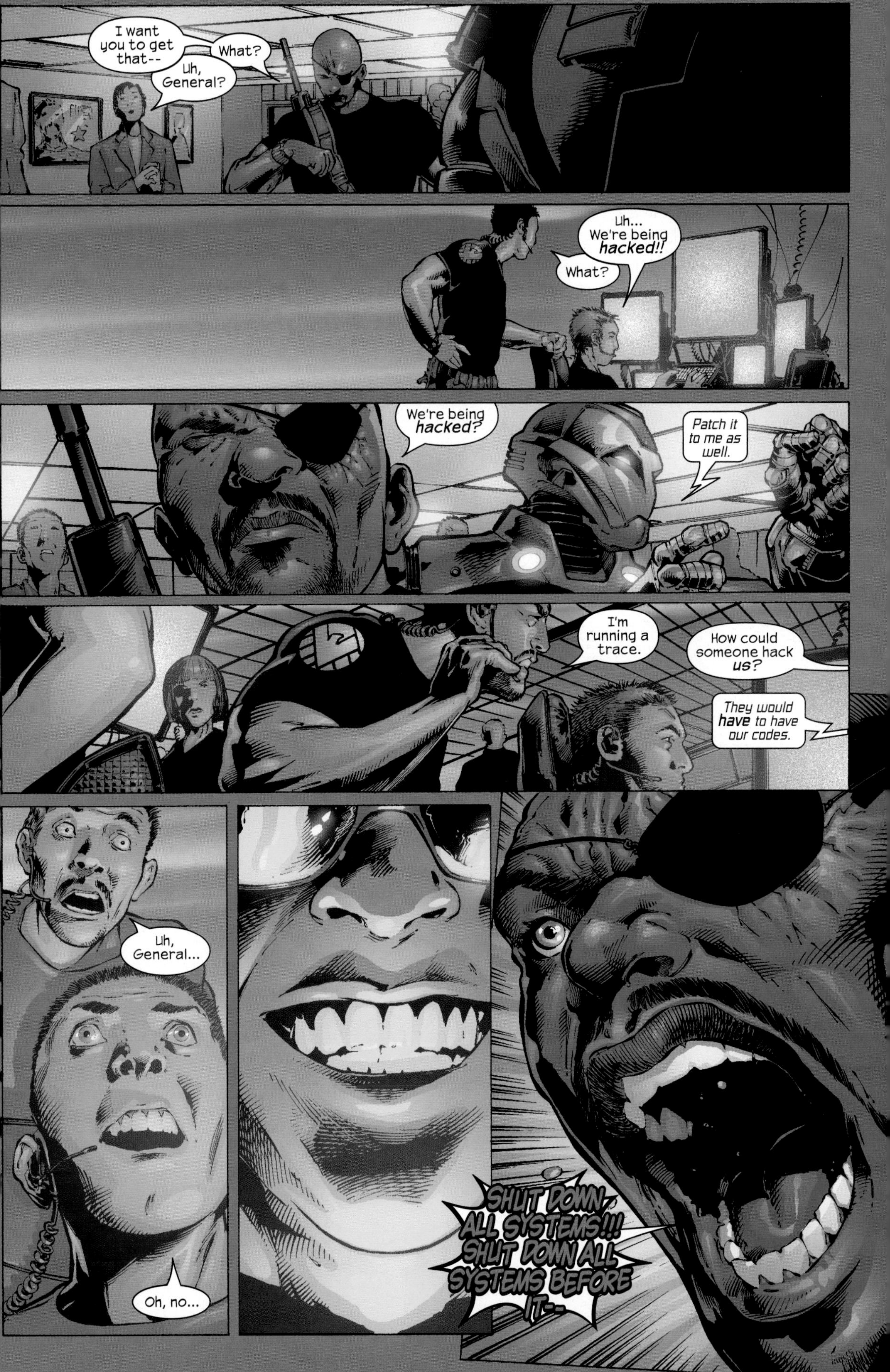
I want you to get that--
What?
Uh, General?
Uh... We're being hacked!!
What?
We're being hacked?
Patch it to me as well.
I'm running a trace.
How could someone hack us?
They would have to have our codes.
Uh, General...
Oh, no...
SHUT DOWN ALL SYSTEMS!!! SHUT DOWN ALL SYSTEMS BEFORE IT--

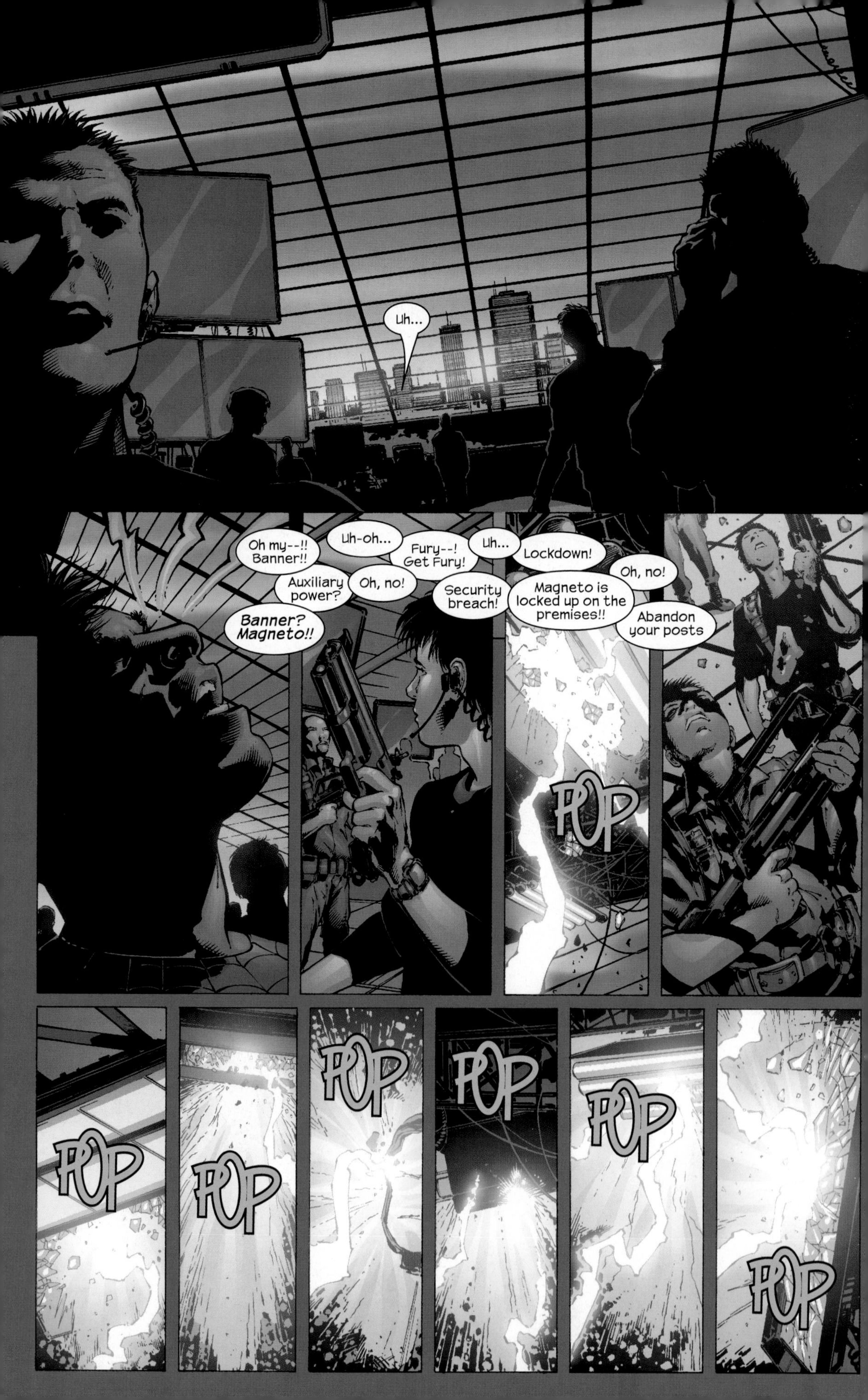
Uh...
Oh my--!! Banner!!
Uh-oh...
Fury--! Get Fury!
Uh...
Lockdown!
Auxiliary power?
Oh, no!
Banner? Magneto!!
Security breach!
Magneto is locked up on the premises!!
Oh, no!
Abandon your posts
POP
POP
POP
POP
POP
POP
POP

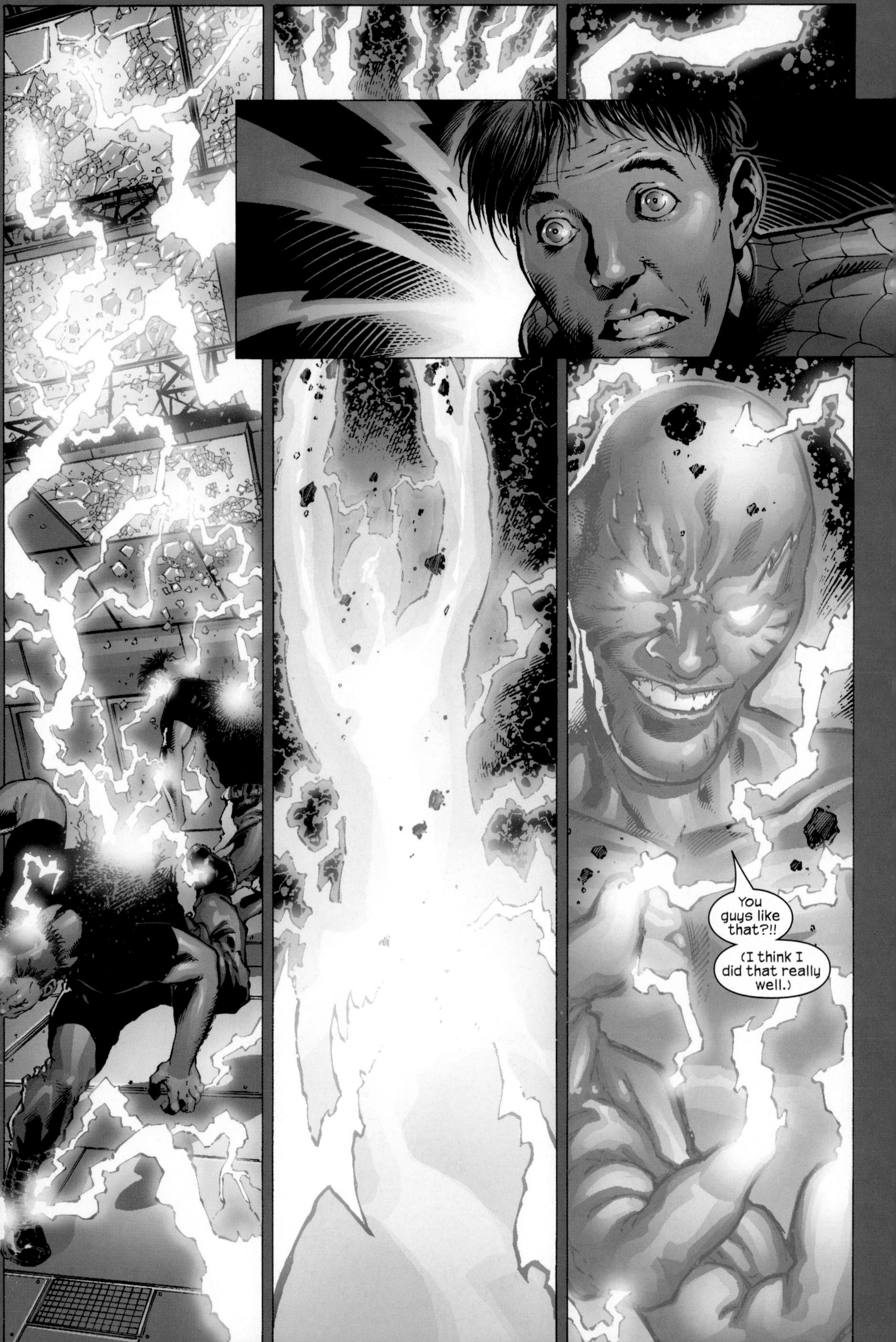
You guys like that?!!
(I think I did that really well.)

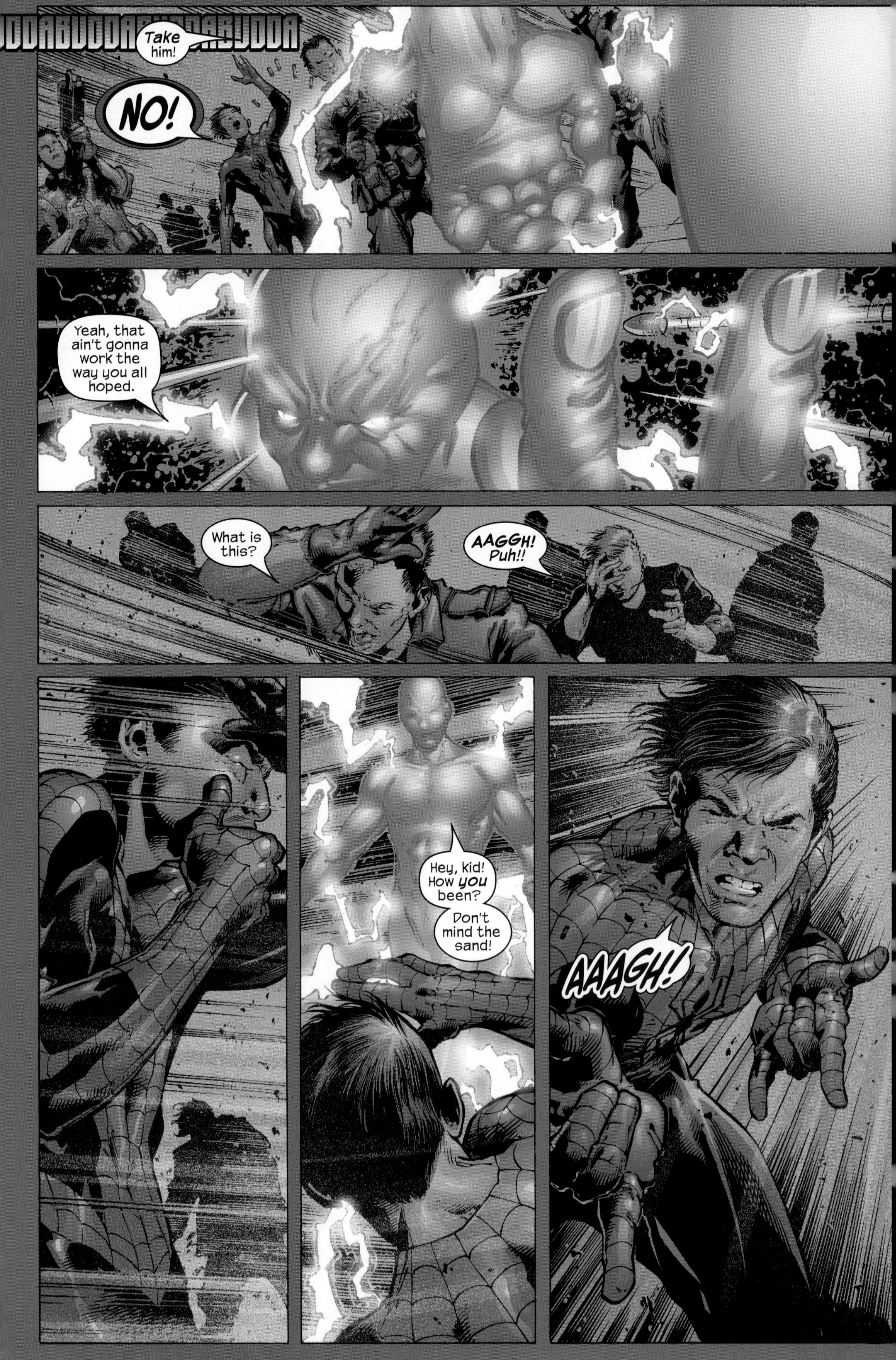
Take him!
NO!
Yeah, that ain't gonna work the way you all hoped.
What is this?
AAGGH! Puh!!
Hey, kid! How you been?
Don't mind the sand!
AAAGH!

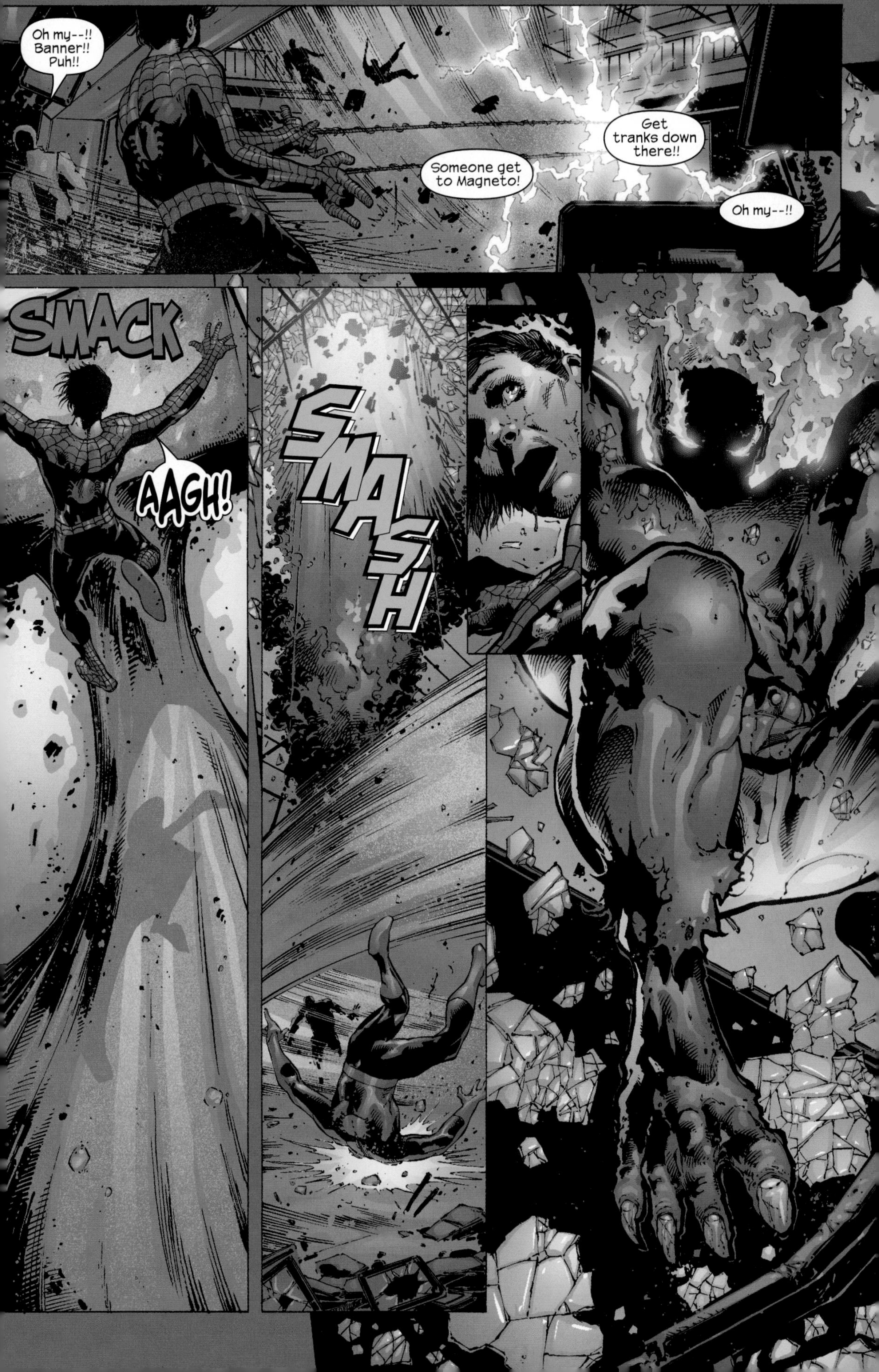

Oh my--!! Banner!! Puh!!
Someone get to Magneto!
Get tranks down there!!
Oh my--!!
SMACK
AAGH!
SMASH

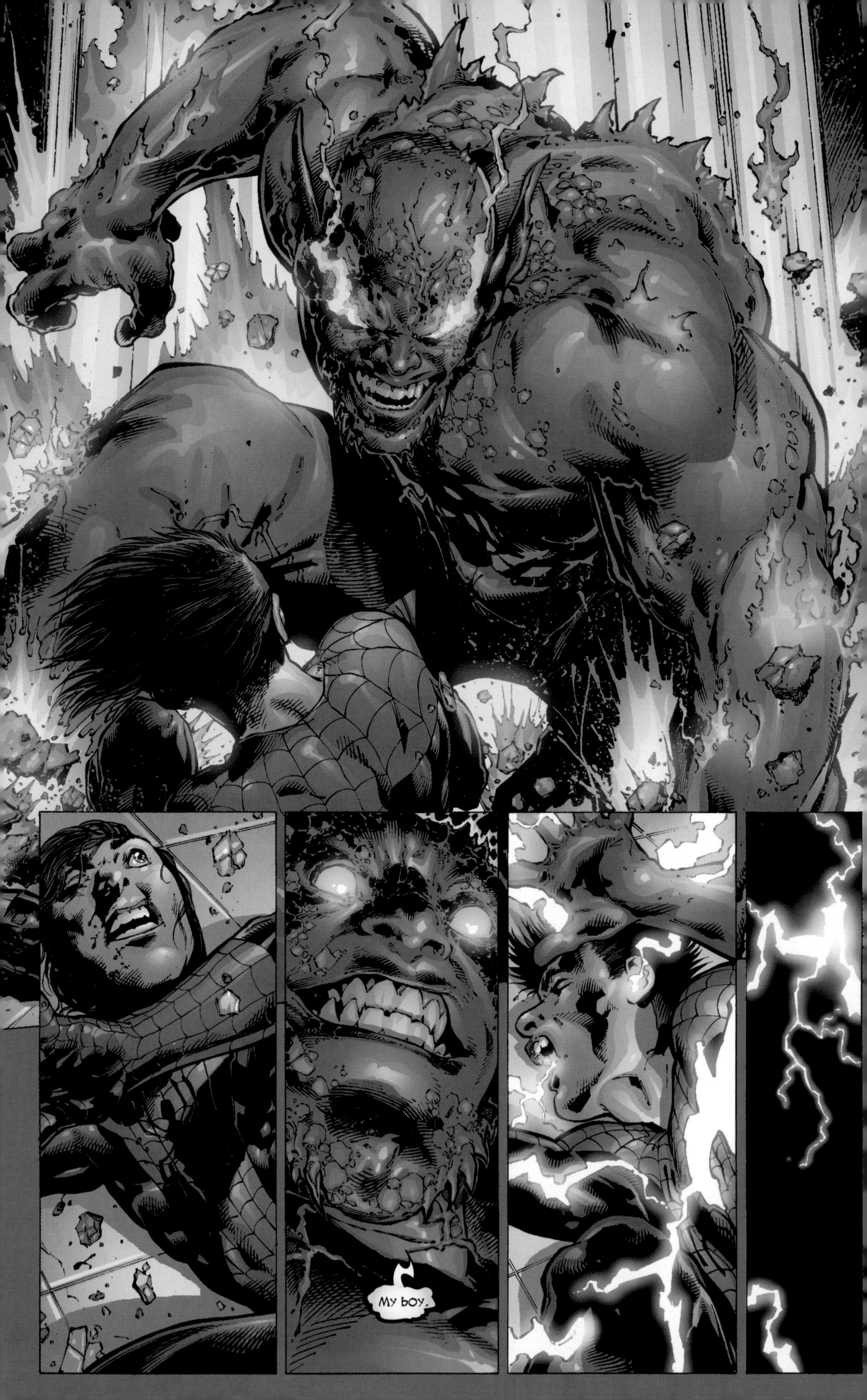
My boy.

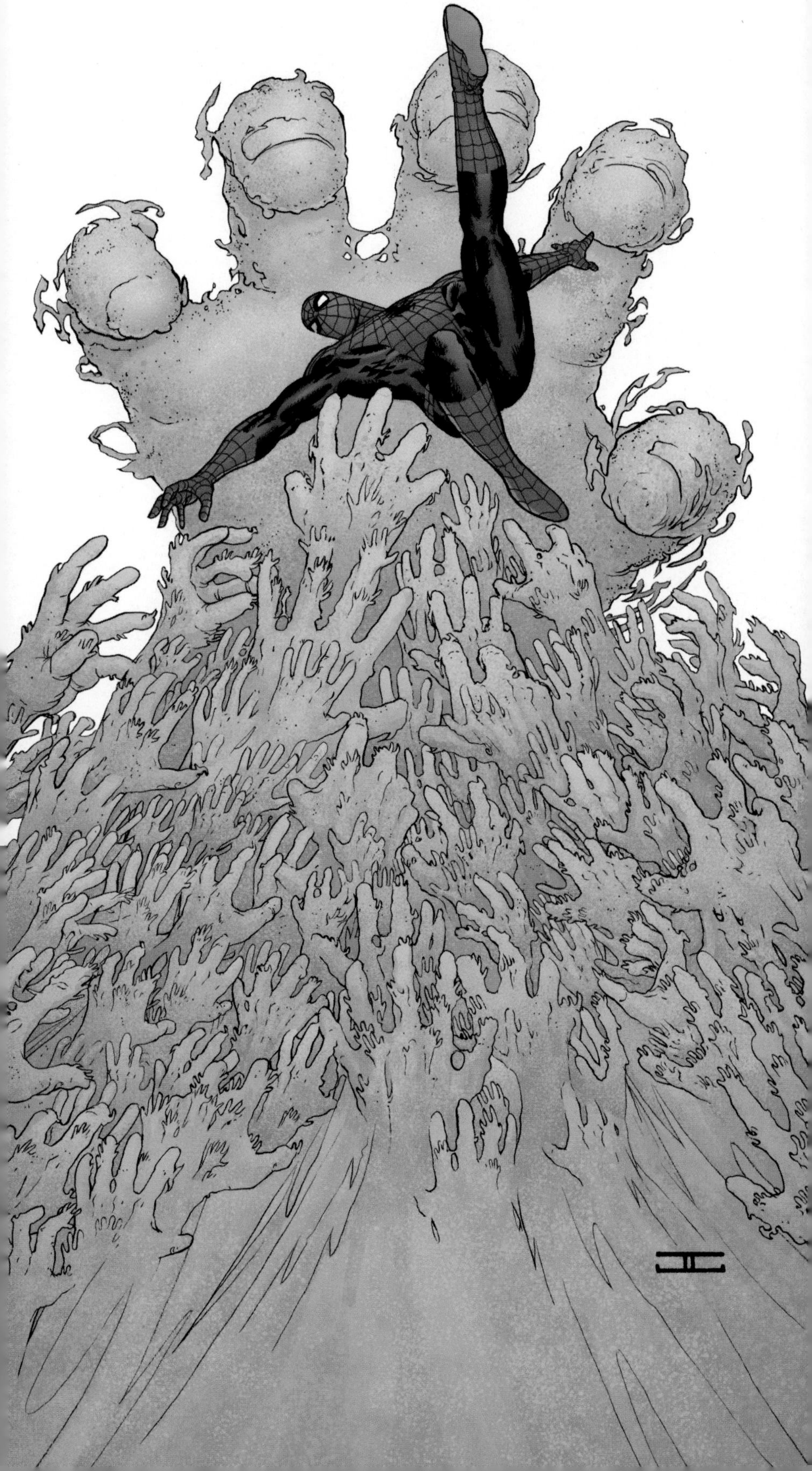

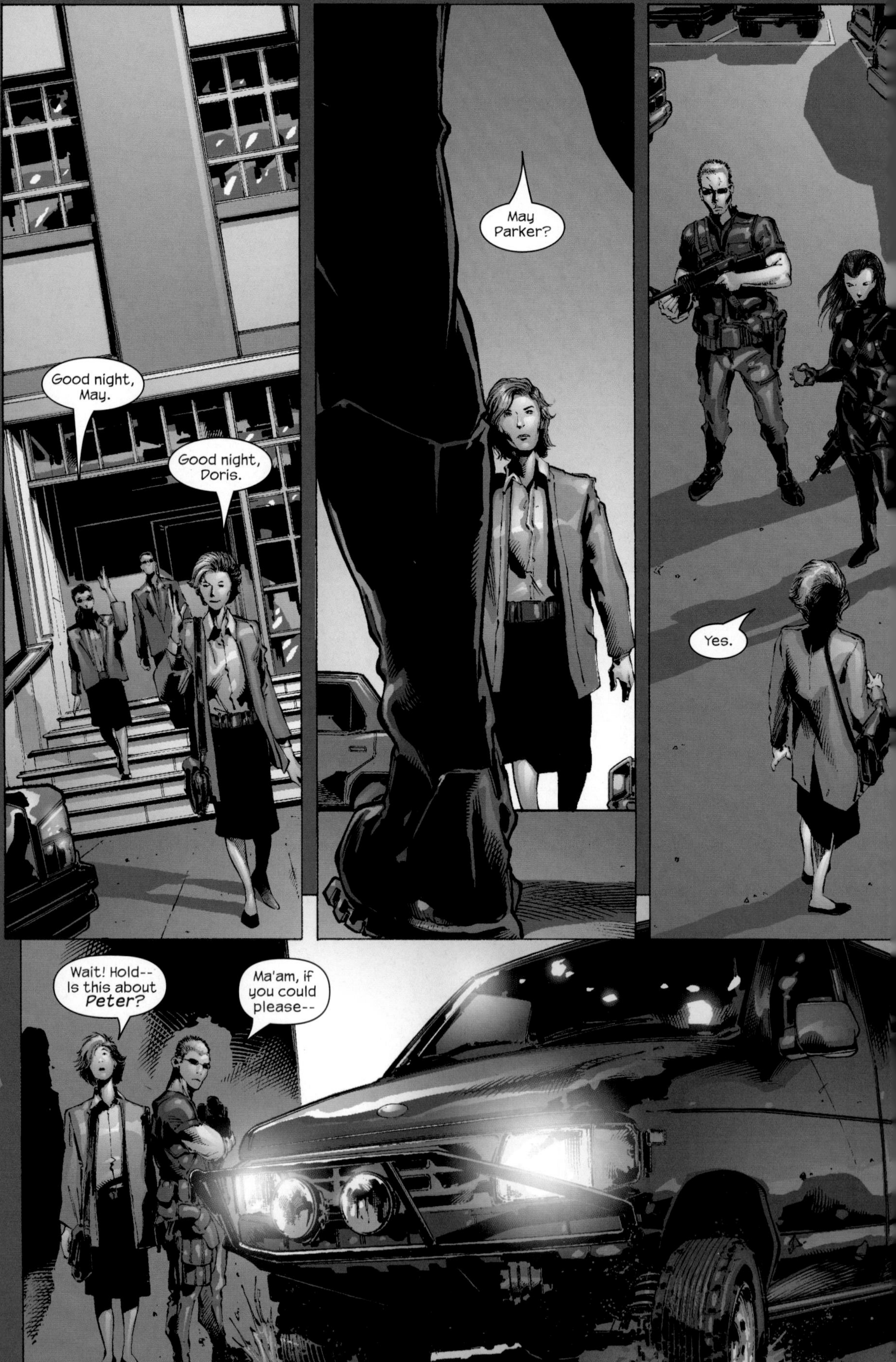
Good night, May.
Good night, Doris.
May Parker?
Yes.
Wait! Hold-- Is this about *Peter?*
Ma'am, if you could please--

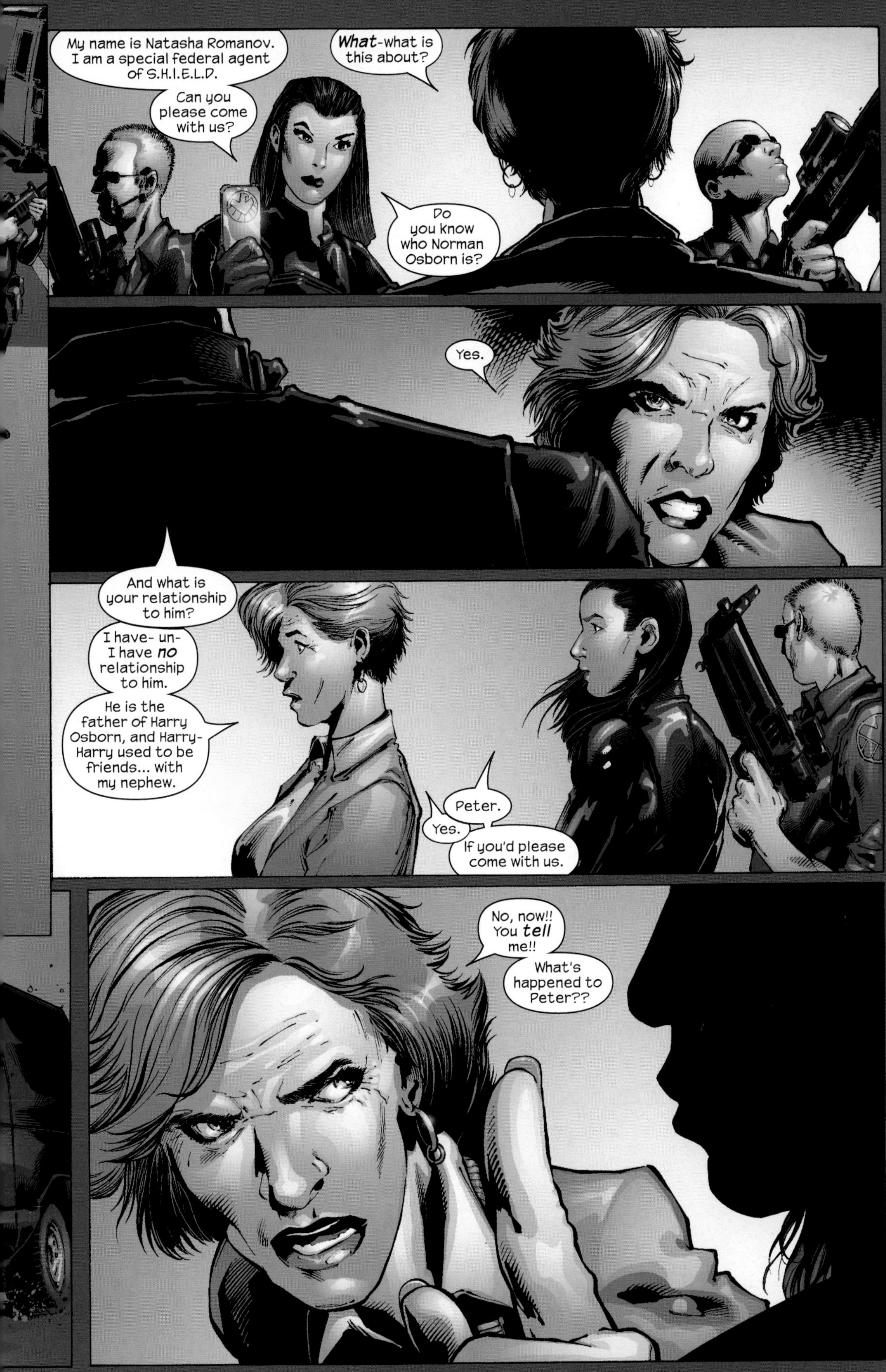
My name is Natasha Romanov. I am a special federal agent of S.H.I.E.L.D.
Can you please come with us?
What-what is this about?
Do you know who Norman Osborn is?
Yes.
And what is your relationship to him?
I have- un- I have *no* relationship to him.
He is the father of Harry Osborn, and Harry- Harry used to be friends... with my nephew.
Peter.
Yes.
If you'd please come with us.
No, now!! You *tell* me!!
What's happened to Peter??

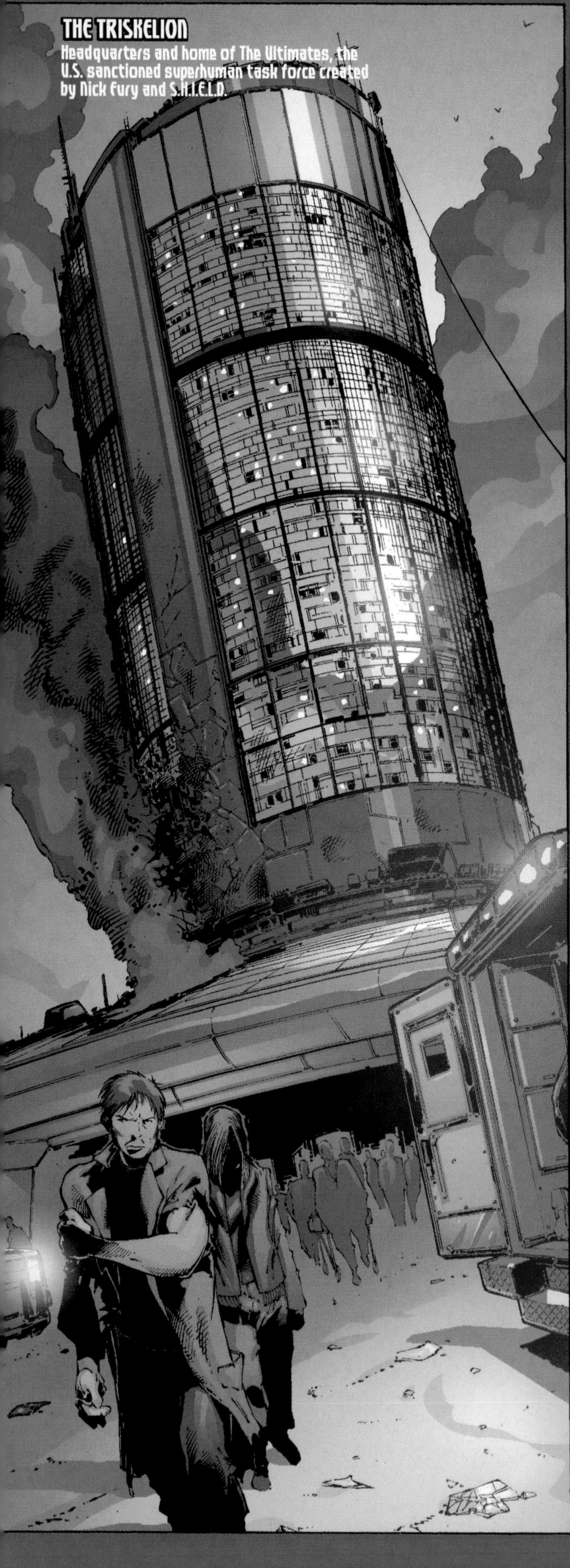
THE TRISKELION
Headquarters and home of The Ultimates, the U.S. sanctioned superhuman task force created by Nick Fury and S.H.I.E.L.D.

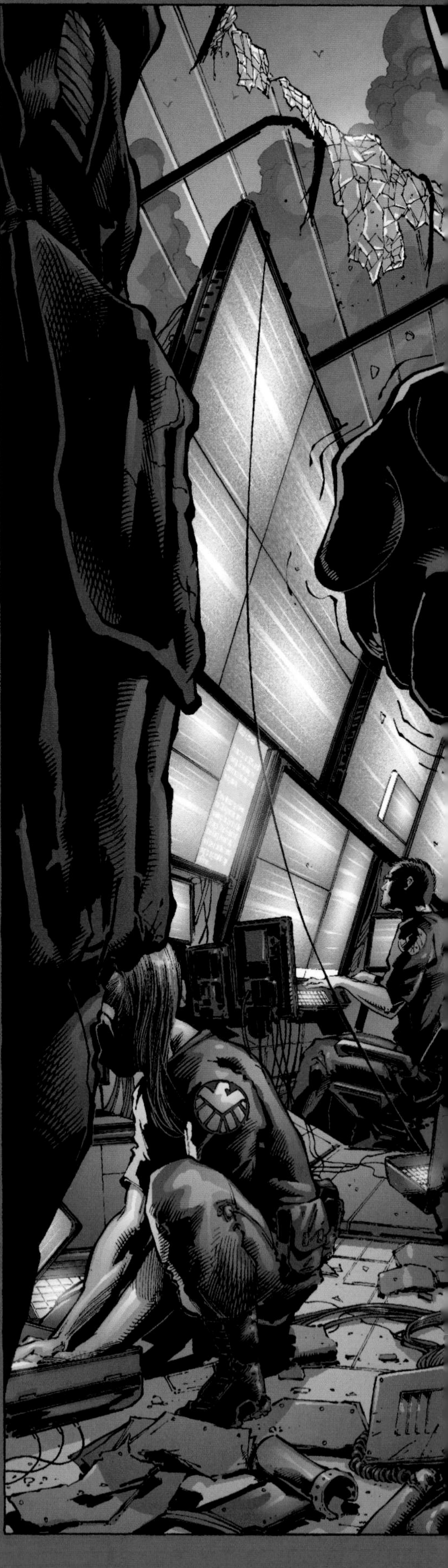

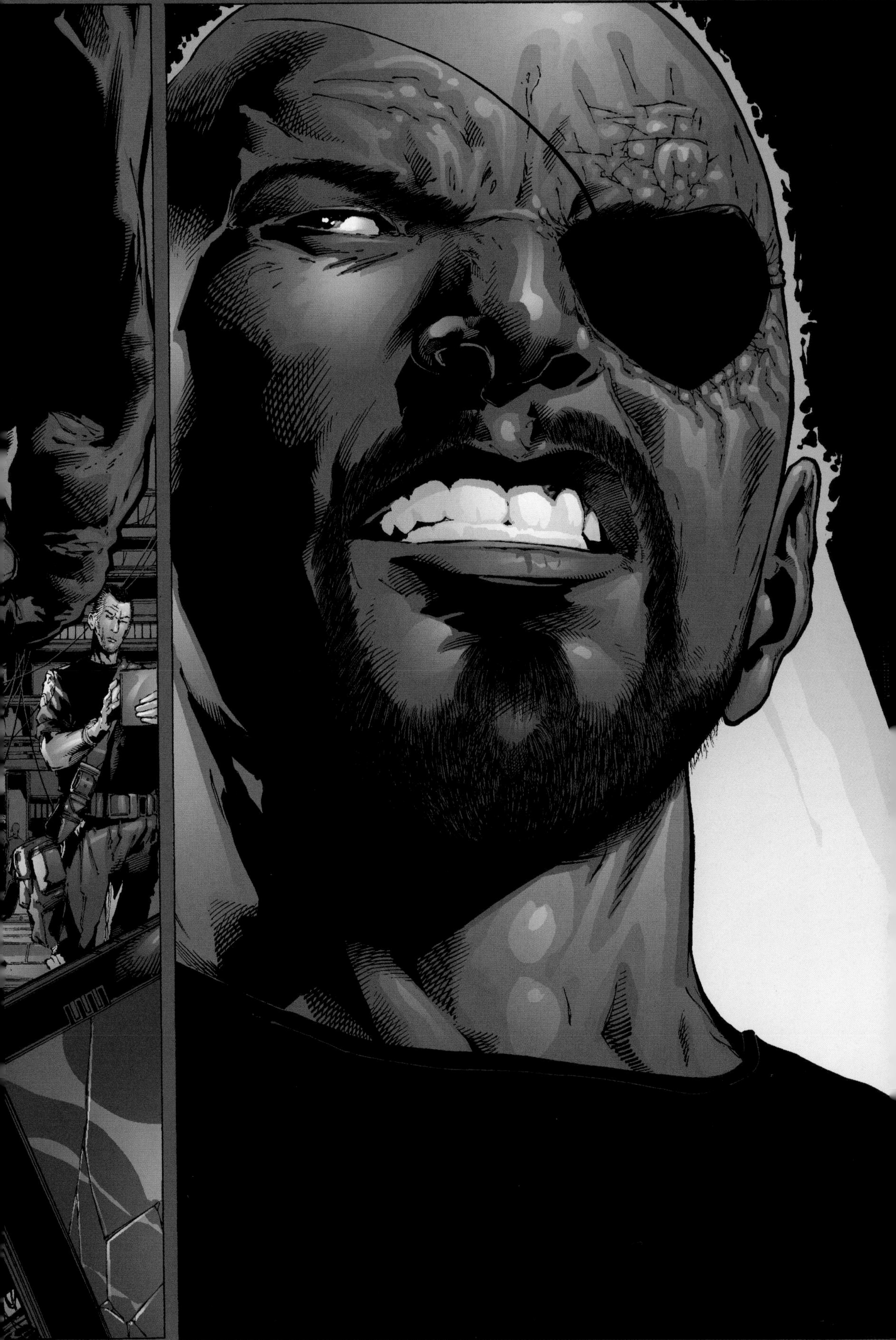

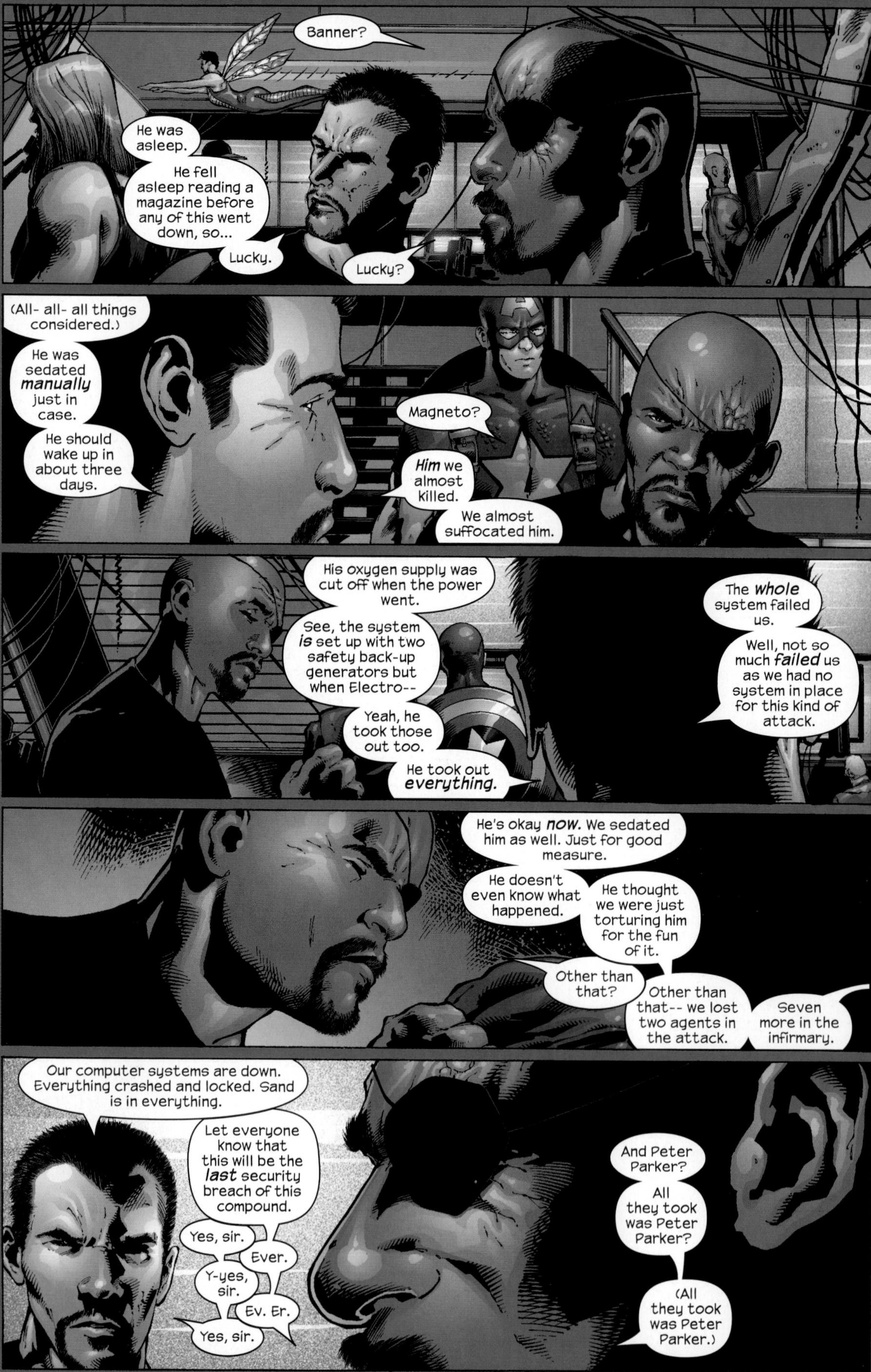
Banner?
He was asleep.
He fell asleep reading a magazine before any of this went down, so...
Lucky.
Lucky?
(All- all- all things considered.)
He was sedated manually just in case.
He should wake up in about three days.
Magneto?
Him we almost killed.
We almost suffocated him.
His oxygen supply was cut off when the power went.
See, the system is set up with two safety back-up generators but when Electro--
Yeah, he took those out too.
He took out everything.
The whole system failed us.
Well, not so much failed us as we had no system in place for this kind of attack.
He's okay now. We sedated him as well. Just for good measure.
He doesn't even know what happened.
He thought we were just torturing him for the fun of it.
Other than that?
Other than that-- we lost two agents in the attack.
Seven more in the infirmary.
Our computer systems are down. Everything crashed and locked. Sand is in everything.
Let everyone know that this will be the last security breach of this compound.
Yes, sir.
Ever.
Y-yes, sir.
Ev. Er.
Yes, sir.
And Peter Parker?
All they took was Peter Parker?
(All they took was Peter Parker.)

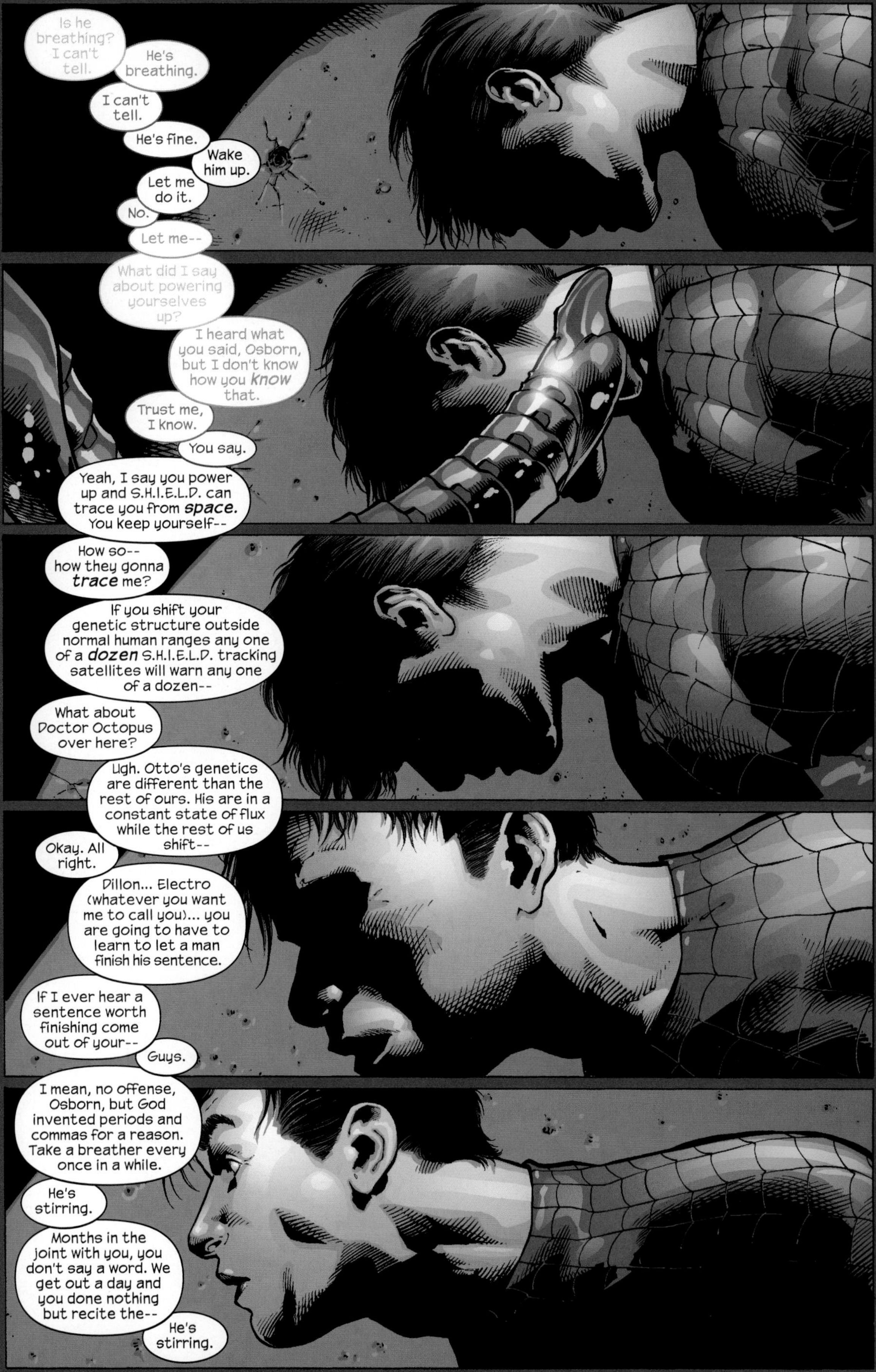
Is he breathing? I can't tell.
He's breathing.
I can't tell.
He's fine.
Wake him up.
Let me do it.
No.
Let me--
What did I say about powering yourselves up?
I heard what you said, Osborn, but I don't know how you know that.
Trust me, I know.
You say.
Yeah, I say you power up and S.H.I.E.L.D. can trace you from space. You keep yourself--
How so-- how they gonna trace me?
If you shift your genetic structure outside normal human ranges any one of a dozen S.H.I.E.L.D. tracking satellites will warn any one of a dozen--
What about Doctor Octopus over here?
Ugh. Otto's genetics are different than the rest of ours. His are in a constant state of flux while the rest of us shift--
Okay. All right.
Dillon... Electro (whatever you want me to call you)... you are going to have to learn to let a man finish his sentence.
If I ever hear a sentence worth finishing come out of your--
Guys.
I mean, no offense, Osborn, but God invented periods and commas for a reason. Take a breather every once in a while.
He's stirring.
Months in the joint with you, you don't say a word. We get out a day and you done nothing but recite the--
He's stirring.

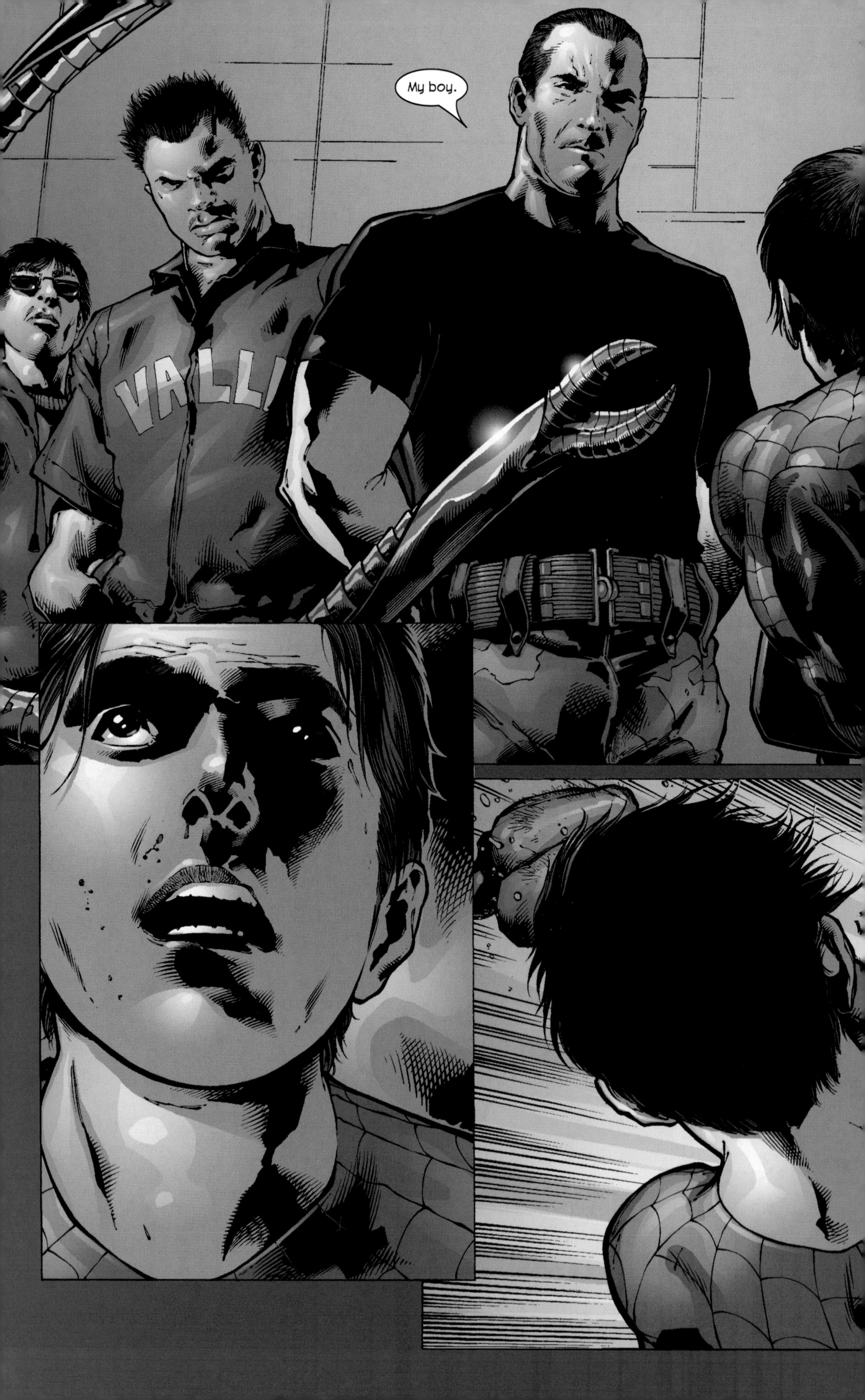
My boy.
VALLI

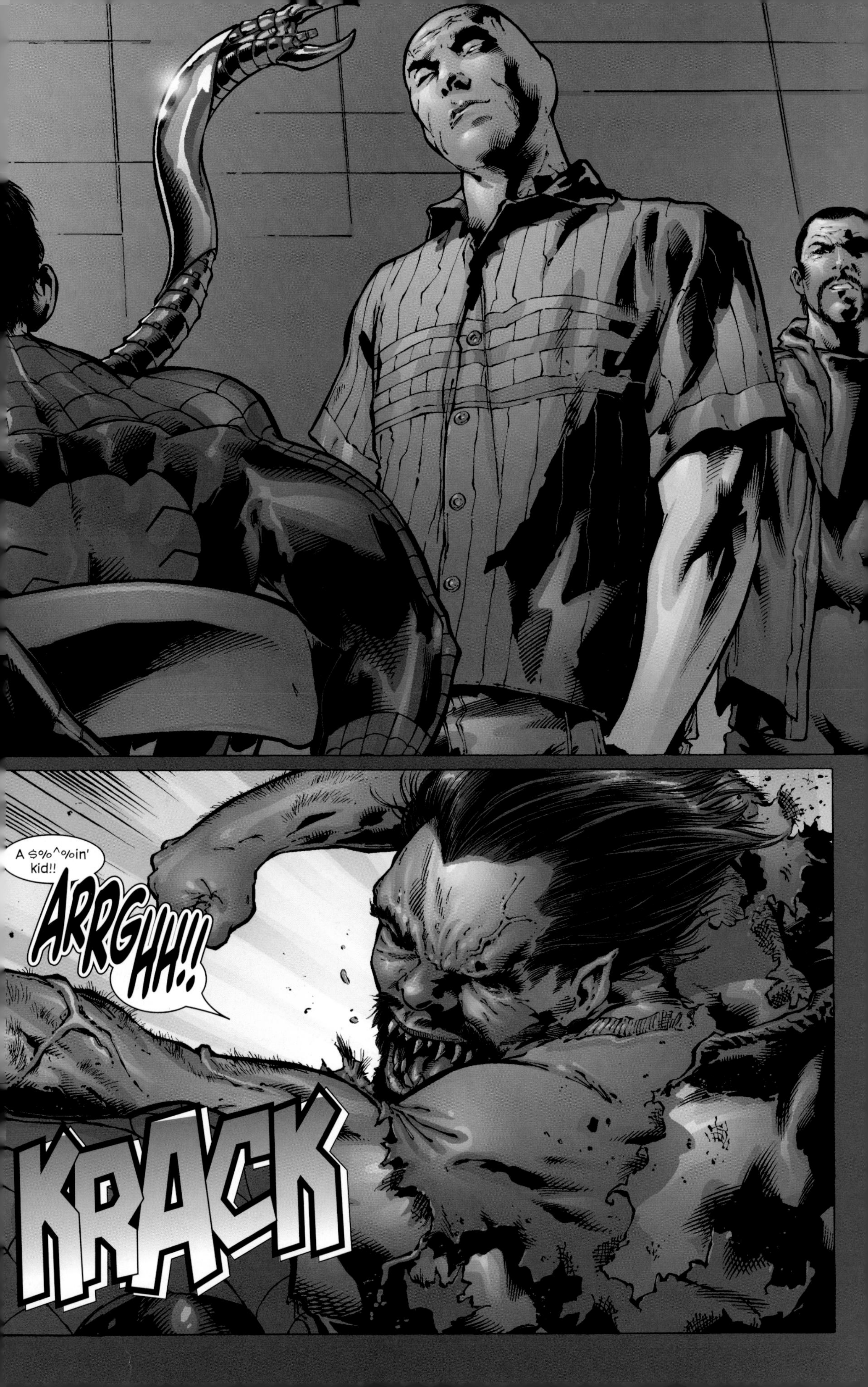
A $%^%in' kid!!
ARRGHH!!
KRACK

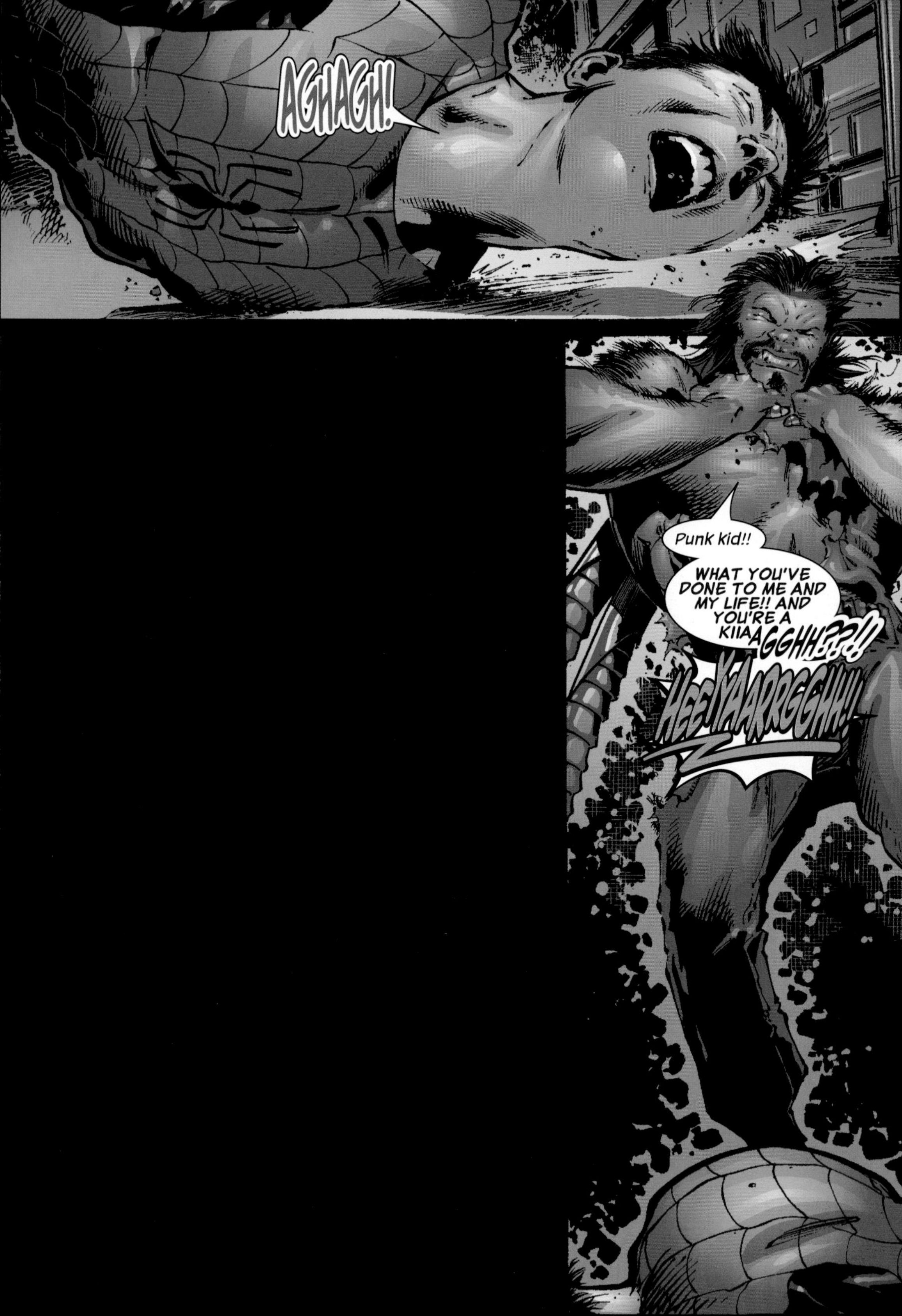
AGHAGH!
Punk kid!!
WHAT YOU'VE DONE TO ME AND MY LIFE!! AND YOU'RE A KIIAAGGHH!?!!
HEEYAARRGGHH!!

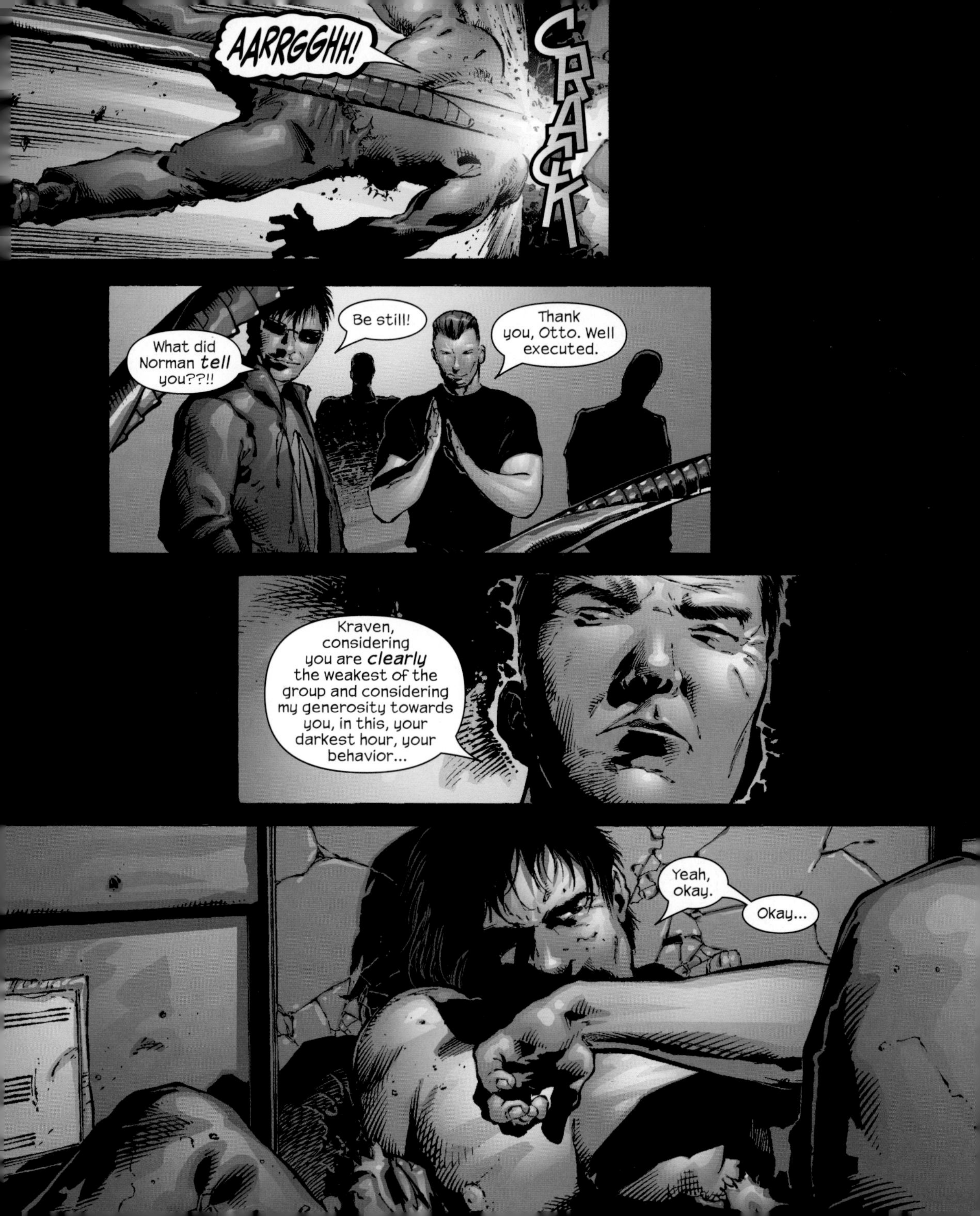
AARRGGHH!
CRACK
What did Norman tell you??!!
Be still!
Thank you, Otto. Well executed.
Kraven, considering you are clearly the weakest of the group and considering my generosity towards you, in this, your darkest hour, your behavior...
Yeah, okay.
Okay...

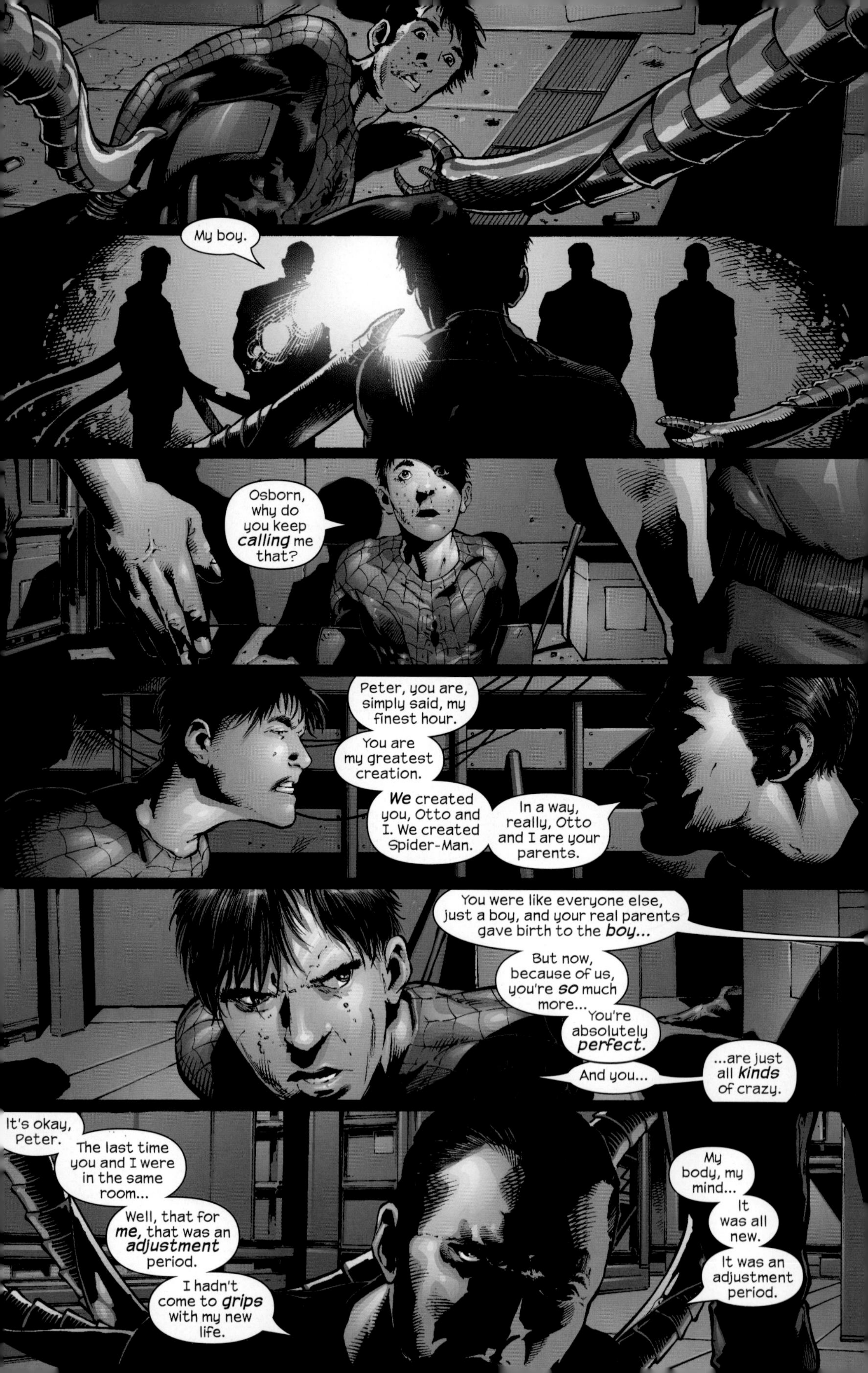
My boy.
Osborn, why do you keep *calling* me that?
Peter, you are, simply said, my finest hour.
You are my greatest creation.
We created you, Otto and I. We created Spider-Man.
In a way, really, Otto and I are your parents.
You were like everyone else, just a boy, and your real parents gave birth to the *boy...*
But now, because of us, you're *so* much more...
You're absolutely *perfect.*
And you...
...are just all *kinds* of crazy.
It's okay, Peter.
The last time you and I were in the same room...
Well, that for *me,* that was an *adjustment* period.
I hadn't come to *grips* with my new life.
My body, my mind...
It was all new.
It was an adjustment period.

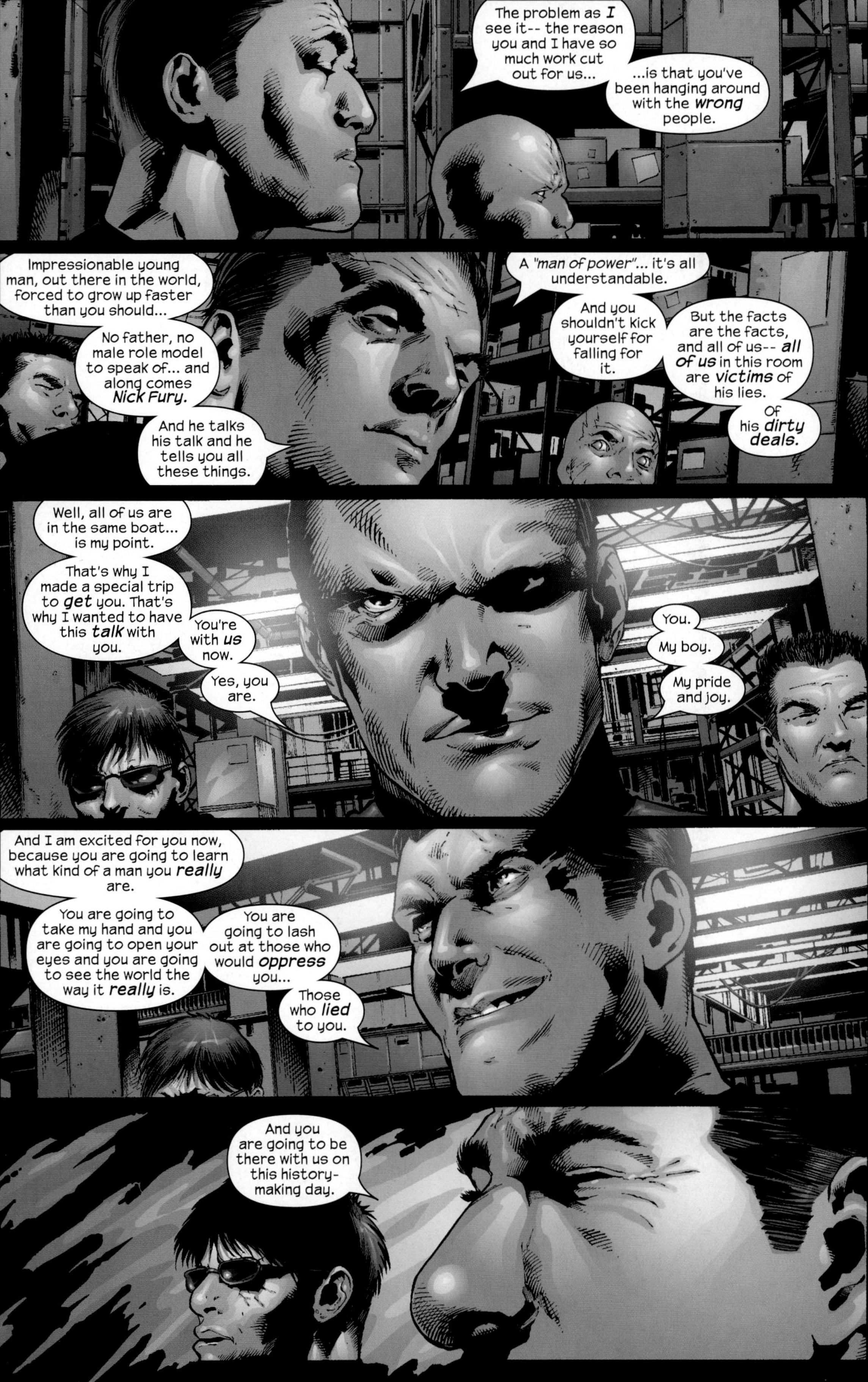
The problem as I see it-- the reason you and I have so much work cut out for us...
...is that you've been hanging around with the wrong people.
Impressionable young man, out there in the world, forced to grow up faster than you should...
No father, no male role model to speak of... and along comes Nick Fury.
And he talks his talk and he tells you all these things.
A "man of power"... it's all understandable.
And you shouldn't kick yourself for falling for it.
But the facts are the facts, and all of us-- all of us in this room are victims of his lies.
Of his dirty deals.
Well, all of us are in the same boat... is my point.
That's why I made a special trip to get you. That's why I wanted to have this talk with you.
You're with us now.
Yes, you are.
You.
My boy.
My pride and joy.
And I am excited for you now, because you are going to learn what kind of a man you really are.
You are going to take my hand and you are going to open your eyes and you are going to see the world the way it really is.
You are going to lash out at those who would oppress you...
Those who lied to you.
And you are going to be there with us on this history-making day.

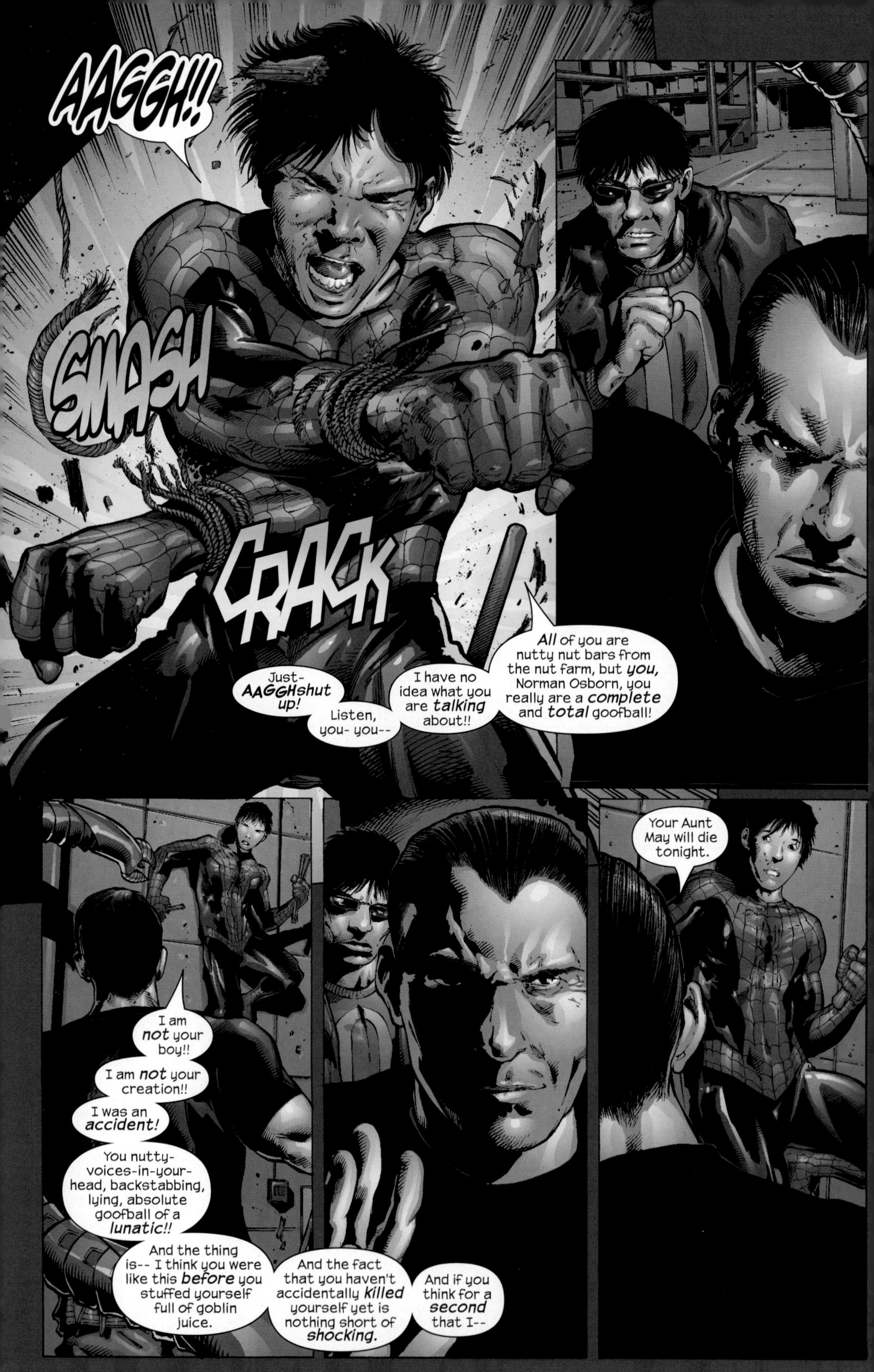
AAGGH!!
SMASH
CRACK
Just- AAGGHshut up!
Listen, you- you--
I have no idea what you are talking about!!
All of you are nutty nut bars from the nut farm, but you, Norman Osborn, you really are a complete and total goofball!
I am not your boy!!
I am not your creation!!
I was an accident!
You nutty-voices-in-your-head, backstabbing, lying, absolute goofball of a lunatic!!
And the thing is-- I think you were like this before you stuffed yourself full of goblin juice.
And the fact that you haven't accidentally killed yourself yet is nothing short of shocking.
And if you think for a second that I--
Your Aunt May will die tonight.

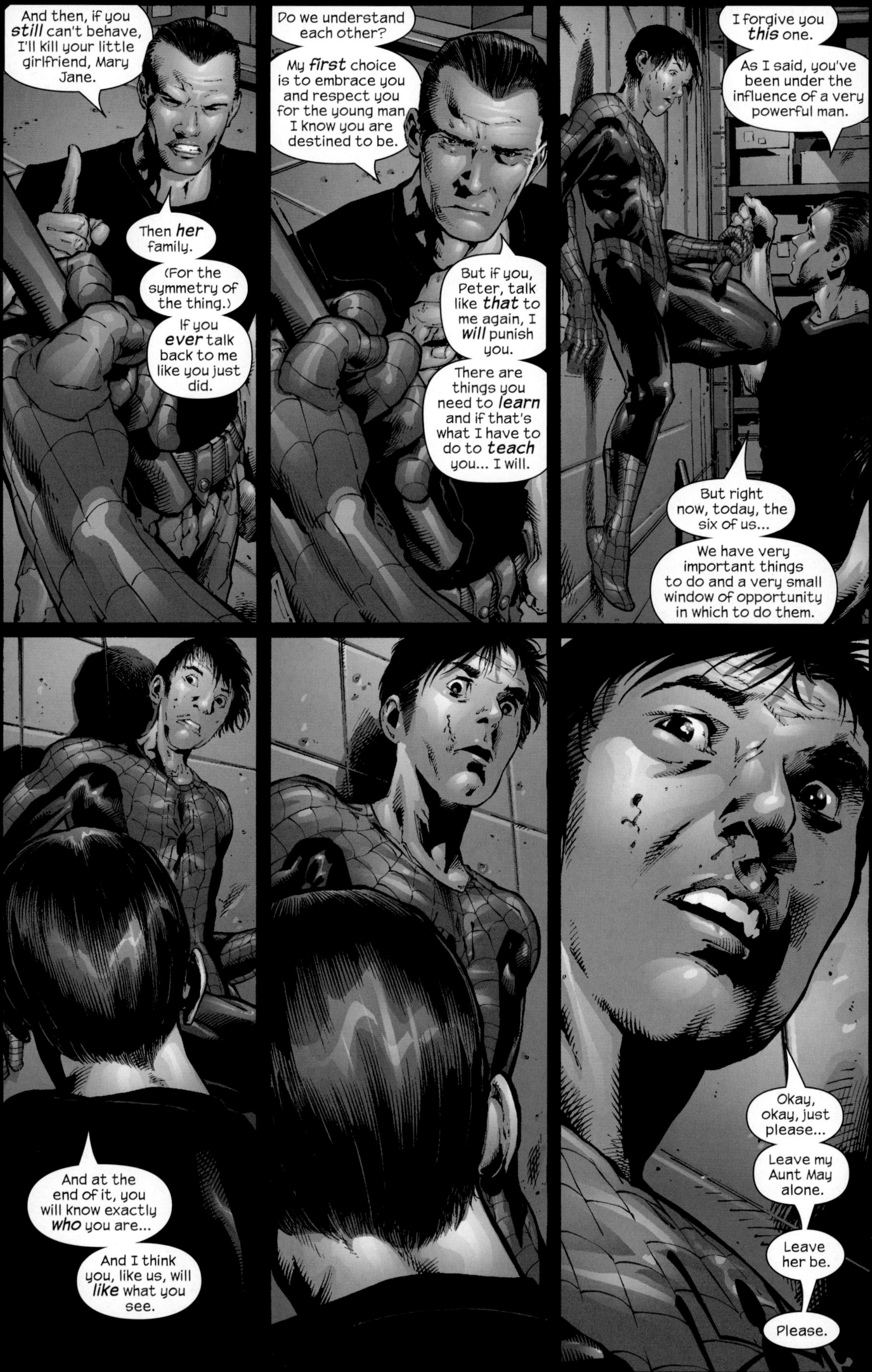
And then, if you still can't behave, I'll kill your little girlfriend, Mary Jane.
Then her family.
(For the symmetry of the thing.)
If you ever talk back to me like you just did.
Do we understand each other?
My first choice is to embrace you and respect you for the young man I know you are destined to be.
But if you, Peter, talk like that to me again, I will punish you.
There are things you need to learn and if that's what I have to do to teach you... I will.
I forgive you this one.
As I said, you've been under the influence of a very powerful man.
But right now, today, the six of us...
We have very important things to do and a very small window of opportunity in which to do them.
And at the end of it, you will know exactly who you are...
And I think you, like us, will like what you see.
Okay, okay, just please...
Leave my Aunt May alone.
Leave her be.
Please.

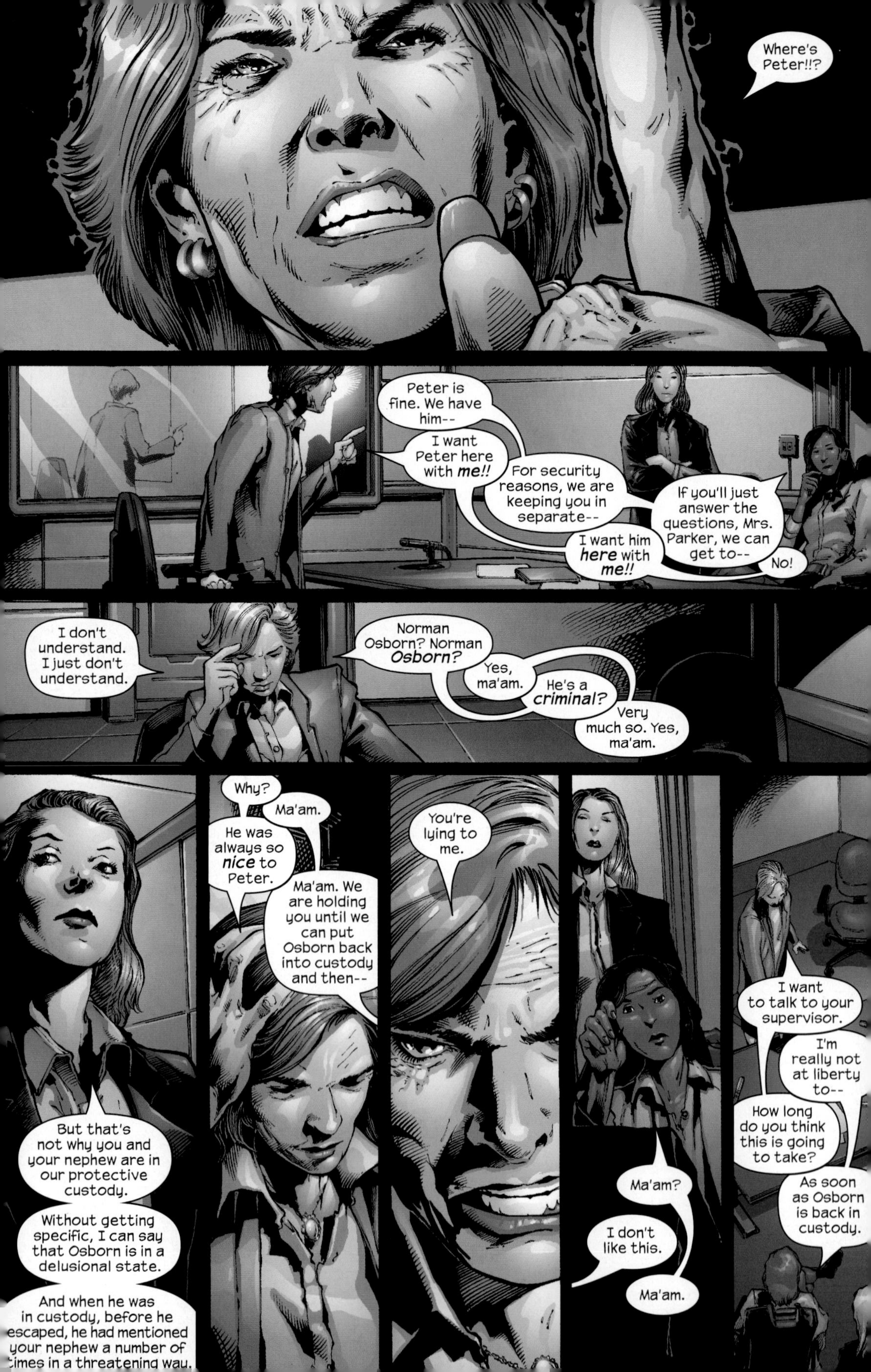

Where's Peter!!?
Peter is fine. We have him--
I want Peter here with *me!!*
For security reasons, we are keeping you in separate--
I want him *here* with *me!!*
If you'll just answer the questions, Mrs. Parker, we can get to--
No!
I don't understand. I just don't understand.
Norman Osborn? Norman *Osborn?*
Yes, ma'am.
He's a *criminal?*
Very much so. Yes, ma'am.
But that's not why you and your nephew are in our protective custody.
Without getting specific, I can say that Osborn is in a delusional state.
And when he was in custody, before he escaped, he had mentioned your nephew a number of times in a threatening way.
Why?
Ma'am.
He was always so *nice* to Peter.
Ma'am. We are holding you until we can put Osborn back into custody and then--
You're lying to me.
Ma'am?
I don't like this.
Ma'am.
I want to talk to your supervisor.
I'm really not at liberty to--
How long do you think this is going to take?
As soon as Osborn is back in custody.

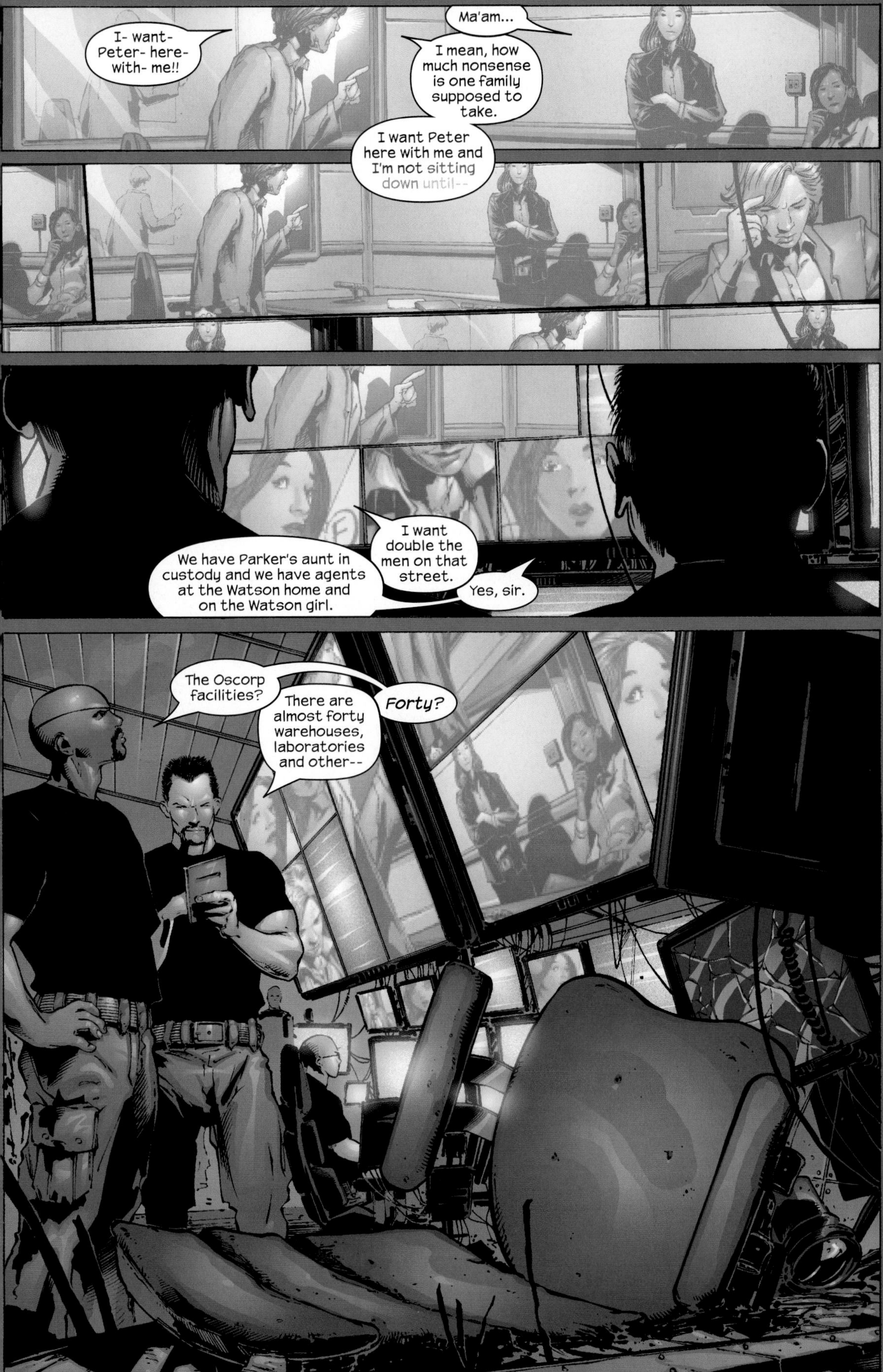
I- want- Peter- here- with- me!!
Ma'am...
I mean, how much nonsense is one family supposed to take.
I want Peter here with me and I'm not sitting down until--
I want double the men on that street.
We have Parker's aunt in custody and we have agents at the Watson home and on the Watson girl.
Yes, sir.
The Oscorp facilities?
Forty?
There are almost forty warehouses, laboratories and other--

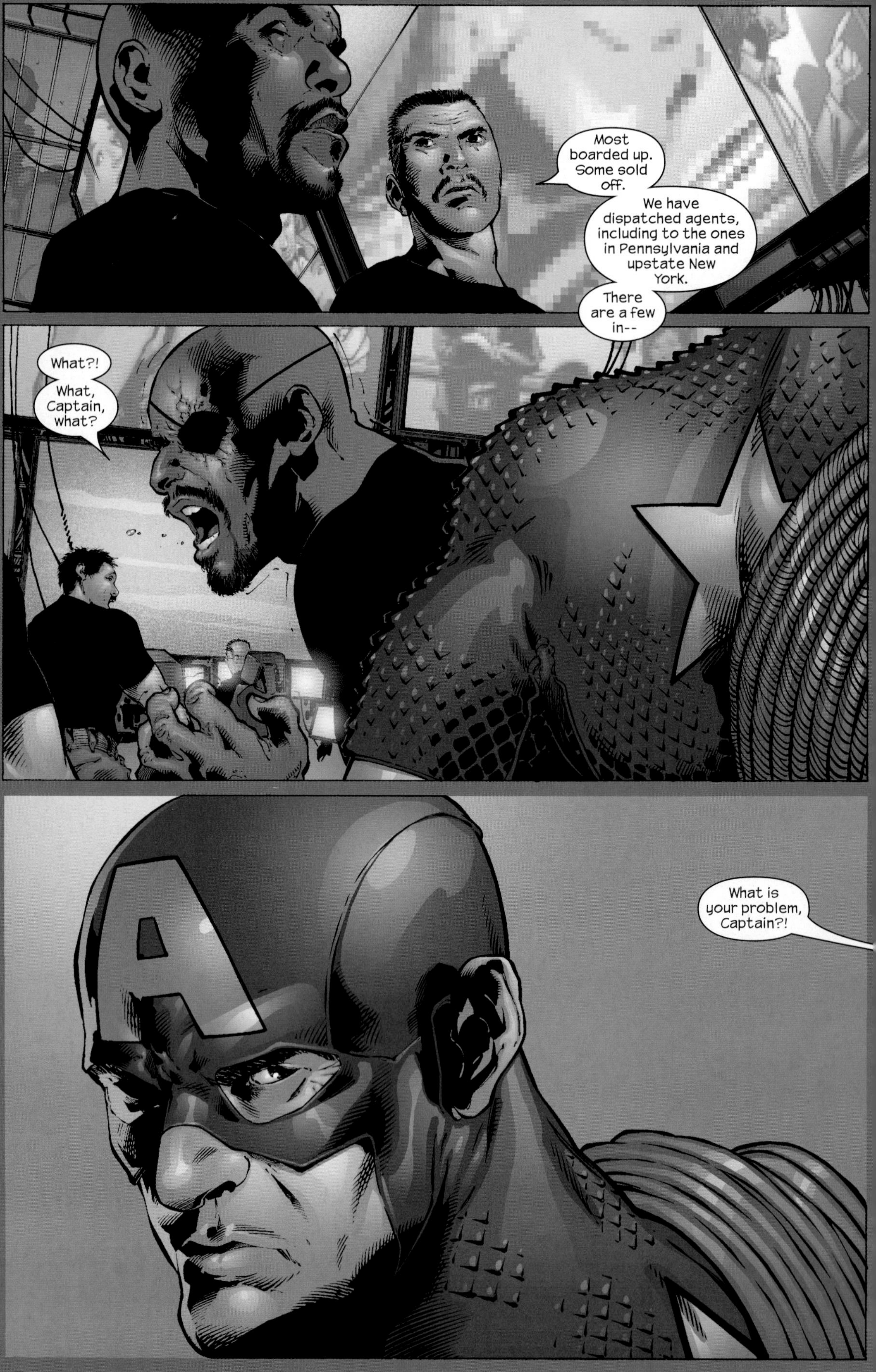

Most boarded up. Some sold off.
We have dispatched agents, including to the ones in Pennsylvania and upstate New York.
There are a few in--
What?!
What, Captain, what?
What is your problem, Captain?!

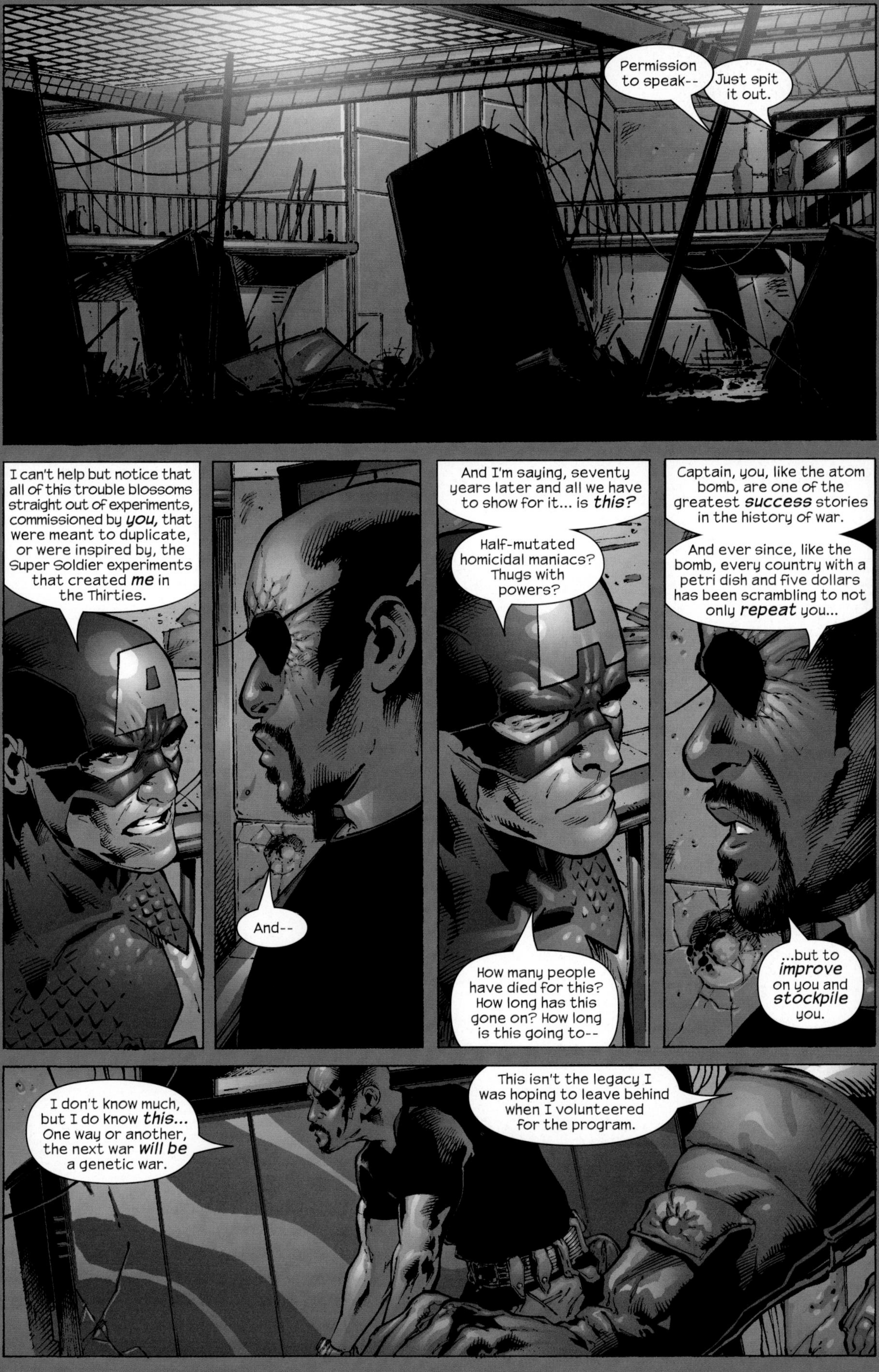
Permission to speak--
Just spit it out.
I can't help but notice that all of this trouble blossoms straight out of experiments, commissioned by *you,* that were meant to duplicate, or were inspired by, the Super Soldier experiments that created *me* in the Thirties.
And--
And I'm saying, seventy years later and all we have to show for it... is *this?*
Half-mutated homicidal maniacs? Thugs with powers?
How many people have died for this? How long has this gone on? How long is this going to--
Captain, you, like the atom bomb, are one of the greatest *success* stories in the history of war.
And ever since, like the bomb, every country with a petri dish and five dollars has been scrambling to not only *repeat* you...
...but to *improve* on you and *stockpile* you.
I don't know much, but I do know *this...* One way or another, the next war *will be* a genetic war.
This isn't the legacy I was hoping to leave behind when I volunteered for the program.

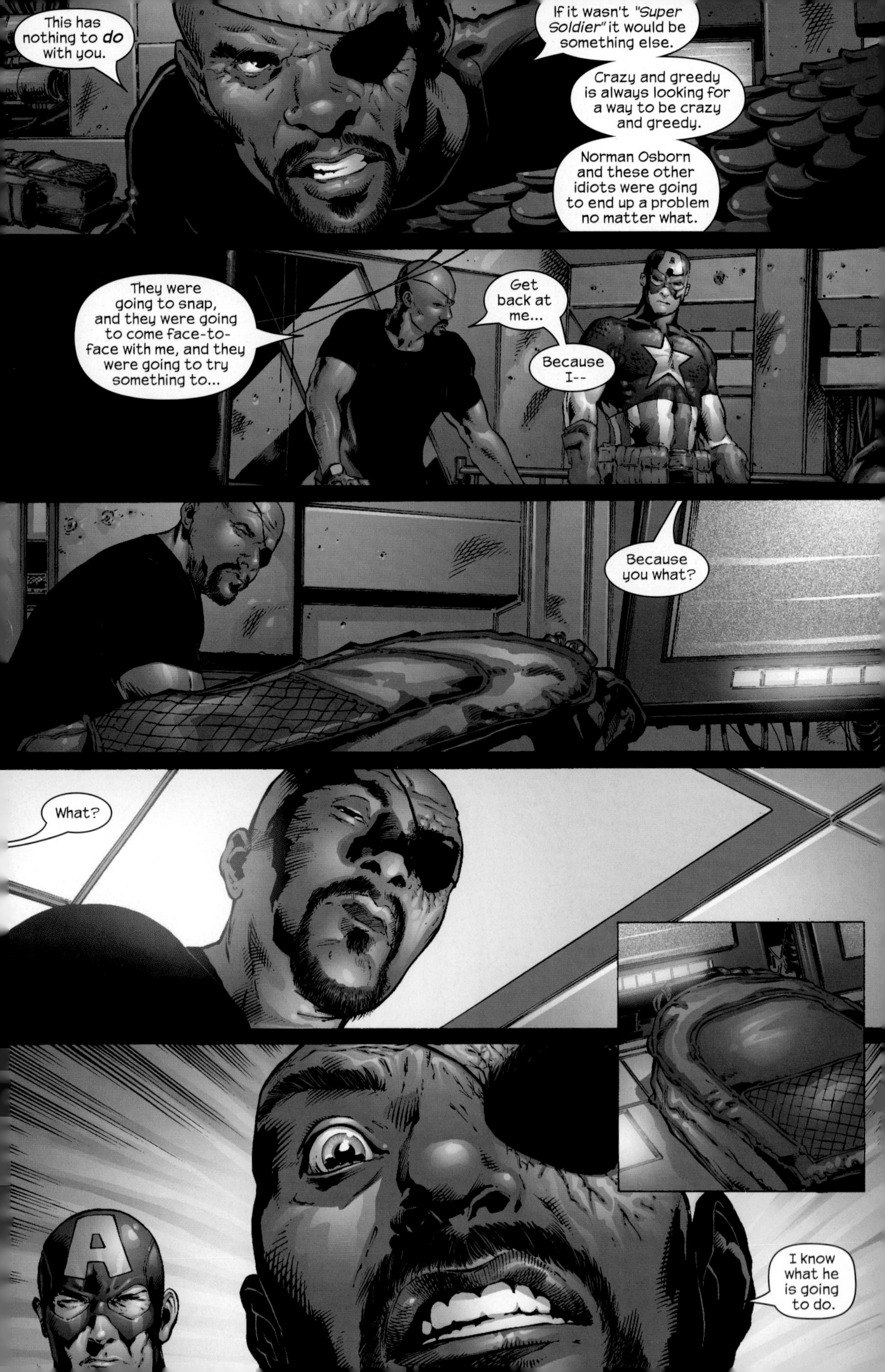
This has nothing to *do* with you.
If it wasn't *"Super Soldier"* it would be something else.
Crazy and greedy is always looking for a way to be crazy and greedy.
Norman Osborn and these other idiots were going to end up a problem no matter what.
They were going to snap, and they were going to come face-to-face with me, and they were going to try something to...
Get back at me...
Because I--
Because you what?
What?
I know what he is going to do.

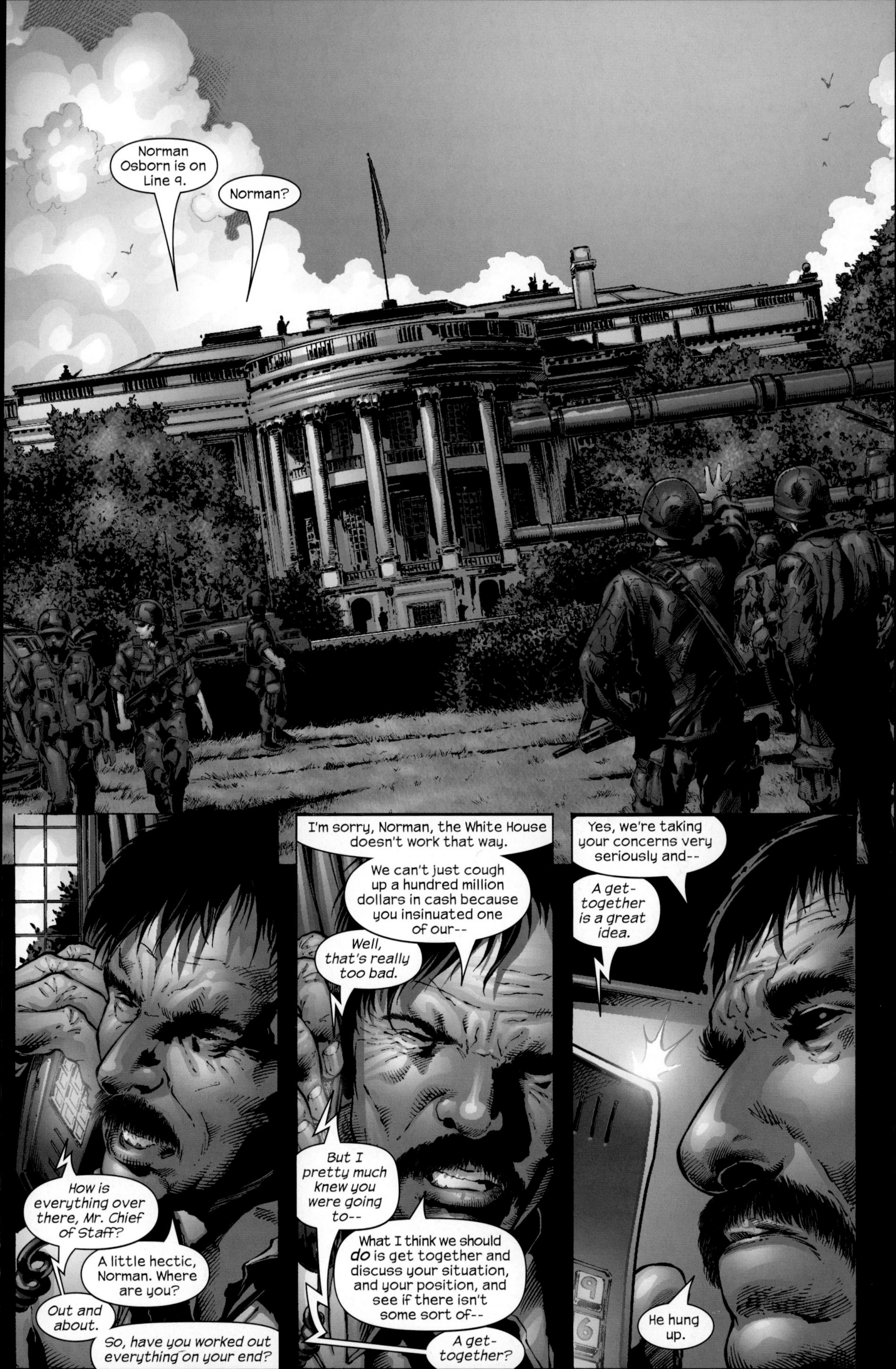

Norman Osborn is on Line 9.
Norman?
How is everything over there, Mr. Chief of Staff?
A little hectic, Norman. Where are you?
Out and about.
So, have you worked out everything on your end?
I'm sorry, Norman, the White House doesn't work that way.
We can't just cough up a hundred million dollars in cash because you insinuated one of our--
Well, that's really too bad.
But I pretty much knew you were going to--
What I think we should **do** is get together and discuss your situation, and your position, and see if there isn't some sort of--
A get-together?
Yes, we're taking your concerns very seriously and--
A get-together is a great idea.
He hung up.

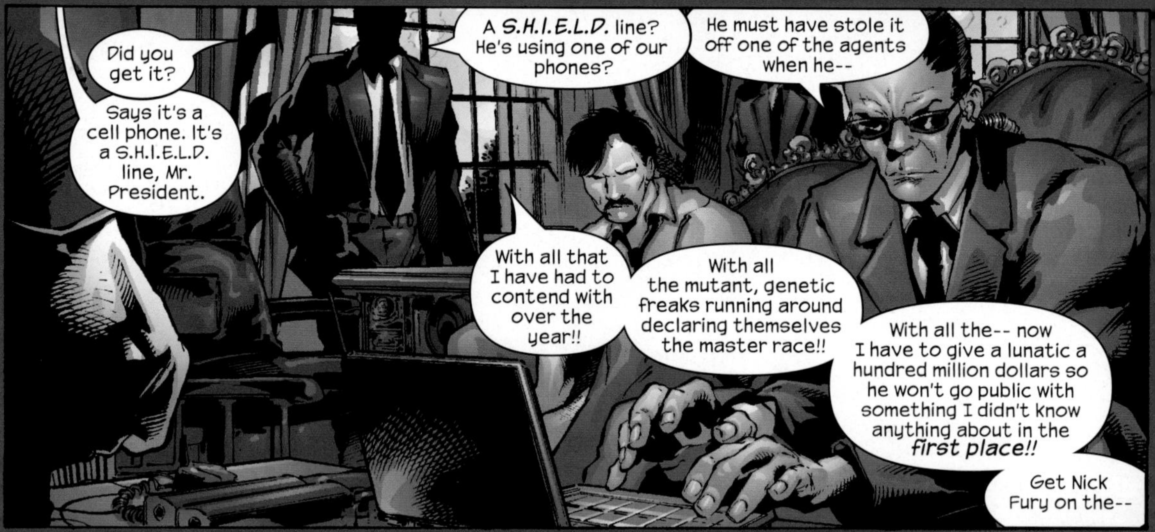
Did you get it?
Says it's a cell phone. It's a S.H.I.E.L.D. line, Mr. President.
A S.H.I.E.L.D. line? He's using one of our phones?
He must have stole it off one of the agents when he--
With all that I have had to contend with over the year!!
With all the mutant, genetic freaks running around declaring themselves the master race!!
With all the-- now I have to give a lunatic a hundred million dollars so he won't go public with something I didn't know anything about in the first place!!
Get Nick Fury on the--

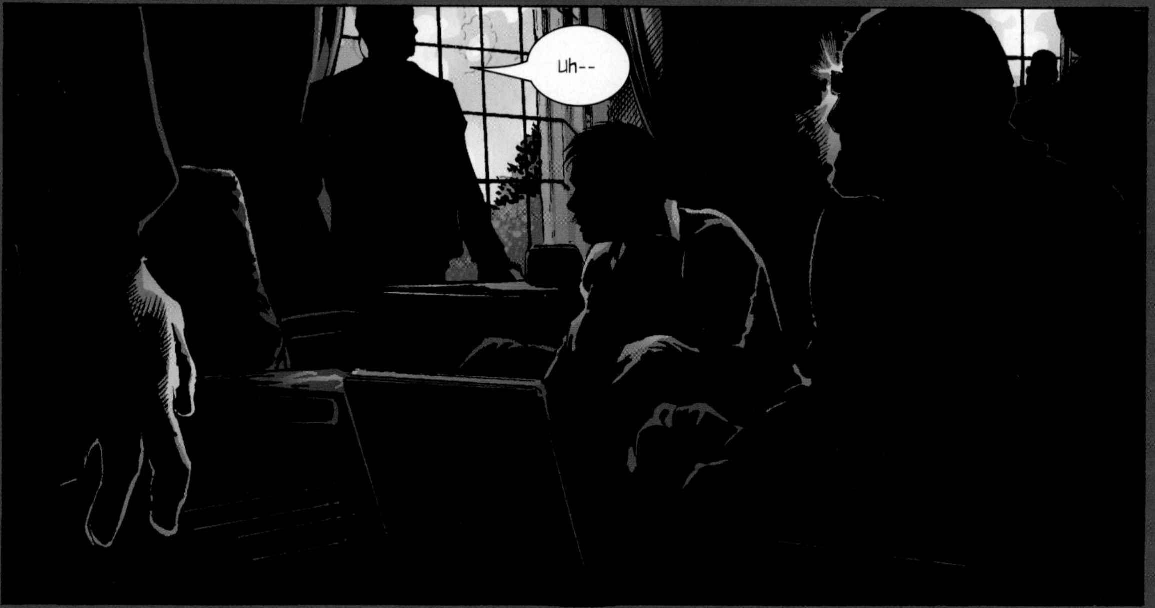
Uh--

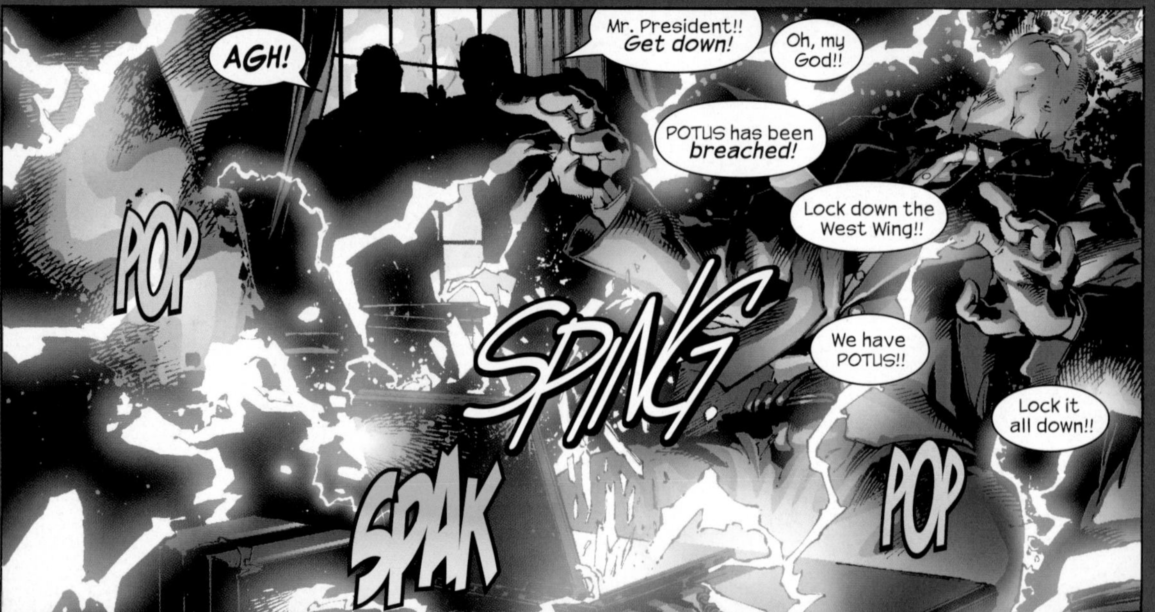
AGH!
Mr. President!! Get down!
Oh, my God!!
POTUS has been breached!
Lock down the West Wing!!
POP
SPING
We have POTUS!!
Lock it all down!!
SPAK
POP

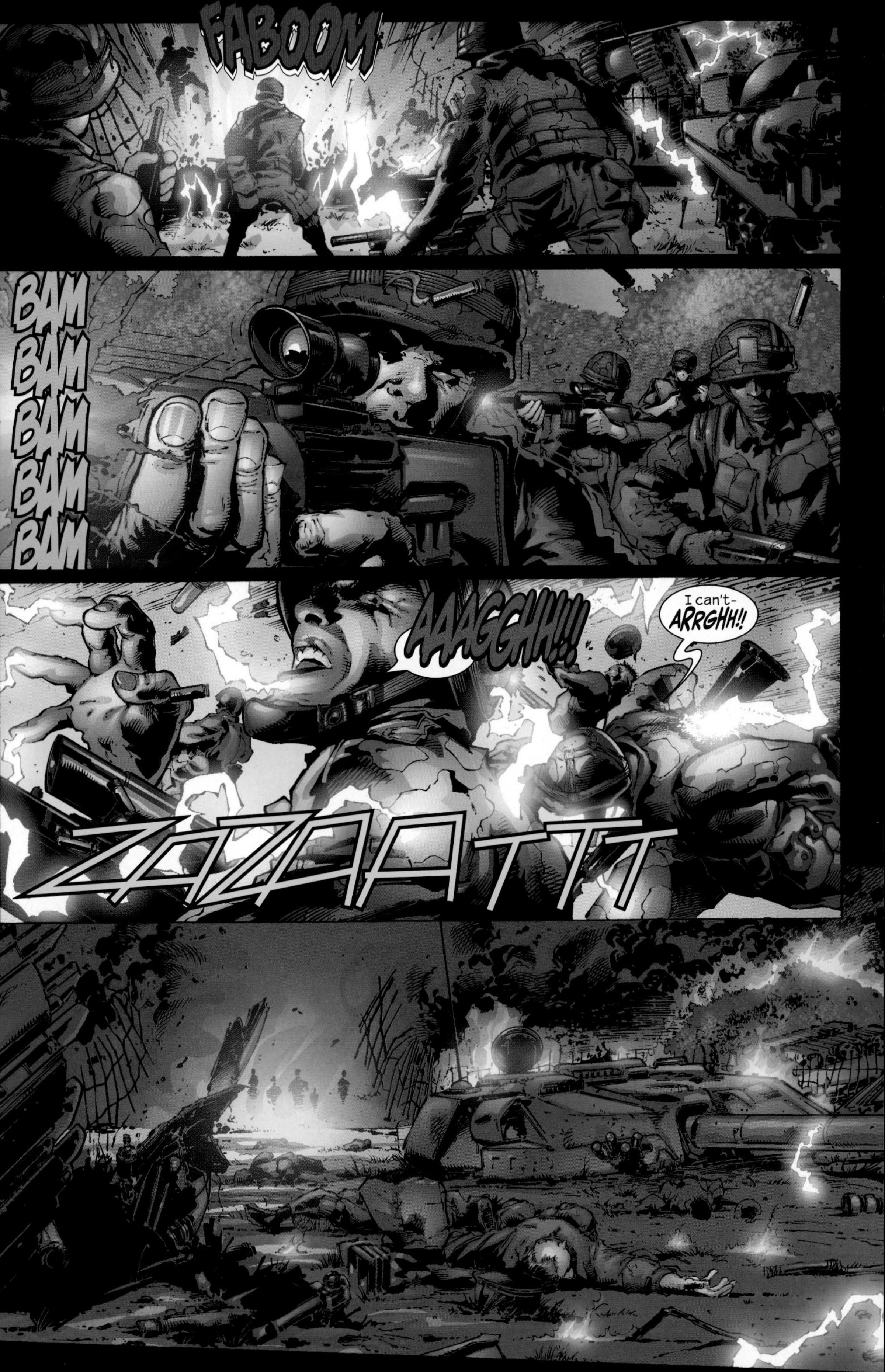
FABOOM
BAM
BAM
BAM
BAM
BAM
AAAGGHH!!!
I can't-
ARRGHH!!
ZAZAAATTT

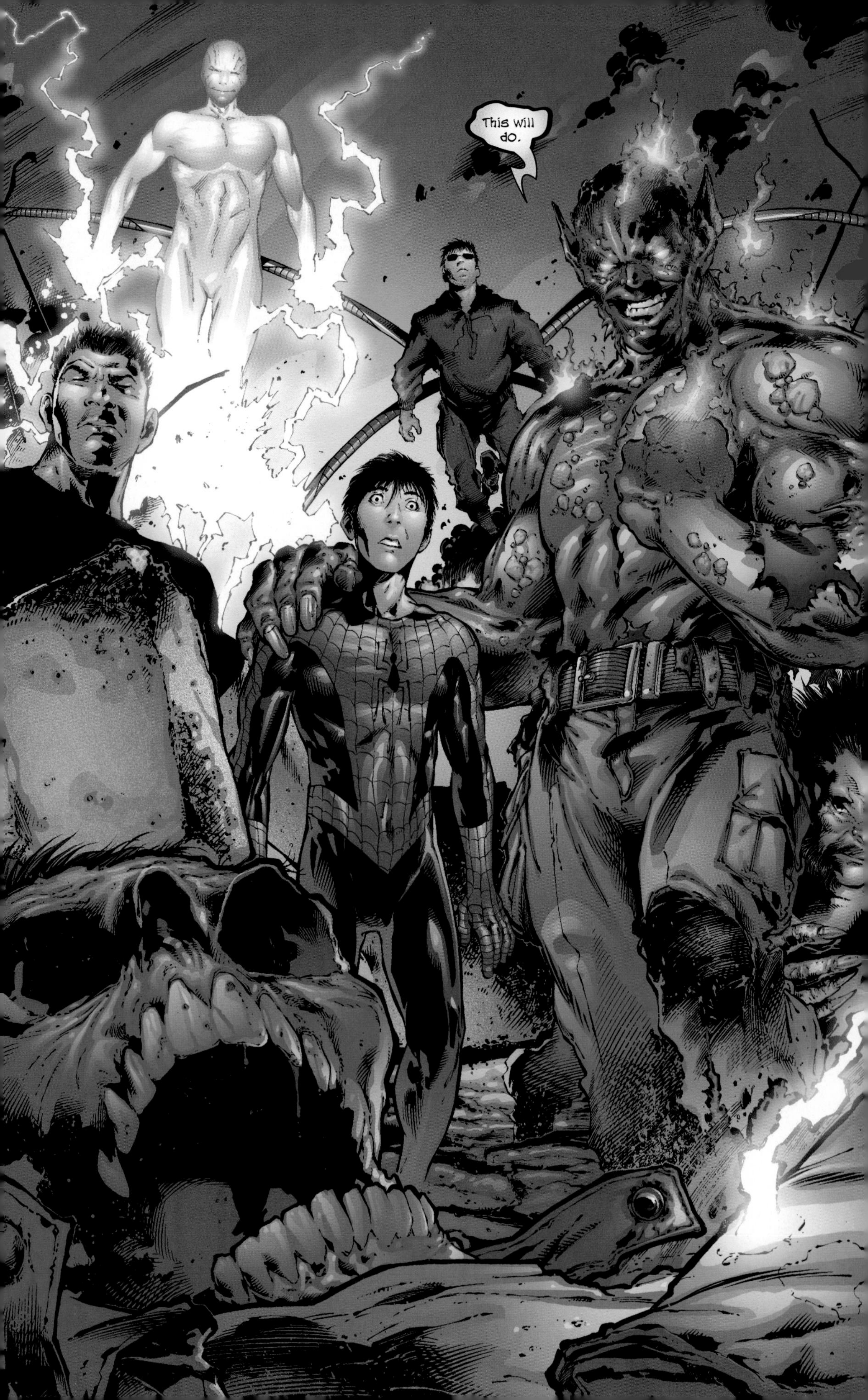
This will do.

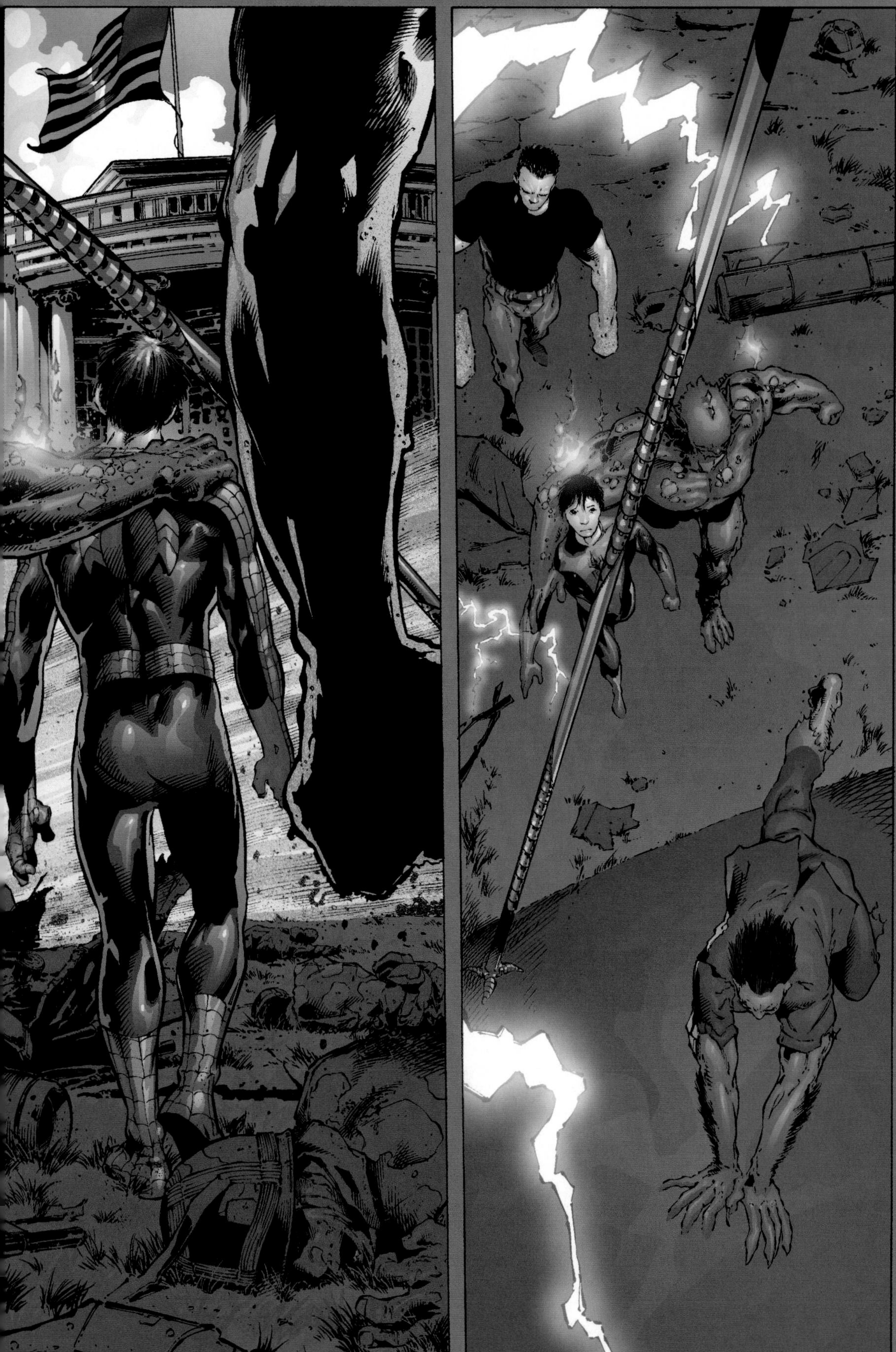

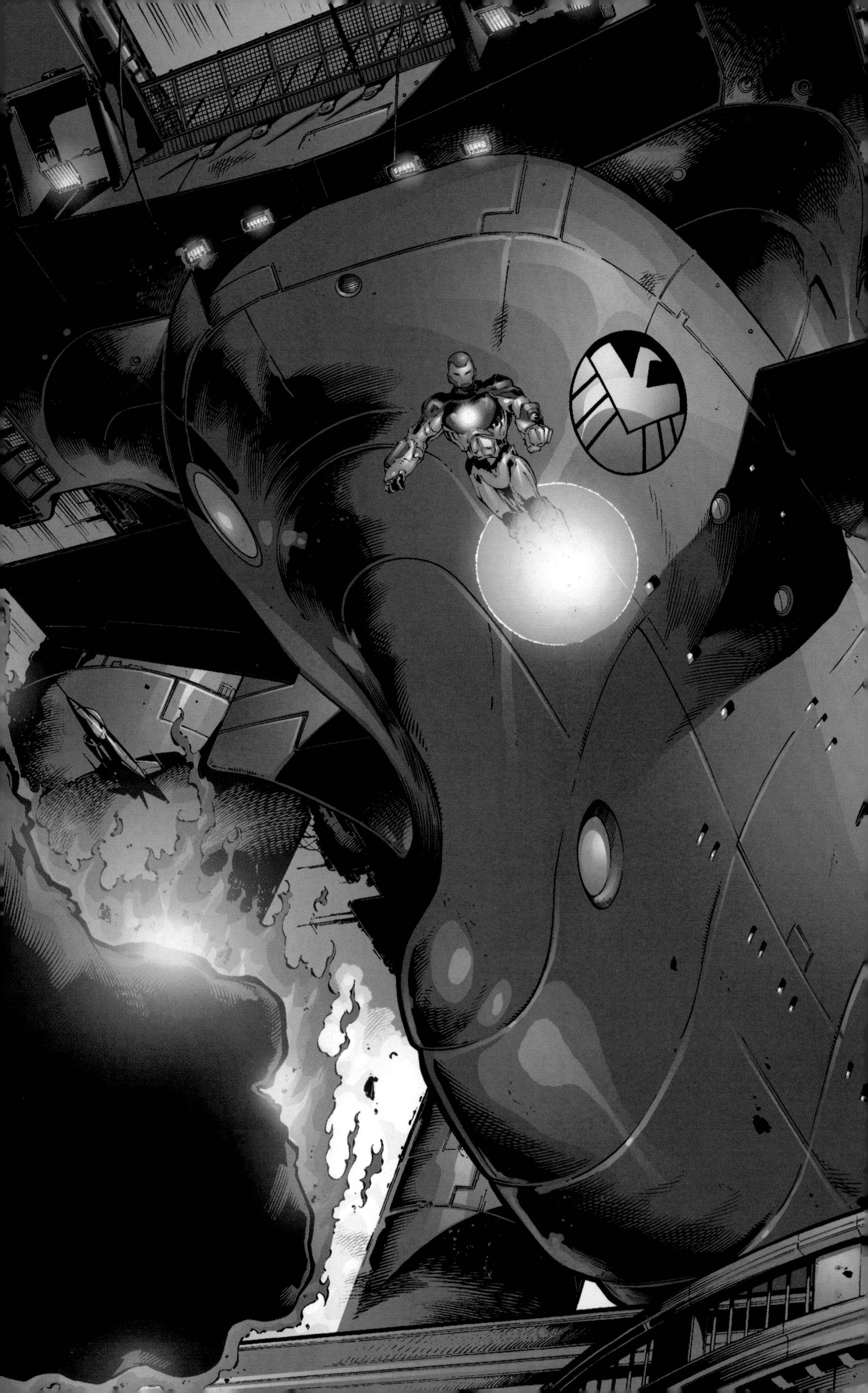

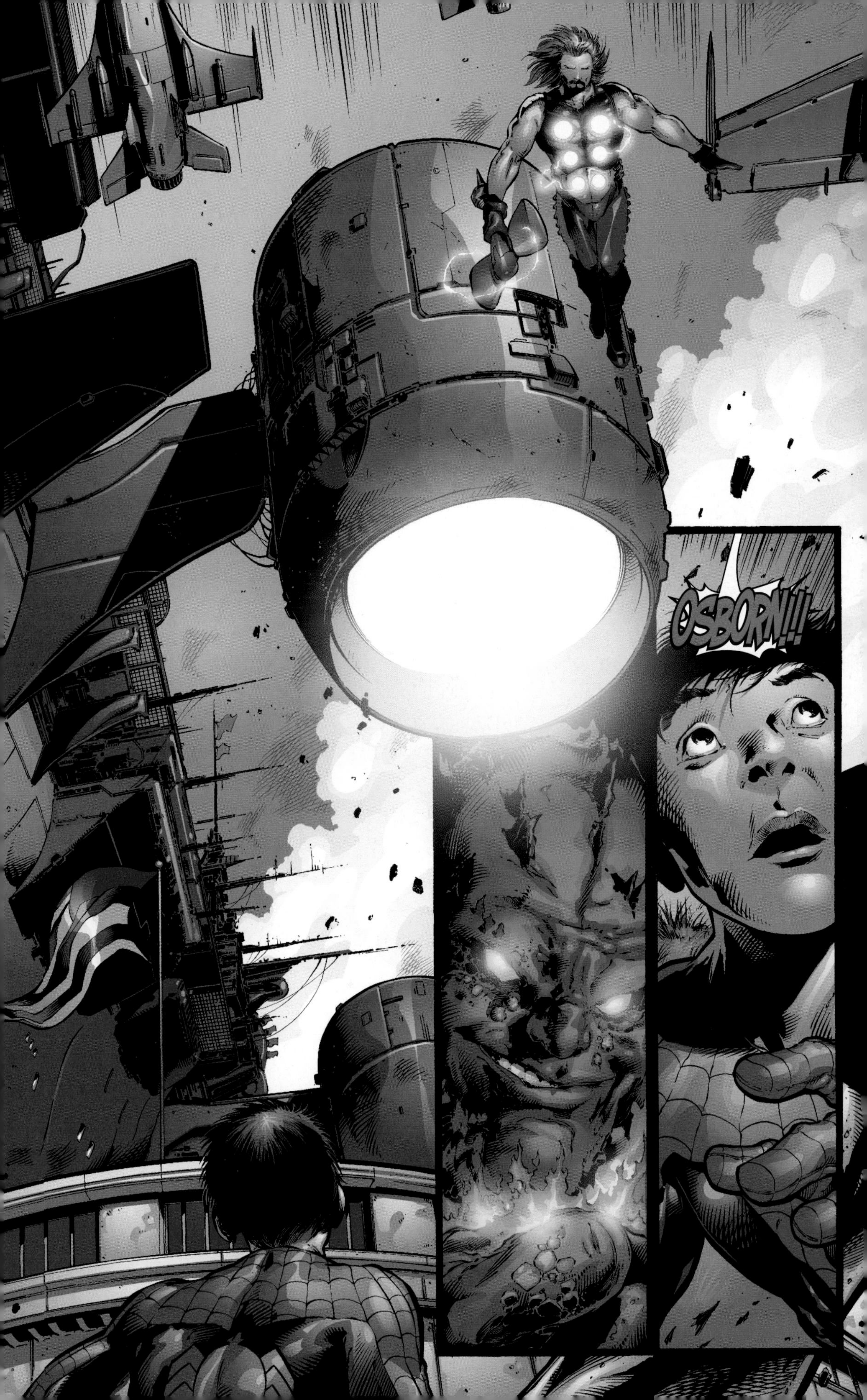
OSBORN!!!

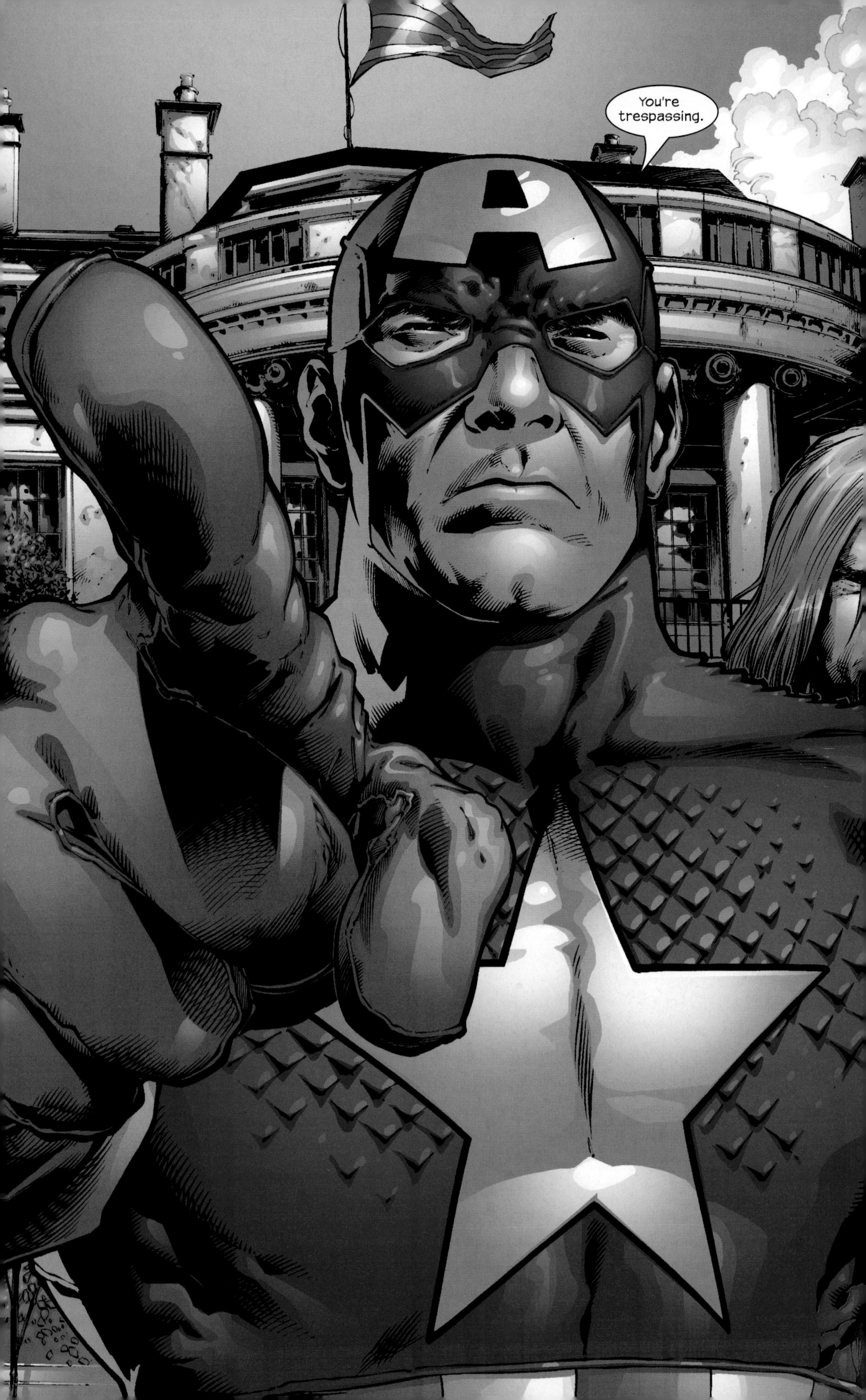
You're trespassing.

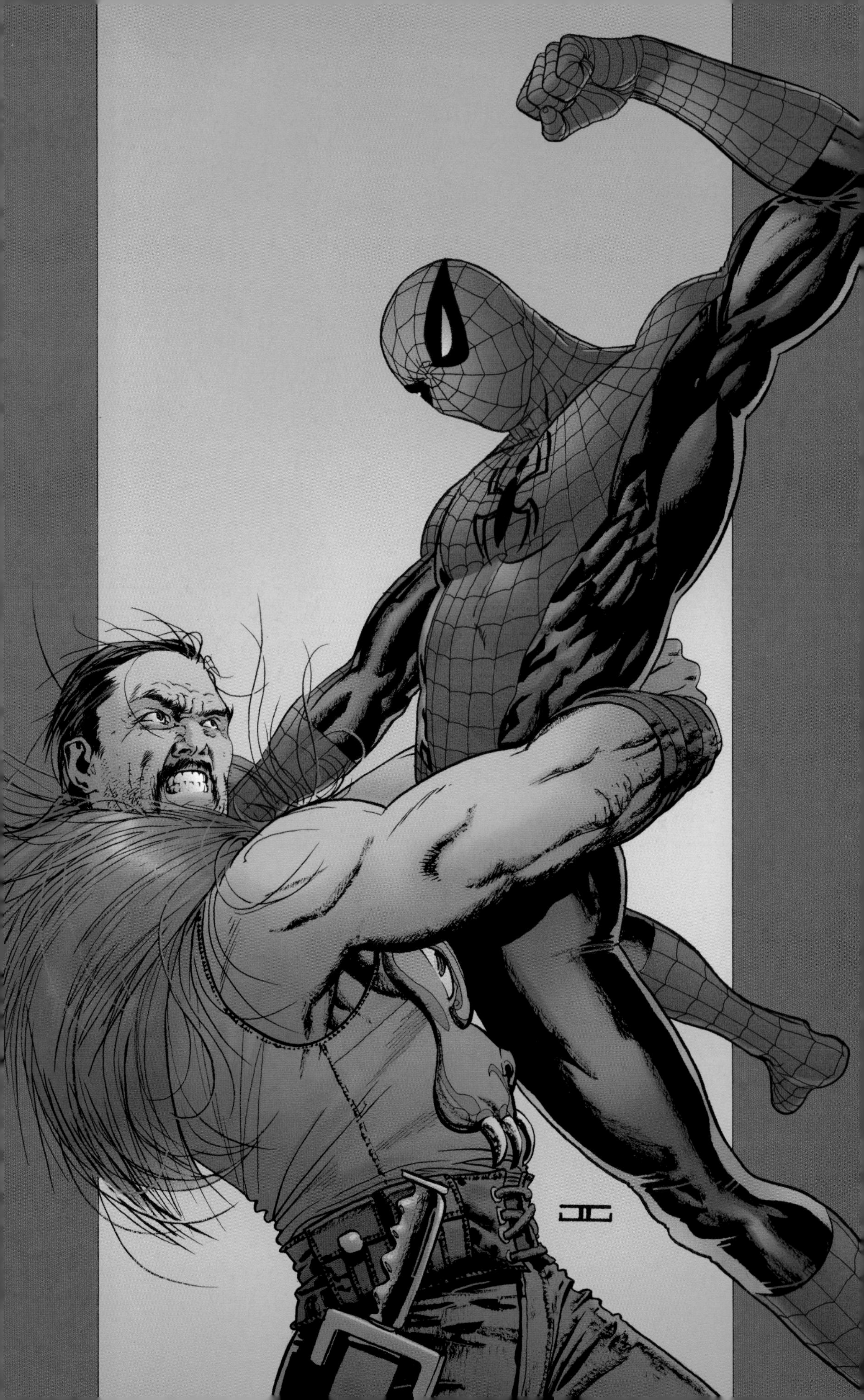

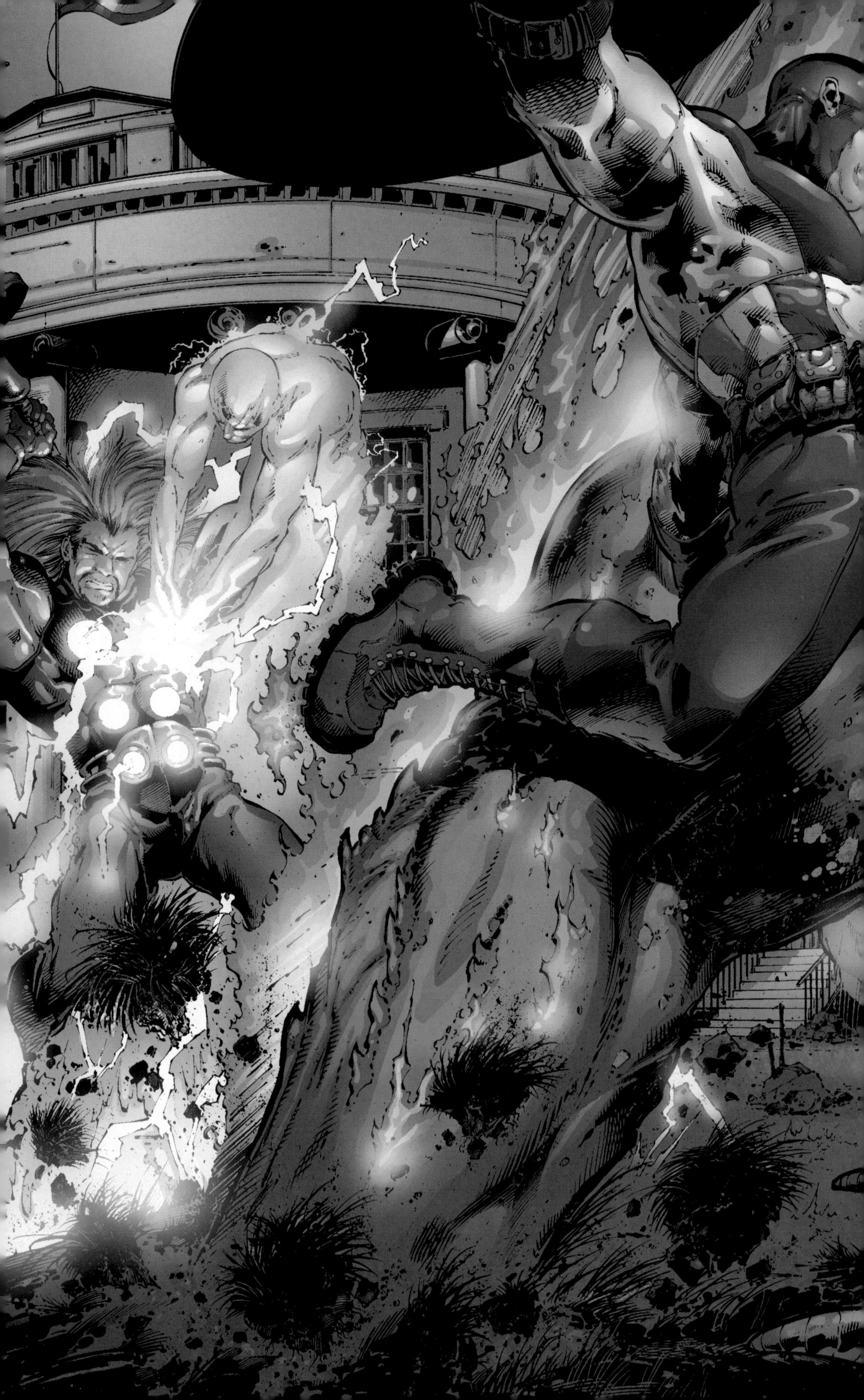

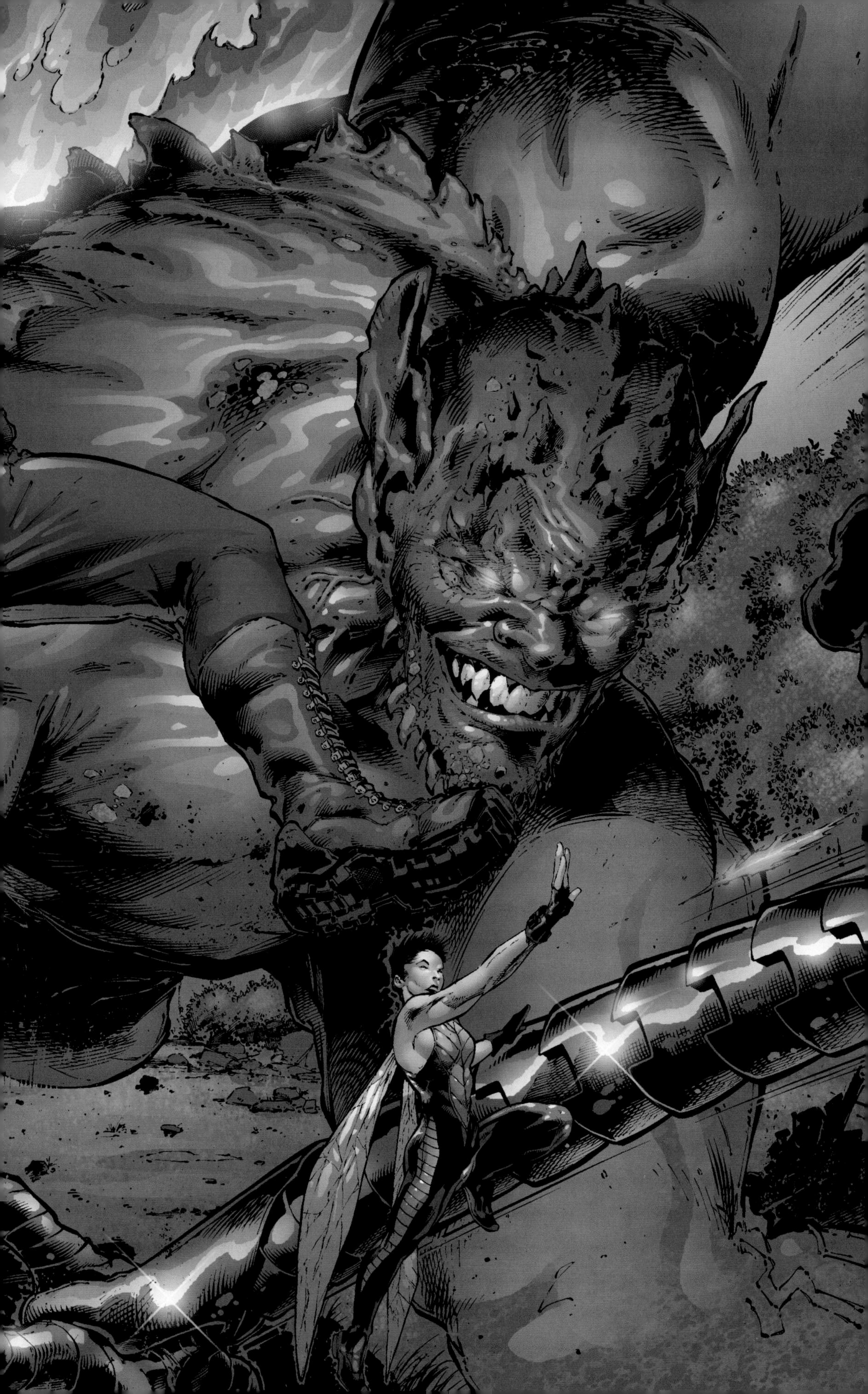

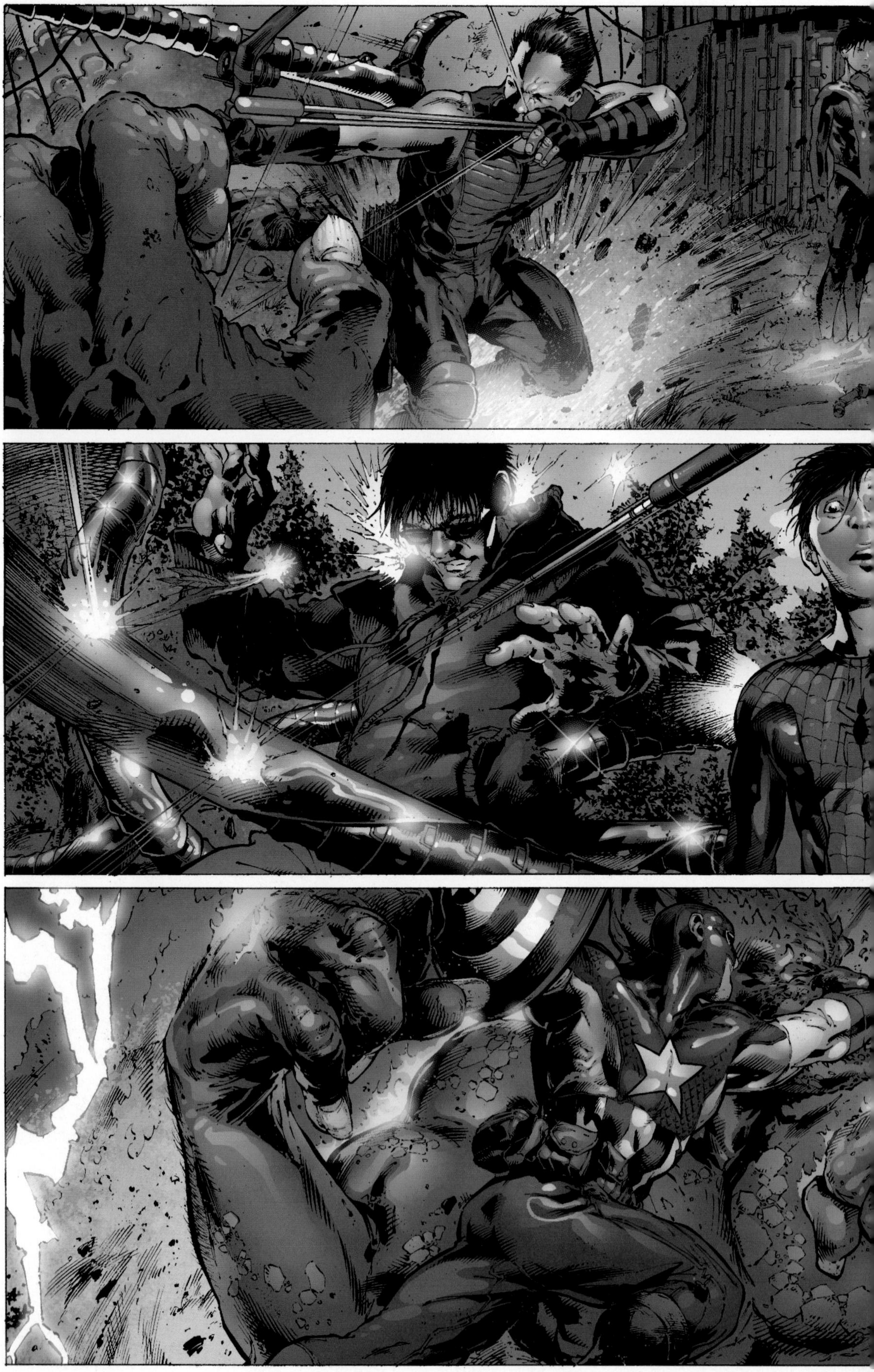

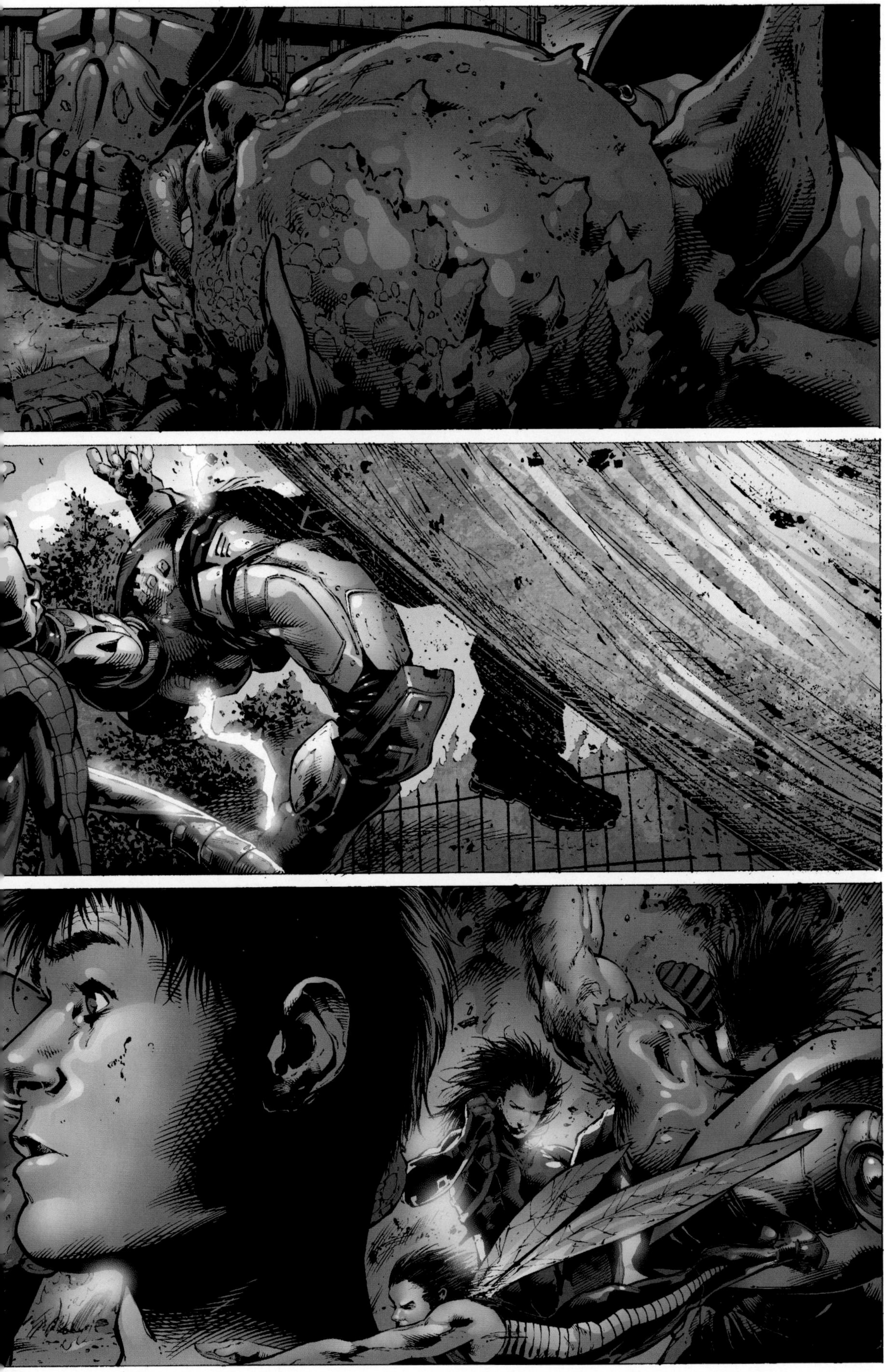

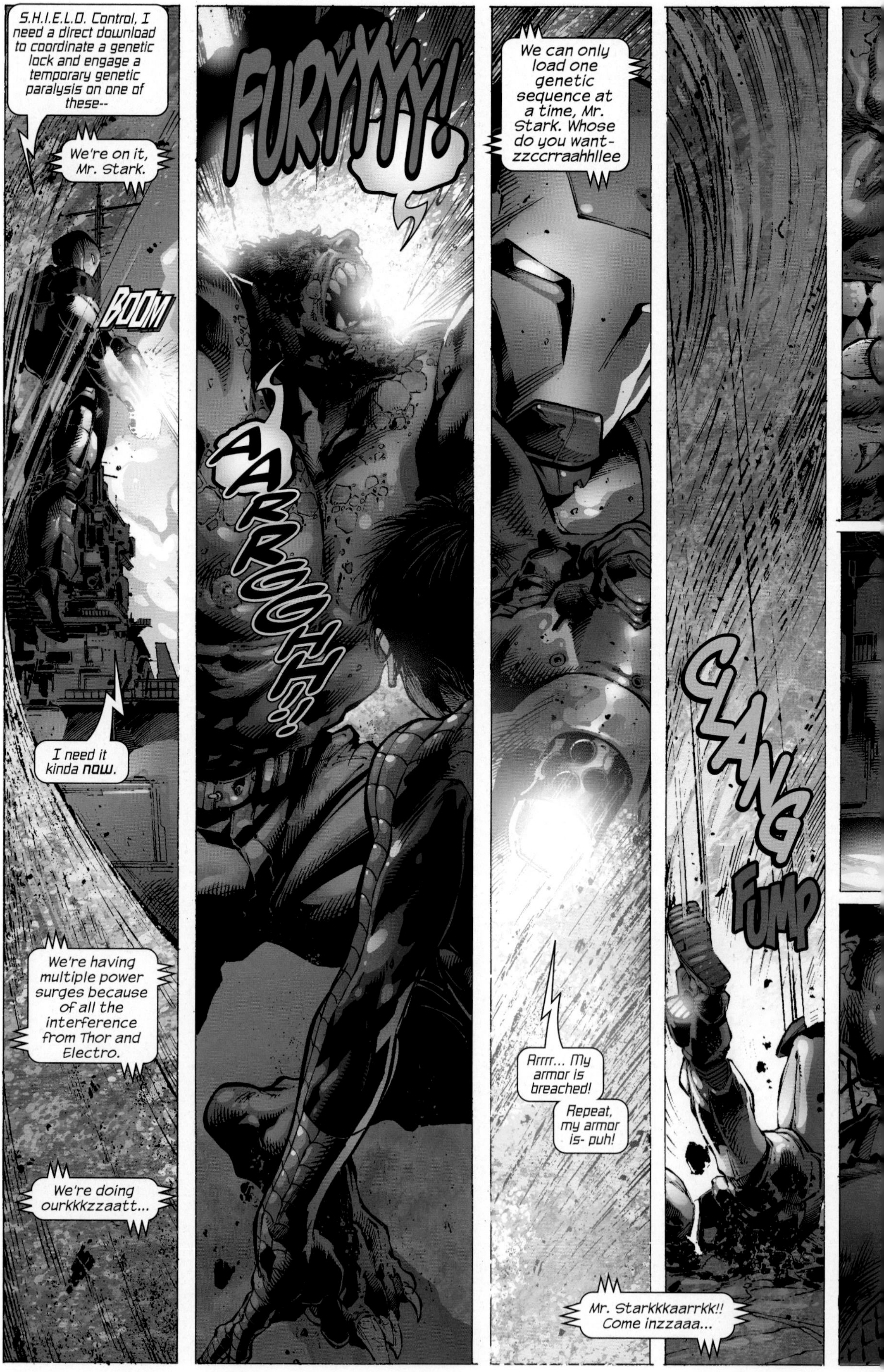
S.H.I.E.L.D. Control, I need a direct download to coordinate a genetic lock and engage a temporary genetic paralysis on one of these--
We're on it, Mr. Stark.
BOOM
I need it kinda now.
We're having multiple power surges because of all the interference from Thor and Electro.
We're doing ourkkkzzaatt...
FURYYYY!
AARRGGHH!!
We can only load one genetic sequence at a time, Mr. Stark. Whose do you want-zzccrraahhllee
Arrrr... My armor is breached!
Repeat, my armor is- puh!
CLANG
FUMP
Mr. Starkkkaarrkk!! Come inzzaaa...

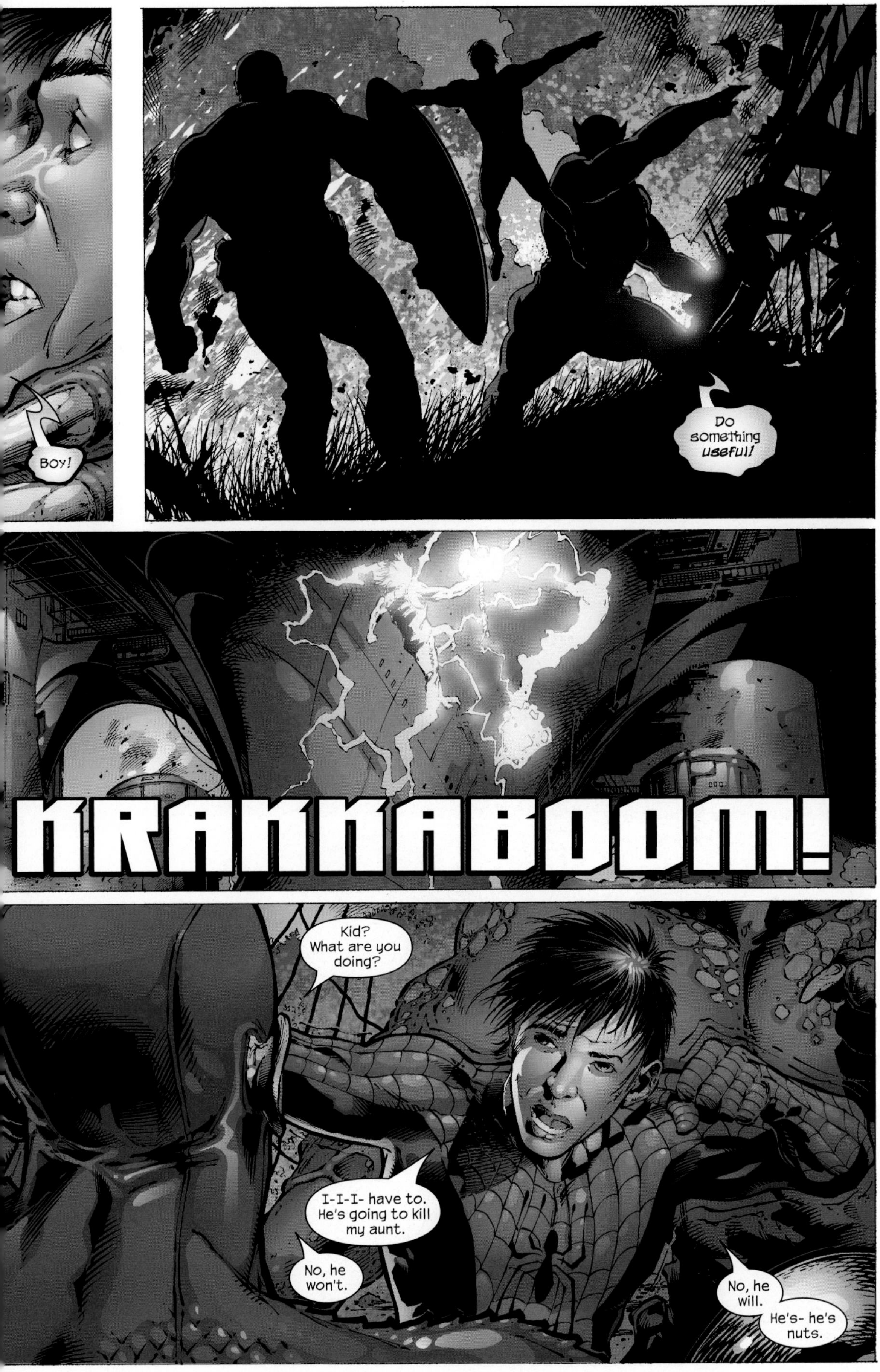
Boy!
Do something useful!
KRAKKABOOM!
Kid? What are you doing?
I-I-I- have to. He's going to kill my aunt.
No, he won't.
No, he will.
He's- he's nuts.

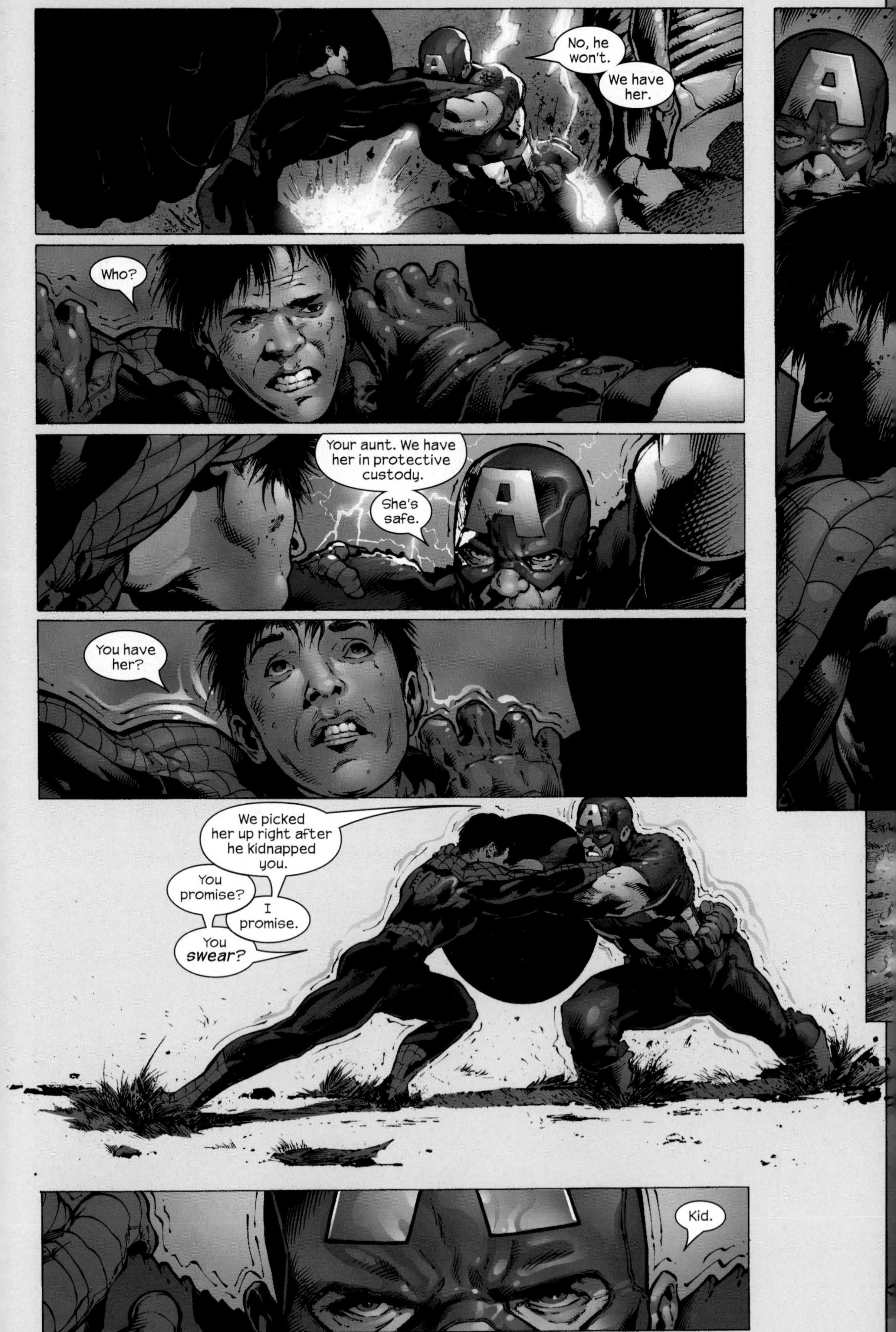
No, he won't.
We have her.
Who?
Your aunt. We have her in protective custody.
She's safe.
You have her?
We picked her up right after he kidnapped you.
You promise?
I promise.
You swear?
Kid.

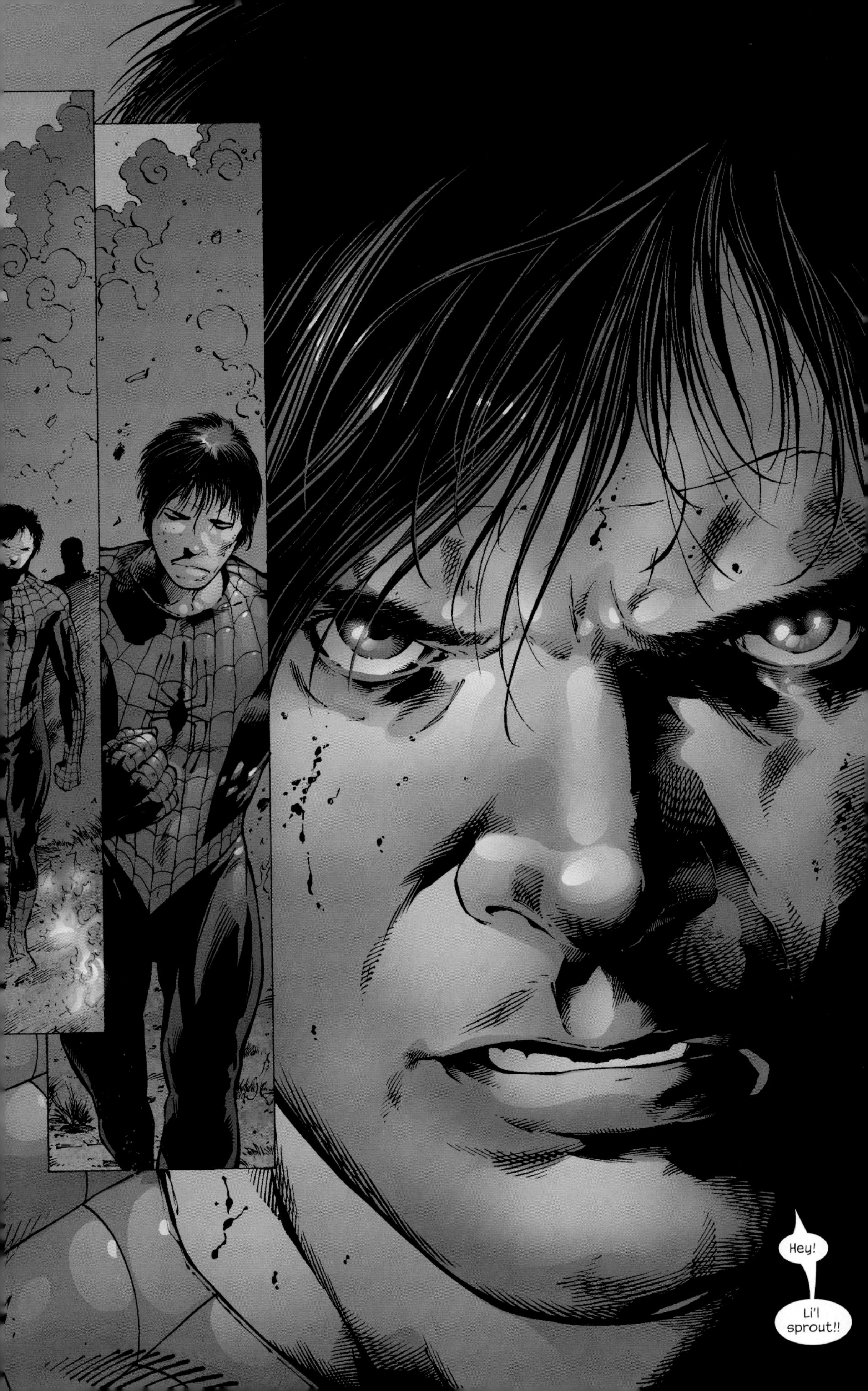
Hey!
Li'l sprout!!

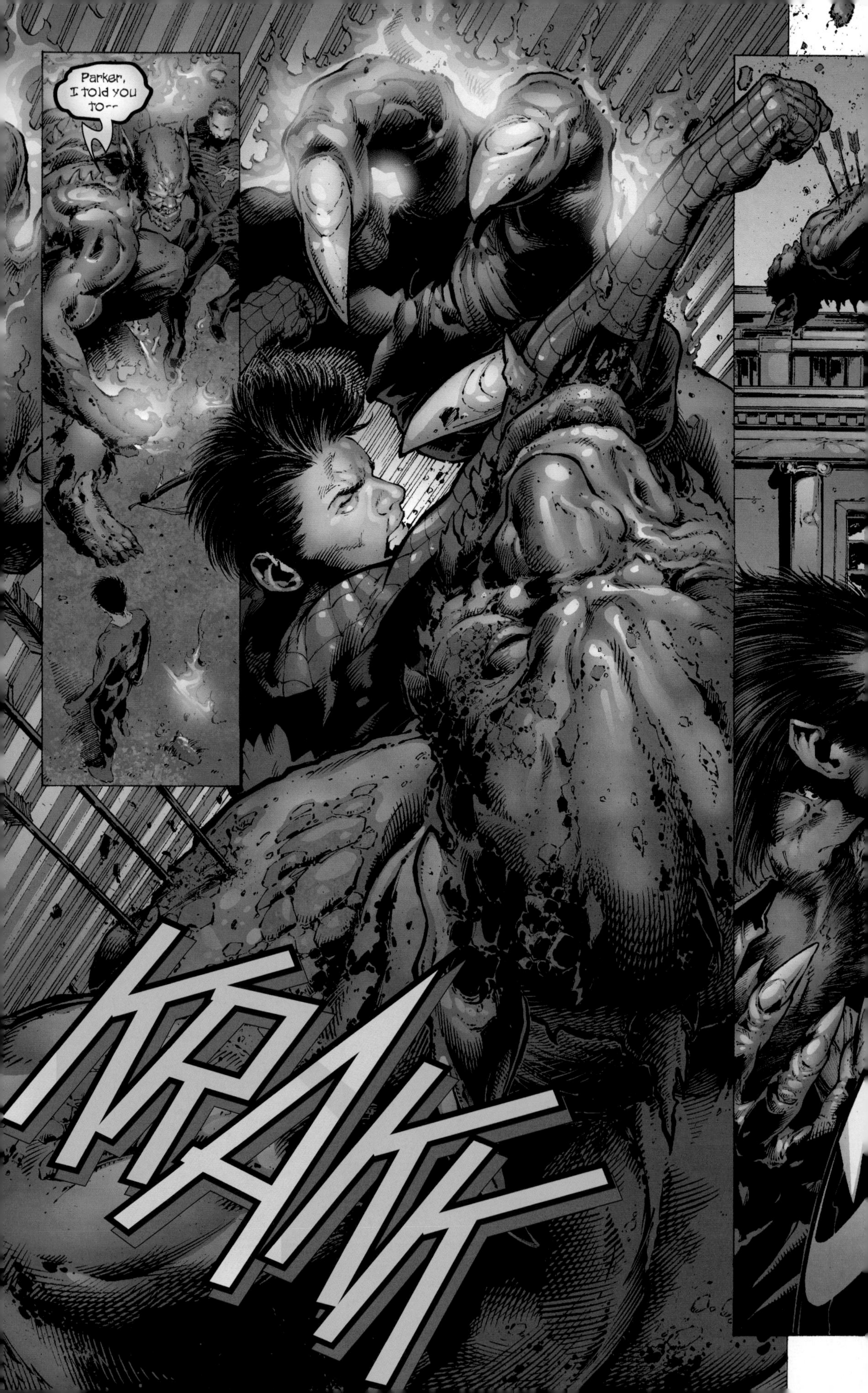
Parker, I told you to--
KRAKK

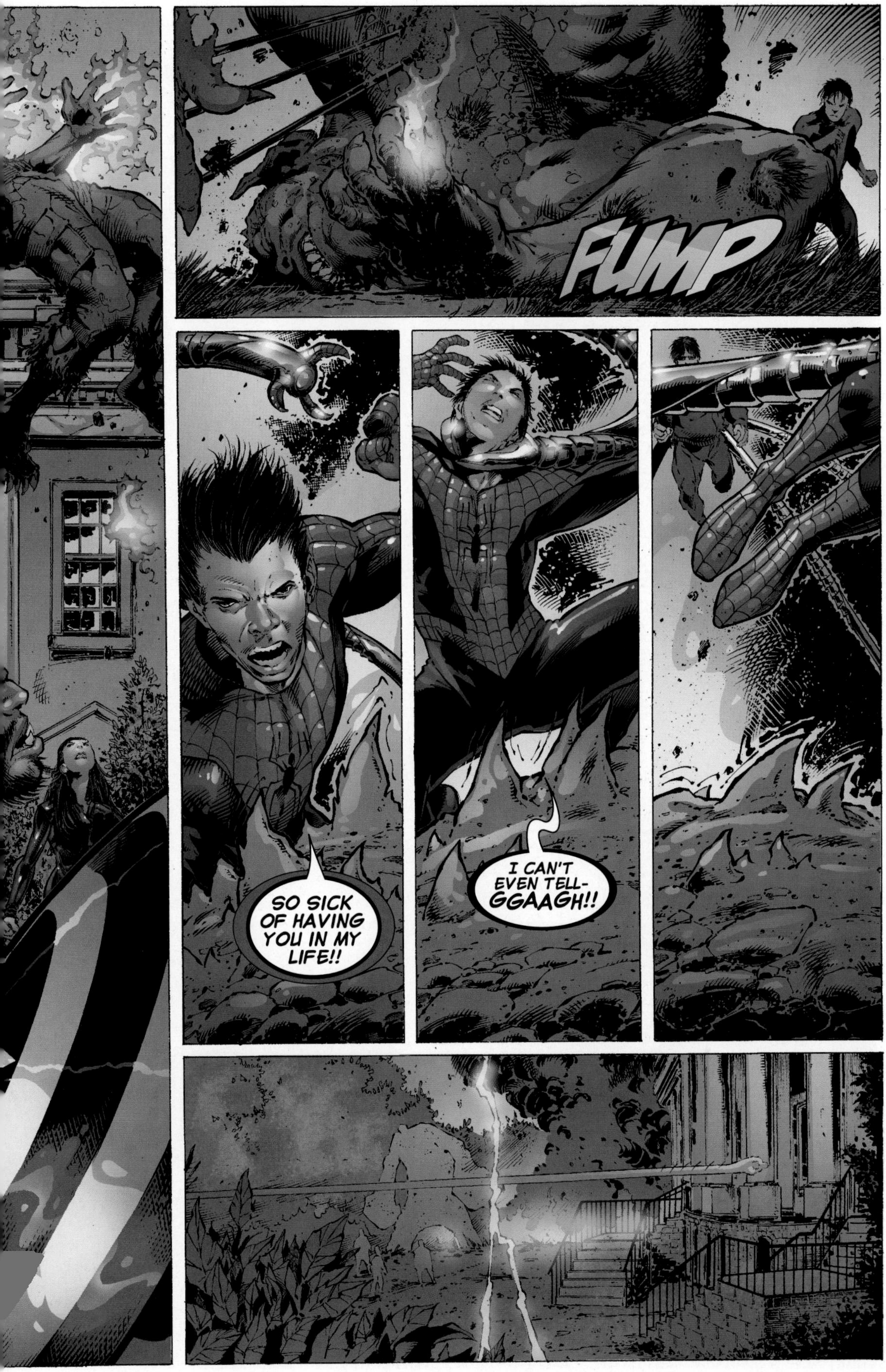
FUMP
SO SICK OF HAVING YOU IN MY LIFE!!
I CAN'T EVEN TELL-GGAAGH!!

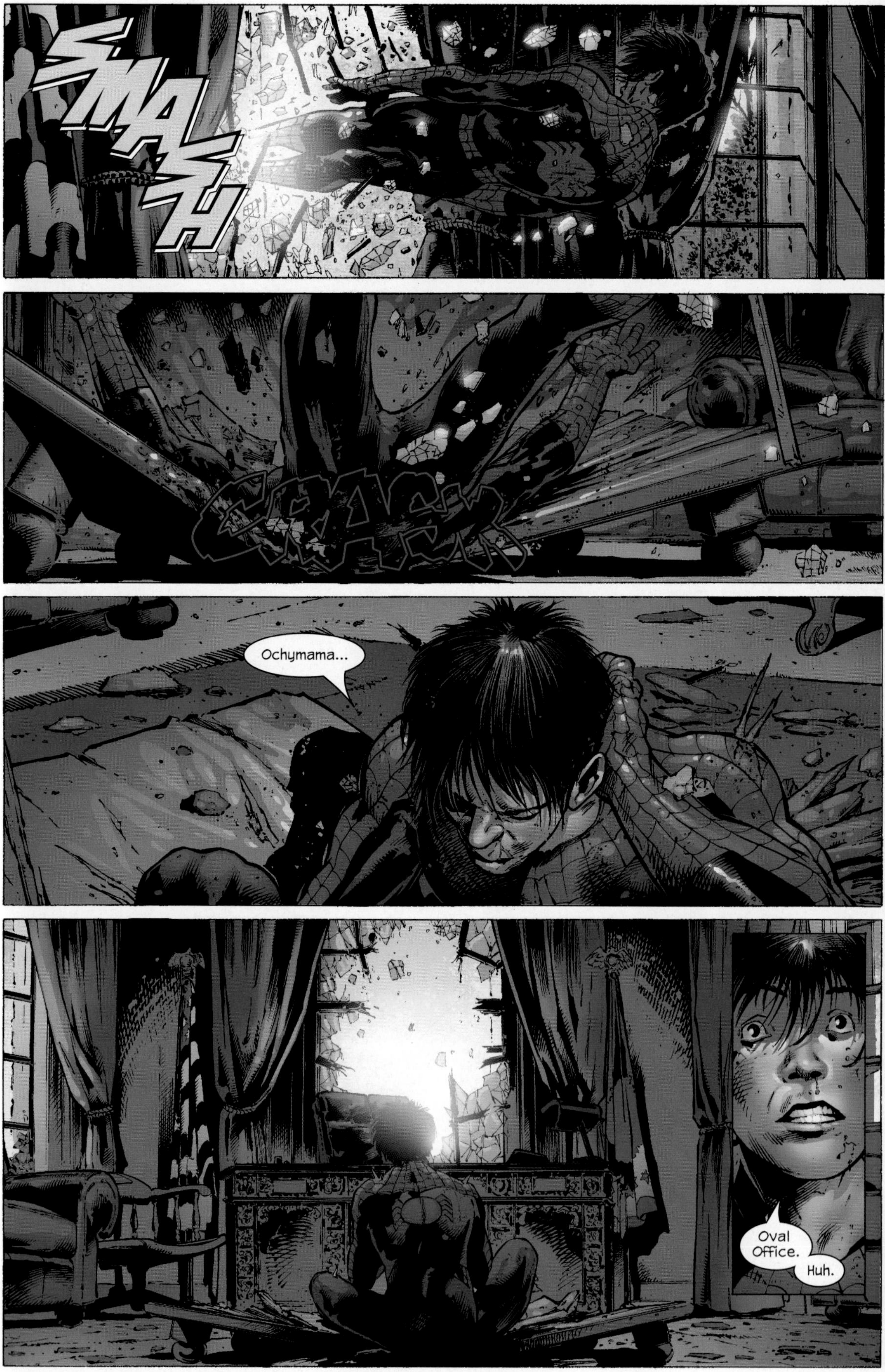
SMASH
CRASH
Ochymama...
Oval Office.
Huh.

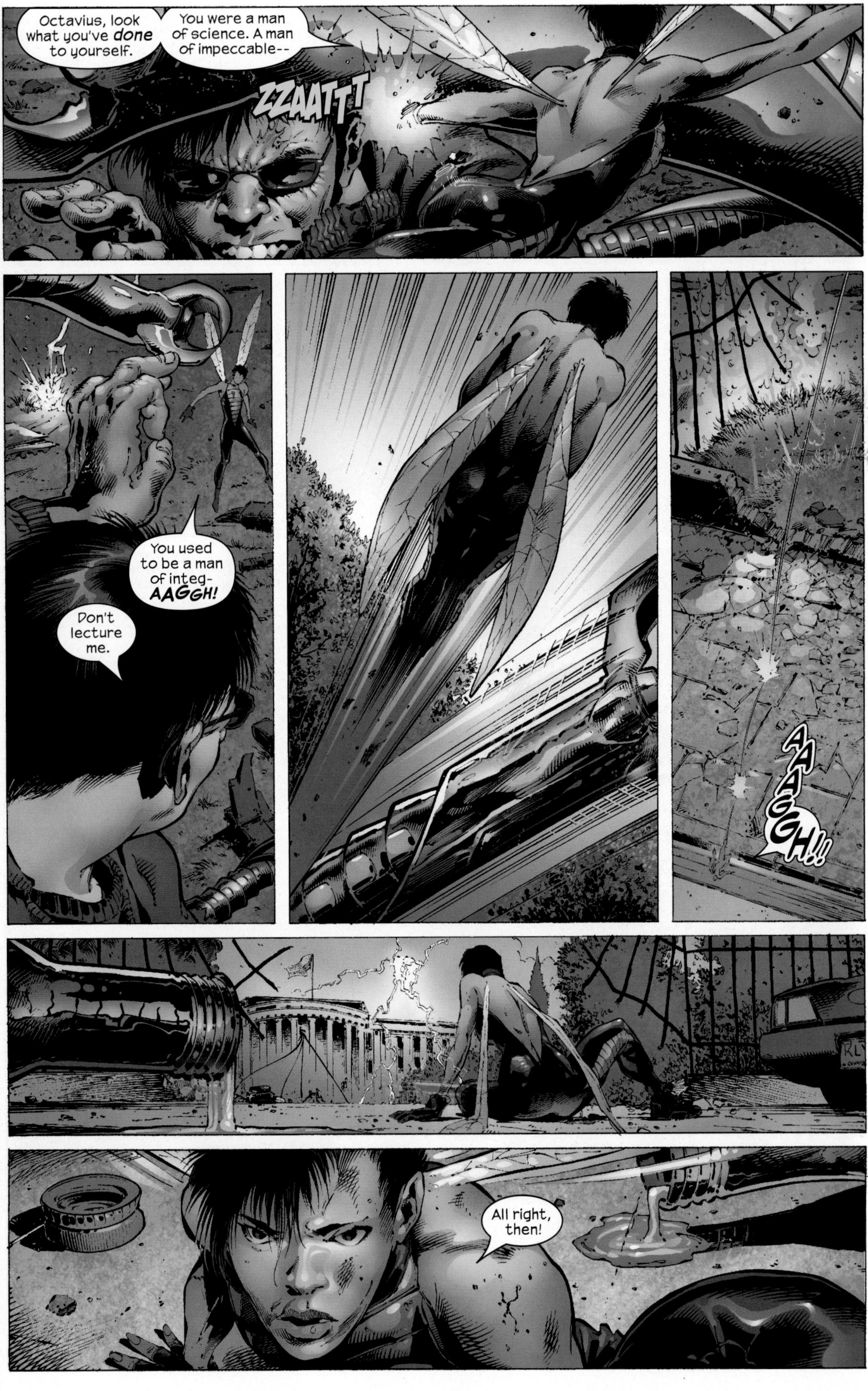

Octavius, look what you've **done** to yourself.
You were a man of science. A man of impeccable--
ZZAATTT
You used to be a man of integ-
AAGGH!
Don't lecture me.
AAAGGH!!
All right, then!

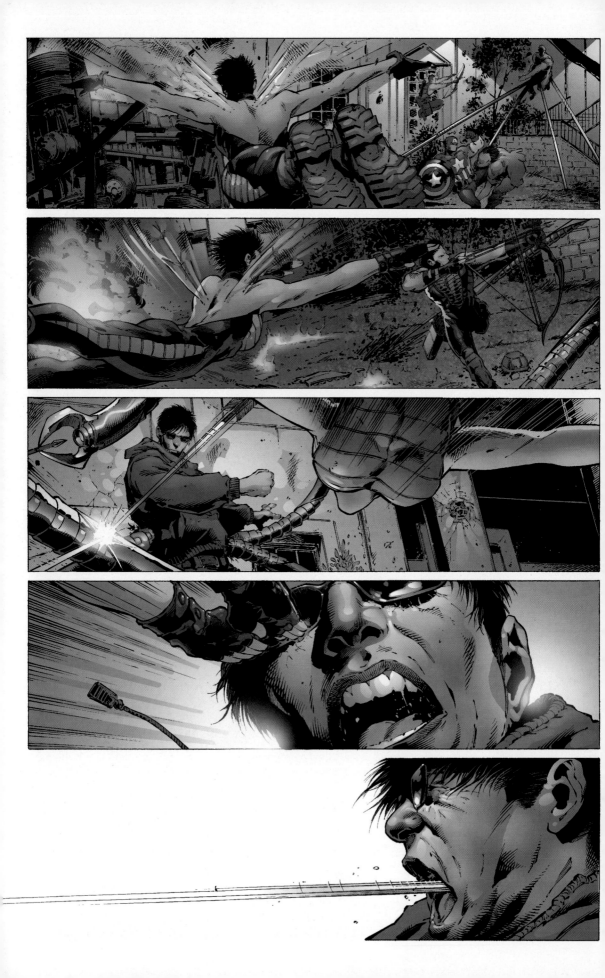

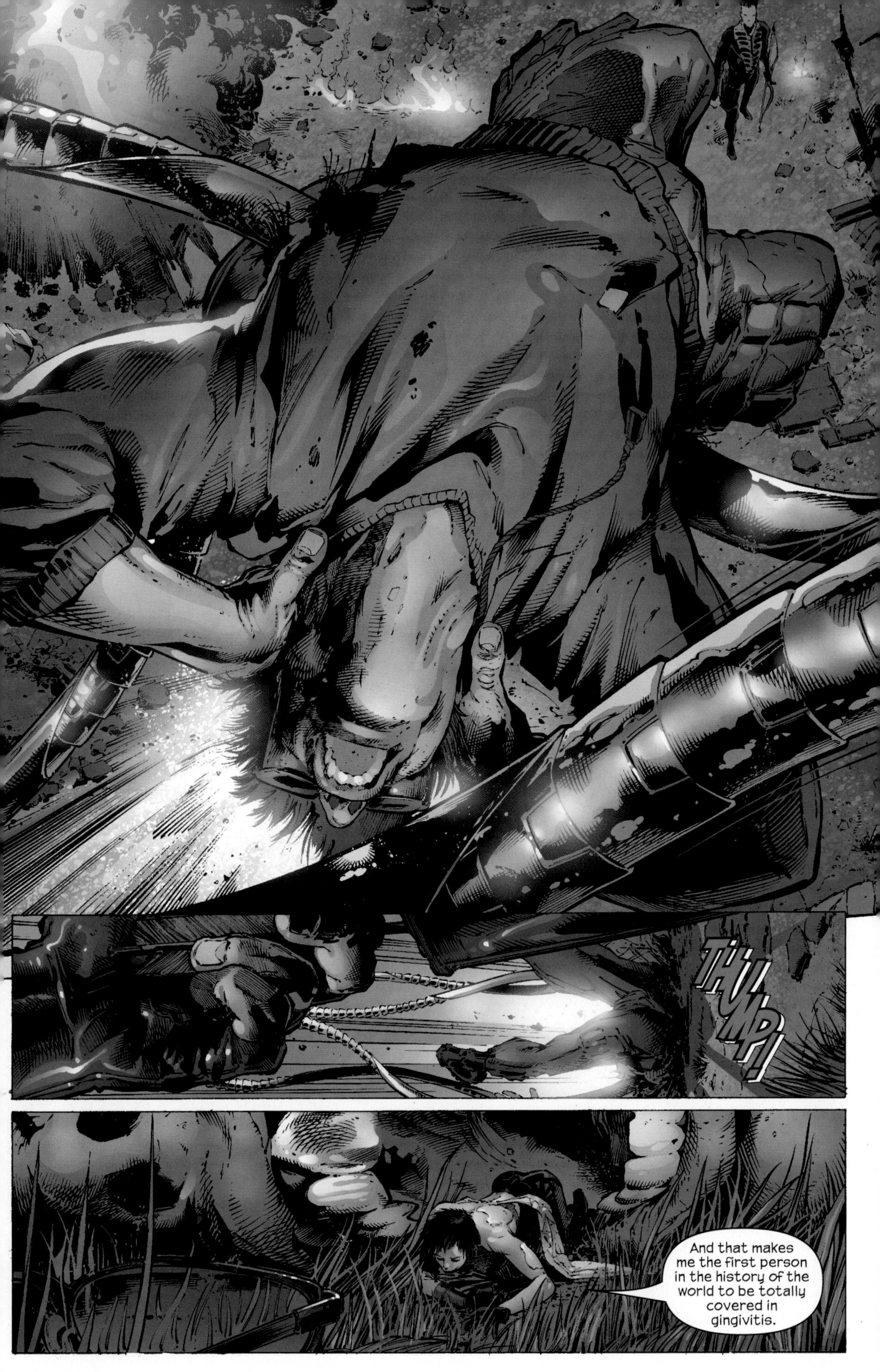
THUMP!!
And that makes me the first person in the history of the world to be totally covered in gingivitis.

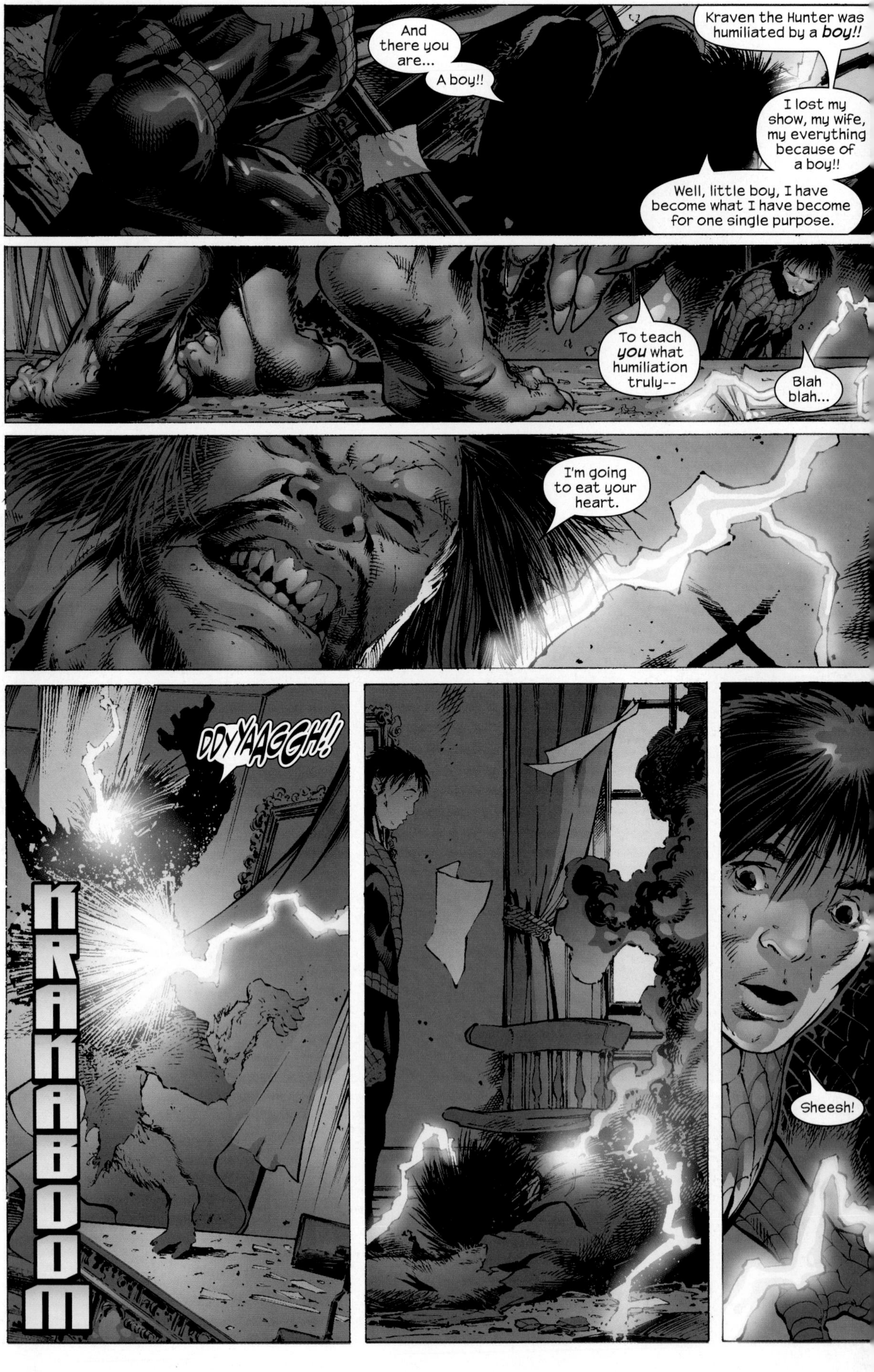

And there you are...
A boy!!
Kraven the Hunter was humiliated by a *boy!!*
I lost my show, my wife, my everything because of a boy!!
Well, little boy, I have become what I have become for one single purpose.
To teach *you* what humiliation truly--
Blah blah...
I'm going to eat your heart.
DDYYAAGGH!!
KRAKABOOM
Sheesh!

HHRRAAGGHH!!
Mr. Stark, we're back online.
Which genetic code sequence do you want first?
Raggh! Hold on, my armor has to reboot.
WHAM
Holding...
I'm going to go with the Sandman file.
File upload complete.
File received.

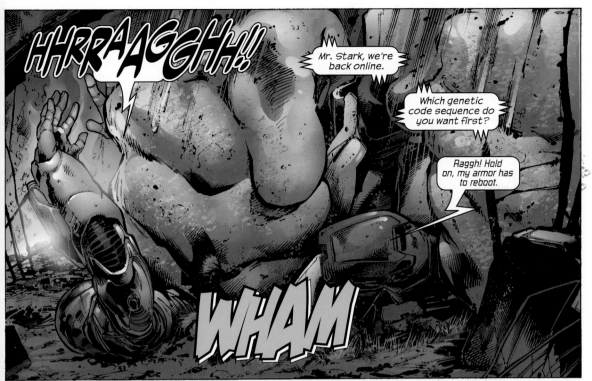

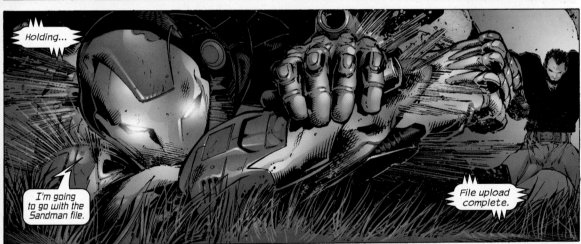

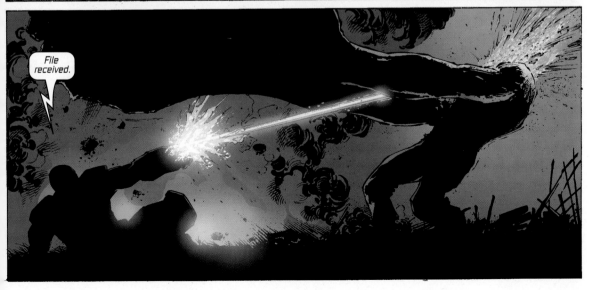

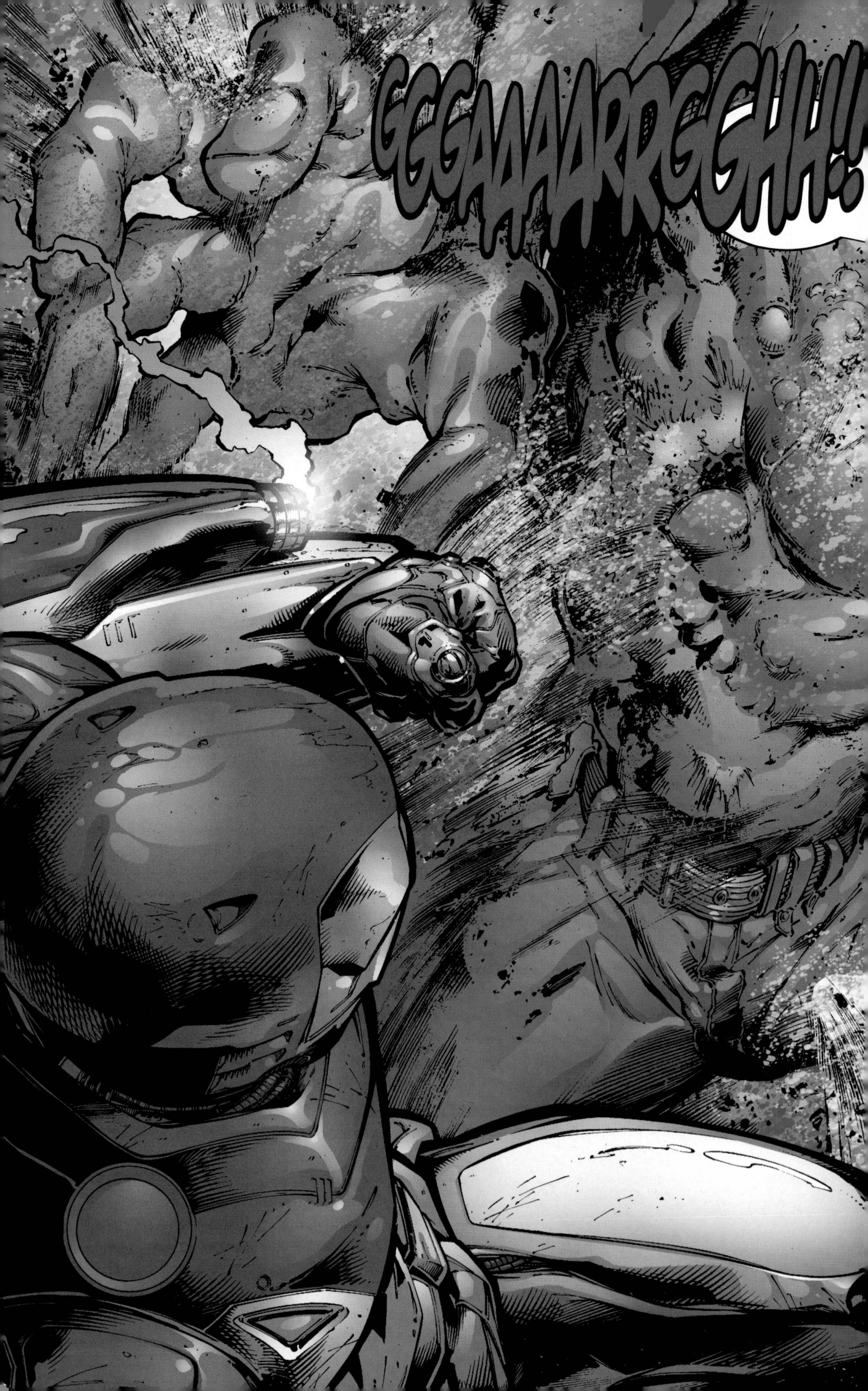
GGGAAAARRGGHH!!

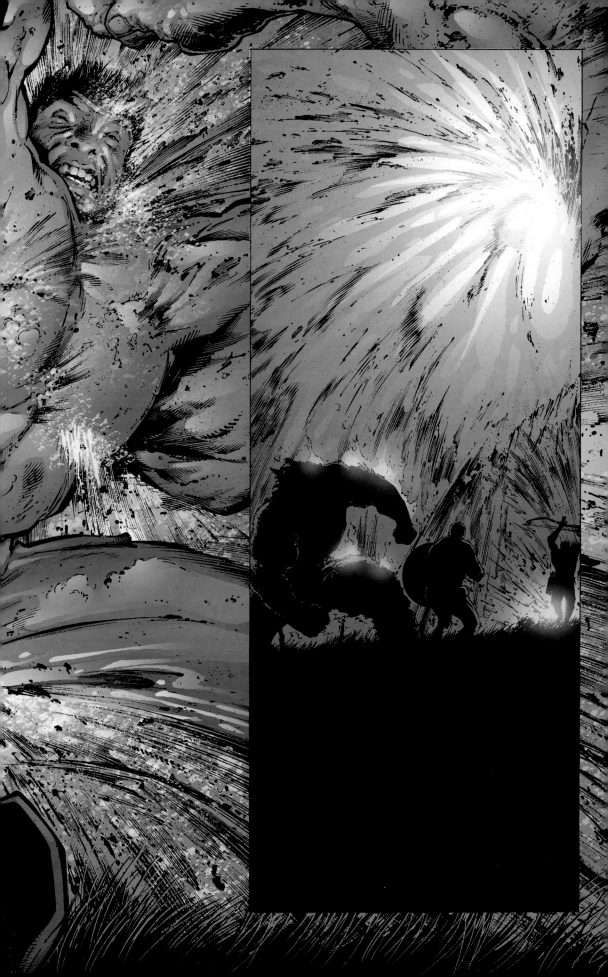

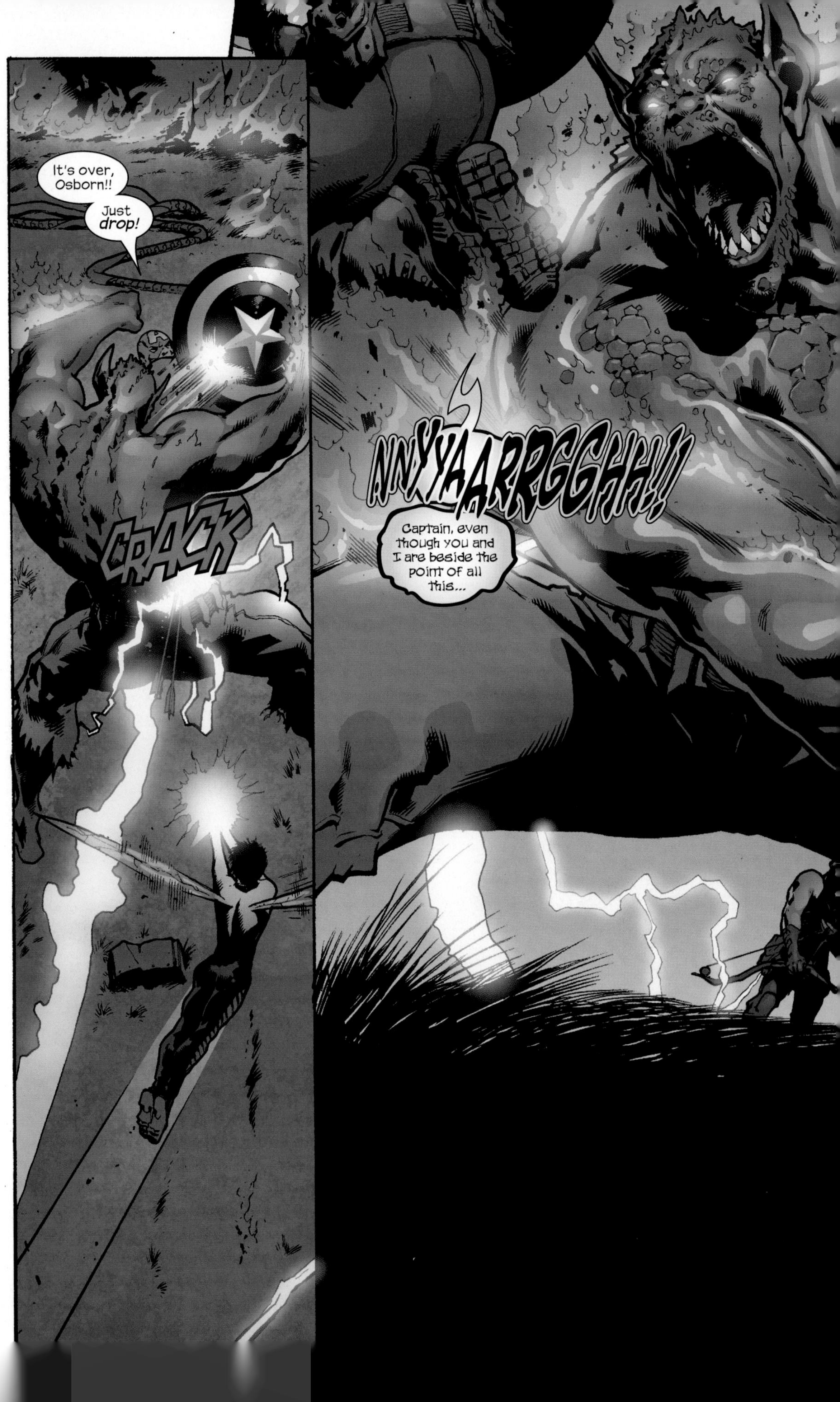
It's over, Osborn!!
Just drop!
CRACK
NNYYAARRGGHH!!
Captain, even though you and I are beside the point of all this...

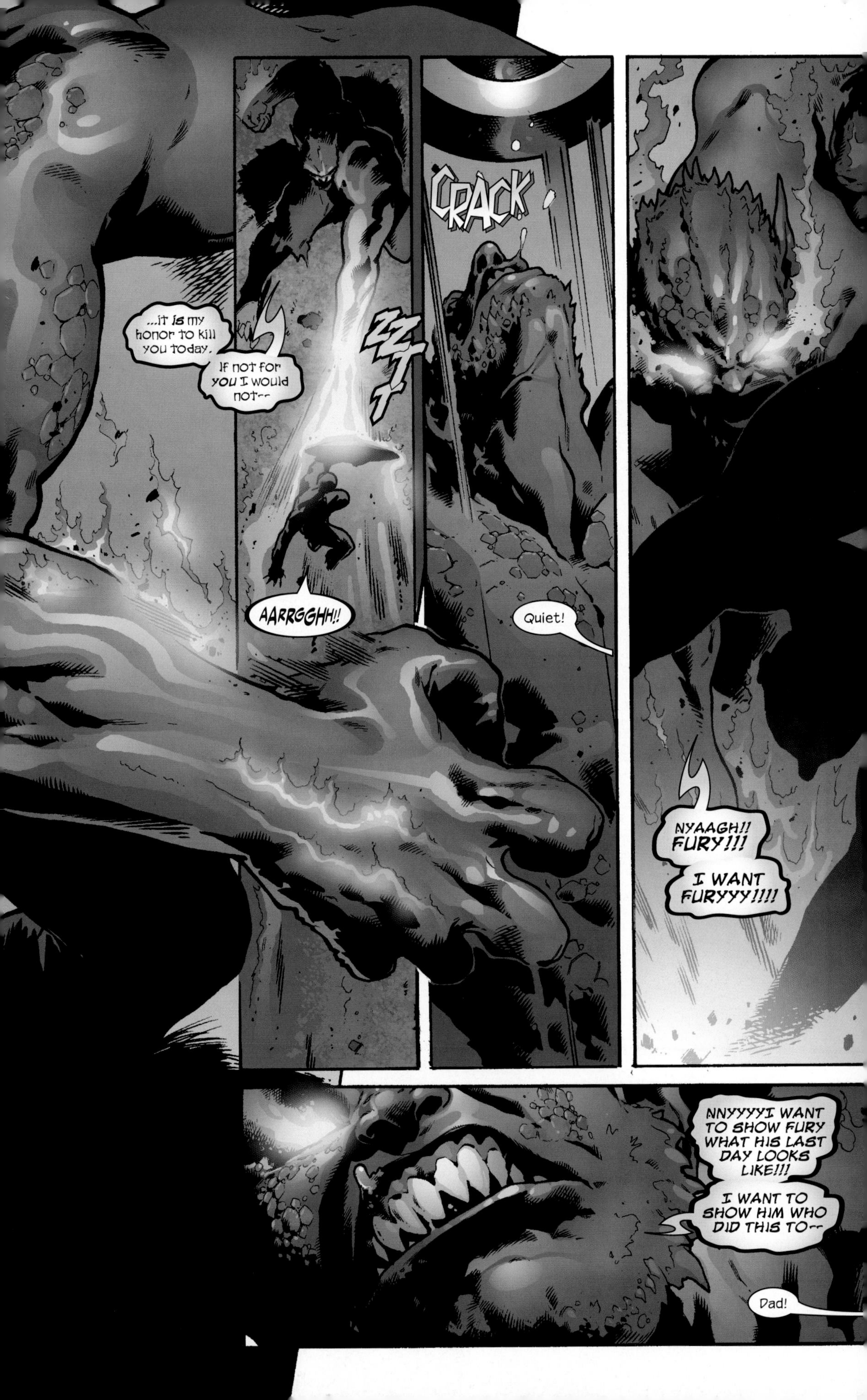
...it is my honor to kill you today.
If not for you I would not--
ZZT
AARRGGHH!!
CRACK
Quiet!
NYAAGH!! FURY!!!
I WANT FURYYY!!!!
NNYYYYI WANT TO SHOW FURY WHAT HIS LAST DAY LOOKS LIKE!!!
I WANT TO SHOW HIM WHO DID THIS TO--
Dad!

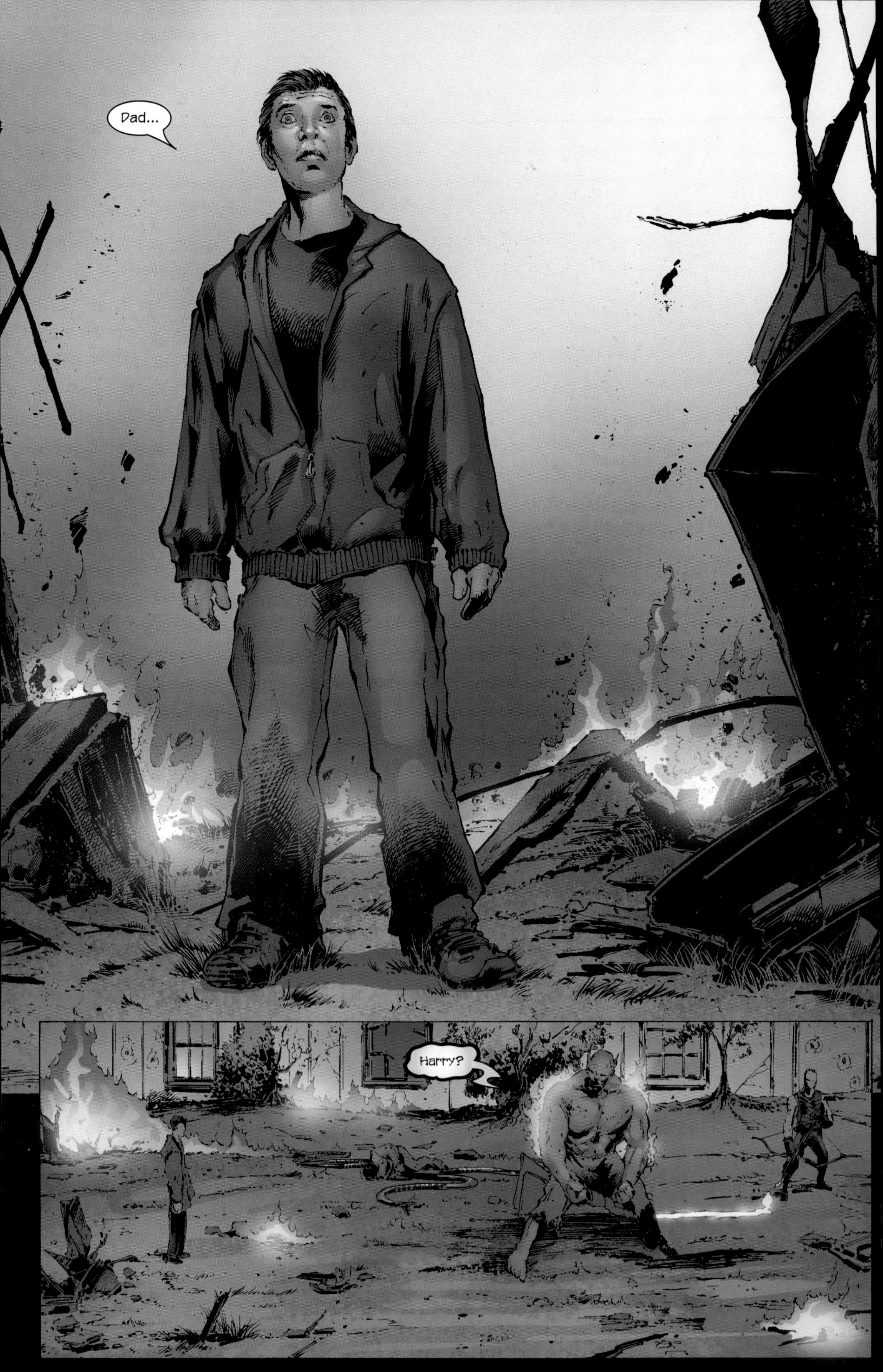
Dad...
Harry?

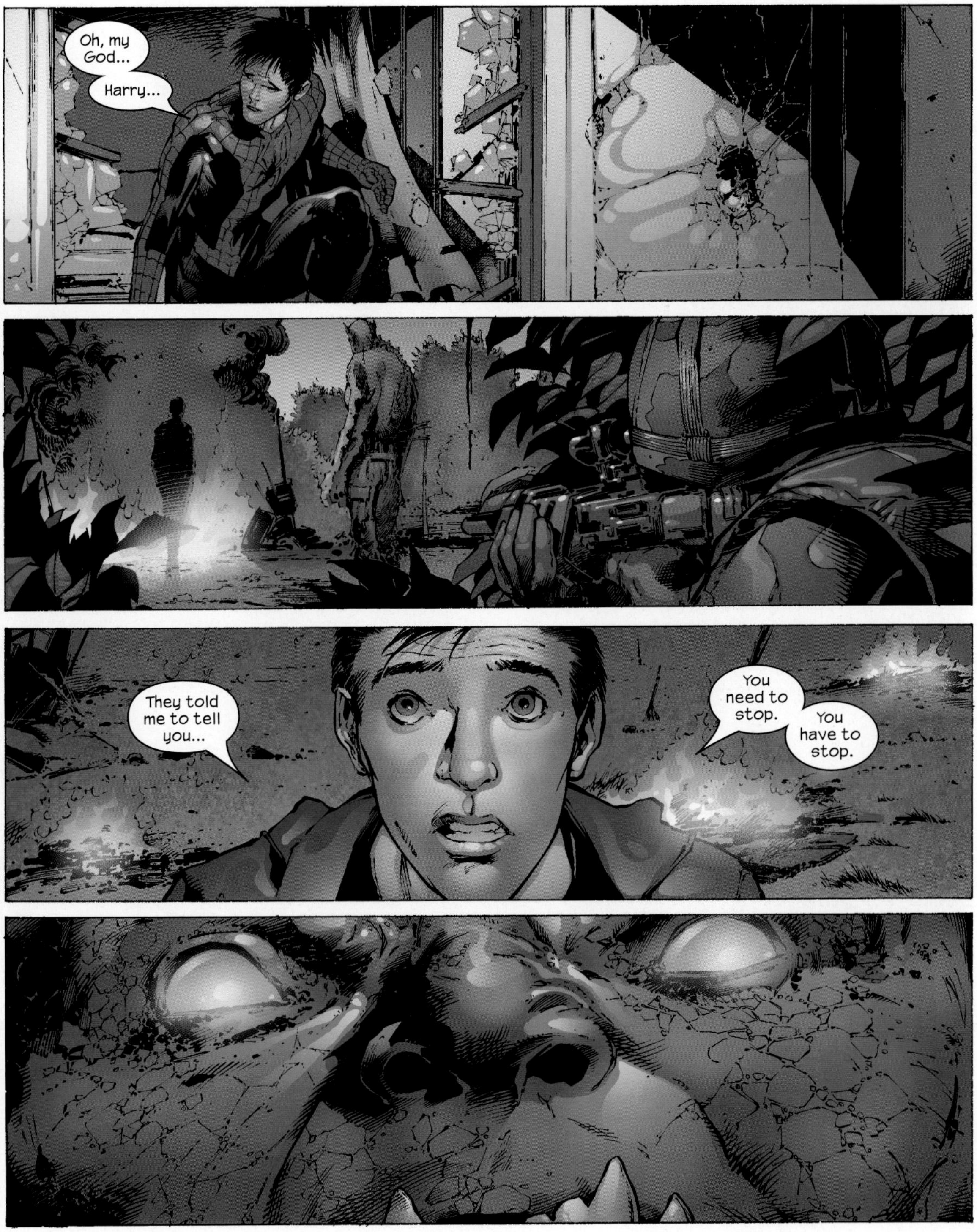
Oh, my God...
Harry...
They told me to tell you...
You need to stop.
You have to stop.

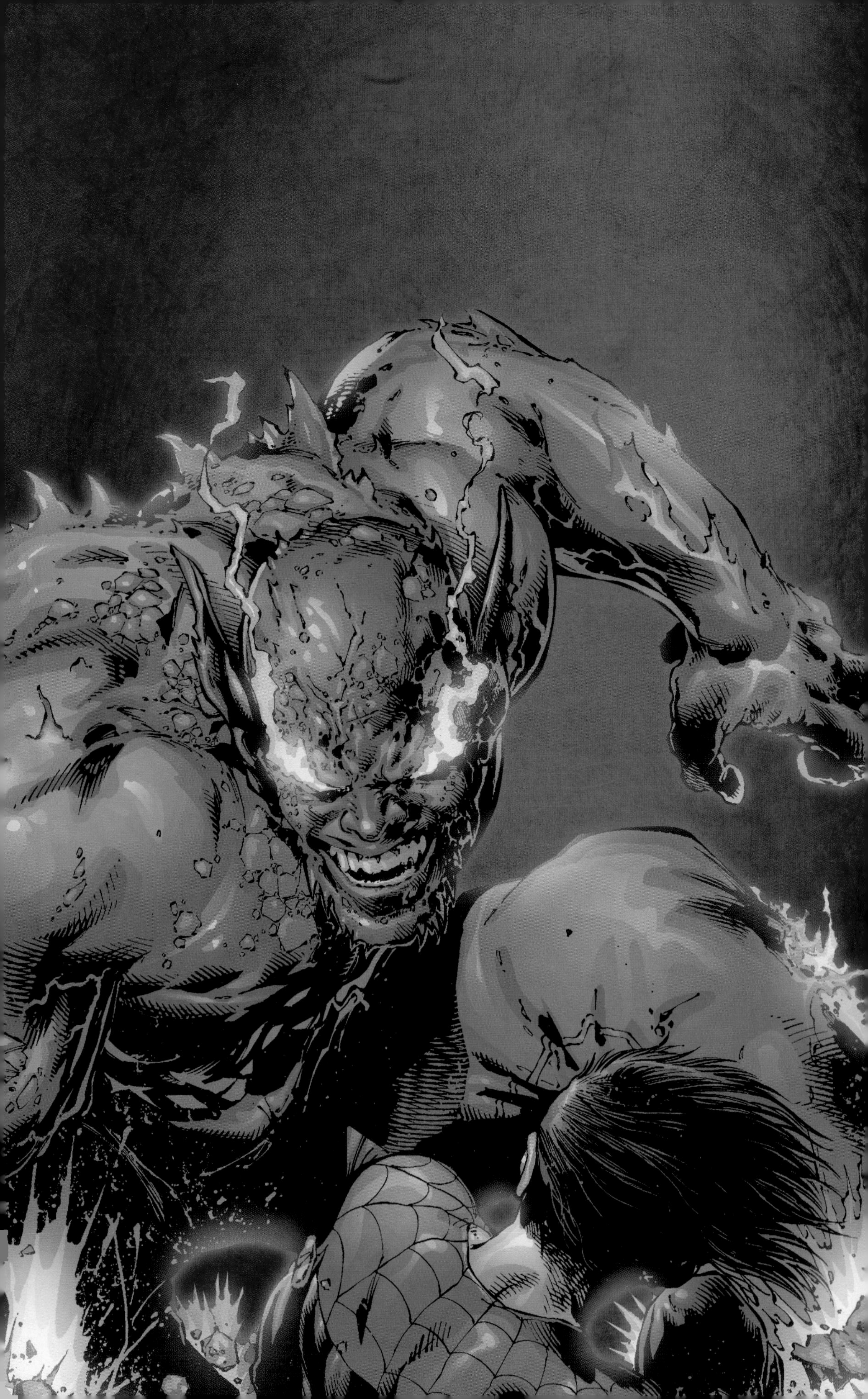

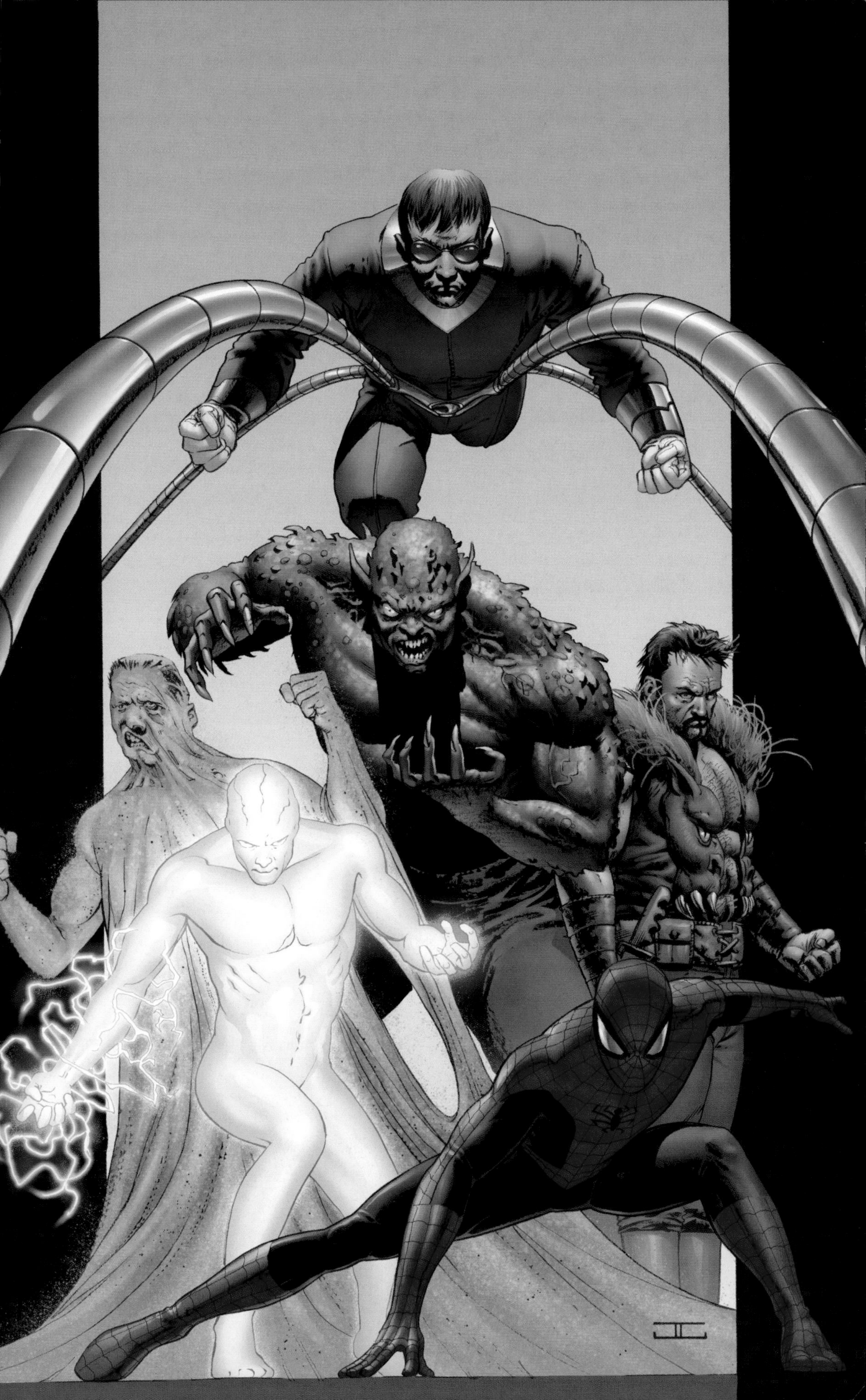

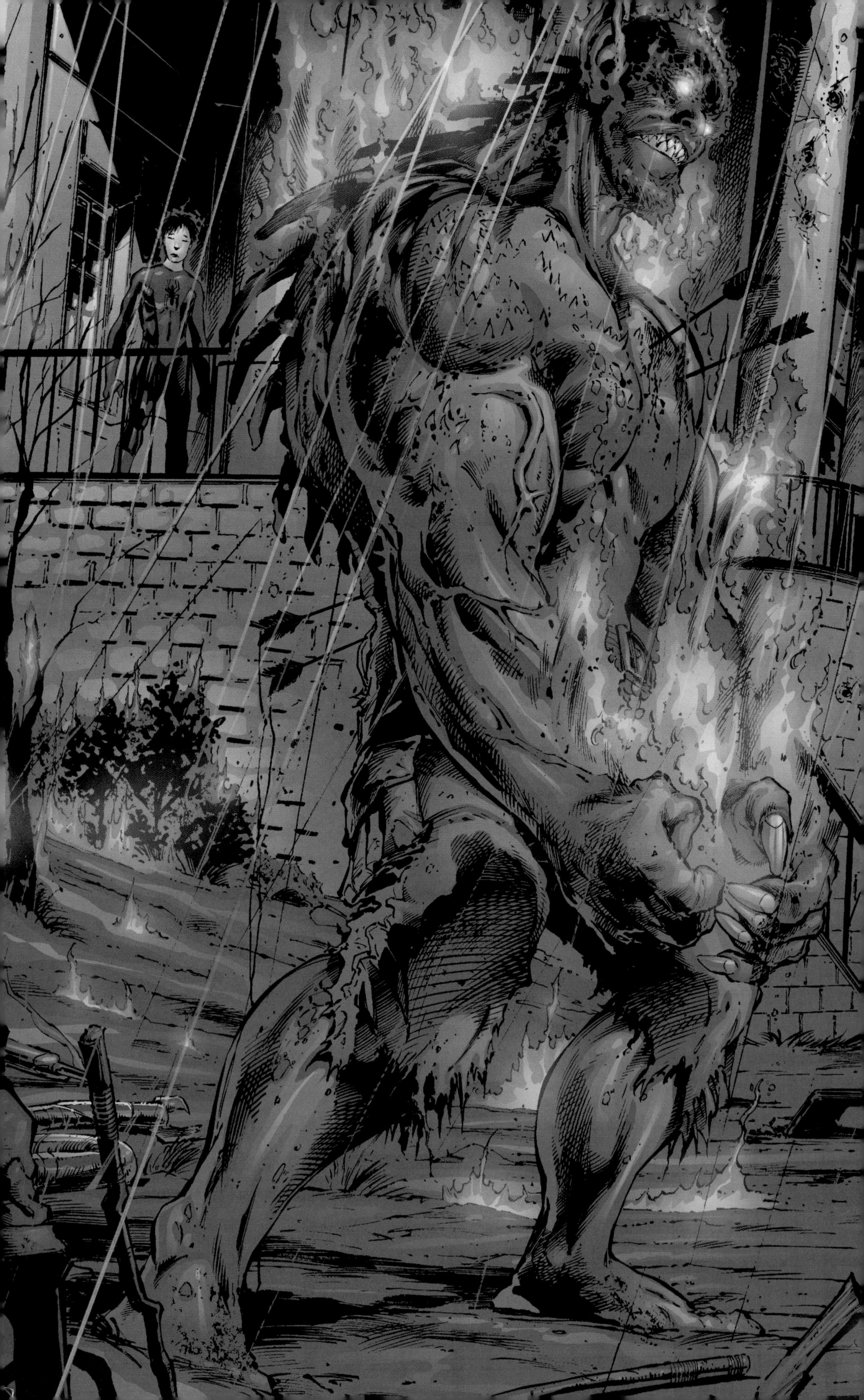

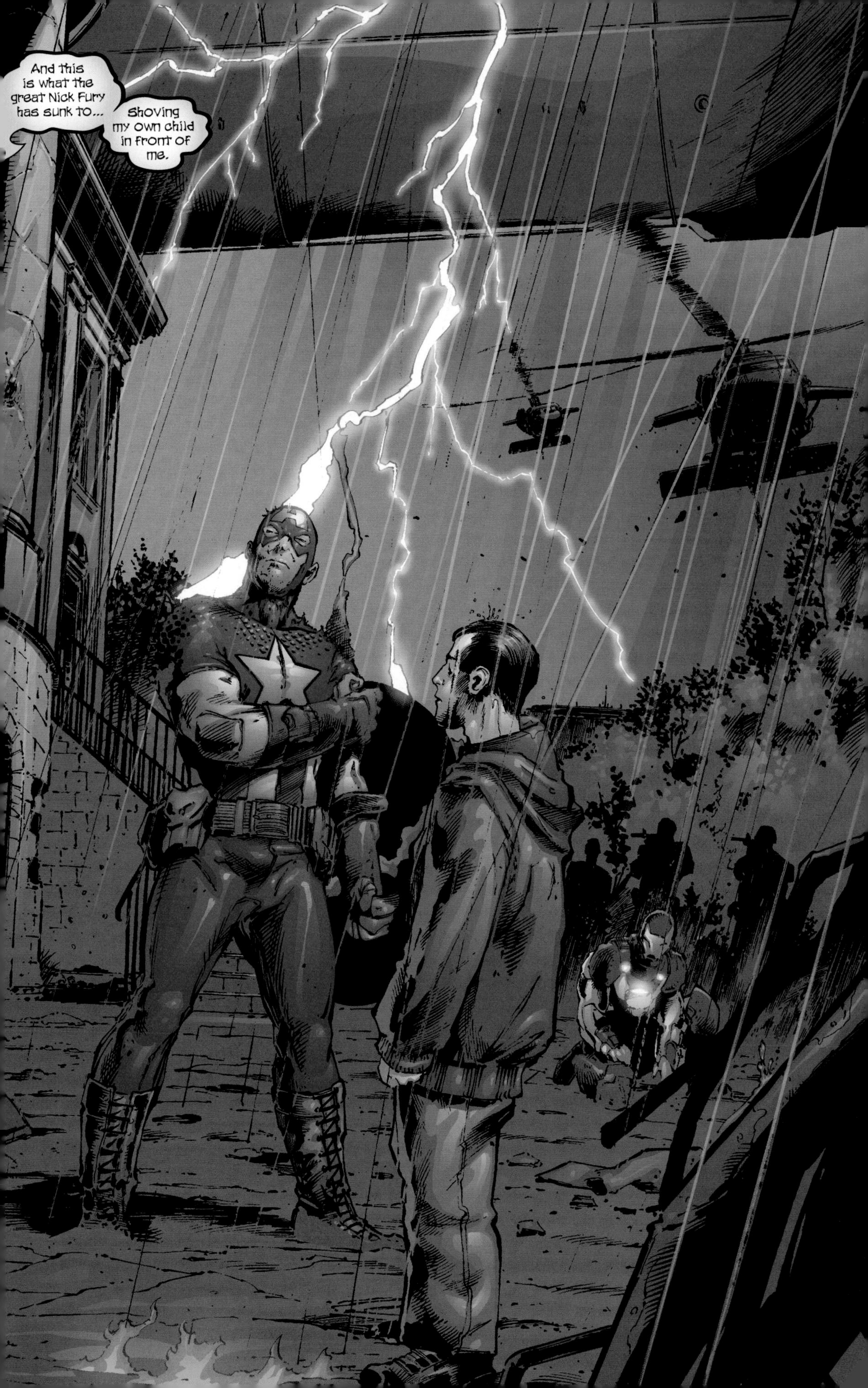
And this is what the great Nick Fury has sunk to...
Shoving my own child in front of me.

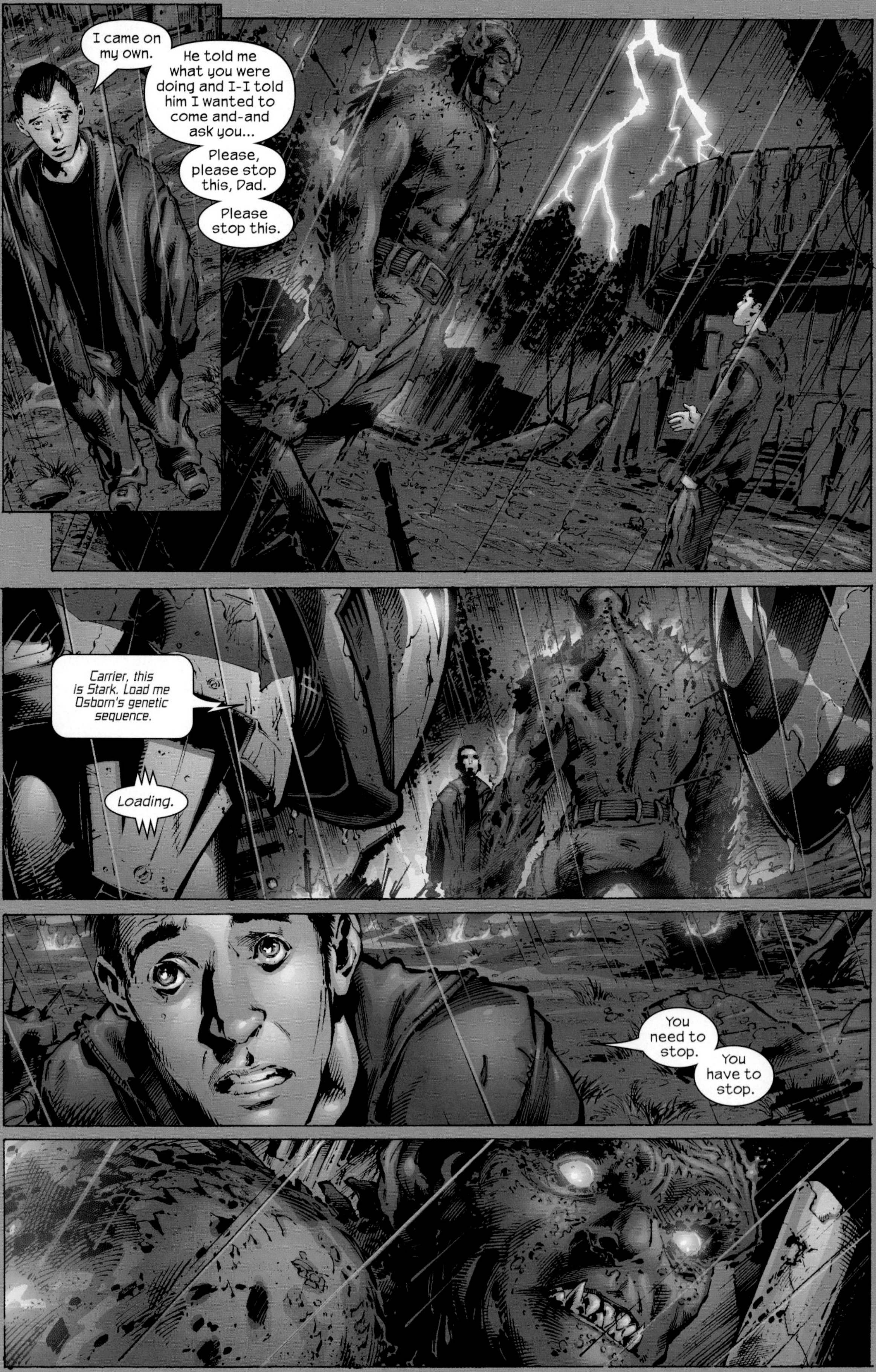
I came on my own.
He told me what you were doing and I-I told him I wanted to come and-and ask you...
Please, please stop this, Dad.
Please stop this.
Carrier, this is Stark. Load me Osborn's genetic sequence.
Loading.
You need to stop.
You have to stop.

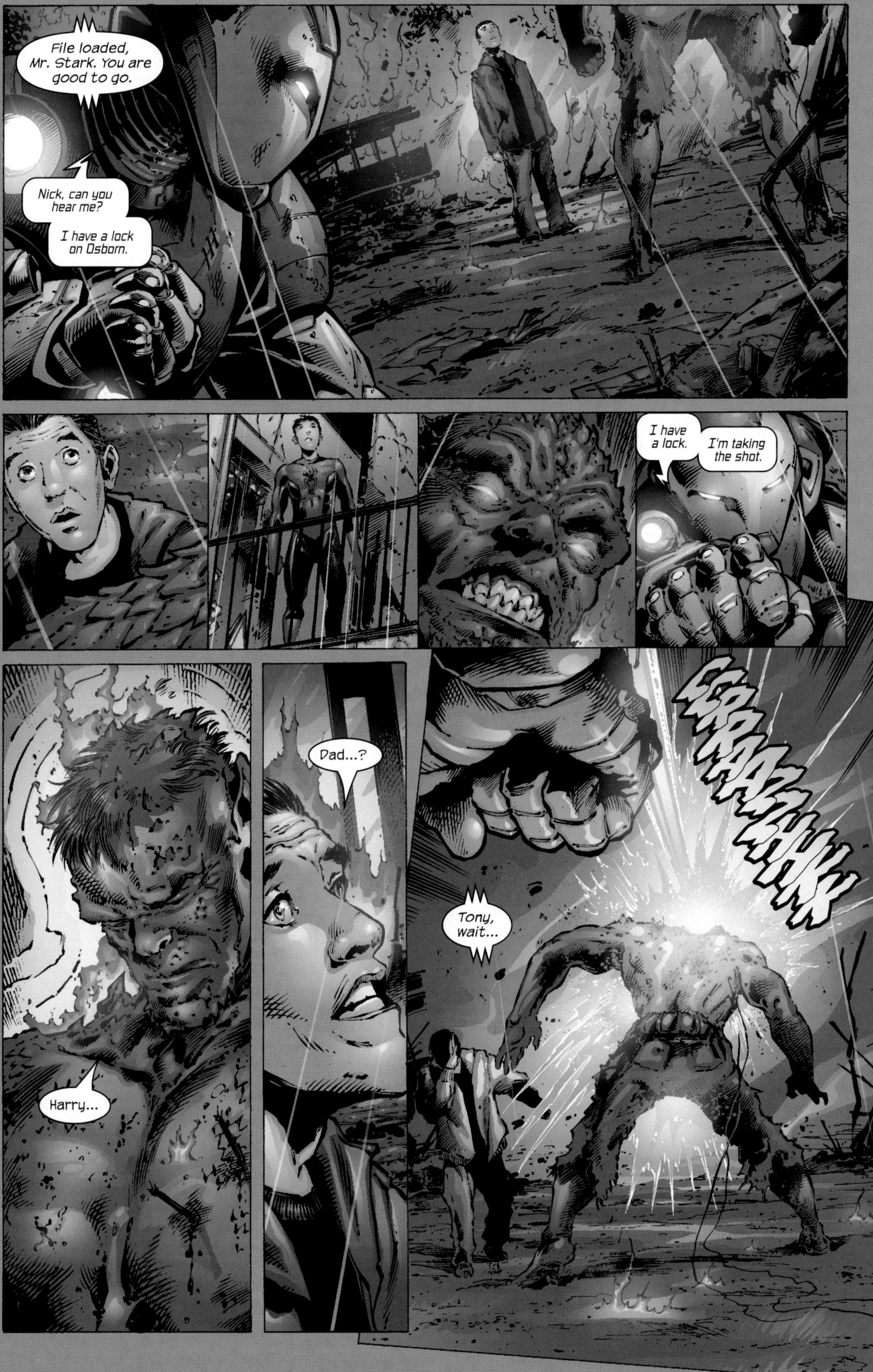
File loaded, Mr. Stark. You are good to go.
Nick, can you hear me?
I have a lock on Osborn.
I have a lock.
I'm taking the shot.
Harry...
Dad...?
CCRAAKHHKK
Tony, wait...

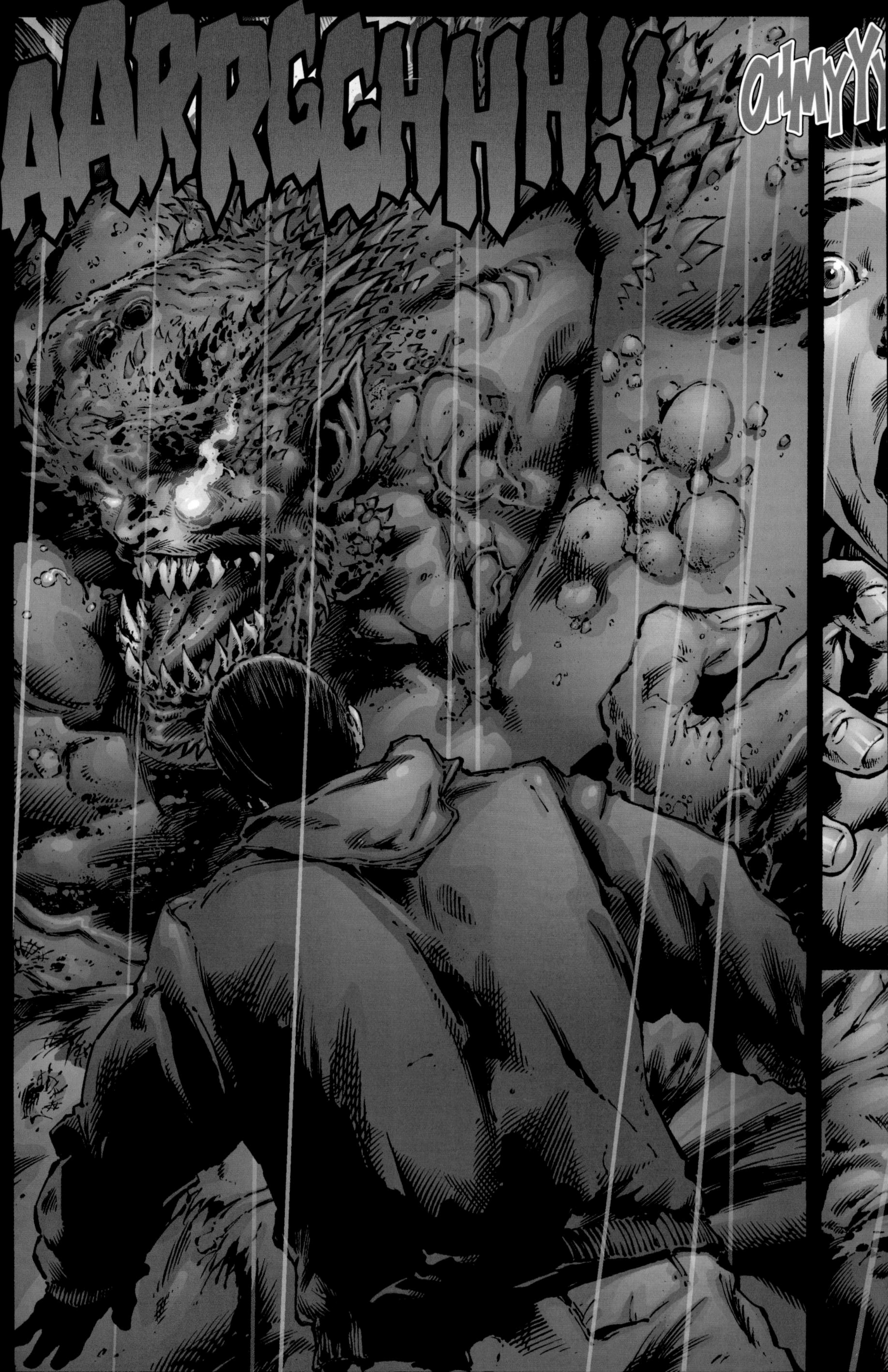
AARRGCHHH!!
OHMYY

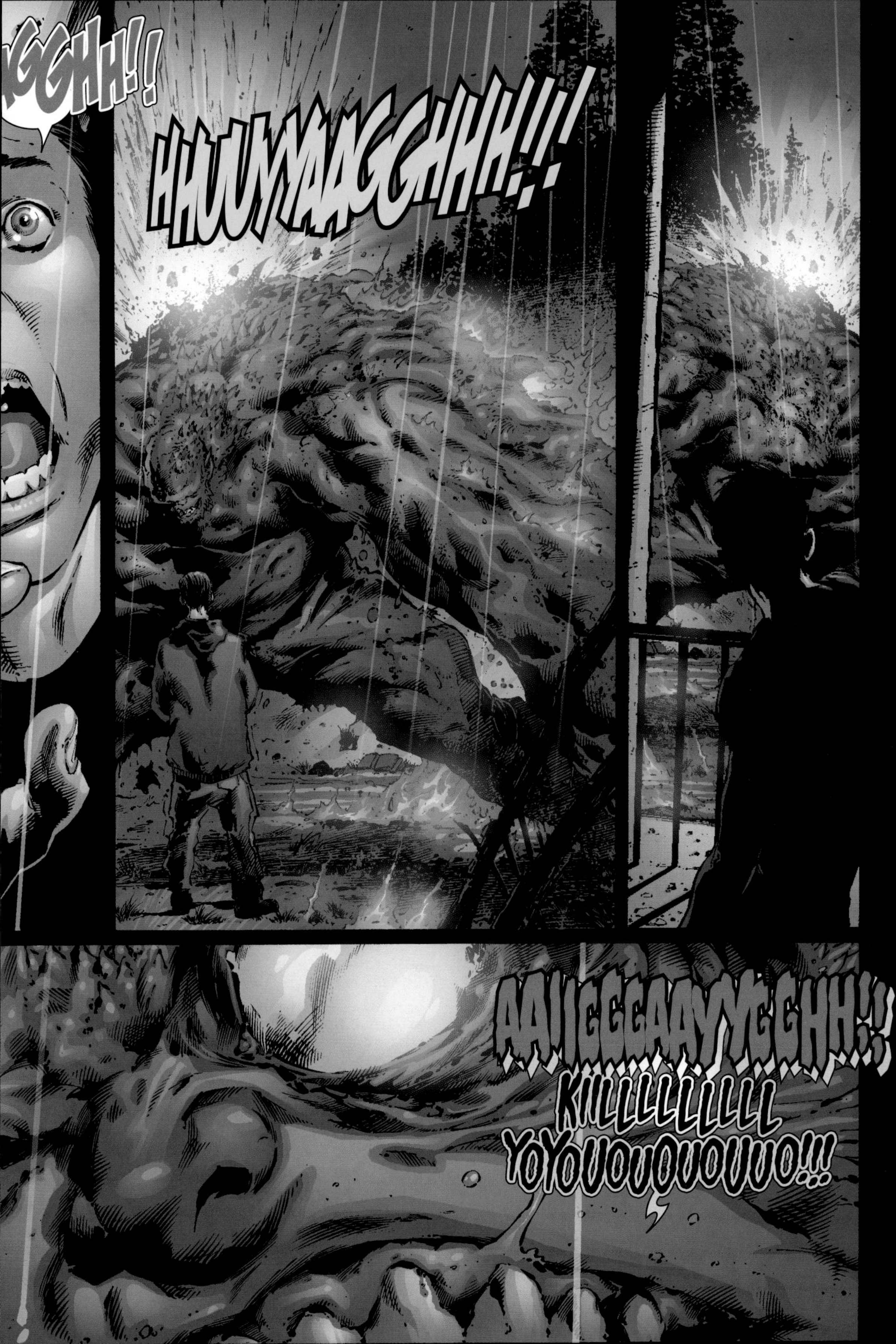
GGHH!!
HHUUYAAGGHHH!!!
AAIICCCAAYYGGHH!!!
KIILLLLLLLLL
YOYOUOUQUOUUO!!!

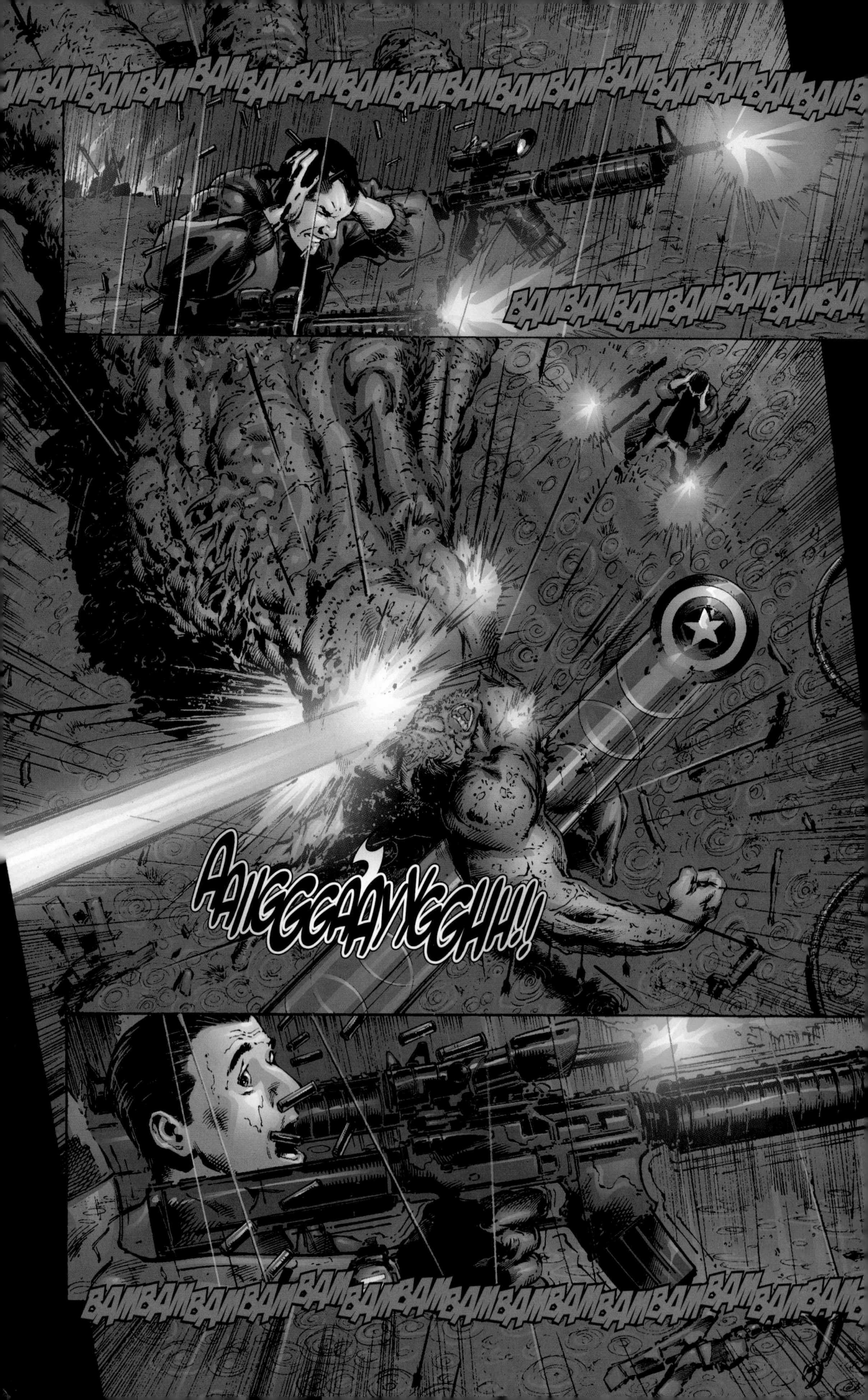
AMBAMBAMBAMBAMBAMBAMBAMBAMBAMBAMBAMBAM
BAMBAMBAMBAMBAMBAMBAM
AAIGGGAAYXGGHH!!
BAMBAMBAMBAMBAMBAMBAMBAMBAMBAMBAMBAMBAM

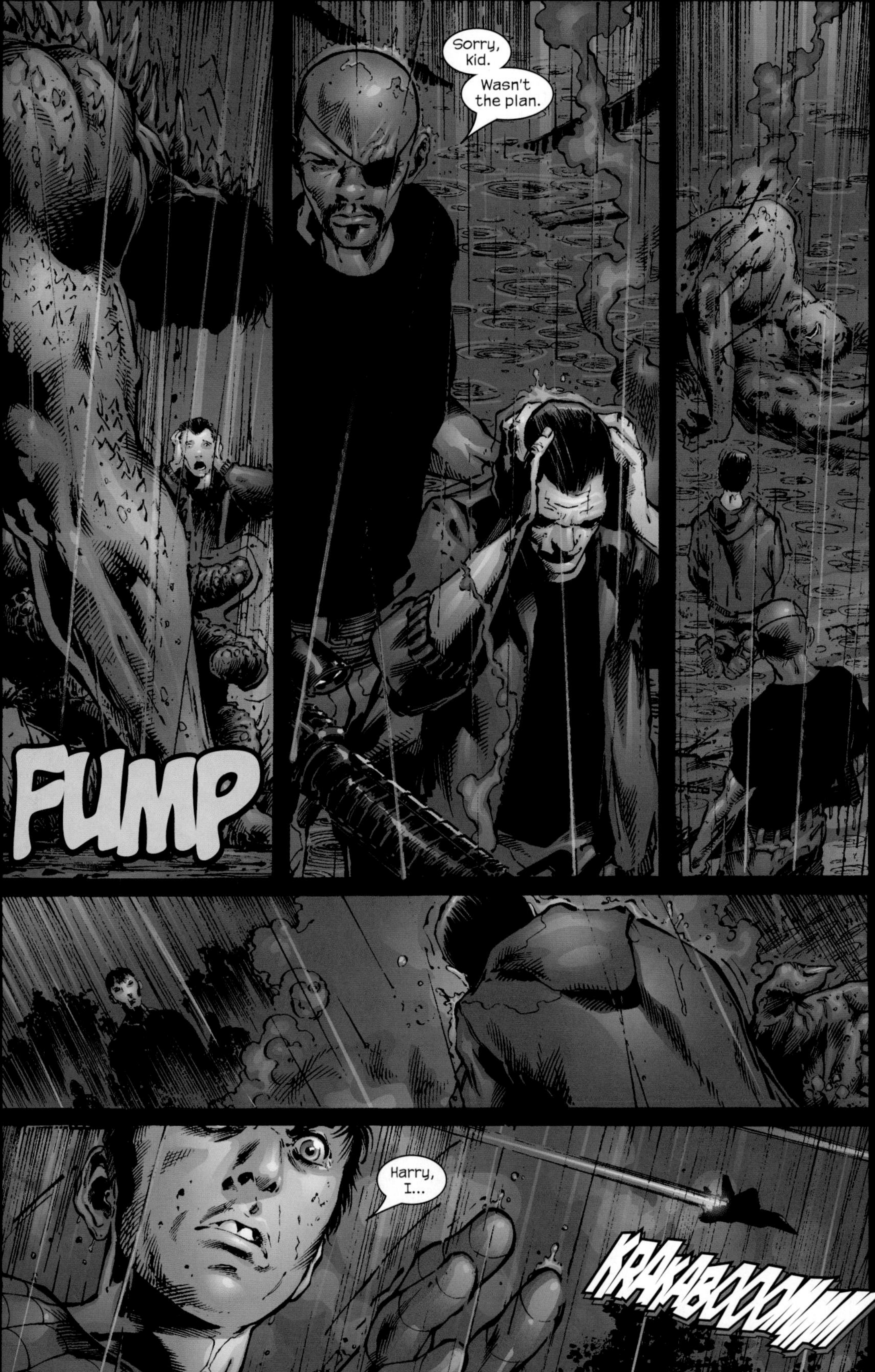
FUMP
Sorry, kid.
Wasn't the plan.
Harry, I...
KRAKABOOOMMM

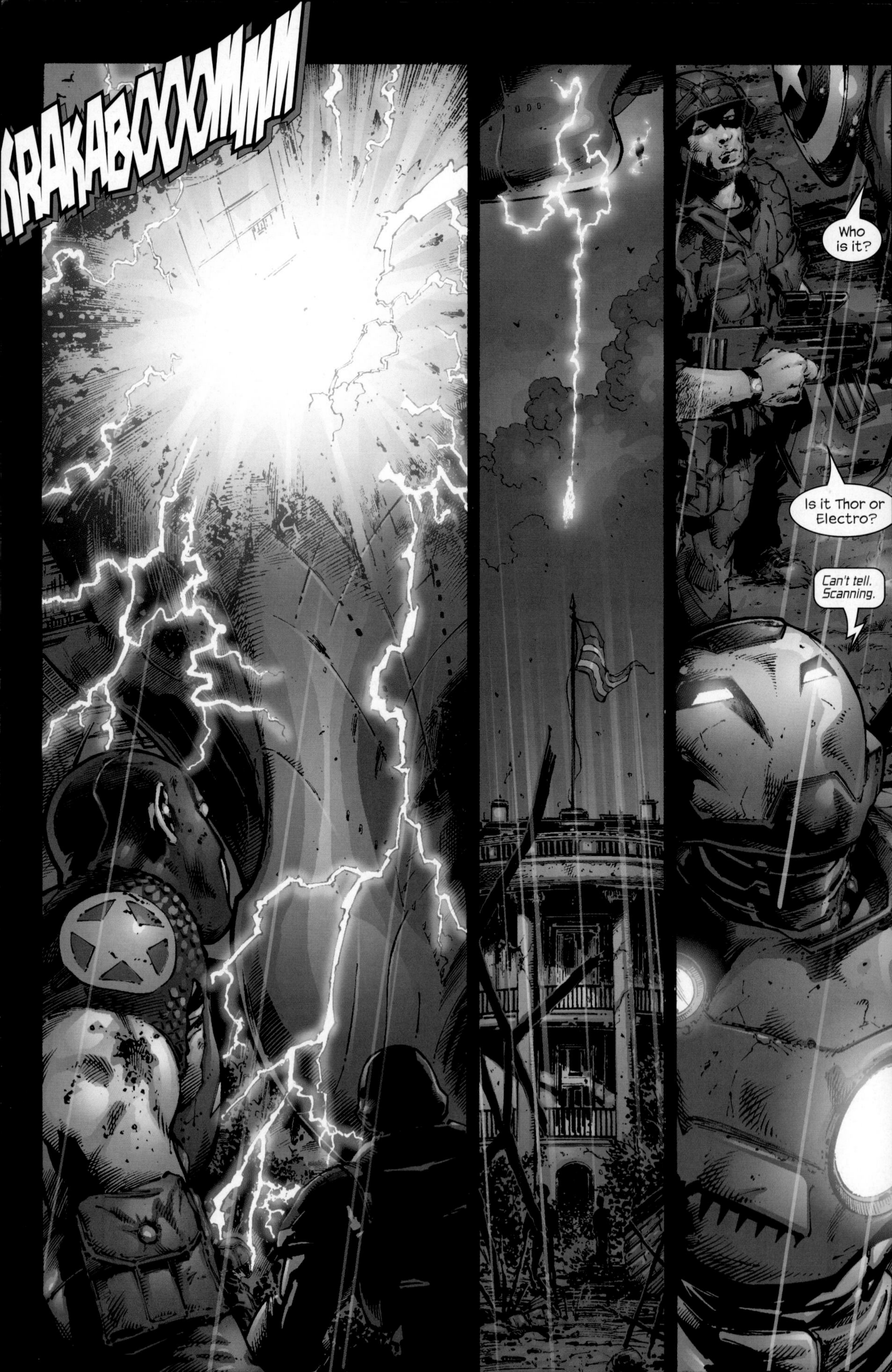
KRAKABOOOMMM
Who is it?
Is it Thor or Electro?
Can't tell. Scanning.

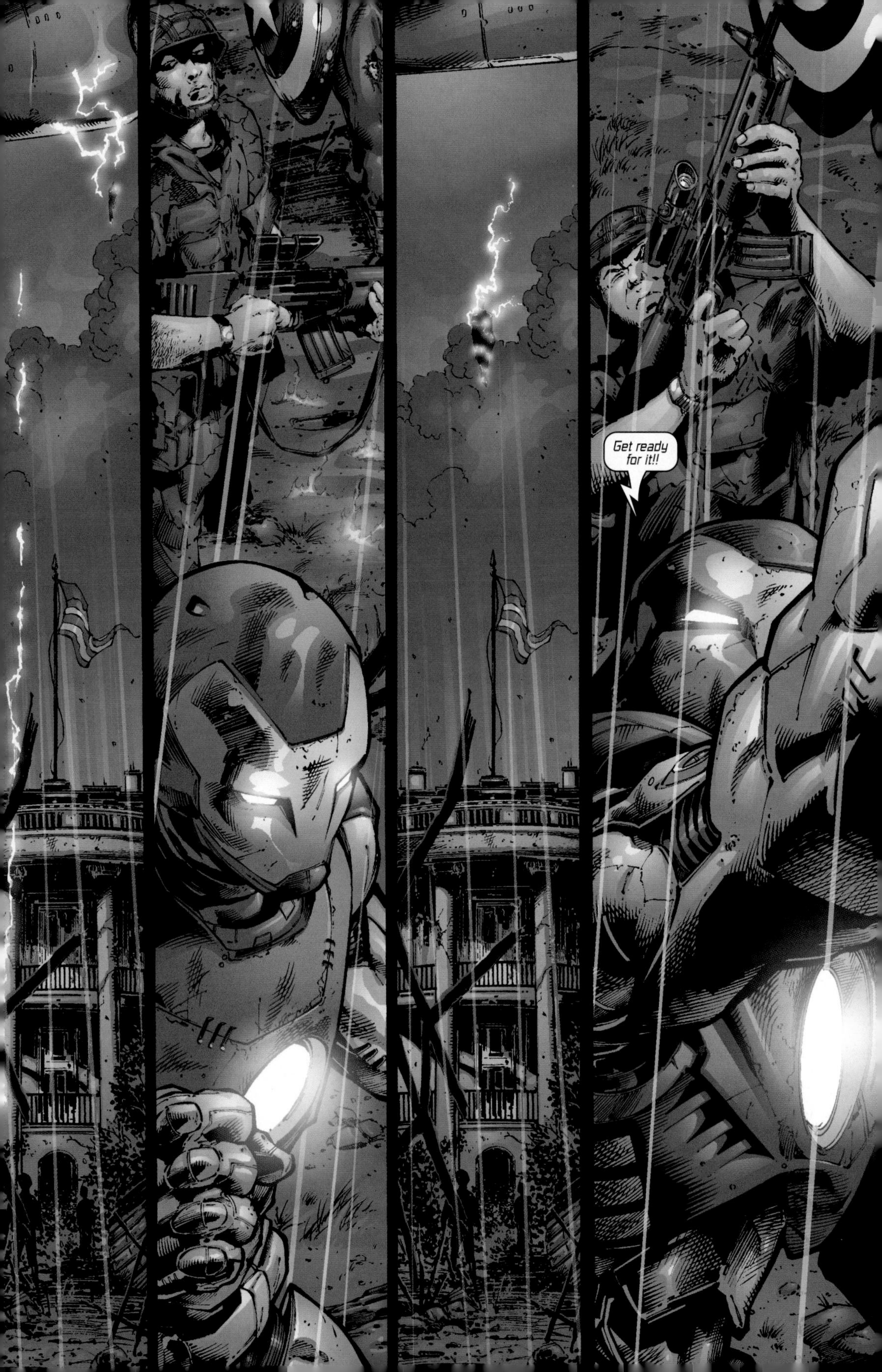
Get ready for it!!

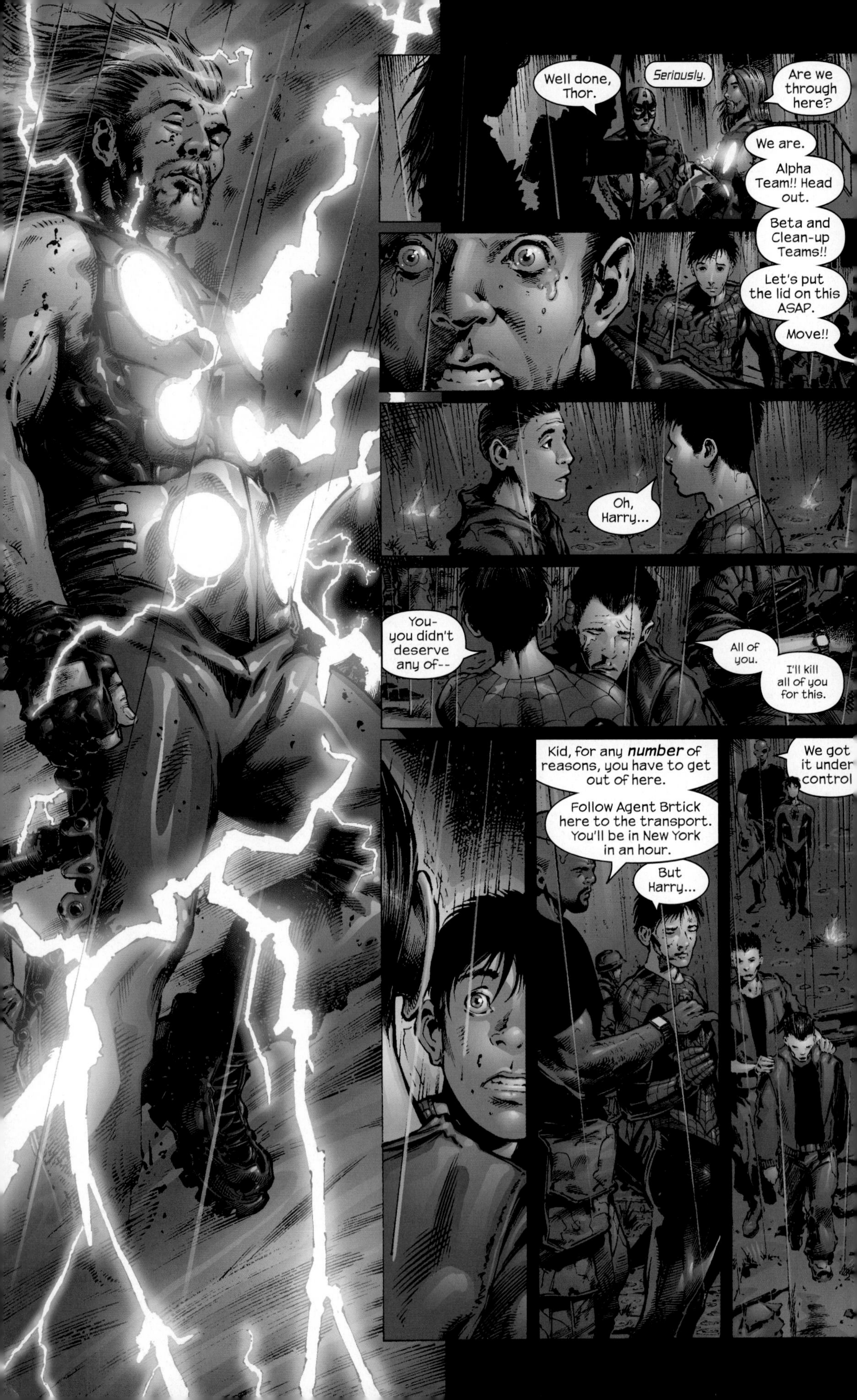
Well done, Thor.
Seriously.
Are we through here?
We are.
Alpha Team!! Head out.
Beta and Clean-up Teams!!
Let's put the lid on this ASAP.
Move!!
Oh, Harry...
You-you didn't deserve any of--
All of you.
I'll kill all of you for this.
Kid, for any number of reasons, you have to get out of here.
Follow Agent Brtick here to the transport. You'll be in New York in an hour.
But Harry...
We got it under control

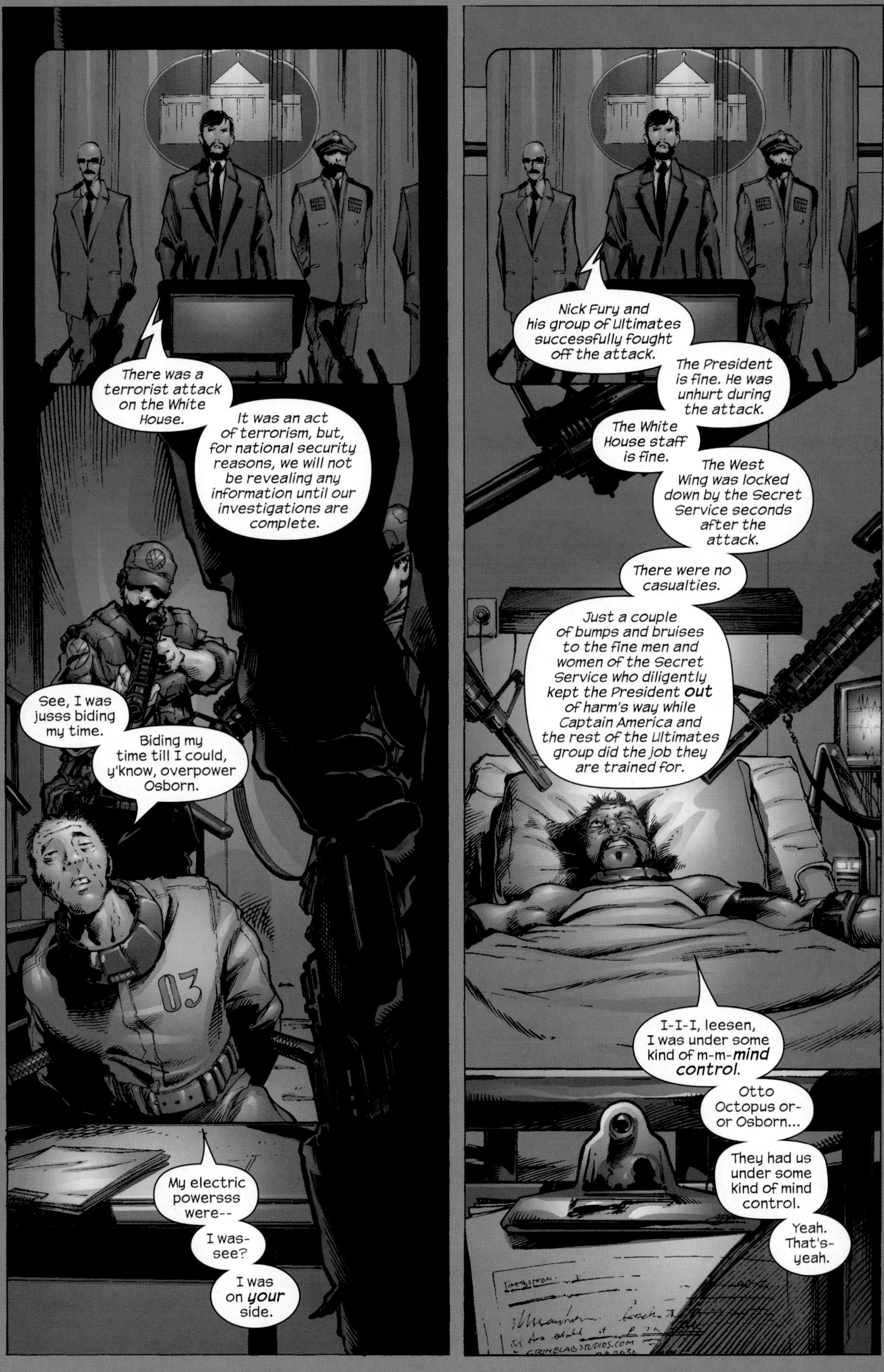
There was a terrorist attack on the White House.
It was an act of terrorism, but, for national security reasons, we will not be revealing any information until our investigations are complete.
See, I was jusss biding my time.
Biding my time till I could, y'know, overpower Osborn.
My electric powersss were--
I was-see?
I was on *your* side.
Nick Fury and his group of Ultimates successfully fought off the attack.
The President is fine. He was unhurt during the attack.
The White House staff is fine.
The West Wing was locked down by the Secret Service seconds after the attack.
There were no casualties.
Just a couple of bumps and bruises to the fine men and women of the Secret Service who diligently kept the President **out** of harm's way while Captain America and the rest of the Ultimates group did the job they are trained for.
I-I-I, leesen, I was under some kind of m-m-***mind control***.
Otto Octopus or- or Osborn...
They had us under some kind of mind control.
Yeah. That's- yeah.

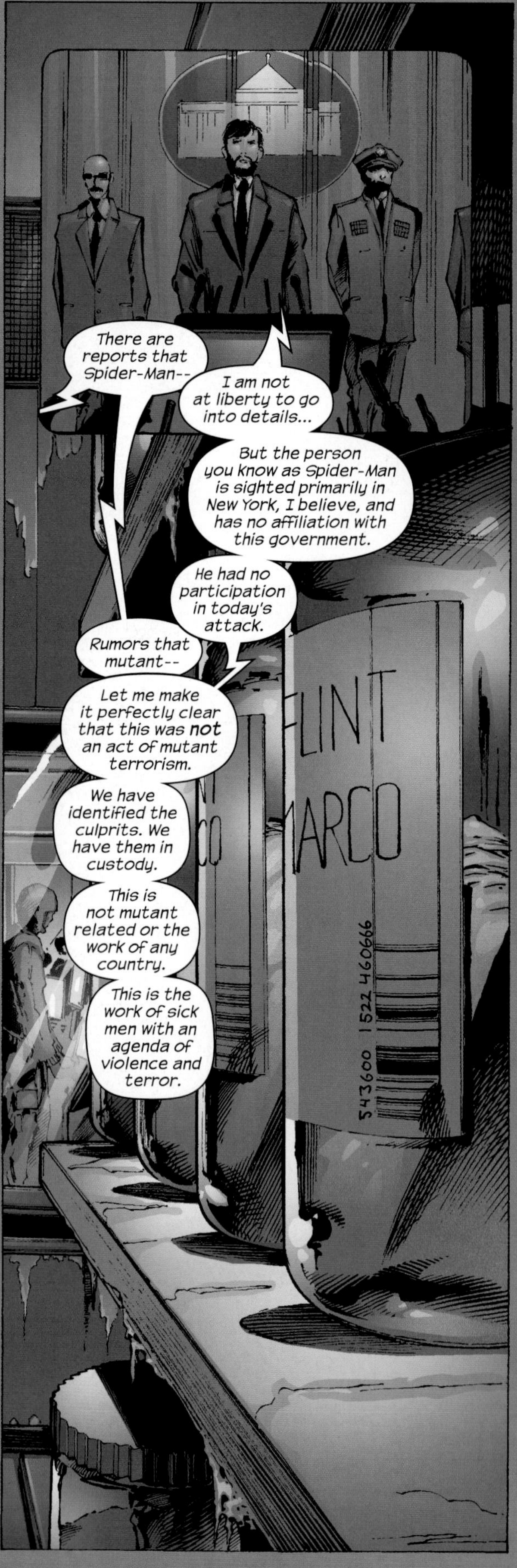
There are reports that Spider-Man--
I am not at liberty to go into details...
But the person you know as Spider-Man is sighted primarily in New York, I believe, and has no affiliation with this government.
He had no participation in today's attack.
Rumors that mutant--
Let me make it perfectly clear that this was **not** an act of mutant terrorism.
We have identified the culprits. We have them in custody.
This is not mutant related or the work of any country.
This is the work of sick men with an agenda of violence and terror.
FLINT MARCO
543600 1522 460666

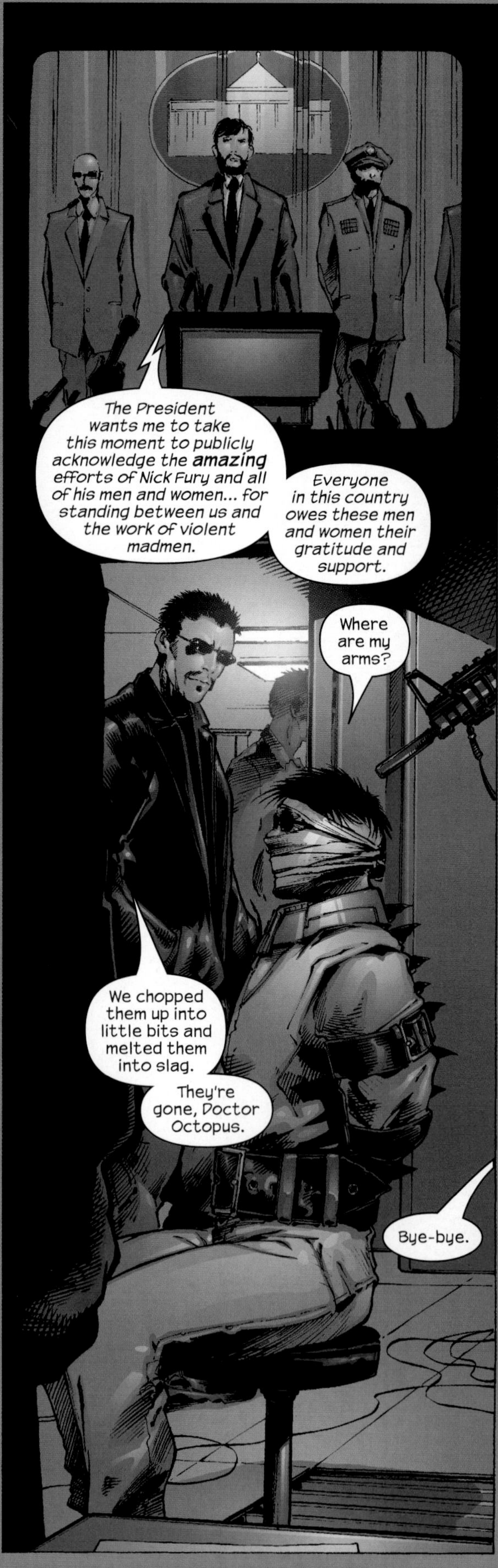
The President wants me to take this moment to publicly acknowledge the **amazing** efforts of Nick Fury and all of his men and women... for standing between us and the work of violent madmen.
Everyone in this country owes these men and women their gratitude and support.
Where are my arms?
We chopped them up into little bits and melted them into slag.
They're gone, Doctor Octopus.
Bye-bye.

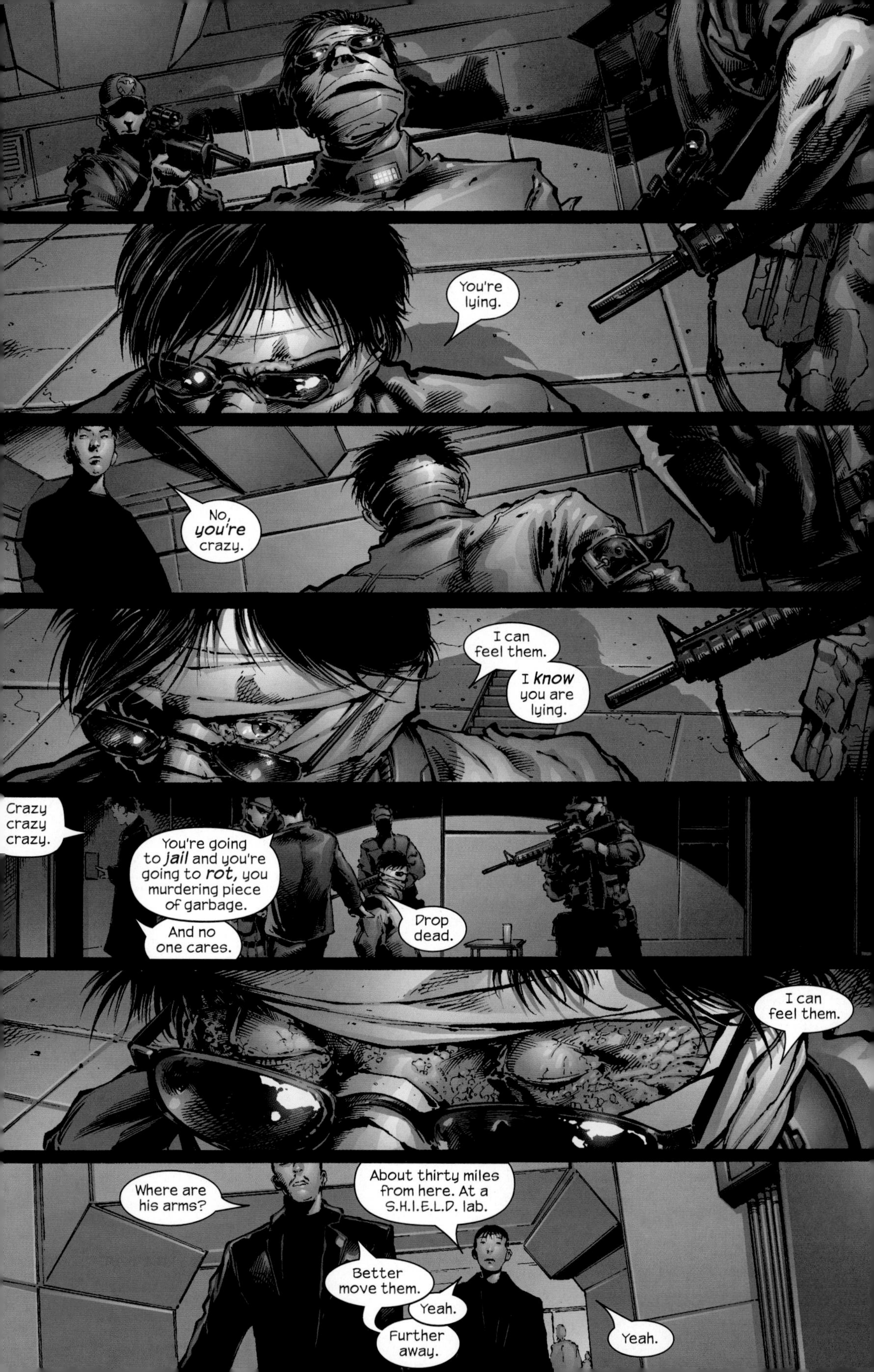
You're lying.
No, *you're* crazy.
I can feel them.
I *know* you are lying.
Crazy crazy crazy.
You're going to *jail* and you're going to *rot*, you murdering piece of garbage.
And no one cares.
Drop dead.
I can feel them.
Where are his arms?
About thirty miles from here. At a S.H.I.E.L.D. lab.
Better move them.
Yeah.
Further away.
Yeah.

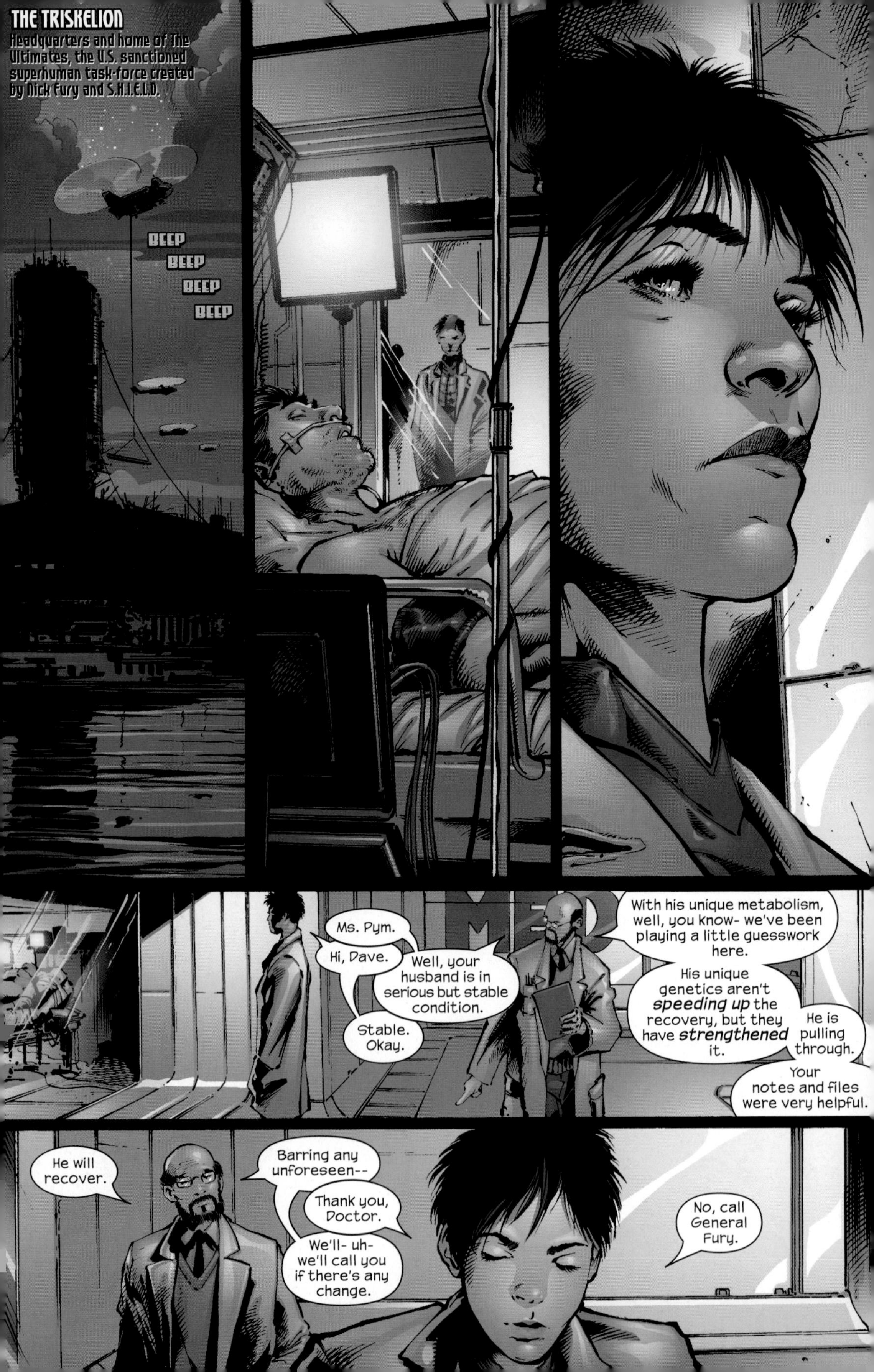
THE TRISKELION
Headquarters and home of The Ultimates, the U.S. sanctioned superhuman task-force created by Nick Fury and S.H.I.E.L.D.
BEEP
BEEP
BEEP
BEEP
Ms. Pym.
Hi, Dave.
Well, your husband is in serious but stable condition.
Stable. Okay.
With his unique metabolism, well, you know- we've been playing a little guesswork here.
His unique genetics aren't *speeding up* the recovery, but they have *strengthened* it.
He is pulling through.
Your notes and files were very helpful.
He will recover.
Barring any unforeseen--
Thank you, Doctor.
We'll- uh- we'll call you if there's any change.
No, call General Fury.

Mr. Parker, please hurry up.

Are you taking me home?

Both you and your aunt.

My aunt is here?

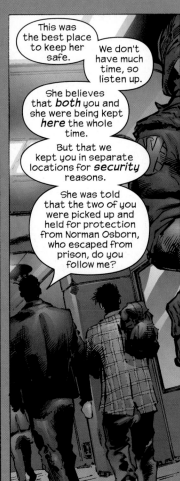

This was the best place to keep her safe.

We don't have much time, so listen up.

She believes that *both* you and she were being kept *here* the whole time.

But that we kept you in separate locations for *security* reasons.

She was told that the two of you were picked up and held for protection from Norman Osborn, who escaped from prison, do you follow me?

So she thinks both she and I have been here the whole time in separate--

Exactly. And you don't *know* anything.

Nothing?

You don't know *anything.*

Is she okay?

She's fine.

No, I mean, like, is-is she mad?

Dunno.

On a scale of one to ten...

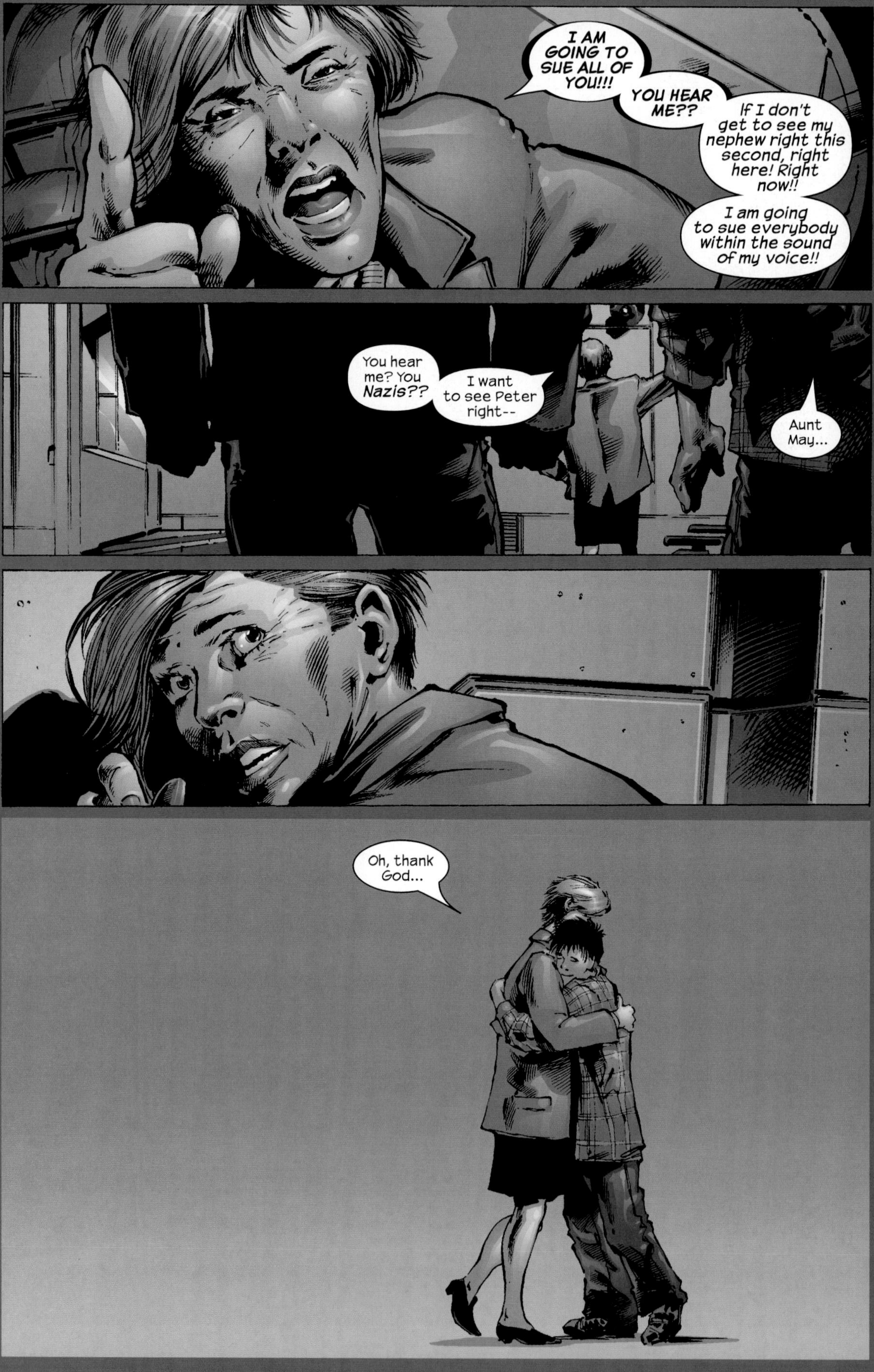
I AM GOING TO SUE ALL OF YOU!!!
YOU HEAR ME??
If I don't get to see my nephew right this second, right here! Right now!!
I am going to sue everybody within the sound of my voice!!
You hear me? You *Nazis*??
I want to see Peter right--
Aunt May...
Oh, thank God...

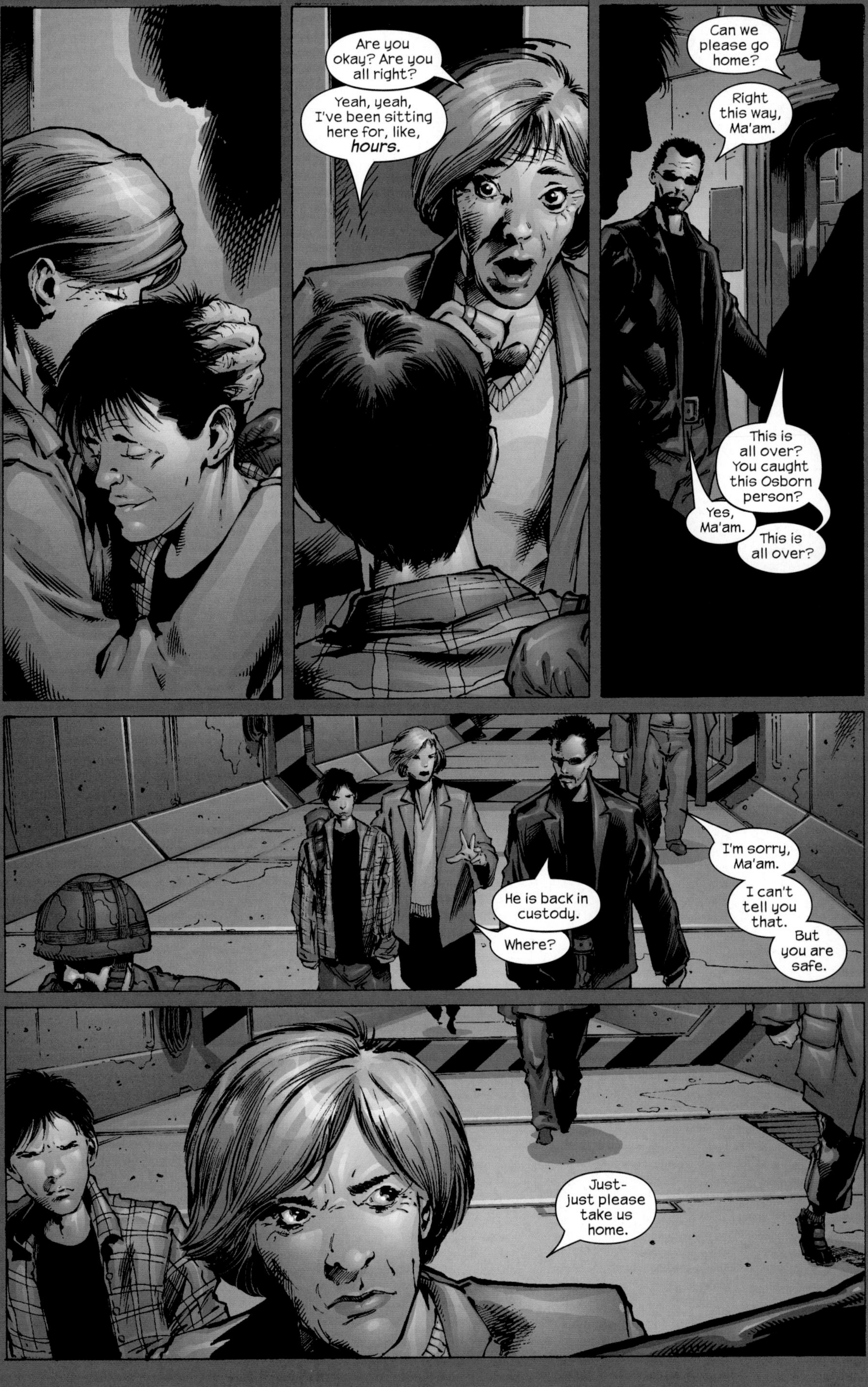
Are you okay? Are you all right?
Yeah, yeah, I've been sitting here for, like, *hours.*
Can we please go home?
Right this way, Ma'am.
This is all over? You caught this Osborn person?
Yes, Ma'am.
This is all over?
He is back in custody.
Where?
I'm sorry, Ma'am.
I can't tell you that.
But you are safe.
Just- just please take us home.

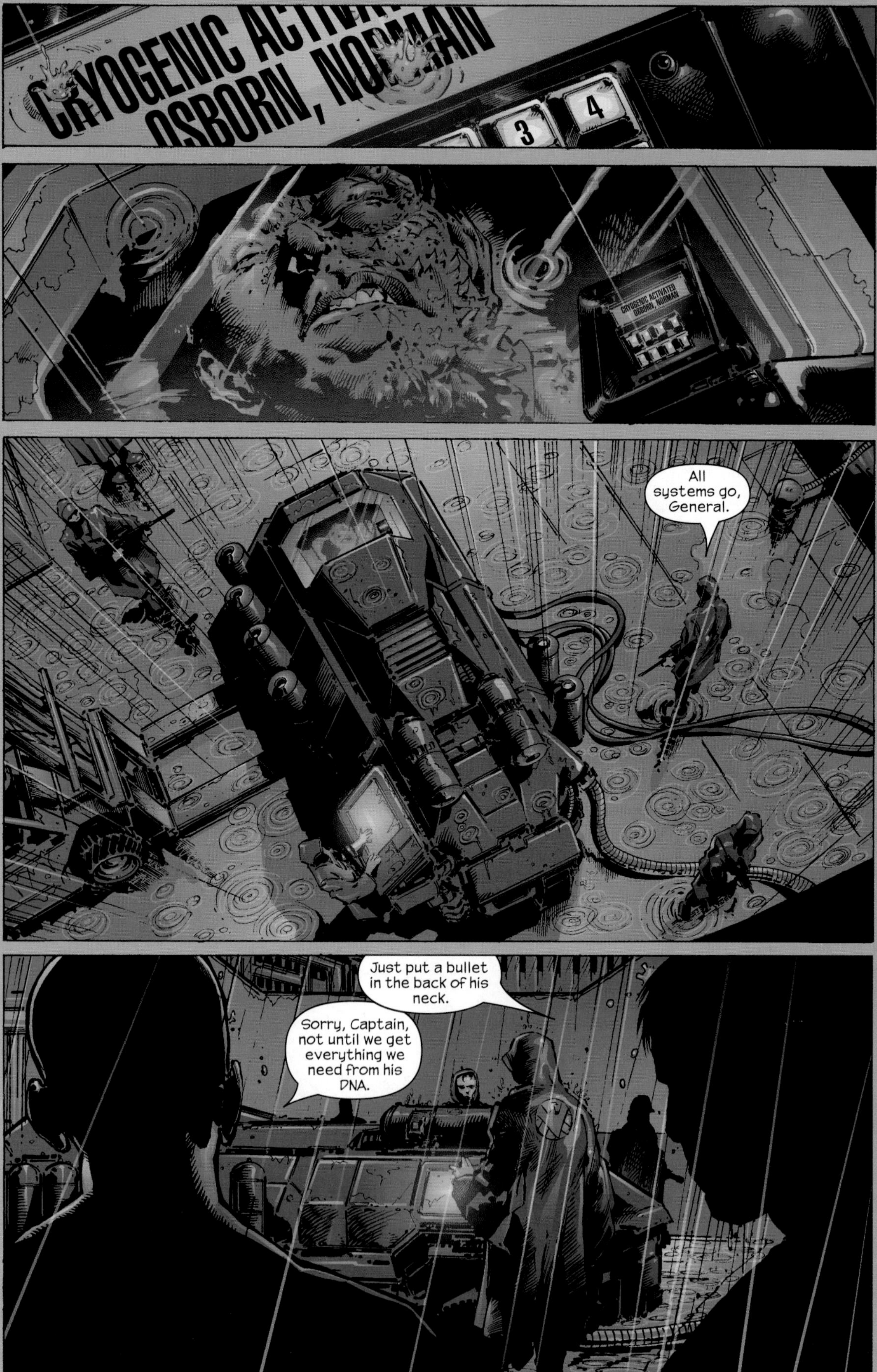
CRYOGENIC ACTIVATED
OSBORN, NORMAN
All systems go, General.
Just put a bullet in the back of his neck.
Sorry, Captain, not until we get everything we need from his DNA.

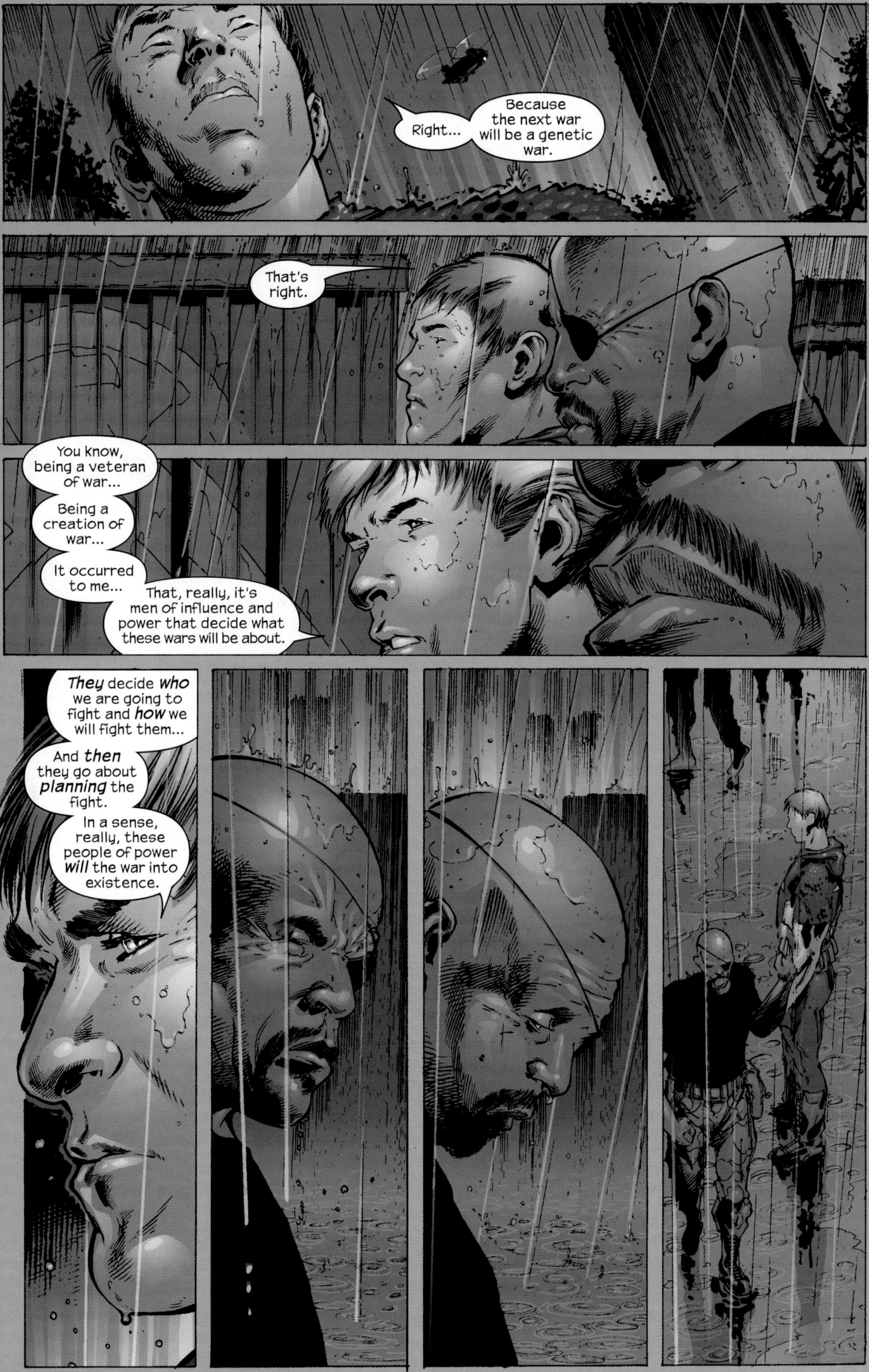
Right...
Because the next war will be a genetic war.
That's right.
You know, being a veteran of war...
Being a creation of war...
It occurred to me...
That, really, it's men of influence and power that decide what these wars will be about.
They decide who we are going to fight and how we will fight them...
And then they go about planning the fight.
In a sense, really, these people of power will the war into existence.

Next: Hollywood

ULTIMATE SANDMAN by MARK BAGLEY

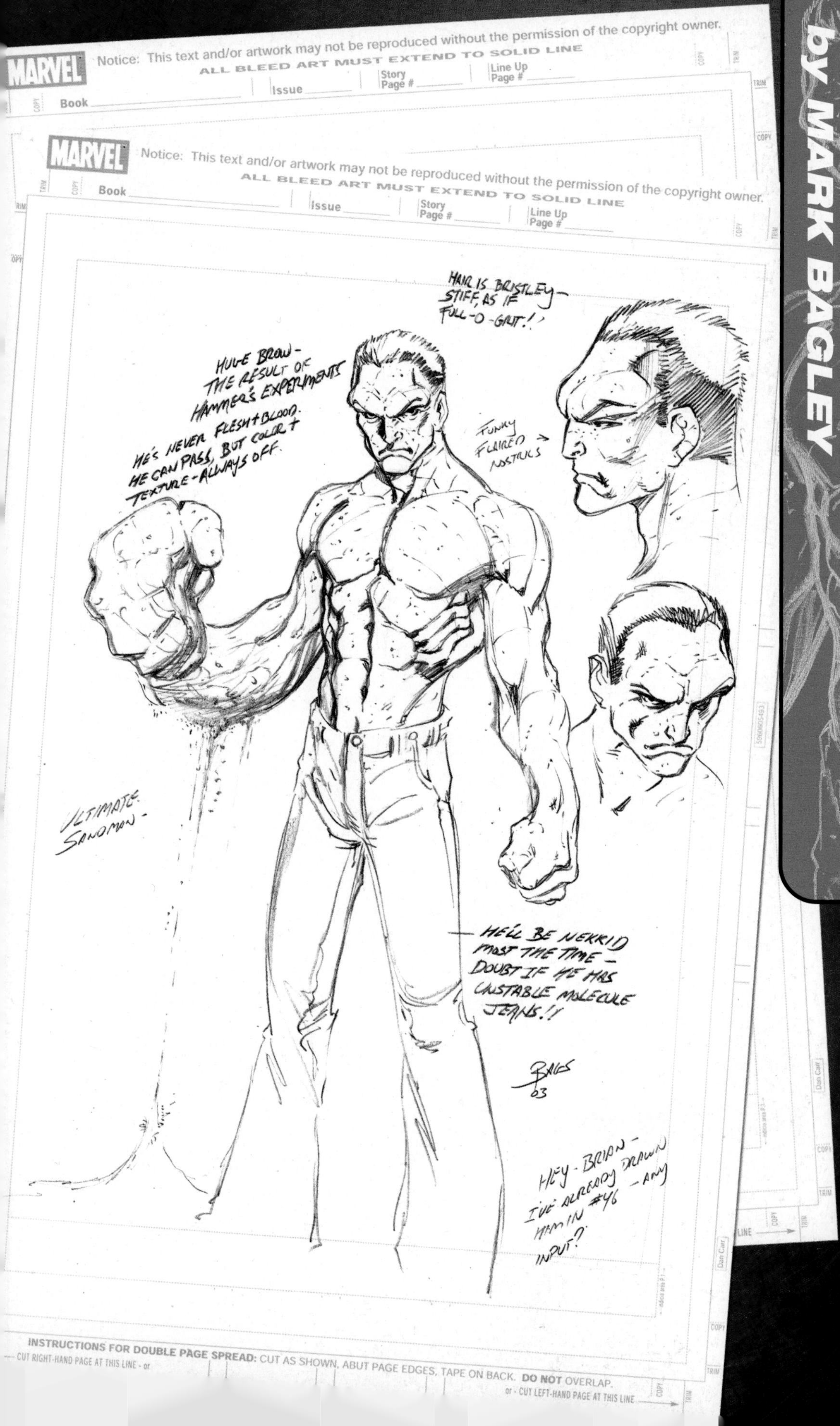

MARVEL
Notice: This text and/or artwork may not be reproduced without the permission of the copyright owner.
ALL BLEED ART MUST EXTEND TO SOLID LINE
Book
Issue
Story Page #
Line Up Page #
HAIR IS BRISTLEY- STIFF, AS IF FULL-O-GRIT!!
HUGE BROW- THE RESULT OF HAMMER'S EXPERIMENTS
HE'S NEVER FLESH+BLOOD. HE CAN PASS, BUT COLOR + TEXTURE- ALWAYS OFF.
FUNKY FLAIRED NOSTRILS
ULTIMATE SANDMAN-
HE'LL BE NEKRID MOST THE TIME- DOUBT IF HE HAS UNSTABLE MOLECULE JEANS!!
BAGS 03
HEY- BRIAN- I'VE ALREADY DRAWN HIM IN #46 - ANY INPUT?
INSTRUCTIONS FOR DOUBLE PAGE SPREAD: CUT AS SHOWN, ABUT PAGE EDGES, TAPE ON BACK. DO NOT OVERLAP.
CUT RIGHT-HAND PAGE AT THIS LINE - or
or - CUT LEFT-HAND PAGE AT THIS LINE

MARVELS

10TH ANNIVERSARY EDITION

MARVEL®

CELEBRATE 10 YEARS OF MARVELS!
KURT BUSIEK • ALEX ROSS